THE FRENCH NOBILITY IN THE EIGHTEENTH CENTURY

REASSESSMENTS AND NEW APPROACHES

edited by JAY M. SMITH

THE PENNSYLVANIA STATE UNIVERSITY PRESS
UNIVERSITY PARK, PENNSYLVANIA

Library of Congress Cataloging-in-Publication Data

The French nobility in the eighteenth century : reassessments and new approaches /
edited by Jay M. Smith.
p.   cm.
Includes bibliographical references and index.
ISBN 0-271-02898-X (cloth : alk. paper)
1. Nobility—France—History—18th century.
2. Social classes—France—History—18th century.
3. Nobility—France—Historiography.
I. Smith, Jay M., 1961– .

HT653.F7F74 2006
305.5'22094409033—dc22
2006007769

A longer version of Chapter 2 originally appeared in the journal
*1650–1850: Ideas, Aesthetics, and Inquiries in the Early
Modern Era 2* (2005): 443–509. Used with permission of
AMS Press, New York.

Chapter 6 originally appeared in
Mita Choudhury's *Convents and Nuns in Eighteenth-Century
French Politics and Culture*. Copyright © 2004 Cornell
University. Used with permission of Cornell University Press.

FOR *Alyssa and Connor*

CONTENTS

ACKNOWLEDGMENTS

The original versions of the essays collected here were presented at a symposium held at the National Humanities Center (NHC) in Research Triangle Park, North Carolina, in 2002. The symposium was made possible by a generous grant from the Florence Gould Foundation and by the good will, experience, and encouragement of the staff at the NHC. I would particularly like to thank John Young at the Gould Foundation, who surpassed all reasonable expectations of generosity, and at the National Humanities Center, David Rice, Pat Schreiber, Joel Elliott, Kent Mullikin, and the former director of the Center, Robert Connor. Connor had the courtesy and grace not to dismiss the whole idea when he first heard of our scheme in fall 2001, and the others provided crucial assistance and logistical support without which the symposium could not have succeeded as it did.

At the symposium, the authors of the following essays received incisive feedback from a panel of experts, whose presence made our weekend conference an exceptionally invigorating exercise. On behalf of the authors, I express our collective gratitude to William Doyle, Steven Laurence Kaplan, and Lloyd S. Kramer, each of whom provided a provocative commentary on a set of related papers and generally pressed the authors whenever they needed pressing. David D. Bien also participated in the symposium, both as an author of a paper and as a co-conspirator and co-organizer of the conference. He deserves special thanks for helping to persuade many of the contributors to join the party and for supplying thoughtful written critiques to the authors of several essays. Because of the great importance of his own work on nobility, and his vital contributions both at the symposium and in the months that followed, this book would be unthinkable without him.

At Penn State University Press, Peter Potter had faith in the project from its beginning and has provided steady encouragement throughout the process of evaluation and publication. The two peer reviewers for the Press were informed, thoughtful, and helpful in their criticisms of specific essays. For their help in providing the publication subsidy—with timely and indispensable support at the very end of the process—I wish to express my sincere thanks to the Departments of History and Romance Languages at the University of North Carolina, the University Research Council at UNC, and, especially, the Gould Foundation. In these difficult economic times for academic presses, one finds comfort in knowing that, in some cases at least, universities, conscientious editorial boards, and generous foundations can combine to promote and sustain scholarship that has little chance of shaking up the best-seller lists.

My wife and children also deserve thanks for their usual support and forbearance—and for peeling me off the backyard deck after a scary fall from the roof (where I was removing leaves from the gutters) on the very day that the NHC conference on the French nobility ended in November 2002. That forceful and ironic reminder of the mind-body dichotomy (Montesquieu in the morning, cracked ribs in the afternoon), along with relentless teasing at home, has helped to keep my feet planted firmly on the ground ever since.

Jay M. Smith
Chapel Hill, 5 October 2005

INTRODUCTION: NOBILITY AFTER REVISIONISM

The purpose of this volume is neither to reassess the French eighteenth century nor to survey the full range of experiences and attitudes characteristic of the French nobility over the course of that century. No single book could do justice to such large subjects in any case, and the title of this volume is actually meant to evoke a more defined problem of historical interpretation. The contributors to this volume were asked to respond to a particular challenge: to reexamine the relationship between the dependent variable of "nobility" and the larger equation of historical change in eighteenth-century France. What difference did the nobility make? How did the nobility influence, and how was it influenced by, processes of historical change in the eighteenth century? In what ways does the history of the nobility illuminate the relationship between the Old Regime and the French Revolution? Where, in other words, should the nobility fit into the twenty-first century's narrative about eighteenth-century France?

In all likelihood, members of the educated reading public would be puzzled by historians' desire to reexamine the nobility's place in the unfolding drama of the eighteenth century, since for them, as for the historians who crafted the standard interpretation of eighteenth-century French history generations ago, the nobility's function in eighteenth-century life was thrown into stark relief by the events that closed the century. According to still-current conventional wisdom and by the light of most scholarly accounts before the 1970s, the nobility exemplified the traditional order in the eighteenth century because of its arrogance, decadence, and parasitic habits, and its increasingly irritating presence in French politics and society had helped to trigger the French Revolution. In films, novels, and popular accounts of the period—and in many a classroom—the nobility's loss of power in 1789, and its eventual destruction in the course of the Revolution, continues to be represented as an inevitability. Common sense has it that the nobility's demise reflected the ascendance of the liberal values characteristic of the middle class, which mobilized the righteous anger of a population eager to be free of aristocratic tyranny.

For specialists of the period, however, these and other venerable assumptions about the nobility's role in eighteenth-century history were brought down by the seismic upheaval of "revisionism" in the 1970s and 1980s.[1] Revisionists, who especially took aim at crude versions of Marxist explanation built on rigid social categories and a teleological vision of class conflict, showed that nobles of the eighteenth century had been as modern and progressive as anyone, that they too were dissatisfied with the existing political order, and that the most forward-thinking among them had helped to spearhead the assault on the old order in 1788–89. Moreover, they showed that avenues of upward mobility remained open for commoners in the decades before the Revolution and that the economic and social resources of French society were not manipulated specifically, or self-consciously, for the benefit of an aristocracy—or at least no more so than in previous generations. As drawn by the leading revisionist historians, then, the picture of the nobility (and of its former sparring partner in the pages of history books, the bourgeoisie) came to be dominated by shades of gray. Except for the accident of legal title, little distinguished the nobility from other citizens who rose above a certain minimum threshold of income and social capital. The members of France's heterogeneous elite owned similar forms of property, read the same books, belonged to some of the same organizations, frequented the same social venues, and assumed the same respectful but increasingly critical posture toward the government. The animosity toward nobility that the abbé Sieyès and other publicists articulated in 1788–89 grew directly from the immediate circumstance of political debate and not from deeply rooted and increasingly stark social differences.

As one specialist of the period recently noted, the revisionists' dismantling of the "social interpretation" of the Revolution in the 1970s left "an indelible mark" on the image of the nobility, and it completely altered the research agenda for specialists of the Old Regime.[2] Heeding George Taylor's famous dictum that the Revolution had been a "political" event with "social" consequences rather than the other way around, historians of the eighteenth century sought new sources for the revolutionary rupture that occurred in 1789, and they naturally began to focus on aspects of eighteenth-century political

1. The debates between the revisionists and the standard bearers of the Marxist interpretation are conveniently summarized in *The French Revolution: Recent Debates and New Controversies,* ed. Gary Kates (London, 1997), 1–20, and William Doyle, *Origins of the French Revolution,* 3rd ed. (Oxford, 1999), 5–34.

2. John Dunne, "The French Nobility and the Revolution: Towards a Virtual Solution to Two Age-Old Problems," *French History* 17 (2003): 96–107.

life—parlementary constitutionalism, Jansenism, political sociability, publishing, language and ideology, reading habits, the shape of the emerging public sphere—that were not easily transposed to the experience of discrete social classes.[3] In France, where revisionism never entirely swept the field and where a long tradition of regional history encouraged work on local nobilities, the nobility continued to attract scholarly attention even after the assault on social interpretations of the Revolution.[4] On the American side of the Atlantic, however, where the key findings of the revisionists coalesced into a new conventional wisdom embraced by most of the leaders of the field, the decline of "the social interpretation" meant that the eighteenth-century nobility increasingly faded from view, just as social history ceded pride of place to cultural history within the discipline as a whole. One of the seminal works of revisionism, Guy Chaussinand-Nogaret's *The French Nobility in the Eighteenth Century: From Feudalism to Enlightenment* (1976), eventually obtained a kind of scriptural status, as specialists of the eighteenth century simply invoked its authority or quickly rehearsed its central conclusions whenever the subject of the nobility became unavoidable in their own analyses.

The essays in this volume thus reflect, at least in part, a desire to compensate for the field's recent record of benign neglect with respect to the eighteenth-century nobility, especially in America.[5] The contributors, all of whom are American, share the assumption that the category of nobility

3. George V. Taylor, "Non-Capitalist Wealth and the Origins of the French Revolution," *American Historical Review* 72 (1967): 469–96.

4. Landmark works include Jean Nicolas, *La Savoie au 18e siècle: noblesse et bourgeoisie*, 2 vols. (Paris, 1977–78), and Maurice Gresset, *Gens de justice à Besançon: de la conquête par Louis XIV à la Révolution française, 1674–1789* (Paris, 1978). More recently, see Mathieu Marraud, *La noblesse de Paris au XVIIIe siècle* (Paris, 2000); Michel Figeac, *L'automne des gentilshommes: noblesse d'Aquitaine, noblesse française au siècle des lumières* (Paris, 2002); Jean Duma, *Les Bourbon-Penthièvre (1678–1793): une nébuleuse aristocratique au XVIIIe siècle* (Paris, 1995), and Natacha Coquery, *L'hôtel aristocratique: le marché du luxe à Paris au XVIIIe siècle* (Paris, 1998).

5. The relative decline in interest in the eighteenth-century nobility is underscored by the very different trajectory followed by American specialists of sixteenth- and seventeenth-century France, for whom the subject of nobility supported an impressive cottage industry between the mid-1970s and the mid-1990s. See, for example, works by Jonathan Dewald, *The Formation of a Provincial Nobility: The Magistrates of the Parlement of Rouen, 1499–1610* (Princeton, 1980); James B. Wood, *The Nobility of the Election of Bayeux, 1463–1666: Continuity through Change* (Princeton, 1980); Kristen B. Neuschel, *Word of Honor: Interpreting Noble Culture in Sixteenth-Century France* (Ithaca, N.Y., 1989); William Beik, *Absolutism and Society in Seventeenth-Century France: State Power and Provincial Aristocracy in Languedoc* (Cambridge, 1985); Ellery Schalk, *From Valor to Pedigree: Ideas of Nobility in France in the Sixteenth and Seventeenth Centuries* (Princeton, 1986); Mark Motley, *Becoming a French Aristocrat: The Education of the Court Nobility: 1580–1715* (Princeton, 1990); Donna Bohanan, *Old and New Nobility in Aix-en-Provence, 1600–1695: Portrait of an Urban Elite* (Baton Rouge, 1992).

must remain a central, rather than a marginal, character (or characters) in any retelling of French history. Each in his or her own way, the authors bring the nobility back toward center stage in the French drama of eighteenth-century transformation.

What makes this effort to reassess the nobility especially timely, however, is the methodological ferment that has taken place within the larger field of French history and, indeed, within the historical discipline as a whole over the last decade. A generation after the halcyon days of revisionism, the ascendancy of cultural history has produced two distinct and conflicting, if not incompatible, imperatives within the discipline.[6] On the one hand, the expositors of a mature "postsocial" history continue to search for the logic of historical change through ever more sensitive analyses of representations, discourses, and necessarily "constructed" realities.[7] On the other hand, historians determined to see some combination of institutions, social groups, and economic change as the engines of history have aggressively contested the primacy of cultural analysis and have inspired a pendulum-like "return" of social history.[8] The appearance of a new professional organization for historians in the late 1990s reflected a growing determination to promote

6. The founding in 2004 of the British journal *Cultural and Social History* reflects the determination of the editors—who surely represent many within the historical profession—to define and enlarge the common ground that unites cultural history and the traditional concerns of materialist history. For an overview of some of the challenges involved in this project of reconciliation, see the lively exchange between Peter Mandler and his respondents in the journal's first volume: Mandler, "The Problem with Cultural History," *Cultural and Social History* 1 (2004): 94–117; Carla Hesse, "The New Empiricism" (vol. 1, 201–7); Colin Jones, "Peter Mandler's 'Problems with Cultural History,' or Is Playtime Over?" (vol. 1, 209–15); Carol Watts, "Thinking about the X Factor, or, What's the Cultural History of Cultural History?" (vol. 1, 217–24); and Mandler, "Problems in Cultural History: A Reply" (vol. 1, 326–32).

7. Miguel Cabrera, *Postsocial History: An Introduction* (Lanham, Md., 2003). See also Patrick Joyce, "The End of Social History?" *Social History* 20 (1995): 73–91, and his introduction to *The Social in Question: New Bearings in History and the Social Sciences,* ed. Patrick Joyce (New York, 2002).

8. For commentary on the return of the social, especially in the context of French revolutionary history, see Rebecca Spang, "Paradigms and Paranoia: How Modern Is the French Revolution?" *American Historical Review* 108 (2003): 119–47. Further evidence of the renewed defense of the social, and the attempt to rethink the methodologies of social history in light of the challenges presented by cultural history and the postmodern sensibility, is provided by the *Journal of Social History,* which devoted a recent issue (vol. 37, 2003) to the subject of "social history today." See, in particular, the articles by Christophe Charle, "Contemporary French Social History: Crisis or Hidden Renewal?" (pp. 57–68); Paula S. Fass, "Cultural History/Social History: Some Reflections on a Continuing Dialogue" (pp. 39–46); Jurgen Kocka, "Losses, Gains, and Opportunities: Social History Today" (pp. 21–28); Mark Smith, "Making Sense of Social History" (pp. 165–86). See also William H. Sewell Jr., "Whatever Happened to the 'Social' in Social History?" in *Schools of Thought: Twenty-Five Years of Interpretive Social Science,* ed. Joan W. Scott and Debra Keates (Princeton, 2001), 209–16.

rigorously empirical research on traditional subjects and, just as clearly, a desire to counter the surging influence of cultural analysis, which many had come to regard as excessively theoretical and abstract.[9]

The essays in the present collection inevitably reflect the influence of this ongoing debate, because the historian who sets out to reassess the eighteenth-century French nobility in the wake of the revisionist earthquake and its successive aftershocks necessarily traverses methodologically conflicted terrain. To revisit the category of nobility, some thirty years after Chaussinand-Nogaret formulated the most comprehensive and influential revisionist statement on the subject, means also to revisit the analytical approaches favored by earlier generations of historians, to reassess their validity, and to consider what has been gained or lost through the adoption of new methods of inquiry in the intervening years. In other words, the essays do not merely suggest *that* the nobility needs to be recovered as an object of focused inquiry, but each also suggests, either explicitly or implicitly, *how* that recovery operation should proceed. How can the insights provided by Marxist analysis be retained and reenergized? Which of the revisionists' conclusions have deservedly and permanently altered the interpretive landscape, and which reveal the methodological limitations under which the revisionists labored? Did their obliteration of the nobility–cum–class foreclose the development of more fruitful variations of social interpretation? If the empirical findings of the revisionists have made it impossible to define the nobility as a socially and economically constituted group, have the techniques and assumptions of cultural history made it possible to reconceive the nobility's role and identity? In short, what *kind* of nobility should be reinserted into the narrative framework of eighteenth-century history, and what are the historian's most reliable routes of access to the nobility and its pertinent contexts?

In seeking their own answers to these questions, the authors have incorporated a mixture of methods and forms of evidence, and the volume actually projects a number of distinct agendas for future research. Some essays emphasize the need to reexamine traditional topics, such as status, property owning,

---

9. See the account of the Historical Society's founding in *Chronicle of Higher Education,* 8 May 1998, p. A12. There Eugene Genovese refers derisively to the "dominant fads and trendy stuff that are of significance only to small groups of people with nothing better to do." The official Web site announces that the society "conducts activities that are intellectually profitable, providing a forum where economic, political, intellectual, social, and other historians can exchange ideas and contribute to each other's work." The category of cultural history is conspicuously absent from this statement of ecumenical intent. See http://www.bu.edu/historic/about.html.

and taxes. Others stress the shaping influence of contemporary language and cultural categories in the experiences of the nobility. Nevertheless, common themes do emerge, and the volume's reassuring message is that the "revival of the social" and the exploration of new frontiers in cultural analysis need not be mutually exclusive. All of the authors both acknowledge the important lessons of revisionism and show an eagerness to reexamine the assumptions on which revisionism was based. But in their reexamination of those assumptions, the authors collectively advocate a methodological eclecticism that makes it possible both to assess changing social realities and to highlight the creative and determining capacities inherent in cultural forms.

Perhaps the clearest evidence of this healthy eclecticism comes in the contributions by Michael Kwass, Gail Bossenga, Robert Schwartz, and John Shovlin. All four recognize a need to implant the eighteenth-century nobility within a context of overarching economic change, but they approach economic change in very different ways, and together their essays show not only the value but also the complementarity of conclusions reached within loosely defined "social" and "postsocial" analytical frameworks. By reconnecting the Old Regime and the Revolution, by joining the traditional concerns of materialist historians to those of cultural historians, and by reconceptualizing the nobility's impact on the consciousness of the later eighteenth century, Michael Kwass's essay perfectly conveys the spirit of respectful reassessment and reformulation that animates the entire book. Kwass analyzes an important aspect of contemporary debates over luxury, and in doing so he reveals fascinating interconnections between political, social, and intellectual change. Beginning with discussion of the controversy over the sartorial guidelines that determined the dress of deputies to the Estates-General at the convocation ceremony in May 1789, Kwass proceeds to demonstrate how, over the course of the second half of the eighteenth century, the fermentation of French economic thought propelled a transformation in basic social attitudes. He argues that the very idea of conspicuous display, which the convocation ceremony brought to the fore by correlating mode of dress with official status, had been thoroughly discredited in previous years by a range of economic and moral theorists who had redefined the meanings of luxury, consumption, and utility. In particular, the works of Rousseau, Mirabeau, and Forbonnais in the 1750s had presented three powerful and influential models for the reinterpretation of luxury and consumption, and although deep disagreements separated the texts, all three authors ultimately renounced as wasteful or counterproductive the traditional linkage between high social status and conspicuous displays of power and wealth. By decisively breaking this link,

Kwass suggests, these three models contributed to "a crisis in social representation" that visibly played itself out at Versailles in the spring of 1789.

Gail Bossenga focuses not on the force of representations but on some of the underlying mechanisms shaping social and cultural change in the eighteenth century. In an essay that draws deftly from the insights of Marx, Weber, and Tocqueville, she highlights the evolving relation between nobility and markets under the Old Regime. She describes the elaboration of two kinds of markets in the eighteenth century—emerging capitalist markets based on the free exchange of goods and services, on the one hand, and the more pervasive markets constructed and regulated by the "patrimonial state," on the other hand. These markets were not mutually exclusive, and the units of value on which they were theoretically based—money in the case of capitalist markets, status and honor in the case of patrimonial markets—actually overlapped in practice. By sensitively detailing the contradictions created and promoted by the state's involvement in market exchange, Bossenga shows how the advanced patrimonialism of the Bourbon monarchy helped to create the grounds for the "delegitimation" of nobility. The Revolution did not facilitate "the rise of the market," as was once believed. Rather, the Revolution's achievement was to change the rules governing the operation of markets, so that those entering contracts could do so from a position of legal equality, "in which status could not make pre-emptive claims."

Whereas Bossenga focuses on the contradictory moral and material pressures brought to bear on the nobility in the markets of the Old Regime, Robert Schwartz uses case studies of noble seigneurialism in Burgundy to show how individual nobles could creatively combine the calculuses of profit and status so well described by Bossenga. Through analysis of the techniques of estate management developed by the Mairetet and Berbis families after about 1750, Schwartz demonstrates that they were motivated to expand and improve their estates through a mixture of motives that reflected a distinctive phenomenon aptly termed "noble entrepreneurship." They continued traditional efforts to protect the rights and incomes attached to their seigneuries, thereby following in the footsteps of ancestors from the sixteenth and seventeenth centuries, but they also applied rational techniques of accounting and negotiation, promoted agrarian capitalism, and saw the defense of their seigneurial prerogatives as "good business." Influenced both by the Enlightened celebration of professional commitment and by their enduring pride in family and position, they cultivated new roles for themselves. By the second half of the eighteenth century, Schwartz suggests, "the attentive seigneur came to see the development of his lordships as a noble profession—work that sustained and legitimized his wealth, power, and status."

Although both Bossenga and Schwartz address key aspects of the cultural environment of the eighteenth century—the changing meaning of status for Bossenga, the new professionalism for Schwartz—they focus especially on structural characteristics of economic life, and they situate the nobility in relation to those characteristics. In contrast, John Shovlin places great interpretive weight on the terms through which contemporaries made sense of changing economic structures and practices. As Shovlin puts it, after about 1750 "the language of political economy became a critical site for debate" about the nobility, and his stimulating essay ties the fate of the nobility in 1789 to the outcome of a competition between different ways of discussing and thinking about French economic life and the nobility's place within it. Echoing and amplifying a point made by Kwass, Shovlin surveys the undeniable evidence attesting the growing importance of economic discussion in the publishing world of the later eighteenth century, and he argues persuasively that the language of political economy evolved through three distinct phases between 1750 and 1789: the first phase hostile to the nobility, the second phase particularly sympathetic to the landowning nobility, and the third phase directed against forms of luxury with which the nobility fairly or unfairly came to be identified. In his insightful discussion of prerevolutionary debates, Shovlin shows that the nobility came under attack not necessarily, or only, because of its own behavior and ideas but because its critics had learned to interpret the nobility through damning categories provided by the language of political economy.

By drawing attention to the political debates of 1789, and thus highlighting the ideological stakes implicit in economic discussion, Shovlin's essay also points to the rich and complicated historiographical legacy of François Furet. Because of the wide and powerful impact of his *Penser la Révolution française* (1978) and later writings, Furet was responsible, more than any other individual, for revisionism's drift away from traditional subjects of social history and the field's increasing attention to discourse and representation.[10] Throughout the 1980s and much of the 1990s, Furet and his many admirers and collaborators—Mona Ozouf, Keith Michael Baker, and Lynn Hunt most prominent among them—focused on the cauldron of political contestation and highlighted the determining power of the languages, ideologies,

10. Translated as *Interpreting the French Revolution,* trans. Elborg Forster (Cambridge, 1981).

and representations that framed and defined such contestation.[11] New and revealing attention was given to the powerful Rousseauian discourse of the general will, the idea of national sovereignty, and the language of ecclesiastical reform, as well as to other distinctly political phenomena. Scholarship treating a discursively defined "political culture" took precedence over the study of social relations, economic structures, and material conditions.

The essays by Rafe Blaufarb, Mita Choudhury, and Thomas E. Kaiser suggest that one of the answers to the provocative question posed recently by Suzanne Desan—"What's after political culture?"—is "more political culture but of a different kind."[12] For in contrast to the interpretive tradition founded by Furet, the essays by Blaufarb, Choudhury, and Kaiser connect political action and attitudes at the end of the Old Regime to contemporaries' culturally inflected reading of their own social and institutional experiences. The essays thus provide a new model for the analysis of political culture, one in which culture is represented simultaneously as a cause of political behavior and as the discernible consequence of social and institutional constraints and realities. As represented in this volume, the new political culture incorporates an endlessly expansive definition of the "political" and a "culture" that is always rooted in the negotiation and articulation of relationships.

Blaufarb takes the long view in order to explain the nature of the stakes involved in political contestation in Provence on the eve of the Revolution. In a careful and illuminating analysis of the intractable but little-studied *procès des tailles* (dispute over noble tax exemption) that occupied Provençal elites for more than two centuries, Blaufarb shows that tensions between different categories of landowners and different kinds of nobles in the eighteenth century reflected both competing material interests and rival understandings of the French legal and social hierarchy. A long and complicated struggle to define and circumscribe the rights and exemptions enjoyed by fief-holding nobles—a struggle that had begun in the middle of the sixteenth century and left property-owning nobles with an increasingly limited range of motion by the 1770s—pitted an imperfectly representative corps of *noblesse* against

11. Keith Michael Baker, *Inventing the French Revolution* (Cambridge, 1990); Mona Ozouf, *Festivals and the French Revolution,* trans. Alan Sheridan (Cambridge, Mass., 1988); Lynn Hunt, *Politics, Culture, and Class in the French Revolution* (Berkeley, 1984). Also of great importance was the four-volume collection of essays in which they and many others collaborated, *The French Revolution and the Creation of Modern Political Culture,* ed. Keith Michael Baker, François Furet, Mona Ozouf, and Colin Lucas (Oxford, 1987–94).

12. Suzanne Desan, "What's After Political Culture? Recent French Revolutionary Historiography," *French Historical Studies* 23 (2000): 163–96.

other landowning elites of the Provençal *communautés,* with the state posi-
tioned between the warring parties. Blaufarb argues convincingly that the
constitutional wrangling that attended the revival of Provence's provincial
Estates-General in 1787, a bickering over representation that historians have
generally seen as an early expression of a novel and prerevolutionary politics,
was firmly rooted in prior conflicts over noble tax exemption. A political
rhetoric that incorporated such newly resonant terms as nation, liberty, representation, and constitution actually channeled passions that stemmed from
a centuries-old struggle over fiscal privilege, one that both parties hoped to
turn to their own advantage in an increasingly unsettled political context.

Using different sources and examining different contemporary problems,
Mita Choudhury likewise reveals the deep roots that underlay the critique of
monarchical authority and the traditional social order in 1789. In an essay
that focuses especially on the image of a particular type of elite woman—the
convent abbess, who almost always came from an aristocratic family—
Choudhury exposes the ways in which gendered assumptions about power,
rationality, and public space informed the construction, and the criticism, of
the category of the "aristocrat" in the eighteenth century. By probing the
issues and rhetoric surrounding several court cases in which abbesses came
under assault by virtue of their status as powerful elite women, Choudhury
suggests that the eighteenth century's critique of arbitrary and despotic
authority was fueled in part by the fusion of mounting suspicions toward
both women and nobles. Carefully situating the legal and literary discussions
about abbesses within the context of the abbesses' actual and perceived living
conditions, Choudhury persuasively links the disapproving rhetoric directed
toward "arbitrary" abbesses—who were accused of abandoning their natural
nurturing role in order to exercise power in unseemly ways—to society's
growing disenchantment with corrupt kings and nobles, whose own "illegitimate authority" was increasingly described as effeminized. In both the legal
discourses involving the abbesses and wider debates about the social order,
Choudhury argues, images of "feminine capriciousness" ran parallel to an
"aristocratic sense of entitlement" and "aristocratic appetites" in the contemp-
tuous eyes of the political critics of the ancien régime.

The cultural and political history of the term *aristocrat* also forms the focus
of Thomas Kaiser's essay, although in this case it is the Revolution itself that
proves to be the critical turning point in French understanding of the term.
Choudhury's essay on the image of the aristocracy actually serves as a fitting
introduction to Kaiser's piece because her concluding argument—that an
image of "bad" nobles had emerged to complicate the political lives of "good"

nobles on the eve of the Revolution—is actually elaborated in rich detail through Kaiser's intricate analysis of the interplay between perceptions and political events after 1787. As Kaiser puts it, by the end of the Old Regime, "sufficient ideological scaffolding was in place to build a powerful indictment against the noble order given the appropriate circumstances," and the power of his essay lies in his explanation of the process whereby "circumstances" ultimately turned the "scaffolding" into an "indictment." In the years preceding the Revolution, he shows, a great many nobles had joined members of the Third Estate in stigmatizing the court and courtiers as the perverse symbols of aristocratic excess. Nobles' complicity in this critique of the court-based segment of the aristocracy proved costly, however, after bitter constitutional disagreements erupted at the Estates-General in spring 1789. The reluctance of Louis XVI to accept the formation of the National Assembly, the well-known machinations of the king's conservative advisors, and, perhaps most damning, evidence (and rumors of evidence) of collaboration between noble deputies in the Assembly and royal agents at court all converged to create the appearance of a vast "aristo-ministerial" conspiracy aimed at reversing the gains of the Third Estate. To simplify a complex argument, one could say that because of their real and imagined links to a discredited court in 1789, nobles in general came fatefully to be assimilated to an image of aristocracy—that of the nefarious conspirator—that had circulated for decades, if not for centuries.

One of the tensions that Kaiser's essay so skillfully brings to light—that between ascribed and self-articulated identity—also permeates the essays of Johnson Kent Wright, Jay M. Smith, and Doina Pasca Harsanyi. The divided, surprising, and sometimes conflicting self-perceptions and affiliations of the French nobility first emerged as an important theme of interpretation for the revisionist historians of the 1970s, who were interested above all to break down the misleading image of the nobility as a relatively homogeneous and self-consciously feudal social class. Wright, Smith, and Harsanyi all acknowledge and build on their predecessors' "revised" image of a socially diverse and ideologically variegated nobility, but they also seek to recover traces of a distinctive aristocratic consciousness that spanned the long eighteenth century, and each of their essays threatens to give new meaning to the long-discredited concept of the "aristocratic reaction." The differing faces of "reaction" shown by the three individuals treated in these essays nevertheless underscore the adaptable and multivalent nature of the "aristocratic" identity defended, asserted, and remembered by nobles over the course of the eighteenth century and beyond.

Wright contributes an elegant and refreshing reassessment of the surprisingly understudied Montesquieu. Until the 1960s, the *président* was most often represented in historical literature as a subtle but determined defender of aristocratic interests, and Wright's essay begins with an appreciative review of the historiographical and theoretical landmarks—works by Mathiez, Ford, Althusser, and Palmer—that marked the parameters of the "social interpretation" of Montesquieu's *Spirit of the Laws* in the prerevisionist age. With the decline of the paradigmatic social interpretation of Old Regime and Revolution from the late 1960s, Wright explains, Montesquieu came to be represented—when he received any attention at all—especially as a liberal political theorist and critic of despotism. Through a close and erudite rereading of Montesquieu's chapters on nobility and monarchical government, Wright impressively manages to reconcile the "social" and "liberal" readings of *The Spirit of the Laws,* thus restoring the "feudal" dimensions to Montesquieu's understanding of French society while simultaneously highlighting the *président*'s resolute commitment to the institutions of modern monarchy. Having willingly accepted the nobility's historic "surrender of political autonomy to absolutism," Montesquieu posed not as a backward-looking reactionary but as an energetic promoter of a status quo that he found favorable both to the interests of the nobility and to the vital cause of political moderation.

The comte d'Escherny, who is the subject of Smith's essay, also reconciled himself to modernity, so much so that he denounced the hereditary privileges of the nobility, consorted with philosophes, and welcomed the Revolution when it came. Embedded within Escherny's liberal and progressive worldview, however, lay a particular understanding of nobility, equality, and social order, an understanding that shaped his reading of the unfolding Revolution in unmistakably "aristocratic" ways. Inspired by Montesquieu's celebration of noble honor, but fiercely critical of the institutions of modern monarchy and sharing the hatred for courtiers that—as Kaiser shows—united many people across the social and political spectrum in the 1780s, Escherny imagined that a regenerated society and a regenerated nobility would emerge together in the wake of 1789's dramatic rupture with the past. The reformed and open-ended nobility he envisioned would have scarcely resembled the aristocratic class that had largely dominated French politics under the Old Regime—Escherny dismissed that fraudulent aristocracy as "monstrous"—but it would have preserved the principles of rank, inequality, and hierarchy that he believed necessary to the preservation of civic attachments in an increasingly egoistic world. The value of Smith's essay lies in its uncovering of the intersection between progressive and potentially reactionary political agendas. At least until the Revolution, ideas favorable to the nobility, and to the maintenance of certain social inequalities, remained compatible with, and could easily be veiled by, ideas associated with liberalism, constitutionalism, and natural rights.

Doina Pasca Harsanyi takes this general point even further in an essay suggesting that the revolutionary vision of Alexandre de Lameth—one of the noble patriots who steered the "liberal" Revolution from 1789 to 1791—was actually rooted, at least in part, in his own distinctly aristocratic sense of duty, civic obligation, and honor. Harsanyi focuses on the retrospective analysis of the Revolution supplied by Lameth in his *History of the Constituent Assembly,* a combination memoir/history written during the period of the Restoration. Like most postrevolutionary memoirs, the work offered convenient rationalizations of past behavior, and, as Harsanyi points out, Lameth used the memoirs to settle scores with many of his old foes. Nevertheless, Harsanyi persuasively argues that in his *History,* Lameth set out to reconcile his commitment to revolution with his identity as a noble, which, he insisted, he had never abandoned. Indeed, Lameth's nineteenth-century recollections of the early political conflicts of the Revolution seem to confirm two eighteenth-century cultural realities stressed by half the essays in this volume: the almost universal repudiation of a decayed "aristocracy" by the last years of the Old Regime and the simultaneous affirmation of "authentic" noble identity. In Lameth's case, nobility implied superiority of talent, character, enlightenment, and, perhaps especially, selflessness. For him, the true nobles of 1789 were marked precisely by their willingness to endorse revolutionary change and by their magnanimous efforts to lead the nation toward the construction of a better world. Although Lameth would never fit anyone's definition of a reactionary, there seems to be little doubt that the process of making sense of his own political engagement in the years following the Revolution made him acutely aware, and belatedly proud, of his identity as a noble. In the *History of the Constituent Assembly,* his expositions of political principle are tinged with cultural nostalgia.

The nineteenth century's memory of the prerevolutionary nobility and, more important, its understanding of the nobility's relationship to the coming of modernity, is the central theme in the overarching essay that concludes this book, Jonathan Dewald's thoughtful meditation on the history of the French nobility *before* revisionism. Dewald opens the essay by pointing out two peculiar features of twentieth-century French historiography. First, he notes, French historians before about 1960 devoted surprisingly little attention to the early-modern nobility, in spite of the nobility's continuing hold on the literary and political imagination of the twentieth century. Second, the impulse to reexamine the social realities of the early-modern French nobility came especially from Anglo-American scholarship, and in particular the field-changing study of Robert Forster on the nobility of Toulouse.[13]

Dewald explains the mystery of French historians' blind spot for the nobility by revisiting the nineteenth century and the narrative of modernization that emerged in the decades after the Revolution. In confronting and making sense of the features of the modern world that enveloped them, historians, novelists, and social scientists assigned to the nobility a necessarily marginal role in the history of French national development. The centralizing monarchy and the bourgeois creators of capitalist markets and values became the bearers of modernity in the nineteenth-century imagination. Nobles thus necessarily figured as "ghostly outsiders to the processes that mattered for French identity," either fruitlessly resisting the advance of modernization, as in the work of the historians Guizot and Renan, or marching cavalierly to their own drummer, as in the novels of Dumas or the literary histories of the Goncourt brothers. Because its values and interests seemed incompatible with the central story line of French history, in other words, the nobility could not be suitably integrated into the historiographical canvas depicting premodern life. Dewald provocatively suggests that this situation changed only after World War II as the French embraced distinctively American assumptions about the relationship between shaping social structures and the elaboration of personal identities and histories. Only the widespread acceptance of the belief that individuals cannot stand outside their own social and historical contexts—and perhaps, one is tempted to add, an emerging postmodern aversion to master narratives of any kind—made it possible for historians to see nobles and the institution of nobility as integral components in the unfolding of the French national past. This changed understanding of the relationship between individuals and society, as much as the developing critique of Marxist thought after 1956, gave birth to the revisionism of the 1960s and to the debates about nobility and eighteenth-century society that have raged ever since.

The contributors to this volume would not presume to announce a similarly momentous shift of interpretive paradigm in the early twenty-first century. The intersection between the revived interest in nobility and the intensifying discussion in historical circles about the very nature of "society"

---

13. Robert Forster, *The Nobility of Toulouse in the Eighteenth Century* (Baltimore, 1960).

nevertheless suggests that the nobility is in the process of becoming a valuable site for the reconceptualization of historical change and for the testing of new methods of social, cultural, and political analysis. The essays collected here represent one sign of the vitality of that process and, we sincerely hope, a stimulant (and friendly invitation) to renewed debate.

I

NOBILITY AND ECONOMY

I

ECONOMIES OF CONSUMPTION: POLITICAL ECONOMY AND NOBLE DISPLAY IN EIGHTEENTH-CENTURY FRANCE

Michael Kwass

In April 1789, only days before a spectacular public procession was to mark the opening of France's first Estates-General in 175 years, the marquis de Brézé, grand master of ceremonies for Louis XVI, sent instructions to deputies stipulating exactly what they should wear to this momentous event. In Brézé's eyes, the Estates-General was an affair of court, and deputies to Versailles were to wear clothing that befitted their rank and station. The clergy was to don its professional attire: red capes for cardinals; purple cloaks and square caps for bishops; cassocks, long coats, and square caps for clergy of second rank. The nobility was to wear black coats and vests trimmed with "magnificent" gold fabric (and gold buttons, if one wished), black breeches, white stockings, a lace cravat, and a beplumed hat à la Henri IV like those worn by Knights of the Order. The Third Estate was instructed to wear plain black suits: black coats, black vests, black stockings, muslin cravats, and black three-cornered hats with no adornment (braids and buttons were strictly forbidden). Everything about these three outfits—their color, fabric, style, and trimming—was designed to give visual expression to the social distinctions of the Old Regime.[1]

Brézé's dress code set off a storm of protest. There were obviously more important issues on the table in spring 1789, but the vivid social symbolism of the court's sartorial prescriptions touched a nerve among Third Estate deputies, many of whom were freshly reminded of the disdain with which

---

1. Georges Lefebvre, ed., *Recueil de documents relatifs aux séances des Etats-Généraux* (Paris, 1953), 1:64–68.

nobles still regarded the lower order. Why should I have to wear a lowly "*chapeau à clabaut*," wondered Dubois de Crancé, Third Estate deputy from the Ardennes, while my noble colleague from the same *bailliage* is allowed to sport a "*superbe panache*"? "I am unable to conceal from you," Dubois told his constituents, "that my humble suit, compared with the chivalrous costume of M. de Ballidart, painfully taught me that I have, for thirty years, lived in ignorance of the divisions that prejudice has fixed between men."[2]

More was at stake in marking such divisions than mere social humiliation. Because it was still unclear how deputies to the Estates-General would cast their votes, the stakes were also political. Would deputies vote by order, according to the traditional "forms of 1614," which would give the two privileged estates an overwhelming political advantage; or would they vote by head, a new procedure that would grant the Third Estate an unprecedented degree of power? Preoccupied by this fundamental question, deputies of the Third Estate discerned in Brézé's instructions an insidious political agenda. "The distinction in clothing," protested the Third Estate deputy Delandine, "can give rise to the idea that other distinctions will be allowed, whether in the presentation of the *cayers* or in the way votes are counted."[3] If distinctions in dress were to set a precedent for distinctions in voting, then the voice of the Third Estate was bound to be drowned out by those of the first two orders.

Alarmed by this politics of appearance, Honoré de Mirabeau printed a remarkable note, reputedly from the journalist Salaville, in the first issue of his *Lettre du comte de Mirabeau à ses comettans.*[4] In the letter, which was immediately reprinted on the front page of *Le Moniteur* (14 May 1789), Salaville acknowledged the social humiliation that "despotism" had visited upon the Third Estate when it forbade the order from wearing feathers and lace. But he was more concerned with the dress code's political implications. Given the influence that appearances exercise over the minds of men, "to give a different costume to deputies of different orders is to reinforce this unfortunate distinction of orders that can be regarded as the original sin of our nation, and of which it is absolutely necessary that we be purified if we expect to regenerate ourselves." Deputies to the Estates-General were not "to regard themselves as deputies from such or such an order,

---

2. *Lettre de M. Dubois de Crancé, député du département des Ardennes, à ses commettans* (Paris, 1790), 4.

3. Lefebvre, 1:69.

4. Honoré Gabriel Riqueti de Mirabeau, *Lettre du comte de Mirabeau à ses comettans* [Paris, 1789], 13 – 15.

but as true representatives of the universality of the kingdom." Here, in a well-publicized letter concerning the politics of dress, we find an early formulation of the mandate-breaking rhetoric that the Third Estate and its allies in the nobility and clergy would soon use to declare themselves the nation's representatives and seize power.[5] Thus, far from inspiring the kind of awe and respect that had contributed to the second order's domination of past Estates-General, noble display in 1789 served to galvanize Third Estate opposition and emboldened that order's deputies to claim a powerful role in a new political order.

This anecdote illuminates the crisis in social representation that plagued France at the end of the Old Regime. In the eighteenth century, as Enlightenment writers and literate French citizens entertained new notions of the individual, family, society, and nation, the social categories that defined the traditional ordering of the French kingdom became highly problematic. Some scholars have recently asserted that the social categories of the society of orders—clergy, nobility, Third Estate—were becoming increasingly obsolete as French men and women gradually ceased to think in terms of old social taxonomies.[6] I would suggest an alternative hypothesis: that instead of making traditional social categories obsolete, the Enlightenment provoked a heady process of reevaluation. Old social categories, in other words, were not so much abandoned as redefined and reassessed.[7] Indeed, the history of the origins of the French Revolution could easily be told in terms of prerevolutionary attempts to recast traditional social taxonomies in response to the political, social, and philosophical challenges of the eighteenth century.

In this chapter I will consider one aspect of this crisis in social representation by examining how writers in the burgeoning field of political economy

5. The revolutionary implications of antimandate rhetoric are analyzed by Ran Halévi, "La révolution constituante: les ambiguités politiques," in *The Political Culture of the French Revolution,* ed. Colin Lucas (Oxford, 1988), 69–96.

6. Sarah Maza, "Luxury, Morality, and Social Change: Why There Was No Middle-Class Consciousness in Prerevolutionary France," *Journal of Modern History* 69 (June 1997): 199–229; Sarah Maza, *The Myth of the French Bourgeoisie: An Essay on the Social Imaginary, 1750–1850* (Cambridge, Mass., 2003); David A. Bell, *The Cult of the Nation: Inventing Nationalism, 1680–1800* (Cambridge, Mass., 2001), chap. 1; William H. Sewell Jr., *A Rhetoric of Bourgeois Revolution: The Abbé Sieyes and What Is the Third Estate?* (Durham, N.C., 1994), chap. 4.

7. Mathieu Marraud, *La noblesse de Paris au XVIIIe siècle* (Paris, 2000), 370–400, argues that Parisian nobles in the late eighteenth century abandoned exterior signs of rank, creating a style of life that ran counter to the society of orders. However, he also acknowledges that Versailles continued to operate according to an older social framework based on birth, which encouraged recent and less wealthy nobles to falsify their genealogy to bolster their rank. Clearly, for the nobility at least, old social taxonomies coexisted with new ones, creating a kind of social identity crisis.

reconceptualized the relation between consumption and social status. The study of representations of nobility in eighteenth-century political economy has, in general, focused on issues of economic production. Historians, for example, have analyzed the Coyer debate, which considered the possibility of a commercial nobility.[8] Here, I would like to look at the other side of the economic coin: that is, how the social order and the nobility's place within it was reimagined in literature on consumption. Admittedly, literature on consumption did not always deal explicitly with nobles, but it did raise fundamental questions about conspicuous consumption and social rank that inevitably implicated the Second Estate.

The high Enlightenment smiled on political economy. From 1750 to 1789, as French literary production tripled in general, economic literature in particular increased no less than sevenfold.[9] For the historian of social representations, this corpus of printed work constitutes one of the richest literary troves of the Old Regime. As writers addressed a host of economic problems in the decades before the French Revolution, they not only analyzed how their society functioned but proposed a variety of alternative socioeconomic models to growing numbers of readers. In this essay I will dip into this body of literature to examine three seminal texts from the 1750s, the decade that launched political economy on its brilliant Enlightenment career. The texts are: *Discours sur l'économie politique* (1758) by Jean-Jacques Rousseau; *L'ami des hommes* (1756–60) by the marquis de Mirabeau; and *Elemens du commerce* (1754) by François Véron de Forbonnais. These works document the nearly simultaneous emergence of three basic vocabularies in eighteenth-century political economy: classical republicanism, physiocracy, and Gournay-school commercialism.

It would be an exaggeration to say that these three languages denoted distinct ideologies, for the boundaries between them were far too porous. Nor did the three idioms encompass the full range of ideas found in the political economy of the day. Nonetheless, the texts represent three main streams in French political economy, each of which evinced a new concern to analyze the social implications of consumption. Rousseau's classical republicanism attacked conspicuous consumption, severing the connection between

8. Jay M. Smith, "Social Categories, the Language of Patriotism, and the Origins of the French Revolution: The Debate over *Noblesse Commerçante*," *Journal of Modern History* 72 (2000): 339–74.

9. Christine Théré, "Economic Publishing and Authors, 1566–1789," in *Studies in the History of French Political Economy: From Bodin to Walras,* ed. Gilbert Faccarello (New York, 1998), 21.

material display and noble status. Mirabeau's prephysiocratic work also challenged conspicuous consumption. However, by prescribing a new regime of consumption, it sought to restore the preeminence of the nobility. Forbonnais's commercial treatise added utilitarian meaning to the definition of luxury, creating a fluid relation between consumption and social class.

Published originally in 1755 in the *Encyclopédie* under the entry "Économie (Morale et Politique)," Rousseau's *Discours sur l'économie politique,* which appeared in a separate edition in 1758, was the third and final installment of his trilogy of discourses.[10] Because Rousseau's concerns in the third discourse were overwhelmingly political and moral, some may object to characterizing the work as a treatise on political economy. But political economy in the Enlightenment was hardly an autonomous field with well-defined parameters. On the contrary, it remained deeply enmeshed in moral and political philosophy, never completely freeing itself to form an autonomous "economic science."[11] Thus, it can be argued that although Rousseauian classical republicanism concentrated on the political question of civic virtue (the quality by which the individual citizen acted on behalf of the common good), it also made its own distinct contribution to the development of Enlightenment political economy. In deploying a language of opposition to an increasingly commercial society, classical republicanism engaged with economic questions of the day, if at times only to refute the arguments of more commercially minded writers.[12]

Working within the idiom of classical republicanism (while adding a radical version of natural law theory), Rousseau's 1755 discourse on "economy" set out to establish a set of principles for the creation of "legitimate or popular government," that is, a polity "in which unity of interest and will reigns between the people and the rulers."[13] Rousseau began the essay by noting that in political society, unlike the family, rulers had no "natural interest" in the happiness of those over whom they ruled.[14] In fact, it was not uncommon

---

10. Rousseau's first two discourses, *Discours sur les sciences et les arts* (1751) and *Discours sur l'origine de l'inégalité* (1755), are still widely read, but his third discourse has been largely passed over by scholars and merits attention.

11. Philippe Steiner, *La "science nouvelle" de l'économie politique* (Paris, 1998); and Alain Béraud and Gilbert Faccarello, eds., *Nouvelle histoire de la pensée économique* (Paris, 1992), 148–50.

12. For French classical republicanism, see Keith Michael Baker, "Transformations of Classical Republicanism in Eighteenth-Century France," *Journal of Modern History* 73 (March 2001): 32–53; and Johnson Kent Wright, *A Classical Republican in Eighteenth-Century France: The Political Thought of Mably* (Stanford, 1997), which stands out for taking questions of political economy seriously.

13. Jean-Jacques Rousseau, *Discours sur l'économie politique* (Paris, 1990), 64.

14. Ibid., 59.

for rulers to seek their own happiness in the misery of their subjects. To rise above this tragic political situation, Rousseau called for a "reign of virtue" in which rulers and citizens alike followed a transcendent "general will." "This general will, which tends to the preservation and well-being of the whole and of each part, and which is the source of all laws, is for all members of the State, in their relation to one another and to it, the rule of what is just and unjust."[15] This was the philosopher's first formulation of the general will, a concept he would go on to develop, famously, in *The Social Contract*.[16]

A truly popular government was extremely difficult to achieve, however. In fact, the bulk of the *Discours sur l'économie politique* was devoted to identifying threats to popular government and proposing means to neutralize them. According to Rousseau, popular government faced two principal dangers: lack of patriotism and excessive inequality of wealth. The former allowed a culture of self-interest to flourish, sapping the political body. Rousseau's solution to this problem was to create a system of public education that would instill civic feeling in children and turn them into good citizens. The latter threat bears directly on the question of consumption. It was in the course of analyzing the problem of the inequality of wealth that Rousseau elaborated a distinctly republican economic theory that had important implications for noble display. The chief evil of wealth inequality, he explained, was that it permitted the rich to impose a tyrannical social compact on the poor: "'You need me, because I am rich and you are poor. Let us therefore make an agreement. I will permit you to have the honor of serving me, on condition that you will give me what little you have left for the trouble I will take to command you.'"[17] Because such an absurdly lopsided compact violated the general will and blunted the force of law and justice, it was imperative that popular governments act to abate extremes of wealth and poverty.

The most effective institutional instrument available for redressing economic inequality and consequently strengthening popular government was taxation. It was here, in his long discussion of taxation, that Rousseau worked out a theory of consumption and social status.[18] Certain forms of taxation, he reasoned, could mold society in such a way that it would become capable

---

15. Ibid., 61.

16. For Rousseau's appropriation of earlier uses of the general will, see Patrick Riley, *The General Will Before Rousseau: The Transformation of the Divine into the Civic* (Princeton, 1986).

17. Rousseau, *Discours sur l'économie politique*, 93.

18. For the Genevan context of Rousseau's ideas on taxation, see Helena Rosenblatt, *Rousseau and Geneva: From the First Discourse to the Social Contract, 1749–1762* (Cambridge, 1997), 191–203.

of sustaining government by general will. It was not enough to levy taxes "in an equitable and truly proportional manner," that is, according to the value of one's property.[19] All things being equal, Rousseau admitted, a person with ten times more property should pay ten times more in taxes. But all things were not equal, he insisted, since property had different uses. At this point, the political philosopher turned economist to introduce a basic distinction between two forms of property: that which is consumed from "necessity" and that which consists of "superfluity." "He who has only basic necessity should pay nothing at all; [whereas] the tax of the person who has some superfluity may go, according to need, up to all that which exceeds his necessity."[20] In levying taxes, governments should avoid touching "necessary" property and pursue superfluous wealth exclusively.

This proposed tax policy rested on a specific understanding of conspicuous consumption. "As long as there are rich people, they will want to distinguish themselves from the poor, and the State cannot establish a less onerous nor more certain revenue than the one based on this distinction."[21] Since the whole purpose of superfluous wealth was to show it off and thereby distinguish its possessor, material expressions of such wealth constituted the perfect fiscal target. Rousseau did not hesitate to list the most brilliant markers of status on which taxes should fall: liveried domestics, equipages, mirrors, chandeliers, furniture, fabric, gilding, townhouse courts and gardens, entertainments, and idle professions (dancers, singers, players)—"in a word, on this mass of objects of luxury, of amusement and idleness, which strike the eyes of all, and which can all the less be hidden since their sole purpose is to appear, and since they would be useless if they were not seen."[22]

It is possible to place Rousseau's tax plan in a conservative context and interpret it simply as a restatement of an old critique of the newly monied bourgeoisie. The philosopher certainly had little sympathy for this or any other upstart social group: "nothing is more disastrous to mores and to the republic than continual changes in rank and fortune among citizens."[23] In

---

19. Rousseau, *Discours sur l'économie politique,* 93.

20. Ibid., 91.

21. Ibid., 98.

22. Ibid., 97. "One enjoys luxury only by showing it," Rousseau later wrote to the maréchal de Luxembourg. *Correspondance complète de Jean-Jacques Rousseau* (Banbury, U.K., 1972), 50, letter of 20 January 1763.

23. Such changes, he continues, are "the proof and the source of a thousand disorders, which overturn and confuse everything, and by which those who were brought up for one thing find themselves destined for another; neither those who rise nor those who fall are able to

fact, one historian has attempted to link Rousseau's disdain for commercial wealth and social mobility to a long-standing noble ideology.[24] Rousseau's tax plan, however, easily defies such an interpretation. Although the main social division in the plan is that between the categories of rich and poor, Rousseau clearly has the high nobility, not the wealthy bourgeoisie, in his sights. Note how in the following defense of his tax proposal the rich man materializes as a *Grand*, the highest of nobles: "To this [my tax plan] he [who possesses superfluity] will say that, with regard to his rank, that which would be superfluous for an inferior man is necessary for him; but this is a lie: for a *Grand* has two legs just like a herdsman, and has but one stomach, no more than he. Moreover, this claimed necessity is so little necessary to his rank, that if he knew how to renounce it for a praiseworthy cause, he would only be more highly respected for it. The people would bow down before a minister who would go to council on foot, for having sold his carriages for a pressing need of State. In short, the law prescribes magnificence to no man, and propriety is never an argument against right."[25]

Rejecting the argument that for *les grands* superfluity was in fact a social necessity, Rousseau introduced a blast of radicalism into his discourse. In this passage, Rousseau marshals two highly subversive arguments to counter the widely held belief that men and women of high status were obliged to spend according to rank and were thus entitled to higher thresholds of necessity. Based on an anthropological conception of man that reduced all to a single biological identity, the first argument defined necessity and superfluity in physical rather than social terms. All men and women required the same minimum of consumption to meet the same basic physical needs. Therefore, all objects of consumption beyond such basic needs were superfluous, no matter the social position of the men and women who possessed or consumed them. If "a *Grand* has two legs just like a herdsman, and has but one stomach, no more than he," why should the *grand* be entitled to a higher level of consumption? This first argument severed the connection between *les grands* and the ostentatious possessions that were commonly, if mistakenly, believed to express their elevated status.

The second argument in the passage widened the division between status and consumption. High levels of consumption were not at all essential to

---

assume the maxims or the knowledge suitable to their new position [*état*], still less discharge its duties." Rousseau, *Discours sur l'économie politique*, 83.

24. Renato Galliani, *Rousseau, le luxe et l'idéologie nobiliaire: étude socio-historique* (Oxford, 1989).

25. Rousseau, *Discours sur l'économie politique*, 91.

the maintenance of rank, Rousseau contended. In fact, consumption could be antithetical to rank as in the case of a minister who stands to gain public esteem by renouncing objects of display. The royal minister who patriotically sacrificed his carriage for the good of the state would be more highly regarded than the minister who continued to consume conspicuously. Thus, Rousseau concludes, the possession of superfluous goods was wholly incidental to rank and esteem and should not be seen as an essential part of the social identity of any individual: "the law prescribes magnificence to no man." In formulating this double argument, Rousseau recategorized the luxurious material world of *les grands*. What had customarily been characterized as social necessities were now labeled biological superfluities—superfluities that had nothing to do with social esteem.[26]

Finally, Rousseau argued that both state and society stood to reap great benefits from this reclassification of consumption. If the crown adopted the tax plan and levied taxes on the superfluous consumption of the rich, two positive outcomes were possible. If despite new luxury taxes the rich continued to consume conspicuously, then the royal coffers would overflow with revenue. This fiscal surplus would allow the state to relieve poor farmers of their heavy tax burdens and, as a result, would revive agriculture. Excessive inequalities of wealth would in turn moderate as fortunes drew closer to that "*médiocrité* which constitutes the true strength of a State." If, alternatively, the rich reformed their decadent ways in order to avoid new taxes, such taxes "would produce the effect of the best sumptuary laws," curtailing luxury and choking the circulation of signs of social inequality.[27] In this case, the state would save a great deal of money. As superfluous spending declined among elites, government expenses (much of which Rousseau undoubtedly

26. This anthropological vision of necessity and luxury is discussed at greater length in my article, "Ordering the World of Goods: Consumer Revolution and the Classification of Objects in Eighteenth-Century France," *Representations* 82 (spring 2003): 87–116.

27. Although his third discourse did not describe how superfluity corrupted society, Rousseau explained in *Dernière réponse [à Bordes]* that "everything beyond physical necessity is a source of evil. Nature already gives us too many needs; and it is extremely foolish, to say the least, to multiply them needlessly." Superfluity was immoral in part because it deprived the poor of necessity: "Luxury may be necessary to give bread to the poor: but, if there were no luxury, there would be no poor. . . . We need sauce in our kitchens; which is why so many ill people lack bouillon. We need liqueurs on our table; which is why the peasant drinks only water. We need powder for our wigs; which is why so many poor do not have bread." Jean-Jacques Rousseau, *Oeuvres complètes* (Paris, 1964), 3:79. In a more psychological vein, Rousseau's "Le luxe, le commerce et les arts" suggests that "since the words poor and rich are relative, there are poor people only because there are rich people." Henry C. Clark, ed., *Commerce, Culture, and Liberty: Readings on Capitalism Before Adam Smith* (Indianapolis, Ind., 2003), 399.

believed subsidized aristocratic expenditure) would shrink along with it.[28] Either way, state finances would improve. Either way, the polity would be less vulnerable to the "tyranny of the rich."

Rousseau's *Discours sur l'économie politique* set out to establish the economic conditions in which a popular government based on the general will could survive. The main threat to such a government was certainly not the existence of a nobility. Rather, it was the concentration of wealth in the hands of the few. But in protesting against the tyranny of the rich, Rousseau implicated the nobility in two ways. First, he at times cast the high nobility—the *Grands*—in the role of the vicious rich. Second, and more important, he claimed that the conspicuous consumption of the *Grand* was completely unjustified. Severing the link between consumption and public esteem, Rousseau rejected the social function of material display. Display was but an empty form of distinction and as such made a perfect target for the state treasury.

Rousseau's discourse on political economy was published at the same time as the marquis de Mirabeau's *L'ami des hommes,* a passionately written if verbose book that took the literary world by storm and became an instant best-seller.[29] Like Rousseau, Mirabeau worried about the decline of France and lamented the depopulation of the countryside, the growth of vice and idleness in the capital, the waning of patriotism, the spread of luxury, and the financial corruption of the monarchical state. In fact, Mirabeau was so struck by the similarities in their ideas on political economy that he would later attempt to recruit the philosopher for the physiocratic cause.[30] Yet there remained crucial differences between the two, especially regarding nobility and the economics of consumption.

The first edition of *L'ami des hommes* appeared in 1757 (though it was dated 1756) and did not bear the physiocratic influence of François Quesnay.[31] For historians interested in social vocabulary, there is a singular advantage in looking at this prephysiocratic text. Whereas physiocracy would develop an economic vocabulary that masked traditional social categories, substituting "landowners" for "nobles" for example, *L'ami des hommes* still employed

28. Rousseau, *Discours sur l'économie politique,* 98.

29. While most moderately fashionable books in this period went through three or four editions, *L'ami des hommes* ran through twenty editions in its first three years and perhaps forty editions over the century. For a fuller treatment of the work and its popularity, see Michael Kwass, "Consumption and the World of Ideas: Consumer Revolution and the Moral Economy of the Marquis de Mirabeau," *Eighteenth-Century Studies* 37 (2003): 187–214.

30. Louis de Loménie, *Les Mirabeau: nouvelles études sur la société française au XVIIIe siècle* (Paris, 1889), 2:265–76.

31. Parts 4–6, which reflect Mirabeau's move toward Quesnay, were added in later editions.

traditional social language in its attempt to illuminate the laws of economic prosperity and demographic growth.

For Mirabeau, unlike Rousseau, the nobility was key to both the moral and economic rejuvenation of France. "Love the *grands*," the marquis urged his readers. Although Mirabeau admitted that *les grands* were presently "taken with wealth," pursuing vain riches at the expense of honor, he asked his readers to consider these great nobles as they had existed in the distant feudal past when they had lived a rougher life (sleeping on straw beds and going about on horseback), had cared for the poor and humble, and had fought valiantly for the king.[32] In this feudal environment, Mirabeau emphasized with more than a tinge of nostalgia, material display had never been a problem. If those of high rank exhibited their status through magnificence (*faste*), they did so without triggering the nefarious effects of luxury: "In days of old, the peasant went to his seigneur's on Sunday to see a Venetian Mirror two square feet in size; he returned home astonished by this magnificence, but instead of being shocked and envious, he appropriated a share of this magnificence. . . . Nothing in all this excited desire or greed."[33]

Although Mirabeau did not detail the mechanics by which the peasant of the past managed to appropriate the magnificence of his lord without inflaming his own consumer desire, the marquis made it clear that the Golden Age in which this wholesome culture of consumption operated had long passed. By the eighteenth century, Mirabeau observed, material display had completely changed its meaning. In a kingdom run amuck by the pursuit of wealth, conspicuous consumption symbolized greed, not power. "Precious furniture, magnificent clothes, sumptuous houses, coaches and entourages, and so on inevitably draw the attention of the multitude, and this is what men take and will always take as a sign of distinction. In their original constitution these things served to designate power; but as soon as they designate no more than wealth, from that moment on, I say, luxury reigns. Emulation then turns toward wealth, but emulation of wealth is nothing but greed."[34]

---

32. Victor de Riqueti, marquis de Mirabeau, *L'ami des hommes, ou Traité de la population* (Avignon, 1756, reprint of 1970), vol. 1, pt. 1, pp. 69, 78−79, and 107. Alexis de Tocqueville's own nostalgic representations of medieval nobility may owe something to Mirabeau, whose works Tocqueville studied closely.

33. Mirabeau, vol. 1, pt. 2, p. 102. On the meaning of "magnificence," see Richard A. Goldthwaite, *Wealth and the Demand for Art in Italy, 1300−1600* (Baltimore, 1993), 75, 204−20; and Philippe Perrot, *Le luxe: une richesse entre faste et confort, XVIIIe−XIXe siècle* (Paris, 1995), chap. 2.

34. Mirabeau, vol. 1, pt. 2, p. 106.

Mirabeau did not pinpoint which social groups were responsible for this transformation. But he lamented the fact that the nobility of the mid-eighteenth century did not stand above the common fury for money and luxury. Quite the contrary. Like the rest of the social order, the nobility was spending all its income on useless decoration. Consider the ambitious land-scaping plans of an absentee landlord who finally visits his country estate.

> He arrives, the avenue is too narrow and asymmetrical, another must be staked out, with two side paths, thirty *toises* wide and as far as the eye can see. The land of a good *métairie* becomes an avenue, and the revenue zero. The park, tree-lined walkways, quincunx, labyrinth, topiary, another zero. Three hundred acres of this kind is not too much. The vegetable garden is too narrow, it needs some borders, some dividing walls, a water pump, a few greenhouses, an *orangerie*. Gravel terraces, pruning, the upkeep of vegetable gardens from which the first fruit of the season will be brought to the city, the maintenance of the pumps, the raking of all the paths, etc.: if all this costs no more than 10,000 *livres,* it's not too much. . . . The land is worth 15,000 *livres* of annual income; it cost 400,000 *livres* plus expenses; 60,000 *livres* were spent to make the estate worthy of its master. The newly decorated land reduced income by 4,000 *livres*. It costs 11,000 to maintain it. Nothing is left for Monseigneur.[35]

This kind of spending not only reflected a corrupt system of symbolic capital in which modern luxury had eclipsed medieval magnificence. It also wreaked havoc on the kingdom's physical condition, destroying French agriculture and decimating the population. Since it sharply reduced agricultural output, decorative display was literally lethal. For every culti-vated field that was turned into a park, the subsistence of hundreds of men and women was obliterated. In Mirabeau's eyes, misguided spending was tantamount to homicide.[36]

Yet all was not lost, the marquis declared. If the nobility reformed its wayward expenditure, it could save the kingdom from falling into deca-dence and restore itself to a position of leadership. The solution lay not in a return to medieval life; for all of his nostalgia, Mirabeau knew there was no

35. Ibid., pt. 1, p. 53.
36. Hence, Mirabeau called Voltaire's witticism that the superfluous was necessary a "homi-cidal axiom." Mirabeau, vol. 1, pt. 3, p. 15.

going back. Rather, the path to noble restoration and national revival lay in a new mode of expenditure that would transform corrupt noble spendthrifts into virtuous consumers. Rather than spending irresponsibly on decoration, the new self-disciplined landowner would exercise virtue by managing his land and spending his revenue in an economically productive fashion. "If he uses his leisure time to acquire knowledge regarding the improvement of his patrimony and revenue [*superflu*]; if he makes every effort to exploit them, he fulfils his duty and maintains his position, which is a virtue."[37] If the "grand seigneur" took on the virtues of the "country gentleman" by taking his land in hand, he could produce "in his lifetime more assets for his family, for his neighbors, for the poor, for the State, finally for his *patrie,* than the greatest minds ever imagined."[38]

Like Rousseau, Mirabeau's political economy called for a reign of virtue. But whereas Rousseau clung to the civic virtue of the ancients, Mirabeau transposed the idea of civic virtue from an ancient political context to a modern economic one. Whereas acts of ancient civic virtue had taken place outside the household in political assemblies or on the battlefield, civic virtue in modern France would be enacted on the landed estate, where citizen property owners sacrificed expenditure on fine goods to devote themselves to the productivity of the *patrie.*

It is not difficult to see how these ideas about noble consumption and production were, in the 1760s, incorporated into physiocratic doctrine. Indeed, if we look at the zigzags of François Quesnay's famous *Tableau économique* in light of Mirabeau's preoccupations with consumption, they look less like the first graphic depiction of circular economic flow, as historians of economic thought like to claim, and more like a stiff prescription for proper spending. If in the *Tableau* the social category of noble gave way to that of property owner, the message remained the same: wealthy landowners should restrict their spending on finished luxury products fabricated in towns and direct their consumption toward more productive agricultural channels. To underscore this message, the physiocrats drew an explicit distinction between *luxe de décoration,* decorative luxury that harmed the reproduction of wealth, and *luxe de subsistance,* an agriculturally based and therefore benign form of

37. Ibid., pt. 1, p. 71.
38. Ibid., pt. 1, p. 79–80. Mirabeau's social vocabulary in these passages is highly ambiguous. By turn, he refers to *"propriétaires," "la Noblesse,"* and *"Seigneurs,"* reflecting a degree of uncertainty as to what, precisely, this new productive elite would look like. No doubt the nobility would comprise the bulk of it, but Mirabeau does leave room for the inclusion of non-noble large landowners.

luxury. Thus, Mirabeau, Quesnay, and other physiocrats used the *Tableau* to instruct landowners not so much to save money—saving was a dubious activity, associated with hoarding and the idleness of rentiers—as to spend it productively. "This entire work," Mirabeau wrote of his physiocratic textbook, *Philosophie rurale* (1764), "is, in a word, based only on the development of the influence of expenditure on wealth."[39]

If the physiocrats asserted that the act of spending net income from the land functioned as the economy's principal engine, they did not believe that the landowner was free to dispose of that income as he or she wished. The "natural order" prescribed exactly how it should be consumed, setting definite limits on the amount the landowner could spend on finished goods. If a landowner violated the natural order by spending too much on "decorative luxury," he did so at the direct expense of the kingdom's prosperity. Taking this principle to heart, the physiocrat Baudeau would characterize excessive spending on decorative display as "theft," a "crime" against the public good.[40]

Physiocracy would go on to become the first fashionable (albeit highly controversial) economic ideology of the modern age. But until it caught on among the learned in the 1760s, the true vanguard of economic thought lay within a small circle of writers led by Jacques-Claude Vincent de Gournay.[41] An *intendant* of commerce from 1751 to 1759, Gournay coined the free-trade slogan "laissez faire, laissez passer" and actively promoted the work of economic thinkers who, like him, wanted to free France from the interventionist legacy of Jean-Baptiste Colbert. Equally important for our purposes was the group's willingness to take seriously the commercial development of France. Although the members of Gournay's circle did not deny that agriculture was the most important part of the French economy (who could deny such a thing in the eighteenth century?), its study of "commerce" was broad enough to encompass questions of urban industry, nonagricultural commercial exchange, and colonial trade—economic sectors that both classical republicans and physiocrats devalued. In other words,

---

39. Mirabeau, *Philosophie rurale ou économie générale et politique de l'agriculture* (Amsterdam, 1764, reprint of 1972), vol. 3, chap. 12, p. 261.

40. Nicolas Baudeau, *Principes de la science morale et politique sur le luxe et les loix somptuaires* (1767; Paris, 1912), 32.

41. The circle included Plumard de Dangeul, François Véron de Forbonnais, Anne-Robert-Jacques Turgot, Simon Clicquot-Blervache, Georges-Marie Bûtel-Dumont, Gabriel François Coyer, and André Morellet. As director of the book trade, Chrétien Guillaume Lamoignon de Malesherbes was also instrumental in helping the group's publications to see the light of day. Gournay's circle is finally getting the historical attention it deserves; for a brief introduction, see Béraud and Faccarello, eds., *Nouvelle histoire de la pensée économique*, 199–203.

Gournay and his disciples set out to explore "merchant France," a part of the economic landscape that was, in the words of Daniel Roche, "more open, more mobile [than peasant France], and equipped, if not with its own culture, then at least with its own form of communications and social relations characteristic of a commercial society."[42]

It is in this context that we should consider the forward-looking approach to material culture found in François Véron de Forbonnais's *Elemens du commerce* (1754), a book-length elaboration of the author's essay on "commerce" published in the *Encyclopédie*.[43] Forbonnais's discussion of consumption was complex. On the one hand, like Rousseau and Mirabeau, he noted that in archaic societies the purpose of goods was to signify status and mark the social and political boundaries that defined hierarchy. Tracing the origins of luxury back to the original formation of society, he explained that when legislators and judges were created to correct the injustices arising from the unequal division of property, they invented luxury in order to distinguish themselves from those whom they judged. "Ostentation and pomp was one of the privileges of these powerful men; rare things were destined for their use, and luxury was known. It became the object of ambition of inferiors, because every one likes to distinguish himself."[44] At the dawn of society, the purpose of luxury was to set off a political and judicial elite from the rest of society.

On the other hand, in stark contrast to his classical republican and physiocratic contemporaries, Forbonnais emphasized that the consumption of nonsubsistence goods took on greater utilitarian meaning as commerce developed and as the world of consumer goods expanded. Not that the world of goods in his day no longer marked status: "real inequality" (that is, material inequality) continued to delineate "an inequality of opinion among citizens."[45] But in contemporary commercial society, the purpose of goods broadened to include the provision of comfort, pleasantness (*agrément*), and happiness. In linking material abundance to such utilitarian virtues, Forbonnais's argument converged with that put forward by a small but controversial group of writers (notably, Bernard Mandeville, Jean-François Melon, Voltaire, and David Hume) who had for years been defending the

42. Daniel Roche, *France in the Enlightenment,* trans. Arthur Goldhammer (Cambridge, Mass., 1998), 110.

43. That the editors of the *Encyclopédie* assigned "political economy" to Rousseau and "commerce" to Forbonnais suggests the great range of economic thought in the Enlightenment.

44. Forbonnais, *Elemens du commerce* (Leyde, 1754), 10.

45. Ibid., 227.

production and consumption of luxury. Forbonnais joined in this defense of
luxury by elaborating a new system for classifying the world of goods that
would have far-reaching implications for noble display.[46]

The world of goods, he argued, was divided into three categories: necessity,
convenience (*commodité*), and luxury. Necessities included basic goods, such as
food, lodging, and clothing, all of which satisfied the most basic "physical
needs." Above the level of necessity, people invented conveniences, goods that
not only helped to assure their survival but which made "the preservation
of their being more agreeable." Convenience was a particularly important
category of consumption for Forbonnais, and to emphasize its significance
he contrasted the material lives of two families, one representing necessity
and the other convenience. The first family was poor, lived in a small drafty
cottage, wore scraps of cloth in the middle of winter, and subsisted on roots;
it survived at the threshold of physical necessity. Their neighbors, by contrast,
enjoyed thick wool fabric, cider, and an abundance of meat—conveniences
that existed "between physical necessity and luxury" and that allowed the
second family to live a more secure, pleasant, and agreeable life. At the level
of convenience, then, the purpose of goods went beyond the satisfaction of
primitive needs to improve the material condition of human existence.[47]

What of Forbonnais's third category, luxury? Did the purpose of consumption shift toward status accumulation when one considered the far more
controversial category of luxury? No, Forbonnais insisted. In a commercial
society, luxury did not constitute a qualitatively different category from
convenience. On the contrary, luxury was but an extension of a broader
sphere of convenience. When those who enjoyed a measure of convenience
found their possessions lacking in comparison to those of others, the goods
that they lacked and now desired were called luxuries. Luxury was simply a
comparatively higher degree of convenience.[48]

46. He also joined in the defense of luxury by establishing a conceptual link between commercial progress and intellectual and moral progress. Here, Forbonnais followed Hume rather
closely, quoting the following passage from Hume's "Of Refinement in the Arts" (originally
titled "Of Luxury" in 1752): "We cannot reasonably expect, that a piece of woollen cloth will
be wrought to perfection in a nation, which is ignorant of astronomy or where ethics are
neglected." Forbonnais, 238.
47. Ibid., 3–4, 54–55, 223–28.
48. Ibid., 4, 224, and 227–30. Voltaire's poem, *Le mondain,* introduced the notion that luxury
was merely part of living a reasonably enjoyable life on earth. Forbonnais developed this theme
in his book, but it would be another member of Gournay's circle, Butel-Dumont, who would
provide the century's most elaborate formulation of this idea. For Butel-Dumont, see Kwass,
"Ordering the World of Goods."

Forbonnais's idea of a modern commercial society in which objects were meant to be enjoyed, not just displayed, had important implications for the material culture of the nobility. First, once associated with convenience, all forms of luxury took on a benign quality, including the luxury of *grands* and landed seigneurs to which Rousseau and Mirabeau, respectively, objected. By highlighting the convenient face of luxury and downplaying luxury's capacity to project social status, Forbonnais sought to redeem the category of luxury for all orders. How innocuous the pursuit of private comfort seemed in comparison to ostentatious public display. Second, in a developed commercial society, the expenditure of wealthy nobles could become a progressive social force. Forbonnais encouraged *les grands* and "all those to whom the public order accords a rank distinguished from others" to spend freely, not because it sustained their status (which, he believed, it most certainly did), but because such spending redistributed wealth and improved the quality of life for the less fortunate. Forbonnais could characterize the luxury of *les grands* in positive social terms since according to his economic model it was "inseparable" from the material advancement of the lower orders.[49]

Unlike Rousseau and Mirabeau, then, Forbonnais did not implicate the nobility in a critique of material display. Yet, in supporting the growth of commercial society and emphasizing the free flow of consumer goods, he did imagine a social order in which luxury goods and articles of convenience were no longer associated strictly with the high nobility. Further, Forbonnais's approach to consumption conferred honor upon groups outside the nobility, such as merchants. Merchants, particularly overseas merchants known as *négociants,* were essential to the development of commercial society, he argued, because they served as mediators between wealthy elites and ordinary people. As merchants distributed goods, they extended superfluous consumption well beyond the elite, lifting the artisan and *laboureur* above the threshold of necessity and introducing them to the world of convenience. In Forbonnais's social taxonomy, merchants were assigned the heroic role of agents of material progress. Nobles and other wealthy elites were cast somewhat less heroically as big spenders.[50]

To emphasize this point, Forbonnais invited the reader to imagine what would happen to society if commerce were to thrive no longer. If commerce receded, Forbonnais warned, "the natural order of circulation" would be

---

49. Forbonnais, *Elemens,* 232. The idea that luxury spending improved the lives of the lesser orders was consistently emphasized by such proluxury writers as Mandeville, Melon, Voltaire, and Hume.

50. Ibid., 232–33.

reversed and the "equilibrium" among the classes would be destroyed. A small elite in one or two cities would come to dominate consumption and reintroduce an unhealthy culture of vanity and display. In this commercially desiccated society, pride would take the place of honor, ridicule would be heaped on the poor, and education would become merely a mark of luxury. No longer seeking honor or comfort, men would pursue wealth for the sole purpose of "showing it off."[51] And as the rich introduced new, expensive practices of consumption, others would attempt to imitate them and fall into debt. Describing in detail the disastrous consequences that inevitably followed from the waning of commerce and the narrowing of consumption, Forbonnais drove home the point that commerce alone redeemed nonsubsistence consumption. It did so by adding utilitarian meaning to a form of consumption whose original purpose was to bestow social status and by opening the world of goods to formerly excluded sections of the social order.

All three texts under consideration attempted to recast the relation between consumption and social hierarchy, a project that contributed to the reassessment of nobility in the eighteenth century. Elaborating a classical republican economy, Rousseau not only implicated the nobility in the tyranny of the rich over the poor, but also severed the tie between conspicuous consumption and noble status. Condemning all forms of superfluity as immoral, since the only purpose of superfluity was to satisfy human vanity and put social distinction on display, Rousseau lambasted the conspicuous consumption of elites and imagined an alternative moral economy of necessity in which consumption was anchored to the biological needs of man.

It is not all that surprising to find criticism of noble display in a classical republican tract like Rousseau's *Discours sur l'économie politique*. Yet both Mirabeau and Forbonnais raised questions about noble consumption as well. Mirabeau had no objections to superfluity and display in and of themselves. The problem was that the material culture of his own day had degenerated to the point where display represented wealth instead of power. To regenerate the kingdom and restore the preeminence of the Second Estate, Mirabeau created a new role for nobles as productive consumers. By abandoning decorative display and directing their consumption toward productive ends, the nobility could lead France toward a prosperity that would be both moral and durable.

The least troubled by the consumer society taking shape in midcentury France, Forbonnais did not directly question the morality of noble consumer

51. Ibid., 240–41.

practices. He did, however, establish a more fluid relationship between consumption and class. By claiming that the purpose of the world of goods was not only to project status but to make life more agreeable, Forbonnais deliberately confused the category of exclusive luxury with that of simple convenience. And by asserting that society could sustain high levels of consumption only if commerce acted to redistribute goods from the nobility to the middling orders, he valorized merchants and challenged the nobility's theoretical monopoly on luxury consumption.

Having considered how three key works of political economy reassessed the relation between status and consumption, it is worth returning to the anecdote about revolutionary costume with which this essay began. Historians have generally interpreted the conflict over Brézé's dress code of 1789 with reference to Rousseau. Edna Lemay, for example, gave voice to those who protested against the court-imposed dress code in the following terms: "Had it [the monarchy] not read Rousseau? Politically equal men do not have to wear suits which separate them, arbitrarily, from one another according to the three estates of the Old Regime."[52] Jean Starobinski, a Rousseau specialist, provided a similar interpretation of the crowd's sympathy for the black-suited Third Estate and its negative reaction to the lavishly dressed upper orders: "It was an important moment when the magic of ostentation stopped having an effect on spectators who had learned to add up the cost: expense no longer inspired respectful awe." According to Starobinski, even the nobility was under the spell of Rousseau in 1789: "It [the nobility] had an uneasy conscience. It had listened to its accusers, such as Rousseau and Beaumarchais, and it had dreamed of reforms and philanthropy and regeneration. But it had not thrown off the habit of indulging in expensive amusements; so it ran headlong to its ruin."[53]

It is not difficult to understand why historians have painted revolutionary reactions to noble display against a Rousseauian background. Of the three

52. Edna Lemay, *La vie quotidienne des députés aux états généraux 1789* (Paris, 1987), 25–26.

53. Jean Starobinski, "Reflections on Some Symbols of the Revolution," *Yale French Studies,* no. 40 (1968): 51; and *1789: The Emblems of Reason,* trans. Barbara Bray (Charlottesville, 1982), 19. Historians of dress also emphasize Rousseauian undercurrents. Philippe Perrot based his own interpretation of the 1789 dress code on Starobinski, while Jennifer Jones emphasized Rousseauian shifts in women's fashion at the end of the Old Regime. Perrot, *Fashioning the Bourgeoisie: A History of Clothing in the Nineteenth Century,* trans. Richard Bienvenu (Princeton, 1994), 19 and 201, n. 19; Jones, "Repackaging Rousseau: Femininity and Fashion in Old Regime France," *French Historical Studies* 18 (fall 1994), 939–67.

economies of consumption examined in this essay, Rousseau's republican model launched the most vigorous attack on aristocratic display. Indeed, there is little doubt that the philosopher of virtue was, in some measure, present in the minds of many Third Estate deputies who proudly embraced the modest black suit as their official costume. Rousseauian attitudes toward display certainly informed the proposition of 25 May 1789, by which a minority of deputies in the Third resolved to make "the ridiculous vanity of the rich disappear" by continuing to wear their sober, court-sanctioned clothes.[54]

To consider more fully the development of attitudes toward noble display in the second half of the eighteenth century, however, it is instructive to move beyond Rousseau. By placing so much emphasis on Rousseauian critiques, historians have lost sight of a broad range of prerevolutionary efforts to reconceptualize the relation between consumption and social status. As we have seen, imaginative reformulations of the role of noble display appeared in a wider literature of political economy produced by physiocrats and members of Gournay's circle, groups that in their own ways seem to have anticipated the coming of a new politics of consumption. This lively prerevolutionary debate on consumption and status, I would suggest, helped to establish the context of the 1789 dispute.

Although physiocracy aimed to restore the noble landowner to the pinnacle of society, the case of Mirabeau reminds us that such restoration could take place only if the nobility renounced excessive decorative display. Seen from this angle, the nobility's foppish costume of 1789 represented a gross departure from the kind of political and economic leadership that Mirabeau envisioned for his order. Favorable to the nobility and yet critical of display, the physiocratic perspective may help explain why the Third was not the only estate to bristle at Brézé's instructions. Certain noble deputies were also troubled by their official costume, evincing something similar to a Mirabeauian critique. "I will see what the others do," wrote the noble deputy Garron de La Brévière who was annoyed by the steep cost of outfitting himself for the Estates-General. "In general, it is thought that we might well have been spared this expense. . . . It is unbelievable that the government thought to hold us to this formality on the very eve of the opening [of the Estates-General]."[55]

54. Jean-Marc Devocelle, "D'un costume politique à une politique du costume," in *Modes & Révolutions, 1780–1804* (Paris, 1989), 84.

55. Quoted in Lemay, *La vie quotidienne*, 22–23. Similar sentiments were expressed by a

For Garron, the nobility's true business at Versailles had little to do with the formality and expense of courtly ceremony. Founder of a provincial society of agriculture in 1783 and contributor to the *Journal d'agriculture,* Garron would undoubtedly have preferred that the second order focus its efforts on truly serious matters, such as agricultural reform.[56]

The commercial logic of a Forbonnais also provides an interesting interpretive lens. Unlike Rousseau and Mirabeau, Forbonnais had few qualms about the burgeoning commercial life of midcentury France. Commerce was beneficial to society, he argued, because it prevented consumption from lapsing into an archaic state in which it would have been monopolized and put on display by an exclusive elite. Members of Third Estate would thus find in Forbonnais not only a potent criticism of moribund courtly consumption but a validation of their own middling status. How relevant Forbonnais's model seems when we realize that as many as a third of Third Estate deputies refused to abide by Brézé's sartorial instructions and wore the bright colors and fine embroidery befitting well-off and fashionable (albeit non-noble) citizens. Far from embracing the somber outfit they were instructed to wear, these deputies defiantly wore elegant clothes which, they believed, better reflected their true station in life. "I will keep my clothes, and my character, and my liberty," announced one provincial deputy.[57] In the Third Estate, such sentiment was strong enough to defeat the Rousseauian proposition of 25 May 1789, which would have obliged deputies of the Third to wear their black costumes.[58]

In sum, none of the economies of consumption that in the 1750s helped to lay the foundations of modern political economy would have easily accommodated the rigidly hierarchical dress code imposed by the marquis de Brézé. Nor were such economies of consumption consistent with the traditional forms of political representation that Brézé's dress code implied. Indeed, the fermentation of economic thought not only raised issues of *social* representation but led to reconsiderations of *political* representation as well. For many writers, questions about the meaning of material display (what did display signify? who had the right to consume conspicuously?)

---

noble pamphleteer who, though sympathetic to the idea of a distinct uniform for noble deputies, wished that it did not take the form of "lavish ostentation." Lefebvre, 1:75.

56. Edna Hindie Lemay, ed., *Dictionnaire des constituants, 1789–1792* (Oxford, 1991), 1:391.

57. *Lettre d'un provincial, député aux Etats-Généraux, sur le costume de cérémonie* (n.p., 1789), 7.

58. Devocelle, "D'un costume politque," 84. The Constituent Assembly officially suppressed Brézé's costumes on 15 October 1789.

were tied to political questions concerning the proper distribution of power among various socioeconomic groups.

Rousseau's economy of consumption was certainly the most overtly political, as the author of the *Discours sur l'économie politique* went on to formulate a powerful theory of democracy in *The Social Contract*. The "general will" that Rousseau invoked briefly in the earlier work would become the cornerstone of his radical political theory. But Rousseau was not the only writer to pass from the economic to the political. Beyond the Rousseauian camp, the physiocrats formulated a theory of political representation rooted in specific ideas about economic production and consumption. The physiocrats imagined a political system of provincial assemblies in which representation would be distributed according to the amount of landed income one produced. Citizens with greater net income would exercise greater voting power than those with less net income.[59] Hence, nobles and other large landowners who rejected wasteful display and shifted their resources from the symbolic to the economic realm were to enjoy the lion's share of political power. Although the nobility was to maintain power in the physiocratic schema, such power no longer stemmed from the order's juridical privileges or the material signs of distinction that reflected such privileges. Plainly, physiocratic political theory did not rest on the same set of connections between display, rank, and political representation that underpinned Brézé's dress code. Nor, finally, were the ideas of the commercially minded writers of the Gournay school consistent with a simple correspondence between consumption and political power. By deemphasizing the display value of goods and imagining a more open social order in which utilitarian commodities flowed freely among all who, regardless of rank, enjoyed a measure of wealth, Forbonnais implicitly rejected the kind of sharp sociopolitical divisions that Brézé intended to resurrect.

By 1789, deputies to the Estates-General and the learned public had, for decades, been exposed to an economic literature that reconceptualized links between consumption, social rank, and civic status. Although there was no clear consensus on how best to realign the economic, social, and political orders, it was evident to many that Brézé's last-ditch effort to reaffirm traditional sociopolitical categories would not do. Brézé's dress code provoked a chorus of protest. No doubt such protest owed something to the spread of Rousseauian attitudes, but we should be careful not to interpret it as mere

---

59. Michael Kwass, *Privilege and the Politics of Taxation in Eighteenth-Century France: Liberté, Egalité, Fiscalité* (Cambridge, 2000), 256–66.

Rousseauian reflex. Since the 1750s, wider currents in the literature of political economy had encouraged readers to reconsider the meaning of noble display and to imagine new relations between consumption, social status, and political order. This may explain why something so seemingly trivial as a dress code helped to incite the first great power struggle of the French Revolution.

2

A DIVIDED NOBILITY: STATUS, MARKETS, AND THE PATRIMONIAL STATE IN THE OLD REGIME

Gail Bossenga

Of the grand narratives of the French Revolution, only one, the Marxist, explicitly offered an interpretation of the relation of markets and nobility to the origins of 1789. The story is a familiar one. Two classes existed: one, the nobility, was based in the land; the other, the bourgeoisie, was a product of the market. Despite accumulating vast wealth from the spread of commercial capitalism, the bourgeoisie remained excluded from formal political power. It was only a matter of time until, in 1789, the bourgeoisie overthrew the nobility and made its political power commensurate with its economic resources. By implementing a program of economic liberalism, the bourgeois revolution also guaranteed the growth of free markets for future generations.[1]

On a commonsense level, this interpretation, simultaneously simple and grand in scope, was appealing, but it proved to be unsatisfactory on many counts. After several decades of intensive research, historians emerged knowing a great deal more about the nobility than ever before but still no closer to a coherent interpretation of the relation of markets or nobility to the origins of the French Revolution. Two quite different interpretations

I would like to thank David Bien, Hank Clark, Tom Kaiser, Steve Kaplan, Filippo Sabetti, Jay Smith, and participants at the conference on the "French Nobility in the Eighteenth Century" for their comments. A longer version of this essay appeared as "The Patrimonial State, Markets, and the Origins of the French Revolution," in *1650–1850: Ideas, Aesthetics, and Inquiries in the Early Modern Era,* vol. 2 (2005).

1. See Georges Lefebvre, *The French Revolution,* vol. 1, trans. Elizabeth Moss Evanson (London and New York, 1962), 42; and Albert Soboul, *The French Revolution, 1787–1799: From the Storming of the Bastille to Napoleon,* trans. Alan Forrest and Colin Jones (New York, 1974).

emerged. The first argued for a model of noble and bourgeois fusion, and drew upon studies of social mobility and ownership of wealth. Through the mechanism of ennobling venal offices, it was shown, thousands of commoners, more than 6,500 of them, acquired the legal status of noble during the century before the Revolution. In addition, nobles and the bourgeoisie invested their wealth in similar kinds of markets—in land, urban property, government bonds, and venal offices—which carried social status and remained removed from the volatile world of commercial capitalism. Although proprietary wealth was the investment of choice for nobles and wealthy bourgeois alike, a small but significant portion of the nobility chose to invest in capitalistic enterprises, including government chartered trading companies, estate-based manufactures of glass and textiles, and mining enterprises.[2] From this evidence, some historians concluded that these resourceful nobles played an important role in promoting the development of capitalist markets. "The nobility gave proof of ability to throw itself into innovation," declared Guy Chaussinand-Nogaret, "to join the ranks of modern capitalism, to throw off the weight of tradition, and to play a part of breaking out of 'feudal' forms of production."[3]

Other historians, however, directed their attention toward fission between nobles. This type of interpretation looked at many kinds of divisions within the nobility but generally ignored the market as a causal factor. Nobles were fragmented by differences of wealth, birth, dynastic pretensions, provincial affiliation, profession, religion, court connections, and political outlooks. Numerous *parlements,* for example, restricted membership in their corps to those with three or more generations of nobility, while the Ségur law of 1781 limited recruitment into the army officer corps to those with four generations of nobility.[4]

Evidence such as this led historian Peter Jones to conclude: "If neither a fusionist nor a conflictual schematisation does justice to the sheer complexity of *ancien-régime* social structure, we are left with a conceptual void. The best

2. On ennobling offices, see David Bien, "La réaction aristocratique avant 1789: l'exemple de l'armée," *Annales: E.S.C.* 29 (janvier-février 1974): 23–48; (mars-avril 1974): 505–34; and "Manufacturing Nobles: The Chancelleries in France to 1789," *Journal of Modern History* 61 (1989): 445–86. On investments, see George Taylor, "Noncapitalist Wealth and the Origins of the French Revolution," *American Historical Review* 72 (1967): 469–96.

3. Guy Chaussinand-Nogaret, *The French Nobility in the Eighteenth Century: From Feudalism to Enlightenment,* trans. William Doyle (Cambridge, 1985), 113.

4. Jean Egret, "L'aristocratie parlementaire française à la fin de l'ancien régime," *Revue Historique* (1952): 1–14; David Bien, "La réaction aristocratique avant 1789," and his "The Army in the French Enlightenment: Reform, Reaction and Revolution," *Past and Present* 85 (1979): 68–98.

way to fill it is to abandon any notion of smooth-edged elites locked in one-dimensional confrontation. By the reign of Louis XVI the ordering of society was in disarray: honour was no longer a foolproof guide to rank, nor yet was wealth. Confusion resulted and it took the outward form of a series of parallel hierarchies often overlapping at the base and with no clear sense of preeminence at the top."[5] Given this interpretive imbroglio, it is not surprising that the search for a social interpretation of the Revolution petered out and that the study of political culture proved attractive to scholars.

In this essay, I would like to revisit elements of "confusion" in the nobility, including the "parallel hierarchies" within it, by reference to the market. To do so means looking at old evidence from social history through conceptual lenses different from those framing the Marxist-revisionist debate. First, rather than framing this study in terms of "class," I am interested in examining the power of "status," an important concept that has been far too neglected in social analyses of the Old Regime. Second, it is important to jettison the progressive view of markets that colored both Marxist and revisionist interpretations of the Revolution and follow the lead of institutional economic historians who see markets as institutions embedded in structures of social and political power and subject to their constraints.[6] In the Old Regime, markets often exacerbated traditional inequities and hierarchies rather than eroded them. Third, in both Marxism and revisionism, little attention was paid to how states shaped social structure, including markets. In his work on "patrimonial states," by contrast, Max Weber emphasized the central role of the state in setting up markets in traditional societies. This perspective is useful for challenging historians to explore how the monarchy in the Old Regime created and protected markets to advance its fiscal interests, and how state-sponsored markets might alter both the identity of nobles and the distribution of resources among them.

Why Status?

So much attention has been placed on showing why class was not an organizing principle in the early modern period that not nearly enough attention

---

5. Peter Jones, *Reform and Revolution in France: the Politics of Transition, 1774–1791* (Cambridge, 1995), 71–72.

6. For example, Lee J. Alston, Thráinn Eggertsson, and Douglas North, eds., *Empirical Studies in Institutional Change* (Cambridge, 1996); and Douglas North "The New Institutional

has been directed to the distinctive logic of status. Roland Mousnier was one historian who did make status a defining feature of a society of "orders" as opposed to a society of "classes." His analysis, however, suffered from a teleological viewpoint by which status, something characterizing the early modern period, turned into class, a set of relations structuring modern societies. Thus for Mousnier, the dynamic leading to the Revolution still ended up being one of class conflict, and his analysis of the causes of 1789 actually shared common themes with a Marxist one.[7] Because of this implicit transformation of status into class, Mousnier's interpretation seriously underestimated status as a kind of ongoing power in its own right and was unable to ask how the Revolution changed the nature of status. By removing class from the focus of attention, it is possible to see that the Revolution was a revolution in status, not class. It did not usher in the reign of a rising bourgeoisie, but that of the "citizen." After 1789, the title of citizen, rather than any title derived from membership in an order, corporate group, and other privileged entity, became the basis for enjoying rights in the state. The legal recognition of the "citizen," whose fundamental rights were codified in the famous Declaration of the Rights of Man and of the Citizen, made the institutionalized perquisites of status of the Old Regime illegal and opened up new paths for the operation of status in the new regime.[8]

Status may be defined in several interrelated ways, cultural and juridical, formal and informal. First, status can be considered a system of graded social positions in society based upon shared perceptions of honor and esteem.[9] In

---

Economics," *Journal of Institutional and Theoretical Economics* 142 (1986): 230–37. Douglass North notes the earlier contribution of Karl Polanyi's work in "Markets and Other Allocation Systems," *Journal of European Economic History* 6 (1977): 703–16.

7. See, for example, chap. 1 of *The Institutions of France Under the Absolute Monarchy, 1598–1789,* vol. 1, *Society and the State,* trans. Brian Pearce (Chicago, 1979). "In the last quarter of the 18th century a whole movement of ideas manifested itself which was aimed at sweeping away the ancient constitution of French society in orders and estates and replacing it by a class society" (p. 36).

8. Rogers Brubaker, *Citizenship and Nationhood in France and Germany* (Cambridge, Mass., 1992), chap. 1; Pierre Rétat, "The Evolution of the Citizen from the Ancien Régime to the Revolution," in *The French Revolution and the Meaning of Citizenship,* ed., René Waldinger, Philip Dawson, and Isser Woloch (Westport, Conn., 1993); Gail Bossenga, "Monarchy, Status, *Corps:* Roots of Modern Citizenship in the Old Regime," in *Tocqueville and Beyond: Essays on the Old Regime in Honor of David D. Bien,* ed. Robert Schwartz and Robert Schneider (Newark, Del., 2003); William H. Sewell Jr., "Le Citoyen/la Citoyenne: Activity, Passivity, and the Revolutionary Concept of Citizenship," in *The French Revolution and the Creation of Modern Political Culture,* ed. Colin Lucas (Oxford, 1988), 105–23.

9. As defined by Max Weber, *Economy and Society: An Outline of Interpretive Sociology,* 2 vols., ed. Claus Wittich and Guenther Roth, trans. Ephraim Fischoff et al. (Berkeley, 1978), 1:302–7.

the Old Regime, it was taken for granted as the part of the natural order that men and women were entitled to a place in the social hierarchy according to their degree of honor, from nobles at the top down to "base" individuals at the bottom. The honor inherent in a status position had both genealogical and performative aspects. Honor was considered an intrinsic quality conferred on a person through birth. One connotation of the word birth (*naissance*), according to the dictionary of the Académie Française in 1694 was "the good or bad qualities with which one is born."[10] Yet honor also demanded that individuals follow a code of conduct appropriate to their social station and that "inferiors" publicly defer to "superiors." Status, in other words, was far more than a set of static cultural norms described by jurists. It was a way of thinking and acting that was continually replicated, and sometimes transformed, through patterns of daily life. Degrees of honor were continually made visible in everyday forms of address such as *Monseigneur*, in the rankings of groups in public ceremonies, and in rituals of deference whereby those of lesser status removed their hats in the presence of those of higher status.

Finally, status had a formal, legal dimension. In the Old Regime, the hierarchically arranged status positions of various groups carried different rights, legal obligations, and duties in the state. As a result, all the important institutions of the Old Regime enforced status distinctions and entitlements in some way. Political representation was organized around divisions between clergy, nobility, and commoners but might also take into account finer distinctions between higher and lower clergy or noble fiefholders as opposed to nonfiefholders. Payment of taxes likewise depended upon one's status as a cleric, noble, or commoner, but it also usually involved subtler gradations, such as ownership of a state office or membership in a privileged town. Access to judicial courts and assignment of penalties varied by status, as did professional opportunities, including service in the army officer corps or various magistracies. At every turn, therefore, formal institutions in the Old Regime recalled status distinctions. Life without such distinctions could only be conceived as formless and chaotic.

Status has received scant attention from many historians because it has not been seen as a true form of power. Often described as a normative or linguistic scheme that existed in people's heads, it supposedly had little effect

---

10. Cited by Jay M. Smith in *The Culture of Merit: Nobility, Royal Service, and the Making of Absolute Monarchy in France, 1600–1789* (Ann Arbor, 1996), 62. Discussions of the concept of honor may be found in Smith's work and Arlette Jouanna, *Ordre social: mythes et hiérarchies dans la France du XVIe siècle* (Paris, 1977).

on the "real" material world.[11] What difference did it make if someone took off or left on his hat? If one wanted to study power, it was essential to study social class. Here the insights of Max Weber are useful to recall. Weber argued that status was an actual form of power, one analytically distinct from class, although in practice the two forms might at times converge.[12] Classes, for Weber, were groups having common interests and economic power derived from ownership of property and position in the market. There was the potential for a class relationship to form, for example, when one group was forced to sell its labor power to another group on the market in order to survive. The power of class, therefore, rested on relations of economic dominance and dependency generated through the market and inequitable distribution of property.

Status groups, by contrast, were formed when individuals came together on the basis of their shared honor, usually functionally defined. Weber argued that, particularly in traditional societies, status was an essential form of social power because it deeply affected the life opportunities of individuals. Notions of honor and esteem played a large role in determining whom individuals could marry, what kind of education they could pursue, what types of occupations were open to them, and whether they could be received in polite society. In 1758, for example, students of the Ecole des Ponts et Chaussées asked the director to recall seven students whose presence dishonored the school, including one who was "entirely without education, without sentiment of honor, of a low birth."[13] Alisdair McIntyre has observed that in traditional societies honor is what is owed to individuals "by reason of their having a due place in the social order."[14] This sense of "dueness," that is, entitlement or preemptive claims on resources by virtue of one's distinguished position, allowed status to operate as a central mechanism of power in the Old Regime. To a striking degree, the organizational networks of the Old Regime were organized around the entitlements of status. Owing to the nobility's reputed intrinsic superiority, institutions continually directed all sorts of advantages to this group as its "due." In the

---

11. Pierre Goubert, for example, wrote that "it need hardly be repeated that this assortment of groups [estates and orders] is the expression of a traditional vision rather than of underlying realities." *The Ancien Régime: French Society, 1600–1789*, trans. Steve Cox (New York, 1969), 216.

12. A good discussion of Weber's distinctions between class and status is found in Anthony Giddens, *Capitalism and Modern Social Theory: An Analysis of the Writings of Marx, Durkheim and Max Weber* (Cambridge, 1971), 119–247.

13. Jean Petot, *Histoire de l'administration des ponts et chaussées* (Paris, 1958), 154.

14. Alisdair McIntyre, *After Virtue* (South Bend, 1981), 46.

period 1682–1700, only 8 percent of the 136 archbishops and bishops were non-nobles, but from 1774 to 1790 this was reduced to a mere 1 percent. In the mid-eighteenth century, nobles monopolized between 80 and 85 percent of all the posts in the army officer corps, and about 90 percent on the eve of the Revolution. All the magistrates in the sovereign judicial courts enjoyed at least personal nobility because anyone serving in those courts was automatically ennobled.[15]

It might be objected that nearly all of the nobles mentioned in the above account were wealthy, and thus that money, not status, was responsible for their position. There is no doubt that money was playing an increasingly important role in the formation of the social hierarchy of the Old Regime, but it would be wrong to assume that the force of money dictated the real social hierarchy. On the contrary, status was important because it continued to shape access to and the use of resources in the Old Regime right up to the Revolution. The case of social mobility in the eighteenth century is instructive. Thousands of men invested substantial sums of money in venal offices so that they could become noble. While some might argue that this shows that money was the key to social mobility in the Old Regime, it also demonstrates that status—the desire to become noble—was powerful enough to define the ends of monetary investment. Status thus was not a mere response to underlying economic relations; it played a central role in determining the socially appropriate uses of money itself and shaped the nature of monetary investments in the first place.[16] By continually coding certain actions as honorable or dishonorable, status exerted a powerful influence on collective decision-making and the flow of social resources. In sum, the relationship between status and markets is complex and difficult to predict, because status was able to influence the operation of markets, and not just the reverse.

Markets as Social Organizers

Markets are often treated as part of a distinct domain called the "economy," but they are perhaps better seen as one important form, among several, of organizing society as a whole. "A market system," writes Charles Lindblom,

15. Mousnier, *Institutions of France,* 324, 162–63, 153; Bien, "Réaction aristocratique," provides a full discussion of patterns of social mobility in the army and judiciary.

16. George Taylor called the purchase of venal offices, many of which conferred prestige but often produced little financial reward for their owners, an "investment in standing. What made it desirable was the status, the respectability that it conferred." "Noncapitalist Wealth," 478–79.

"is a pattern of cooperative human behavior."[17] Markets coordinate the distribution of social resources in return for money. The commodities exchanged on markets are often material items like clothing and food, but markets also coordinate the exchange of human labor, services, and other intangible resources. What things are exchanged on markets is a social decision, and this decision is not a direct result of the mechanism of monetary exchange itself. In the past, for example, it was common in the West to put human beings up for sale on slave markets, something which these societies today decry.

For most of human history, markets served as an adjunct to other methods of coordinating human behavior, such as custom, the traditional obligations of hierarchical society, familial duties, and coercive demands by political authorities (the "state"). In contrast to such methods, which depend on sentiments like duty or fear, markets are oriented around voluntary participation in pursuit of self-interest. Participation, furthermore, is reciprocal: individuals on the market must offer something to sell that will generate an offer to buy in return. The egalitarian connotations of reciprocal exchange were one reason that markets had unsettling effects in a deferential, honor-bound society like the Old Regime, where those of high status traditionally had a preemptive claim on resources.

Although the domains of markets are fluid, there are, according to Lindblom, certain minimal conditions that must exist for markets to serve as coordinators of social behavior. Some degree of legal liberty and rights of property are necessary to give participants control over their time, labor, and goods so that they can make reciprocal offers of exchange. In addition, money, which allows the valuation of a multiplicity of goods according to one common denominator, must be the primary medium of exchange. In markets, monetary price is the only indicator of value. The monetization of worth is the feature of the market that is most often criticized for its dehumanizing qualities since it is easy to move from the idea that labor power can be exchanged for money to the view that the value of people themselves is being expressed in monetary terms. Many things, even body parts, can become commodities, that is, objects offered for sale on the market, if there is a demand for them. The market, however, does impose some constraints on commodification. In particular, only objects or services subject to human control can be commodified. Deep, genuine affection, for example,

17. Charles Lindblom, *The Market System: What It Is, How It Works, and What to Make of It* (New Haven, 2001), 39. The next three paragraphs are drawn from his work.

cannot be sold because human beings cannot create this emotion at will. What the market can sell is simulated affection, or the external marks and signs of affection, to which the enormous greeting card industry is testimony.

What was the effect of the penetration of markets into a society organized hierarchically on the principle of honor and deference? Traditionally, the market was viewed as the cradle of dishonor. Those things that the Old Regime revered as honorable and that supposedly characterized the status of the nobility—distinguished lineage, generosity, a spirit of self-sacrifice, heroism on the battlefield, and indifference to mundane monetary matters— were exactly those things that could not be purchased on the market. In fact, the traditional hierarchy of status in the Old Regime was a social statement of disdain for market forces. The clergy, who interceded to God on behalf of humankind, and the nobility, who shed their blood on the battlefield, formed the two highest estates. At the top of the Third Estate were the liberal professions—the doctors, lawyers, officials, rentiers, and professors—all of whom did not have to sully themselves directly with the operations of buying and selling. Merchants followed next, still above those who worked with their hands but suspect nonetheless. The jurist Jean Domat, for example, praised merchants for supplying the state with goods necessary to life, but he also observed: "Of all professions, there is none more exposed to avarice, and to injustice which is the consequence of it, than that of commerce. For since those who exercise it draw profit from the bare trouble of buying in order to sell again, they can cheat and demand what they please."[18]

Although in principle the traditional attributes of noble status were anti- thetical to the norms associated with the market, in practice the market could offer a supporting role to status. Qualities like pure blood, military valor, and generosity of spirit themselves were beyond assessment in mone- tary terms, but the external marks and trappings of a noble lifestyle were easily enough commodified. There was, moreover, a constant demand for those external marks because although nobility was defined by distinguished birth, nobles also had to demonstrate their superiority constantly through an appropriate lifestyle. The dictates of status thus meant that nobles and their imitators had to become consumers par excellence. The market could supply ostentatious dwellings, works of art, silks, land, sumptuous feasts, fine wines, and even the service of creative genealogists. After "living nobly" for a long enough period, a commoner in the sixteenth or seventeenth

18. Jean Domat, *Les loix civiles dans leur ordre naturel* (Luxembourg, 1702), 460.

century might be able to "usurp" nobility, that is, pass off an aristocratic lifestyle as the natural product of birth.[19]

A variety of regulations were designed to prevent just that and to keep the forces of the market at bay. Sumptuary laws prohibited commoners from appropriating silks and other forms of noble dress. Non-nobles could buy fiefs, but their common status remained visible by the obligation to pay the royal fee known as the *franc-fief*. Except in important port regions, nobles could not practice the occupation of wholesale merchant without fear of derogation, that is, loss of noble status, including customary tax privileges. In some regions, inheritance laws prevented the sale of a noble family's patrimony so that it would be passed down intact to heirs or remain under family control.[20]

In the early stages of the development of markets, it is doubtful that markets posed a grave danger to noble identity. There were just not enough commodities widely available for purchase, and nobles themselves were not oriented to seizing opportunities on markets that might exist. Great nobles regarded land primarily as something to rule rather than as a commodity to buy and sell. Land provided a dignified avenue by which to extract customary labor and fees from dependent peasants and to seal the fidelity of clients by parceling out chunks of territory to lesser nobles. In the sixteenth century, for example, the manor of the important seigneurs of Pont-St-Pierre was still subsistence oriented and had a kitchen that was locally stocked.[21] Thus although variations in wealth existed among nobles, these differences did not give rise to a sustained competition for the acquisition of things, and the market itself did not play a major role in differentiating nobles.

By the mid-eighteenth century, this milieu had changed enormously. Between 1700 and 1789, the French population increased from approximately 21,500,000 to 28,000,000 inhabitants. Internal trade quadrupled, and trade with the French colonies rose tenfold. The substantial expansion of overseas trade, the spread of rural industry, and the emergence of the commercial

---

19. For example, George Huppert, *Les Bourgeois Gentilshommes: An Essay on the Definition of Elites in Renaissance France* (Chicago, 1977), 7–13.

20. Gaston Zeller, "Une notion de caractère historico-social: la dérogeance," *Cahiers internationaux de sociologie* 22 (1957): 40–77; on sumptuary laws, Renato Galliani, *Rousseau, le luxe et l'idéologie nobiliaire: étude socio-historique*, in *Studies on Voltaire and the Eighteenth Century* 268 (1989): 98–117; on noble inheritance rights, Samuel Clark, *State and Status: The Rise of the State and Aristocratic Power in Western Europe* (Montreal and Kingston, 1995), 232.

21. Jonathan Dewald, *Pont-St-Pierre, 1398–1789: Lordship, Community and Capitalism in Early Modern France* (Berkeley, 1987), 193–98, 63.

revolution meant that a dizzying array of consumer goods were offered on the market. Consumers began to regard sugar, coffee, chocolate and tobacco as staples, rather than luxuries. All sorts of items once considered marks of noble status—watches, fans, snuff boxes, mirrors, wigs, ornate clothing, and umbrellas—began to come within the reach of even well-to-do artisans. The customary idea that clothing should reveal the fixed status of a person gave way to "fashion" with its implicit acceptance of social mobility and belief that individuals should keep up with changes in style. After 1750 an onslaught of fashion journals appeared to inform the (female) public what was in vogue. Over the course of the eighteenth century, the value of clothing of even poor Parisian women increased sixfold.[22] In this environment, the pressure upon nobles to consume, and to consume on a scale of unprecedented lavishness in order to maintain marks of their superiority, was enormous. In 1788, 20,000 *livres,* one-third of the duc de Saulx-Tavanes's total annual expenditures, went to purchase clothing and accessories.[23] Nobles of any means left their estates to managers and moved to Paris or provincial capitals to enjoy the good life of theater performances, fine wines, perhaps even a private bathtub. Moralists, most famously Rousseau, denounced the debilitating effects of *luxe* and the soft, artificial, egotistical sentiment that it produced.

Just as threatening to the noble's monopoly on external signs of distinction posed by the market was the market's tendency to evaluate all kinds of worth, even social worth, in monetary terms. Toward the end of the eighteenth century, for example, the philanthropist Piarron de Chamousset proposed to create a hospital run as a mutual aid society in which people would pay into six "classes." The more that individuals contributed, the more privacy and better quarters they would receive when they used the hospital. The proposal provoked outrage from one critic who lamented all the estates would all be "thrown together and confused" and that there would not "be any other distinction than that of money." Can you put a price on "good society,"

22. Colin Jones and Rebecca Spang, "Sans-Culottes, Sans Café, Sans Tabac: Shifting Realms of Necessity and Luxury in Eighteenth-Century France," in *Consumers and Luxury: Consumer Culture in Europe 1650–1850,* ed. Maxine Berg and Helen Clifford (Manchester, 1999), 37–82.; Cissie Fairchilds, "The Production and Marketing of Populuxe Goods in Eighteenth-Century Paris," in *Consumption and the World of Goods,* ed. John Brewer and Roy Porter, 228–48; Jennifer Jones, "Repackaging Rousseau: Femininity and Fashion in Old Regime France," *French Historical Studies* 18 (fall 1994): 939–67; and Daniel Roche, *The Culture of Clothing: Dress and Fashion in the Ancien Régime,* trans. Jean Birrell (Cambridge, 1994), 5, 13, 108.

23. Robert Forster, *The House of Saulx-Tavanes: Versailles and Burgundy, 1700–1830* (Baltimore, 1971), 126. Forster's detailed account shows that expenditures, indebtedness, and interest owed to creditors had all risen sharply in the 1780s, well beyond the duke's ability to pay.

queried this author? "Decency for 20 *sols?* Decency for 30 *sols!* Decency for 1 *ecu,* 4 *francs,* 100 *sols,* What a notion!"[24]

Equally illustrative was a dispute over theater seats. Wearing a rose-colored coat, a sword, and plumed hat, the comte de Moreton-Chabrillant, captain of the guard of the comte de Provence, demanded that Pernot Duplessis, a proctor in the *parlement,* give up his seat to him. Duplessis refused, stating, "I have a right to be here for my money." In reply, the count called on his guards to throw Duplessis out by force. Duplessis immediately took his case to the *parlement,* where his lawyer argued that it was "in the general interest of the public to defend the individual whose simple status as citizen should have warded off any kind of insult in a place where money alone put commoners and nobles on the same footing."[25] The *parlement* ordered the count to pay six thousand *livres* in damages. The traditional "due" accorded to those of superior status, it appeared, was giving way to the homogenizing dictates of cold cash.

Seigneurialism and Markets

The power of money to erode noble distinction was one effect of the market, but not the only one. Markets, as we observed above, are embedded in the existing institutional networks of a society. Even in modern, liberal societies, the voluntaristic nature of market exchange can be checked by elements of compulsion and command, and cultural values strongly affect what becomes commodified. In the Old Regime, the most important mode of organizing rural society was seigneurialism. A seigneury, or lordship, did not simply involve ownership of land as a commodity, but legal jurisdiction over the land and corresponding rights of patronage and distinction. Seigneurial dues, monetary payments owed by peasants to lords, were one way that status had been institutionalized. A payment like the *cens* was not merely a monetary payment but a statement of the noble's lordship over the peasant. The original rationale for the system harked back to a prestatist period when the lord was responsible for protecting his peasants, much as a head of household was supposed to protect his dependents. This justification was quickly being exposed as a convenient fiction now that many seigneurs had become

24. Claude Humbert Piarron de Chamousset, *Vues d'un citoyen* (Paris, 1757; repr. Paris, 1970), which includes the *Lettre critique à l'auteur d'une brochure intitulée: plan d'une Maison d'Association,* quotation at 125.

25. Simon Schama, *Citizens: A Chronicle of the French Revolution* (New York, 1989), 138.

absentee landlords, farmed out the collection of their dues to others, and headed for the soft life in the city.

Discussion of seigneurial dues usually centers on how oppressive they were to the peasantry. Far less is said about the relation of the seigneurial system to markets. In this situation, the importance of seigneurialism lay in its production of market monopolies, which usually ended up being in the hands of nobles. In Picardy, for example, where seigneurial dues were minimal, seigneurs relied on their privileges to draw up lucrative leases that granted merchants logging rights in forests at a time when wood prices were skyrocketing. In Toulouse and Bordeaux, lords used their option rights (*droit de retraite*) to force individuals who had recently acquired land to resell it to the lords. Not only was it vexsome to see a lord corner the market in land, the lack of a statute of limitations on many seigneurial rights allowed a lord to resurrect old dues from ages past, demand immediate payment, and seize land if the peasant could not comply. In Bordeaux, a lord could even use his option rights retroactively to purchase land, so that land purchased years earlier by an individual could be forced back onto the market.[26] These examples suggest that in highly commercialized areas, the value of seigneurial rights was most likely to be found not in the direct exploitation of peasants but in the creation of monopolistic markets benefiting lords. The legal arrangements of seigneurialism, developed far earlier in a nonmarket economy, distorted developing markets by creating arbitrariness and undermining secure property rights. The frustration generated by these unjust practices was recorded in the *cahiers de doléances* (lists of grievances) of 1789 of the Third Estate. According to John Markoff, there was more opposition to "various seigneurial monopolies, the dues on fairs and markets, the compulsory labor services, the seigneurial tolls, or the property transfer dues," than to payments like the *cens*.[27]

One last characteristic of seigneurialism must be emphasized: its inability to distinguish clearly "ownership" from "rulership." This was in large part a legacy of the Middle Ages when a distinct political sphere of the "state" as opposed to "society" did not exist and multiple powerholders wielded

26. Florence Gauthier, "Formes d'évolution du système agraire communautaire en Picardie (fin XVIIIe–début XIXe siècle)," *Annales Historiques de la Révolution Française* 240 (1980): 188–89; Robert Forster, "The Provincial Noble: A Reappraisal," *American Historical Review* (April 1963): 685; Gérard Aubin, "La Crise du prélèvement seigneurial à la fin de l'Ancien Régime," in *Aux origines provinciales de la Révolution,* ed. Robert Chagny (Grenoble, 1990): 23–33.

27. John Markoff, *The Abolition of Feudalism: Peasants, Lords, and Legislators in the French Revolution* (University Park, Pa., 1996), 73. Markoff observed that "The Third Estate had an

authority over subjects of various sorts. Seigneuries were economic units that coordinated the production of food and other necessities, but they were also political units that gave seigneurs legal powers over dependent "subjects." The conflation of public authority and personal patrimony had important implications for markets. When markets developed, judicopolitical authority attached to the land was considered a right of property, so that when seigneuries were sold, their political and judicial rights came with them. The purchase of a seigneurie entitled an individual not only to farm or rent out the land, but also to flaunt a distinguished title (baron or count, for example), exercise seigneurial jurisdiction over his peasants, and possibly enjoy political rights of representation. In Languedoc, for example, a province that still possessed self-governing political estates, only fief-owning nobles could sit in the provincial estates. In these cases, the right to local political representation was inherited or acquired through purchase of a fief. As one historian noted, in such a system "public honors are part of one's patrimony; one inherits the right to sit in the estates like a *métairie.*"[28]

This tendency to conflate political authority and status, on the one hand, with personal ownership, on the other, ran through many institutions in the Old Regime. It meant that it was acceptable to put onto markets things that today would be regarded as off-limits to private, monetary transactions. It could be said that rights to wield political authority or enjoy a particular rank became, in effect, treated as commodities to be sold or farmed out for a profit. When vast sectors of the state were characterized by such activity, we have what Max Weber called a "patrimonial state" and the possibility for forms of market activity that the modern liberal state no longer recognizes and that were, in fact, abolished by the French Revolution.

Markets and the Patrimonial State

In surveying political forms of traditional states, Weber saw that many kingdoms and empires were characterized not by bureaucracy, but by patrimonialism. In these situations, the "state" developed by taking on the form of the ruler's estate writ large. The king ruled as father of his people, while the royal household—

---

anti-seigneurial agenda, particularly focused on barriers to the perfecting of the market" (p. 201). He also noted that there was far more readiness by the bourgeois Third Estate than peasants to indemnify lords if these privileges were dismantled. See the table, p. 112.

28. Paul Rives, *Etude sur les attributions financières des états de Languedoc au dix-huitième siècle* (Paris, 1885), 67.

the court—was simultaneously the seat of the king's domestic life and center of official policymaking. Administrative networks were highly personal, based in patron-client relations and heritable offices whose official functions were not clearly separate from a family's patrimony. The concept of "merit" existed, but it was assumed that blood and birth bestowed on certain groups a natural propensity to perform meritorious tasks. Owing to the low level of technology and lack of an efficient, paid bureaucracy, the state was also liable to farm out tasks to other groups rather than to do them itself.[29]

Whereas the Marxist emphasis on class conflict left little room for the state's independent role, and Tocqueville's thesis of centralization offered little perspective on the relation between government and economy, Weber linked the growth of patrimonial states directly to markets. These kinds of states, he suggested, were instrumental in developing markets not to stimulate the rise of capitalism per se, but to finance their own activities, especially war.[30] Unsurprisingly, the markets that they encouraged mirrored the structure and aims of the state itself. The state hedged in markets with tolls and tariffs that siphoned off revenue for the government; sometimes it created state-sanctioned monopolies with the same goal. The markets were entangled in political and fiscal functions, relied on patronage to get business done, and existed in a climate of legal arbitrariness. The erratic legal environment stemmed from the position of the ruler who, as sovereign, was considered above the law and hence able to engage in activities, like changing terms of contracts, beyond the power of ordinary individuals. The ruler's own self-interest, however, served as a check to complete arbitrariness. He needed economic growth and "the accumulation of wealth, so that he [could] draw on tax-farmers, farmers of official supplies and on credit sources."[31]

---

29. See Max Weber, *Economy and Society,* 2:1006–10. Weber observes that patrimonialism "remained dominant in Continental Europe up to the French Revolution, but the longer patri-monialism lasted, the more it approached pure bureaucratism," 2:1087. Thomas Ertman argues that "Latin Europe" was characterized by "patrimonial absolutism" in *Birth of the Leviathan: Building States and Regimes in Medieval and Early Modern Europe* (Cambridge, 1997). Two studies emphasizing patrimonial characteristics of the French army and bureaucracy in the Old Regime are Guy Rowlands, *The Dynastic State and the Army Under Louis XIV: Royal Service and Private Interest, 1661–1701* (Cambridge, 2002), and Clive Church, *Revolution and Red Tape: The French Ministerial Bureaucracy, 1770–1850* (Oxford, 1981). Jeroen Duindam explores the mingling of aristocratic household and bureaucracy at court in *Vienna and Versailles: The Courts of Europe's Dynastic Rivals, 1550–1780* (Cambridge, 2003).

30. As Weber stated, "scholars have often overlooked one constant that has been historically important in the development of strong, centralized patrimonial bureaucracies—*trade.*" *Economy and Society,* 2:1092.

31. Ibid., 2:1095.

In early modern France, the ruler's fiscal needs, a semi-erratic legal environment, and the blurring of public and private spheres all strongly conditioned markets serving the state. Nobles, and particularly financiers, were central participants in these markets by dint of their economic resources and their connections at court. Financiers made their money by exploiting royal financial institutions, including selling offices, advancing loans to the royal government, skimming revenues off provincial tax flows, speculating in government paper, and investing in state-sanctioned trading monopolies. George Taylor called this network of financially oriented capitalism "court capitalism" and opposed it to other, more familiar types of capitalism based in commerce, industry, and real estate. Economic historian James Riley called the system "capitalism in public functions," while the historian of French banking, Herbert Lüthy, talked of "*regnicole* capitalism." All terms bespeak the mixture of public and private activities typifying this form of capitalism. Court capitalism, rather than the bourgeois variant with which most historians have been concerned, was at the center of the rise and fall of the state in the Old Regime. "The most spectacular operations of Old Regime capitalism," wrote Taylor, "were made possible by royal finance and political manipulation rather than industrial or maritime enterprise."[32]

In his important book on the nobility, Chaussinand-Nogaret used his findings on nobles and markets to try to refute a Marxist interpretation that opposed an enterprising, commercial bourgeoisie to a landed, "feudal" nobility. According to Chaussinand-Nogaret, as we noted earlier, nobles threw off "the weight of tradition" and helped society break out of "'feudal' forms of production."[33] Examination of his evidence, however, suggests that the terms of the Marxist-revisionist debate fail to explain coherently the kinds of activities that he found. Nobles were neither joining the ranks of "modern capitalism" nor were they perpetuating "feudal" forms of production. Rather, they were participating in a vast system of court capitalism generated by the patrimonial state. As Chaussinand-Nogaret himself observed, shareholders in noble-dominated enterprises consisted primarily of the "ubiquitous financial officeholders," men "standing well at Court," and a "circle of army officers." These networks were enhanced by the "colonisation of the Court by financiers" through the marriage of daughters of financiers

---

32. Taylor, "Types of Capitalism in Eighteenth-Century France," *Economic History Review*, 311 (July 1964): 479–97 at 489; James Riley, *The Seven Years' War and the Old Regime in France: The Economic and Financial Toll* (Princeton, 1986), 59–67; Herbert Lüthy, *La Banque protestante en France, de la révocation de l'Edit de Nantes à la Révolution*, 2 vols. (Paris, 1959–61), 2:43.

33. Taylor, "Types of Capitalism," 113.

to courtiers. Chaussinand-Nogaret also remarked that much of the capital was "fiscal in origin" and drew attention to "what confusion there was . . . between public moneys and the financiers' own resources."[34]

Viewed from the perspective of the markets generated by the patrimonial state, then, the Revolution was not about the triumph of "capitalism" over "feudalism." Rather, the significance of the Revolution was that it destroyed court capitalism, the capitalism in public functions, which lay at the heart of the French state in the Old Regime. Much of the resiliency of court capitalism grew out of the impoverished monarchy's need for credit, particularly in times of war. Without a public system of credit, the royal government had relied upon expedients that crystallized into durable institutions spawning powerful interest groups. Several institutions were particularly important to court capitalism in France: venality of offices, tax farming, and government-chartered monopolistic trading companies.

The development of a vast system of court capitalism had important implications for the status of the nobility. Nearly all of the players in the networks of court capitalism, at least in its upper reaches, were either nobles or socially mobile commoners in banking poised to enter the nobility.[35] Certain nobles and wealthy financiers thus stood to make enormous gains from court capitalism, but many other nobles could not participate and arguably were actually hurt by the system. The various markets and practices associated with court capitalism helped to exacerbate inequality within the nobility, sow divisions within it, and ultimately undermine its legitimacy.

Venality

Venality, the sale of offices by the government, was a centerpiece of court capitalism. Its story has been well told.[36] From its inception, venality was denounced as immoral, unwise, and even illegal, but enough powerful groups had a stake in its development and it evolved into one of the defining features

34. Chaussinand-Nogaret, *French Nobility,* 101.
35. On financiers and court capitalism, see Julian Dent, *Crisis in Finance: Crown, Financiers and Society in Seventeenth-Century France* (Devon, 1973); Françoise Bayard, *Le monde des financiers au XVIIe siècle* (Paris, 1988); Daniel Dessert, *Argent, pouvoir et société au Grand Siècle* (Paris, 1984); Richard Bonney, *The King's Debts: Finance and Politics in France, 1589–1661* (Oxford, 1981); Guy Chaussinand-Nogaret, *Les Financiers de Languedoc au XVIIIe siècle* (Paris, 1970); and John R. Bosher, *French Finances 1770–1795: From Business to Bureaucracy* (Cambridge, 1970).
36. Essential works are Roland Mousnier, *La vénalité des offices sous Henri IV et Louis XIII* (Paris, 1971); William Doyle, *Venality: The Sale of Offices in Eighteenth-Century France* (Oxford,

of the early modern French state. Venality exemplified quintessential features of the early modern patrimonial state. The practice contained capitalist elements of markets and credit, but the markets confused public power with private ownership, commodified quasi-moral attributes like status by sale of legal titles, and rested in an insecure juridical environment.

Venality had emerged in the king's domain by the twelfth century, after French kings created charges of *prévôts* to collect revenues from their own domains and these officers began passing them down to their sons in return for large monetary payments to the monarch. The medieval roots of patrimonial offices, however, did not automatically give rise to an ongoing market in offices. This required more "modern" features: greater security in property rights, brokers to coordinate sales of offices over long distances, a system of banking and credit, and ongoing consumer demand, that is, enough individuals with money to purchase offices.[37] In the fifteenth and sixteenth centuries, continual war, the growth of the state, and commercial development created a favorable environment. The first steps in formalizing a market were taken by François I, who in 1522 created the *bureau des parties casuelles* to serve as, in Loyseau's words, a *"boutique* for this new merchandise," that is, newly created offices.[38] Soon professionals, the *partisans,* a type of financier, emerged to sell offices across large regions. These men quickly developed effective marketing techniques by which they scoured France with blank receipts endorsed by the monarchy so that offices could be sold without delay in the vast reaches of the countryside.

Meanwhile, officeholders pressured the monarchy to give them more secure property rights. In 1604, the chronically impoverished king, in effect, sold his agreement by creating the famous fee known as the *droit annuel,* or the Paulette, named after the financier Paulet who devised the policy. By paying a small sum each year, officers could ensure that they could bequeath their offices to their heirs. The *droit annuel,* in effect, made investing in venal offices secure. Families would no longer have to fear that

---

1996); and articles of David Bien, esp., "Offices, Corps, and a System of State Credit: The Uses of Privilege under the Ancien Régime," in *The Political Culture of the Old Regime,* ed. Keith M. Baker (Oxford, 1987), 87–114; "Old Regime Origins of Democratic Liberty," in *The French Idea of Freedom: The Old Regime and the Declaration of Rights of 1789,* ed. Dale K. Van Kley (Stanford, 1994), 23–71, and article cited in note 2, above.

37. As K.W. Swart observes, venality never developed in Eastern Europe where commercial capitalism remained undeveloped. *The Sale of Office in the Seventeenth Century* (The Hague, 1949).

38. Mousnier, *Vénalité,* 37. Offices in the king's household and in the military, although subject to sale, never fell under the control of the *bureau des parties casuelles* (p. 117).

the large monetary sums placed in offices would be lost by the unexpected death of an incumbent. There was a benefit to the royal government as well. Offices with secure property rights would become easier to sell. Nonetheless, the policy was not without social and political costs. The chancellor at the time, Bellièvre, was so opposed to this routinization of venality that he refused to sign the *arrêt*. He foresaw that the king would lose the right to choose his own officers and would never be in the financial position to suppress the system once it was extended. The heavily indebted king at that time, Henri IV, turned a deaf ear. Through the *droit annuel,* the monarchy was assured a regular revenue against which it could borrow from its *partisans* in moments of financial crisis.[39] Thus, firmer property rights for officeholders, more predictable royal revenues, and the possibility of an expanded system of credit advanced together.

Solidification of property rights in offices laid the foundation for a huge expansion of the market in offices. Because most offices had become heritable, the government had to make money by creating and selling new offices. During the Thirty Years' War, the number of offices skyrocketed. Approximately 15,000 offices existed in 1600; four decades later the number had tripled. In addition, current officeholders were also subject to forced loans, known as *augmentation des gages,* by which they were obligated to increase the capital invested in their offices or lose them. More sophisticated credit mechanisms were devised, so that the king could "anticipate" or borrow against future revenues from the *annuel* or other levies on offices. At the time the Fronde broke out in 1640, nearly half of the king's ordinary revenues came from the *parties casuelles.*[40] Eventually the financial squeeze on officeholders and the enormous sale of offices produced a political backlash. Forced loans, the dilution of status stemming from the huge influx of new officers, failure to pay the officeholders' *gages* (interest owed them by the government), and other expedients were a principal reason that the *parlement* of Paris began the revolt known as the Fronde.

The reign of Louis XIV following the chaos of the Fronde is usually presented as a new era in French history, one that promoted "centralization." Looking at the picture from a fiscal perspective, however, reveals that the patrimonial character of the state—its mixture of public functions with private funds—was given even greater institutional guarantees. In the 1640s, trade in offices generated around 23 million *livres* for the royal government,

---

39. Mousnier, *Vénalité,* 50–51, 233–41.
40. Doyle, *Venality,* 6–15; Robin Briggs, *Early Modern France, 1560–1715* (Oxford, 1977), 213.

during the War of the Spanish Succession, it produced about 40 million.[41] To borrow these sums, both the property rights of officeholders and their corporate status had to be strengthened again. In February 1683, the royal government created laws that made mortgage information on offices public. By reassuring potential creditors of an officeholder's creditworthiness, Louis XIV made it easier for officeholders to borrow up to the full market value of their offices. When war broke out in 1689, corps of officeholders began borrowing money for the king corporately for forced loans like the *augmentation des gages,* rather than individually.[42] The long-term effect was to reinforce the independence of officeholders vis-à-vis the crown by shoring up their property rights and solidifying their corporate status. Offices were forms of property; legally they could only be dismantled if officeholders were reimbursed.

Despite its continued importance, as a percentage of royal income the value of venality began to wane, supplying only about 10 percent of the revenues for the Sun King's last two wars.[43] In the eighteenth century, the explosive growth of offices ceased, although the monarchy still tapped this expedient periodically. Most important, because the monarchy perpetually lacked the funds to reimburse officeholders for the sums invested in their offices, the huge legacy of previous creations remained. Thus, in 1664, Colbert counted 45,780 offices in justice and finance alone; a century later Necker estimated that there were 50,969 offices of justice and finance, all of which could be sold or bequeathed to others by their owners. All in all, it is estimated that on the eve of the Revolution approximately one of every one hundred adult Frenchmen owned an office.[44]

Between the Renaissance and the Revolution, therefore, the monarchy had succeeded in creating a new market in status and public functions,

41. Doyle, *Venality,* 6, 59; Briggs, *Early Modern France,* 213.

42. Mark Potter, "Good Offices: Intermediation by Corporate Bodies in Early Modern French Public Finance," *Journal of Economic History* 60 (September 2000): 606–7. On the importance of borrowing as a *corps* (legally incorporated body), see also David D. Bien, "The *Secrétaires du Roi:* Absolutism, Corps, and Privilege Under the Ancien Régime," in *Vom Ancien Régime zur Französischen Revolution: Forschungen und Perspektiven,* ed. E. Hinrichs (Göttingen, 1978), 153–68.

43. Doyle, *Venality,* 51–52. But Potter, "Good Offices," estimates that venality supplied 28.6 percent of royal revenue during the last two wars. He does not comment on the difference between Doyle's and his figures. Doyle suggests that the royal government killed its own goose, in effect, by manipulating the system of venality so blatantly that it became difficult to sell offices or demand forced loans.

44. Doyle, *Venality,* 11, 24–25, 59–60; in contrast to Doyle (p. 60), George Taylor suggested that 2 to 3 percent of adult males may have possessed some kind of office before the Revolution. "Noncapitalist Wealth," 477.

which was widespread, deeply rooted, and capable of mobilizing enormous amounts of capital. Needless to say, this market in offices led neither to the "modernization" nor to the direct downfall of the nobility. Its effects were complex: it expanded the number of nobles wielding privileges, but its commercial mechanism contradicted the nobility's traditional basis of legitimation. Four effects of venality on the nobility are of particular interest here. First, owing to venality, the French patrimonial state became an ardent promoter of social mobility, indeed, a machine for the "manufacture" of nobility.[45] Second, by expanding and securing the property rights of officeholders, the state helped to institutionalize its own opposition, led by the aristocratic *parlements*. Third, the sale of titles made it more difficult to defend noble privileges by reference to traditional noble virtues, such as the valor of ancestors or pure blood and chivalric heroism. Fourth, venality exacerbated tensions within the Second Estate between rich and poor nobles and thereby helped to make a united defense of noble privilege impossible.

Venality tied the fortunes of the French state directly to the process of social mobility. The creation of new nobles was tied to the state's fiscal survival. The primary route of legal social mobility in the Old Regime was ennobling venal offices. Although only a small percentage of offices carried the privilege of ennoblement, they were the most coveted, fetched the highest price, and raised the most capital for the royal government. Offices of secretary of the king (*secrétaire du roi*) and councillor in sovereign courts conferred first-degree, that is, transmissible, nobility on the officeholder and his posterity after twenty years of service or death in office. Certain other judicial offices required two generations to complete the process. It has been calculated that in the period 1774 to 1789, a total of 2,477 men were ennobled. Roughly 350 of them received letters, the rest had purchased offices.[46] All in all, perhaps one-third of all the nobles in France before the Revolution had been ennobled during the eighteenth century. Another way to put this is that nearly one-third of the nobles in the eighteenth century were products, in some form, of the market in public offices. If one adds to this total the number of families ennobled through purchase of office in the seventeenth century, the majority of nobles in France on the eve of the Revolution were outgrowths of this market. The production of new nobles,

45. David D. Bien, "Manufacturing Nobles: The Chancelleries in France to 1788," *Journal of Modern History* 61 (1989): 445–86.

46. Bien, "La réaction aristocratique avant 1789," 514; Michael Fitzsimmons has calculated a similar number: 2,310 *anoblis* between 1772 and 1786. In this period he found 352 ennoblements by letters. "New Light on the Aristocratic Reaction in France," *French History* 10 (1996): 425, 427.

as these statistics make clear, had turned into a predictable feature of the French state. The growth of the patrimonial state and the nobility went together, mediated by a market in public functions.

Although venality was instrumental to the survival of the monarchy, particularly in the seventeenth century, it also helped to institutionalize the potential network of opposition to the state. By gradually securing the property rights of privileged officeholders and multiplying offices in the judiciary, the monarchy created a vast entrenched network of magistrates who stood to lose by any attack on privilege and who could not easily be removed. Because the offices had been purchased, abolishing them required compensation and not to do so was to attack the property rights of the office-holders. As Roland Mousnier's work on the sale of offices in seventeenth-century France showed, the growth of the system of venality depended upon solidifying the property rights of the *parlementaires* in return for loans and registration of critical edicts creating new offices. Although the monarchy gained resources in the short term, over the long run the *parlementaires* and the rest of the judiciary grew in number and carved out a highly independent base of operation. The trend over several centuries, therefore, was for the monarchy to tame the great "feudal" magnates and quell their rebellions, only to face another opponent, which it had to a large degree fashioned itself, the *parlementaires*. It was members of the *parlement* of Paris and other officeholders who began the Fronde, who plagued Louis XIV during his wars, whom Maupeou attempted unsuccessfully to abolish, and who ushered in the "prerevolution" of 1787–88. In short, the potent institutional combination of constitutional powers of registering the king's edicts and property in office made the *parlements* a formidable foe.[47] The French patrimonial state had helped to generate its own opposition.

The ease with which noble status could be purchased made it more diffi-cult for nobles, particularly new nobles, to justify the traditional privileges and honors associated with nobility. Venality had turned the acquisition of status into a commodity, subject to all the associations with "vile gain" and "interest" that transactions on the market implied. Could those who pur-chased ennobling offices claim the honorable qualities—heroism, generosity,

47. One contemporary observer who realized how important the property rights of the *par-lementaires* were was the abbé Véri. The failure of Maupeou's *coup,* he believed, was largely a result of that disregard for property rights. Joseph-Alphonse Véri, *Journal de l'abbé de Véri,* 2 vols., ed. Jehan de Witte (Paris, n.d.). "A man who does not want to fill a charge should not, for that, lose the money that he loaned to the state on this charge. That was an illegal and unjust attack against property, in a time where the word property was becoming sacred in every mouth" (1:73).

indifference to monetary worries—that the nobility traditionally reserved to itself? The answer was never straightforward. On the one hand, men who purchased ennobling offices argued that they did not buy a noble title outright; they purchased an office by which they served the state in an honorable capacity. Nobility was a reward for service. On the other hand, there were those who denounced the acquisition of status through purchase of office as a mercenary venture that debased everything that honor stood for. Montesquieu actually expressed both opinions simultaneously. In his *Spirit of the Laws,* Montesquieu defended the sale of judicial offices because it inspired industriousness in the state. Those who aspired to honors first had to acquire riches. Nonetheless, he railed against ennoblement of tax farmers, most of whom purchased offices of secretary of the king. When tax farmers in a monarchy acquire nobility, he lamented, "the state is ruined. . . . All the other orders of the state are dissatisfied; honor loses its whole value; the gradual and natural means of distinction are no longer respected; and the very principle of the government is subverted. Every profession has its particular lot. That of the tax gatherers is wealth, and wealth is its own reward."[48] Thus Montesquieu argued that wealth or "industriousness" was rightly given its due through ennobling offices, but he also reiterated the traditional prejudice that wealth served as "its own reward" and might even subvert the basis of honor itself.

Despite their drawbacks as a source, the *cahiers de doléances* of 1789 offer the best sample of collective attitudes toward venal ennoblement on the eve of the Revolution. In his analysis of 492 *cahiers* (150 clerical, 153 noble, and 189 Third Estate), William Doyle found that 7.3 percent of the clergy, 51.6 percent of the nobility, and 24.3 percent of the Third Estate attacked ennoblement by venal office.[49] The opposition of the established nobility to venality, which tainted and diluted its status, was longstanding and hardly cause for surprise. Ambiguity within the ranks of the Third Estate was also understandable, as some members undoubtedly were hoping to use venality for their own advance. A debate in Dijon over this issue is instructive. There one group of lawyers drafted a model *cahier* for the province that

48. Montesquieu, *The Spirit of the Laws,* trans. Franz Neumann (New York, 1949), t. I, bk. 5, chap. 19; t. II, bk. 13, chap. 20. Montesquieu does not specifically attack venality in the quotation about the tax farmers (*traitants*), but most of them were ennobled by the purchase of the office of secretary of the king.

49. Doyle, *Venality,* 269. On the problem of the *cahiers* as a source, see Gilbert Shapiro and John Markoff, *Revolutionary Demands: A Content Analysis of the Cahiers de Doléances of 1789* (Stanford, 1998).

stipulated that "nobility will not be able to be acquired for money." Another group of lawyers from the *parlement* of Dijon protested: this would serve "to strip all emulation from the Third Estate and raise a wall of separation between this order and that of the Nobility."[50]

The *cahiers* denouncing venal ennoblement, it should be stressed, were not opposed to the concept of ennoblement or the legitimacy of the nobility per se. The opposition was to the idea that nobility could be purchased. Members of all three estates continued to view the nobility as a superior group: to ensure that elevated status they wanted ennoblement to be solely a reward for service to the state. In a sample of 95 *cahiers* that denounced venal ennoblement in the *Archives parlementaires,* more than two-thirds (66) stipulated that nobility should be given as a reward for such things as "patriotic virtues and devotion to public affairs" or "real, public important services."[51] An anonymous author from Franche-Comté in 1789 summed up the problem of squaring noble honor with the principle of the market. With the advent of "venal nobility," he wrote, "merit was nothing any more than a base piece of parchment; everything was put up for auction. . . . It was truly a nobility to the highest bidder."[52]

Finally, venality exacerbated divisions within the nobility, particularly between the rich and poor, and made it impossible for nobles to unite to defend the prerogatives of the Second Estate. According to Chaussinand-Nogaret, about 40 percent of the nobility were able to live decently if they were frugal and avoided outward show. Another 20 percent faced actual poverty, some of them even destitution.[53] Because service to the state was

50. R. Robin, "La Loge 'la Concorde' à l'Orient de Dijon," *Annales Historiques de la Révolution Française* 41 (1969): 437. Both the *cahier* of the city and *bailliage* of Dijon demanded that nobility no longer be able to be acquired "*à prix d'argent.*" *Archives parlementaires de 1787 à 1860,* 7 vols., ed. J. Mavidal and E. Laurent (Paris, 1867–75), 3:131, art. 10, and 3:141, art. 9.

51. I composed this sample by consulting *cahiers* listed in volume 7 of the *Archives parlementaires* under the heading "Demandes tendant à ce que la noblesse ne puisse s'acquierir par charge et à prix d'argent," 577–78.

52. *Réflexions d'un citoyen de Franche-comté sur les privilèges et immunités de la noblesse* (n.p., 1789). A citizen in Besançon contrasted the positive value of nobility received as reward for duty with the "fiscal nobility that the nation can not hasten too quickly to repress." Cited by Patrice Higonnet, *Class, Ideology, and the Rights of Nobles During the French Revolution* (Oxford, 1981), 50. The old nobility had always attacked ennoblement by venal office. In 1789, the comte de Serrant, who enjoyed a long, distinguished old lineage, appealed to commoners over heads of bourgeois leaders. "Let the people distrust the newly-ennobled, whose so-called rights are but the Dead Sea fruits of the extravagance of kings." Cited by John McManners, *French Ecclesiastical Society under the Ancien Régime: A Study of Angers in the Eighteenth Century* (Manchester, 1960), 11.

53. An income of 500 *livres* or less is the standard applied by historians to measure noble

mediated through sale of offices, impoverishment effectively denied nobles the opportunity for government service.

The situation was most critical in the army officer corps, which by long tradition was the profession par excellence of the nobility. As the marquis de Crenolle stated, the nobility was made for military command: "when subjects made for another profession occupy the place of nobles, it is a contravention of the rule established by the sovereign."[54] Not all commissions in the army were subject to purchase, but those ensuring the fastest route to the top were. The venal commissions were those of captain and colonel, which conferred command of a company and a regiment, respectively. Unlike offices in the judiciary, these posts operated outside the jurisdiction of the *bureau des parties casuelles* and thus were not heritable. A company could cost between 6,000 and 14,000 *livres,* a cavalry regiment could run as much as 120,000 *livres* or more in the most prestigious corps.[55] Venality in the military gave military officers a great deal of independence vis-à-vis their superiors. As one historian of the Seven Years' War observed, "Though [a commander] led the 'King's Army,' in a very real sense that army was not royal property, but the possession of proprietary colonels and captains who trained, equipped, and led their own men."[56] The return for this independence, as in the judiciary, was financial aid to the royal government. In wartime, the financial obligations could be crushing. During the Seven Years' War, cavalry and dragoon captains raised two million *livres* to keep their troops fed and equipped in the field. After the war, the government effectively repudiated this debt owed to its own army officers.[57]

The profound demoralization of the officer corps led Choiseul to transfer supply of food and recruitment of men from proprietary captains to agents of the state. Venality was curtailed, although it remained in the cavalry and the corps of the *Maison du Roi.* From there sons of wealthy *anoblis* continued to buy their way into prestigious military posts. Another great military reformer, Saint-German, complained of "the sons of big merchants of

---

poverty. For the overall picture, see Chaussinand-Nogaret, *French Nobility,* 52–53. In economically underdeveloped areas the number of poor nobles might be even higher. See also Jonathan Dewald, *Pont-St-Pierre, 1398–1789,* 97–98; and Steven G. Reinhardt, *Justice in the Sarladais, 1770–1790* (Baton Rouge, 1991), 42–43.

54. L. Tuetey, *Les officiers sous l'ancien régime: nobles et roturiers* (Paris, 1908), 242.

55. See Robert Forster, *The House of Saulx-Tavanes,* 42, and Rafe Blaufarb, *The French Army, 1750–1820: Careers, Talent, Merit* (Manchester, 2002), 29.

56. Lee Kennett, *The French Armies in the Seven Years' War* (Durham, 1967), 35.

57. Blaufarb, *French Army,* 27.

Lyon, of farmers generals and of *receveurs des finances,* who, thanks to their money or alliances contracted with great houses, care to place themselves on the same line and claim the same rights [as nobles]."[58] In 1775 he ordered the gradual suppression of venality in the cavalry, a policy that was partially reversed by his successor, Montbarey. In general, the problems with military venality were more easily identified than uprooted. The patrimonial state had always lived off the credit and resources of its servants. As the Marshal de Castries observed, "to deprive [the king] of . . . the credit of the captains would take from him a precious resource." Incapable of reimbursing officers the sums they had invested, the chronically impoverished state had only limited avenues for reform. Saint-Germain had to settle for a policy of reducing the price of remaining venal companies by one-quarter with each change of ownership. In 1791 there was still nearly 50,000,000 *livres* bound up in military charges.[59]

Alongside venality, a second obstacle to reform was the influence of Versailles itself, the heart of the patrimonial state. "If the court continues to dominate the army," stated one reformer, the chevalier de Keralio, on the eve of the Revolution, "there will be no hope."[60] After 1760, presentation at court was necessary to obtain a colonelcy, so that this grade and those above remained the preserve of *les grands.*[61] At the end of the Old Regime, the army had moved toward a two-track system of promotion, a slow track for poor and middling nobles who performed the real work of the army, and a fast track that essentially conferred social distinction and honorific titles on those that Keralio mockingly called "*héros courtisans*" (courtier heroes).[62] On the eve of the Revolution, nobles on the slow track were deeply disillusioned by their inability to advance and by the disdain that the great courtiers displayed toward them. In September 1789, a petition to the National Assembly signed by fifty-one noble military officers from the Regiment of Foret summed up the anger common to this group. "Deign to let your regard fall on one of the most useful but from all times the most maltreated classes; we have rights like citizens."[63]

58. Quoted by Rafe Blaufarb, "Aristocratic Professionalism in the Age of Democratic Revolution: The French Officer Corps, 1750–1815" (Ph.D. diss., University of Michigan, 1996), 56.

59. Blaufarb, *French Army,* 28–29; quotation of de Castries at 28.

60. Cited by Smith, *Culture of Merit,* 246.

61. Tuetey, *Officiers,* 101.

62. Blaufarb, *French Army,* 29–37. The reference to "*héros*" was in the "Mémoire de Keralio," *Service Historique de l'Armée de Terre (SHAT),* 1 M 1716.

63. *SHAT,* 1 M 1907, *Reclamations des officiers du Regt. de Foret.*

Financiers and Capitalism in Public Functions

The final category of markets involves cases where the royal government entered into formal business arrangements to lease or farm out tasks to private corporations of entrepreneurs. The entrepreneurs paid the royal government a set amount for the right to perform a designated task, such as collecting taxes, and paid all expenses generated by their work. In return, they were able to keep any profits generated over and above the lease price. Among the most important of these groups were the *munitionnaires,* who supplied the armies with bread; the Company of Farmers General, who leased the right to collect indirect taxes; and privileged chartered trading companies, notably the Indies Company, which held trading monopolies.

These groups had several traits in common. First, to enforce compliance on the part of the populace and to enhance the ability of these entrepreneurs to make a profit, the government usually gave them privileges and powers that were usually reserved to the government itself, such as the right to set up a police force or requisition supplies. Thus, as in the case of judicial and military venality, sovereign functions passed into quasi-private hands. The Farmers Generals employed a large police force to combat smuggling, and the Indies Company had the rather startling power to maintain troops, send ambassadors in the name of the king to indigenous rulers, and even to declare war and conclude peace treaties with these rulers.

Second, the growth of these institutions was directly related to the weak credit of the monarchy. All of these groups served as de facto bankers to the king, particularly in wartime when the need for loans was acute. After the Seven Years' War, the government owed one company of munitioneers 15,512,726 *livres* for provisions for the army. During that same war, the Indies Company borrowed 12 million *livres* in order to arm a flotilla to India.[64] The royal government also routinely borrowed against future tax revenues. By the end of the Old Regime, the government was indebted to the Company of Farmers General to the tune of 68,400,000 *livres*.[65] Another group of financiers, the Receivers General, supervised direct taxation—the *taille, capitation,* and *vingtième.* In 1780, the total capital invested in all the

---

64. Kennett, *French Armies,* 8–9, 11–12, 130; For powers of the East Indies Company and advances, see Henri Weber, *La compagnie française des Indes* (Paris, 1904), 121–30, 203–14, 518–19, 540, 562, 570.

65. George Matthews, *The Royal General Farms in Eighteenth-Century France* (New York, 1958), 13–15.

offices and their required surety bonds, which served as a loan to the royal government, was 68,840,000 *livres*.[66]

Various segments of the nobility played critical roles in these companies. The actual administrators and financiers at the top of these organizations often did not begin their careers as nobles, but most of them acquired nobility, usually by purchasing the ennobling office of secretary of the king. On the eve of the Revolution, only 10 percent of the Farmers General were commoners, and one-third of the daughters of Farmers General were wed to court or other distinguished nobles.[67] A particularly famous case of social ascent is that of the Pâris brothers, sons of a poor Dauphiné tavernkeeper, who founded an immense fortune by supplying bread to the army during the War of the Spanish Succession. Pâris de Montmartel, godfather to the king's mistress, the Marquise de Pompadour, became a powerful financier in the court of Louis XV. His brother Pâris Duverney supplied the army and was so intent on handing out advice on military operations that he was dubbed "General of the Flour Bags."[68]

Far from a "feudal" nobility, noble financiers, as George Matthews commented, formed "a curious aristocracy; for although its economic foundations were not in the land, neither did they rest solidly upon the commercial and industrial enterprises of capitalism." The assets of the Farmers General, he continued, "consisted almost exclusively of capital frozen in the permanent royal debt; their incomes derived from an archaic financial enterprise which lived only because the monarchy could not afford to let it die."[69] Although all members of the Second Estate who owned offices or government *rentes* (annuities and bonds) had part of their wealth bound up in the fate of the state, the socially mobile financiers represented the epitome of a nobility that lived and died by financial capitalism.

By the end of the eighteenth century, financiers had shaken off much of the unsavory reputation that had plagued their forebears and mingled with the highest levels of society. They were patrons of the arts, men of refinement and cultivation who had well-placed patrons among the great nobles and influential women at court. The status distinctions between the two groups, of course, were never effaced. In many ways, the colonization of the court by financiers was a frank exchange of money for valuable court

66. John F. Bosher, *French Finances, 1770–1795*, 76.
67. Yves Durand, *Les fermiers généraux au XVIII siècle* (Paris, 1971), 624.
68. Kennett, *French Army*, 8–9, 111–12, 130; Matthews, *Royal General Farms*, 241.
69. Matthews, *General Farms*, 247–48.

connections. Newly ennobled, financiers remained open to the slur of being "bourgeois," a charge that court nobles threw at new nobles to remind them of their roots. An anecdote reported by Sénac de Meilhan illustrated the disparity. After a somewhat elderly duchess took a young noble financier as a lover, her friend expressed surprise. The duchess responded, "Don't you know then that a duchess is never more than thirty years old for a bourgeois?"[70]

Nobles at court were always eager to find ways to use their privileged status in order to milk the system. To become a financier in the Farmers General, for example, one had to invest a share in the company, and this cost was enormous (1,560,000 *livres* in 1767). To raise this capital, most Farmers had financial backers known as *croupiers* behind them, each of whom received a cut from the Farmer's profits. Although many of these investments were simple business arrangements, the system was open to abuse, especially since favor at court was necessary to gain a share in the company. As a result, it was common for a Farmer to find that he had to share his profits with a royal *croupier,* even if the latter person had not invested the full sum demanded of other backers. One of the company's most notorious leases from the royal government, the Lease David of 1774, contained payments totaling 400,000 *livres* a year to members of the court, including the king himself.[71] The profits of the Indies Company also were directed toward those with court connections. During peacetime, monopolies exercised by the company could be lucrative. From 1726 to 1743, the protected commerce in beaver skins generated effective profits of 26 percent, more than twice the profits considered normal for transatlantic trade. Licencing fees and royalties diverted a good portion of this profit from the colonial merchants into the hands of state officials, financiers, and shareholders in the Indies Company itself.[72]

Conclusion

In conclusion, let us return to the questions posed at the outset. What was the relation of nobles to markets, and what insight can this perspective offer on the parallel hierarchies that existed within the nobility? First, the logic of status, as we noted, is to create ever-finer distinctions and hierarchies within groups.

70. Cited by Yves Durand, *Fermiers généraux,* 221.
71. Ibid., 208–9, 230–37.
72. Dale Miquelon, *New France, 1701–1744* (Toronto, 1987), 78–81.

Given this tendency, it is not surprising that the nobility was characterized by many interior gradations and divisions; it would be surprising if it were not.

Second, there is evidence to support the revisionist thesis that wealth was drawing wealthy commoners and nobles together into a plutocratic elite that presaged the notables of the nineteenth century. The growth of the market played a role in this trend by making it possible to purchase the visible marks associated with status and by making monetary exchange the basis of social relations, thereby gradually undermining the idea that status carried the right to deference and entitlements by dint of its very nature. At the same time, however, the move toward social homogenization of the elite through the market remained limited. One important reason was the enduring nature of status itself and its strong legal presence. In the Old Regime many markets, perhaps most markets, did not operate in a level playing field, that is, in a sphere of legal equality. Instead, markets had been grafted onto traditional institutions characterized by relations of political command, privileges bestowed on those of superior status, and confusion between ownership and rulership. As a result, the markets in which nobles usually participated—those of seigneurialism and others associated with the patrimonial state—were prone to create monopolies. They continued to direct profits toward those wielding power and prestige. The Revolution, from this perspective, was not concerned with facilitating the rise of the market. Rather, the work of the Revolution itself was to change the rules governing the operation of markets so that those making contracts would do so from a position of legal equality, that is, from a position in which status could not make preemptive claims.

Third, although the logic of status helps to explain the fragmentation of the nobility, it would be simplistic to attribute all divisions to its work. Key divisions among nobles were also functional and semiprofessional: the most important nobles played roles in finance, the military, the judiciary, and the administration at Versailles. It is striking how closely these groupings were tied to the rise of the patrimonial state—and to its markets. The nobility as an estate as a whole certainly did not trace its origins to these markets, but by the end of Louis XIV's reign, some form of state-sanctioned market transaction had insinuated itself into virtually all the power centers of the nobility. On the eve of the Revolution, the majority of nobles owed their pedigrees to the purchase of an office made by themselves or their ancestors. Ownership of high posts in the judiciary and finance had turned nobles into creditors of the king. Army officers had been virtual proprietors of their regiments, although after the Seven Years' War the government took steps to remove venality in the army. Even offices in the king's household at the court of Versailles were purchased. As for the *intendants,* although as salaried administrators they were subject to recall by the royal government, they could not be considered fully "bureaucratic" in the modern sense. They, too, entered the administrative world by first buying an office of *maître des requêtes.* The most advanced sector of the bureaucracy did not completely escape the patrimonial dimension of the Old Regime and its peculiar markets in status and power.

As the patrimonial state grew larger, then, it spawned a larger and more differentiated nobility, able to perform the more specialized tasks required by a great power. The patrimonial state was thus central in creating parallel hierarchies in the nobility, but it did not do this bureaucratically. It did so by allowing men to lease, purchase, and inherit the functions it needed to be done in return for payments. It provided a mechanism through its markets by which men of wealth, ambition, and talent could be ennobled in return for their services and their ability to generate wealth. It is not surprising that the nobility on the eve of the Revolution was characterized by so many contradictory traits. There was a growing professional dimension to various sectors of the nobility. In the army, there were noble officers who spent time drilling their troops, perfecting tactics, and enduring various deprivations in preparation for war. The Company of Farmers General, which boasted one of the first formal pension systems in Europe, was a highly efficient tax-collecting machine, which increasingly incorporated mathematical advances to enhance its profitability. Nonetheless, this emerging professionalism—whether in the judiciary, military, or finance—remained embedded in patrimonial networks and beholden to the court at Versailles. Venal offices like secretary of the king were attractive precisely because they ennobled but required no work by the officeholder. Judicial officers could not be easily removed because they owned their offices. Army reformers were constantly butting up against courtiers who had secured high rank through patronage and wealth but left critical details to subordinates. *Croupiers* in the Farmers General reaped rewards from court connections, while the crown's indebtedness to these tax collectors made it nigh impossible to reform indirect taxes.

Thus it can be reiterated that interpretations of the Old Regime based in notions of "centralization," or "bureaucracy" (erroneously applied from Weber's own work) do a grave injustice to understandings of networks of power in the Old Regime. It was not that centralization remained incomplete, a mission that could not be fulfilled, given the technology, communication networks, and other conditions of the time. The royal government actually grew in nonbureaucratic fashion by contracting out the functions it needed in return for payments and blurring public functions with private ownership. In so doing, the patrimonial state called into existence, or at least expanded, the different kinds of nobles needed for its survival, thereby institutionalizing the parallel hierarchies within the nobility noted by Peter Jones. The process also helped to generate strong interest groups that ultimately prevented reform. It is sometimes said that the French Revolution originated in a conflict between a reforming state and vestigial, privileged corporate groups. It seems more accurate to argue that the battles leading to 1789 were created when reformers tried, unsuccessfully, to rein in powerful interest groups, particularly within the nobility, that had been spawned by the patrimonial state itself. The state could survive in the long run only by changing the rules of the game—by ending venality, tax privileges, inefficiencies in tax collection, court favoritism in the army, and the like, all of which the patrimonial state had expanded and sustained through its development.

Finally, it should be stressed that many nobles were excluded from the markets of the patrimonial state and the benefits that they conferred. Provincial nobles of lesser or middling means, who constituted the majority of the Second Estate, simply could not compete. They could not afford the costs of the more prestigious army commission, a prestigious judicial office, or even a fief. They had neither contacts at court nor money to invest in government-backed companies, stocks, and securities. And many of them burned at their exclusion. They resented the monied newcomers who purchased their way into the centers of government power, and they deplored the lack of recognition given to their honorable birthright and, in many cases, hard work. The famous Ségur law of 1781 sought to block the effects of court capitalism by preventing sons of newly ennobled financiers and venal officeholders from swarming into the army and, by dint of their money, passing hardworking, patriotic provincial noble officers by. Thus wealth did profoundly divide the nobility, but mainly because court connections and purchase of posts constituted the institutional means of advance.

In sum, the patrimonial state and a linked system of status had helped to create a larger nobility with more specialized sectors, but one that was demoralized at the bottom and open to attack both from within and without. A quotation from Turgot is sometimes cited to show that by the late eighteenth-century money or "class" had replaced the traditional hierarchical orders as the basis of social hierarchy in the Old Regime. "The cause of the privileged," he argued, had become "the cause of the rich against the poor." In its full context, however, it becomes clear that Turgot was actually critiquing the commodification of legal status characterizing the patrimonial state. "Another reason operates," stated Turgot, "to render privilege most unjust and at the same time less worthy of respect. Where nobility can be acquired by a payment of money, there is no rich man who does not speedily become a noble, so that the body of the nobles includes the body of the rich, and the cause of the privileged is no longer the cause of distinguished families against a common class, but the cause of the rich against the poor."[73] The cause of the privileged was more complex than one of rich and poor. The struggle between the Second and Third Estates in the Estates-General of 1789 would demonstrate that.[74] Yet Turgot's statement pointed up the seriousness of grafting the quest for status and honor onto the operation of the market. Between the fiscal needs of the state and the desire for social ascent, the mighty force of the market had been bent to serve the call of status, yet that very act also set in motion the grounds for the delegitimation of various sectors of the nobility and for setting groups of nobles against one another within the patrimonial state.

73. Cited by Douglas Dakin, *Turgot and the Ancien Régime in France* (New York, 1965), 274.
74. The complexities are analyzed by Timothy Tackett, *Becoming a Revolutionary: The Deputies of the National Assembly and the Emergence of a Revolutionary Culture, 1789–90* (Princeton, 1996).

3

THE NOBLE PROFESSION OF SEIGNEUR IN EIGHTEENTH-CENTURY BURGUNDY

Robert M. Schwartz

The aggressive pursuit of rights to revenue is a commonplace today. Be it Microsoft's effort to strengthen its proprietary grip on desktop computing, pharmaceutical firms rushing to patent traditional curatives, or record companies and film studios suing to stop the free circulation of music and movies on the Internet, enforcing property rights over new or existing resources is a pillar of capital accumulation and wealth creation in the contemporary world.[1] In eighteenth-century France, the vigilant exploitation of revenue-producing rights was already old hat when Louis XV came to the throne.

I wish to thank Madame la Comtesse Legouz de Saint Seine for allowing me to consult the private archives of the Château of Longecourt, and the director and staff of the Archives Départementales de la Côte d'Or for their kind assistance over many years, especially Mlle Françoise Vignier, the former director; Gérard Moyse, the current director; Claire and Maurice Bathelier; and Anthony Devarrewaere who brought to my attention the "Monographie de Minot" by George Potey. I am grateful to David Bien, Jay Smith, and Jeremy Hayhoe whose comments on earlier drafts did much to improve this essay. Thanks also go to Marietta Clement for her keen proofreading skills. Over the years I have been fortunate to receive generous financial support for the research from which this article comes: included are a fellowship and summer stipend from the National Endowment for the Humanities, a research grant from the Harry R. Guggenheim Foundation, and faculty fellowships and grants from Mount Holyoke College.

1. According to Tom Bakos, the U.S. Patent Office received 350,000 new patent applications in 2001 and issued 187,824 patents. See "Patenting Insurance," *Contingencies* (July–August 2002): 33–39, p. 33, http://www.contingencies.org/julaug02/patent.pdf (accessed 20 February 2004). The largely successful efforts of Western pharmaceutical firms to patent medicinal plants that have long been used in the traditional medicine of the Indian subcontinent is summarized by Vandana Shiva, "Protecting our Biological and Intellectual Heritage in the Age of Biopiracy," http://www.vshiva.net/archives/biopiracy/protect_biodiversity.htm (accessed 20 February 2004).

The practice was at the heart of the agrarian political economy, and the defining institution there was seigneurialism. Often referred to as *"féodalité"* by contemporary proponents and critics alike, seigneurialism was complex system of public authority, land tenure, justice, agrarian regulation, and surplus extraction. The system was a potent source of power and wealth, so there was no lack of motivation on the part of eighteenth-century lords and their agents to enforce existing seigneurial rights, most of which were centuries old, and to claim new rights at propitious moments.

In Burgundy during the later sixteenth century the imposition of new dues and obligations, together with the augmentation of those already in existence, spread through the province. In the turbulent century that followed, a second extension of seigneurial rights took place, much facilitated by the increased vulnerability and indebtedness of rural communities that the Thirty Years' War and the upsurge in royal taxes brought about. Then, under the favorable economic conditions of the later eighteenth century, a third phase of seigneurial development made its mark on the political economy of the region. As in the past, so after 1750, new *terriers* (title deeds) were drawn up to specify the rights of lords and the obligations of communities over which they held authority. On these occasions, and especially when a new seigneur took control, old rights that had fallen into disuse were often revived, stirring peasant grievances and prompting negotiations and sometimes court proceedings before the antagonistic parties came to agreement on what rights were to be honored.

In Burgundy and in France generally, the remaking of *terriers* and the attentive exploitation of seigneurial rights after 1750 has come to be known, unfortunately, as the the "feudal" or "seigneurial" reaction. Both terms are misleading because they signify a backward-looking movement, one that sustained retrograde practices that hindered agrarian development and growth.[2] When viewed narrowly as feudal, stubbornly premodern, and newly intensified, eighteenth-century seigneurialism seems a major obstacle

2. Robert Forster, "Obstacles to Agricultural Growth in Eighteenth-Century France," *American Historical Review* 75 (1970): 1600–45. Rather than seigneurialism or the lack of secure title inherent in seigneurial land tenure, Forster emphasized the retarding effects of short leases, the tendency for landlords to raise rents abruptly, and the relative absence, in comparison to their English counterparts, among landlords and tenants of the habit of reinvesting surpluses in agricultural improvements. Thus even when the agricultural product increased, it was not growth in the meaningful sense of increased productivity. More recently Philip Hoffman has made a strong case for agrarian growth through increased productivity in the Paris region, though he sidesteps the role that seigneurialism may have played in hindering or stimulating such growth. See his *Growth in a Traditional Society: the French Countryside, 1450–1815* (Princeton, 1996).

to agrarian capitalism, to the physiocrats' program of agrarian reform, and to the reforms incorporated into state policy through royal edicts encouraging enclosure, the partition of common lands, and the free trade in grain. So viewed, sympathies readily gravitate to the modern ingredients seen in the physiocratic campaign and agronomists' writings. All this reinforces the idea that seigneurialism was little more than an outmoded system of legal and practical constraints on capitalist development and a form of aristocratic domination that was digging its own grave. In this way historical complexity is lost, and we fail to appreciate the novel aspects of the evolving system as well as the ability of lords and their agents to adapt seigneurialism to market conditions and capitalist enterprise.

When writing in the Burgundian context, Pierre de Saint Jacob preferred the more appropriate term "seigneurial offensive" to describe both the renewed exploitation of lordly rights after 1750 and the more far-reaching offensive of the previous century. Drawing on Saint Jacob and existing studies for other regions, William Doyle concluded that the so-called seigneurial reaction of Louis XVI's reign was simply the last manifestation of the long, continuing process of maintaining seigneurial rights.[3] Noting that Robert Forster's study of the Burgundian Saulx-Tavanes was perhaps the exception to the rule, Doyle stressed continuity and challenged historians to demonstrate what, if anything, was new about the so-called seigneurial reaction of the Old Regime.[4] Since then new studies leave little doubt that the eighteenth century did see a renewed seigneurial offensive. And some historians have risen to Doyle's challenge by attempting to show, as did Forster, that seigneurial revenues increased at the expense of peasants after 1750.[5]

3. William Doyle "Was There an Aristocratic Reaction in Pre-Revolutionary France?" *Past and Present* 57 (1972): 97–122, p. 119.

4. Although the duc de Saulx-Tavane was an absentee courtier, Robert Forster showed that the remaking of *terriers* under his orders led to increased revenues mainly through the better collection of the *dîme*. See *The House of Saulx-Tavanes: Versailles and Burgundy, 1700–1830* (Baltimore, 1971), 92–104.

5. Among the most recent works on the issue are Peter Jones, *Liberty and Locality in Revolutionary France: Six Villages Compared, 1760–1820* (Cambridge, 2003); and two articles by Stephen Miller that by and large cover the same Languedocian ground: "Absolutism and Class at the End of the Old Regime." *Journal of Social History* 36, no. 4 (2003): 871–98, and "Lord, Peasant Communities, and the State in Eighteenth-Century Languedoc." *French Historical Studies* 26, no. 1 (2003): 55–88. Introductions to the historiography and additional bibliography can be found in Miller and in Jeremy Hayhoe, "Judge in Their Own Cause: Seigneurial Justice in Northern Burgundy, 1750–1790" (Ph.D diss., University of Maryland, 2001), chap. 8. The increasing revenues for the barony of Pont-Saint-Pierre are clearly demonstated by Jonathan Dewald in his *Pont-St-Pierre: Lordship, Community, and Capitalism in Early Modern France* (Berkeley, 1987).

Rather than focusing on change *or* continuity, in this essay I will explore elements of both. The interpretation offered here recognizes that since the fifteenth century the maintenance and extension of seigneurial rights was an ongoing process, and it attempts to illustrate both what was traditional and what was new about the lordly offensive in Burgundy after 1750 by looking at two seigneurial families of robe ancestry, provincial seigneurs of significant rank and wealth. This group of nobles remained in the region. They were neither drawn to Versailles like the Tavanes nor lived lives of gentile poverty behind decaying château walls. They were provincial lords who carried forward the enterprising habits of mind practiced by their bourgeois and *anobli* (recently enobled) forbears.[6] Like their forebears, they engaged in the management of their estates and regarded their seigneurial titles and powers as constituent ingredients of noble rank as well as good business. As the eighteenth century came to define one's work as the main element of rank and identity, so the attentive seigneur came to see the development of his lordships as a noble profession—work that sustained and legitimized his wealth, power, and status.[7]

However subtle, this shift in outlook is especially evident in successful efforts of Nicolas Philippe Berbis to develop his lordships using new management techniques that helped make the seigneurial enterprise a vehicle of agrarian capitalism. Whereas the sixteenth- and seventeenth-century ancestors of Berbis and his peers introduced many new rights and peasant obligations

6. Gaston Roupnel, in *La ville et la campagne au XVIIe siècle: étude sur les populations du pays dijonnais* (Paris, 1922), gives a full account of the vast accumulation of land in the Dijon region by bourgeois and *anobli* of that city. This remarkable story resembles what Miller suggests was occurring in late eighteenth-century Languedoc, namely, that *anobli* were rushing to buy up seigneuries and using seigneurial rights to squeeze peasants hard, an offensive that enjoyed the full support of the Toulouse *parlement* when newly discovered or invented rights were challenged in court.

7. This interpretation in the making is based on the ways in which the Mairetet and Berbis managed their estates and on studies that treat the Burgundian nobility, including La Cuisine, *Le parlement de Bourgogne depuis son origine jusqu'à sa chute*, 3 vols. (Dijon, 1864); Albert Colombet, *Les Parlementaires Bourguignons à la fin du XVIIIe siècle*, 2nd ed. (Dijon, 1937); Roupnel, *Ville et campagne;* Pierre de Saint Jacob, *Les paysans de la Bourgogne du nord au dernier siècle de l'Ancien Régime* (Paris, 1960); Julian Swann, *Provincial Power and Absolute Monarchy: The Estates General of Burgundy, 1661–1790* (Cambridge, 2003). It draws also from the work of David Bien on the shift in the eighteenth-century meaning of *état* from status and rank to profession and occupation— and on the spread of these notions in the army officer corps and other corporate bodies. Jay Smith, Gail Bossenga, Rafe Blaufarb, and others have developed this idea further. See David D. Bien, "The Army in the French Enlightenment: Reform, Reaction and Revolution," *Past and Present* 85 (November 1979): 68–98; "La réaction aristocratique avant 1789: l'exemple de l'armée," *Annales: E.S.C.* 29, no. 1 (janvier-fevrier 1974): 23–48; no. 2 (mars-avril 1974): 505–34; and "The Ancien Régime in France," in *Perspectives on the European Past: Conversations with Historians,* ed. Norman F. Cantor (New York, 1971), 2:3–26.

and could aptly be called the creators of the Burgundian system, the lords of Louis XVI's era rarely followed this practice. They had no need to invent what was already present in their old *terriers*. And once old rights were discovered, they proved adept at adopting them to new circumstances, reviving *corvées* (entitlements to labor services) to produce money or labor as needed and using *triage* (seigneurial entitlement to appropriate common land) to expand pasture and woodlands at a time when land rents and prices were rising sharply. In so doing, they were apt to press their claims on peasants with less force and connivance than their ancestors had done. Gone were the days of the seventeenth century when rural communities, weakened by the effects of war and unpredicted tax increases, were easily forced to sell common lands to seigneurs or wealthy merchants to meet crushing debts. Likewise, the vast acquisitions of land by the urban wealthy in the same century had been completed, leaving eighteenth-century peasants with considerably less land than before. And as a degree of prosperity returned, communities were in a better position to resist when lords or their agents squeezed too hard. With the bulk of the Burgundian peasants largely landless, enterprising seigneurs sometimes found themselves knocking heads with bourgeois and nobles who had come to own much if not most of the land in their lordships.

To appreciate change *and* continuity and to understand the work of seigneurs, one has to look into the minutiae of contracts, account books, negotiations, and the sine qua non of the regime, the ancient title deeds that defined rights and obligations. This, then, will be a microhistory, one that often follows the well-blazed trails of Pierre de Saint Jacob and Robert Forster into the countryside of northern Burgundy.[8] This journey leads to the châteaux of two families of the robe nobility, the Mairetet of Minot and the Berbis of Longecourt. To get our bearings, we need first to recall the larger economic and political context in which they thought and acted.

The Economy of Agrarian Accumulation

In the mid-eighteenth century, economic trends in Burgundy sometimes favored tenants and sometimes landlords. When the young Berbis took charge in 1753, stable land values and grain prices tended to favor tenants and the

---

8. Saint Jacob, *Paysans;* Forster, *House of Saulx-Tavanes.* Anyone who sets out to describe the rural world of seventeenth- and eighteenth-century Burgundy sooner or later realizes that the result risks being a mere footnote to Saint Jacob. Parts of this article are a case in point, as the first sections so clearly demonstrate.

substantial *fermiers* (leaseholders) who took on the leases for an entire seigneurie or for one or more large farms. This situation shifted dramatically in the late 1760s. Grain prices started moving upward in 1765, and the golden age for landlords opened a few years later, around 1770. Far out-distancing the rise in grain prices, the price of leases rose sharply in 1770–72 and by as much as 60 to 80 percent on the most productive land, with the average being lower. Meanwhile, meadowland needed for fodder in stock-raising shot up in value, rising by 80 to 100 percent during the five-year period 1767–72, as compared to the 15 to 20 percent rise in land values during the same period.[9] Behind this conjuncture was not population pressure but the speculative urge and the search for higher profits.

With rising profits in the offing, there was no shortage of lease seekers, and a new breed of *marchand-fermiers* from Dijon and other towns appeared on the agrarian scene, men who profited both from large leaseholds and from agrarian commerce. Betting that the buoyant prices in grain would continue, they used their connections and financial clout to combine several large leases into a block, portions of which they easily sublet to local peasants at good profit. In the process, local men who had previously leased all or parts of a seigneurial estate now found themselves competing to be subtenants of one or more *fermier général* managing things from afar. As the bidding-up of land values reached a peak, large farmers and merchants strove to lock in leases two or three years in advance. With land, harvest dues, and other revenues to offer, seigneurs found themselves in the driver's seat. In responding to the rising tide of agrarian fortune, attentive seigneurs reviewed their *terriers* and adopted rational management methods to draw greater returns on their property. Merchants and substantial tenant farmers shared in this accumulation, so long as their speculations and contracts were well timed in relation to the rise and decline of grain prices from 1770 to 1787. Those who took on costly nine-year leases after 1780–81 were likely to suffer or go bankrupt as grain prices fell in the mid-1780s.[10] As grain prices declined by 25 to 30 percent from the higher levels of the 1770s, the

---

9. Saint Jacob, *Paysans,* 363–68, 394. Saint Jacob's estimates for the increased price of leases were based on only a few examples, so further research here is needed. In Burgundy, rising prices for leases and rents cannot be attributed to population pressure, for the Burgundian population remained relatively stable in the second half of the eighteenth century. See Archives Départe-mentales de la Côte d'Or, Dijon (here after ADCO) I F 38, "Statistique du Département de la Côte-d'Or," 2 vols. (1807), 1: chap. 8.

10. Saint Jacob, *Paysans,* 383–87, 393–95.

high tide of wealth accumulation ebbed. Consequently, urban merchants and speculators withdrew their investments, many no doubt shifting their money to the moderate but steady returns from bonds (*rentes*) on state, church, or provincial debts. As competition for leases subsided, the upward pressure on land values lessened. Then, as before the boom of the 1770s, seigneurs tended to turn again to local men to farm their estates and lordships. Hence in the 1780s, lords hoping to maintain or increase revenues from their seigneuries had to work intelligently to meet the challenge.[11]

The Burgundian Triangle of Power:
Parlement, Provincial Estates, and the State

One reason why speculating on seigneurial rights and estates was considered a good investment was that the system enjoyed the full backing of the *parlement* of Burgundy in Dijon. As magistrates of the sovereign court for the province, *parlementaires* looked upon the local seigneurial justices as lower courts of first instance whose functioning was theirs to supervise and regulate. Not only did the magistrates of the high court uphold seigneurial rights, they exercised their own regulatory authority over agrarian life and village social order. Attempts by the royal administration or even the Burgundian Estates to encroach upon this authority met with *parlement's* determined and usually successful resistance. Behind this resistance also lay a good measure of self-interest, for about two-thirds of the *présidents* and *conseillers* (magistrates) owned at least one seigneurie and the justice to which it belonged.[12]

In the 1760s, as calls grew loud for institutional reform throughout the kingdom, the combination of judicial authority and self-interest in the *parlement* led to a number of improvements in seigneurial justice. The basis for these was the *parlement's arrêt* of 26 March 1768. By its terms, lords were required to ensure that the annual assizes (*grands jours*) of their justices were in fact held every year and that qualified men were appointed and paid for their service as judge, prosecutor (*procureur d'office*), or clerk (*greffier*). Although most of the provisions restated long-standing regulations, the new ruling

11. Ibid., 470–76.
12. Hayhoe, "Judge in Their Own Cause," chap. 8, p. 27. In 1746, two-thirds of the seventy-seven magistrates owned at least one seigneurie, and most of them owned from one to four. In 1787, 65 percent of seventy-one owned at least one, and the more important judges typically owned more, as did 90 percent of the *présidents*.

had teeth: lords who failed to fulfill their duties within a year were subject to heavy fines.[13]

At other times the actions of the magistrates reflected motives less of judicious reform than of clear material interest. A good example was their support of an initiative taken by the Provincial Estates (*Etats*) in 1770 to regulate the seigneurial right of *triage,* the lord's right to appropriate one-third of a community's common lands. Of medieval origin and codified by a 1669 ordinance of the royal *Eaux et Forets* administration, *triage* was perhaps the most contentious issue over which lords and villages struggled without end. In the reasoning advanced by the Estates, the right was to be exercised only once. But in practice, communities remained vulnerable to successive, and thus illicit, uses of *triage.* Consequently, the argument continued, such repeated attacks on a village's resources diminished its ability to meet its fiscal obligations—the principal concern of the Estates. Attempting to stabilize the situation, the Estates secured the royal letters patent of 27 July 1770 that instituted what it held to be a reasonable policy: henceforth seigneurs whose right of *triage* had not yet been exercised had thirty years within which to do so. However misguided as a measure to prevent the further erosion of village resources, the new policy seemed a welcome and beneficial resolution to seigneurs and *parlementaires.* So, amid *parlement*'s bitter struggle against the monarchy—one so intense as to prompt the crown to suspend sovereign courts throughout the kingdom—the embattled judges rushed to register the new *triage* legislation.[14]

That the sovereign court jealously guarded its regulatory authority over agrarian life and seigneurial law often brought it into conflict with the rival authority of the royal *intendant.* The royal edict of 16 August 1766 encouraging the clearing of wasteland as a means of increasing agricultural production provides an example. An opening act in the physiocratic campaign, the new law offered on newly cleared land generous fifteen-year exemptions from the royal land tax (*taille*) and the ecclesiastical tithe (*dîme*). The right to undertake clearings was also granted to village outsiders. These inducements stimulated a frenzy of *défrichements* and an impressive rise in the arable surface. Nonetheless, *parlement* remained wary. In the view of the judges, the edict threatened to undermine seigneurial policing authority: nonresident speculators now permitted to lay hold of waste would escape

---

13. *Réglemens généraux pour les justices seigneuriales, corrigés & augmentés par un Avocat de cette Ville, en l'année 1779* (Dijon, 1779); Saint Jacob, *Paysans,* 408–9; Hayhoe, "Judge in Their Own Cause," 10.

14. Saint Jacob, *Paysans,* 378–99.

seigneurial regulation, while local inhabitants were treating the edict as a license to steal, as the authority to lay claim to portions of communal lands and seigneurial wood lots. The complaints from *curés* (parish priests) worried about the loss of the *dîme* and from seigneurs concerned about their authority over the village *finage* (territory) sharpened the court's resolve. Accordingly, the judges bypassed the *intendant* and lobbied the royal controller general with some success in order to limit the disruptive effects of the law.[15]

Conflicts grew more intensive and frequent after 1775 because the attempt under Chancellor Maupeou to replace all provincial *parlements* with new courts of appeal reunited the Dijon *parlementaires* as little else could. Once restored, the high court renewed its resistance to royal initiatives of many kinds and to those that seemed to weaken seigneurialism in particular. Attempts by the *intendant* to authorize the leasing of village common lands, for example, were blocked, hindered, or denounced.[16] To be sure, there were instances when the *intendant* and the *parlement* shared reservations about the monarchy's agrarian reforms, as they did with regard to the edict of January 1774 authorizing the division of common lands in Burgundy.[17] Nonetheless, the hostility with which *parlement* continued to regard the *intendant* was nurtured by the court's continuing defense of the seigneurial regime. This and the growing power of the Provincial Estates meant that the *intendant* after 1750 was, as Julian Swann put it, "an increasingly marginal figure."[18]

The Estates constituted the third side of the Burgundian triangle of power. Although the institution had no judicial authority over the seigneurial system, its authority in fiscal affairs and highway administration at times involved it in matters of lordly interest, and its general influence in the province rose to a height under Louis XVI.[19] As noted above, sometimes the initiatives of the Provincial Estates were well received by *parlement* and seigneurs alike, as when its call for the reform of trespass and damage offenses (*mesus*) produced in 1773 a new royal law of good effect.[20] On the other hand, the sovereign court repeatedly blocked the Estates' attempts to reform the royal *taille* and

15. Ibid., 351–52, 358.

16. Ibid., 522–23, describes the judges' renewed activities in regulations issued to govern crop rotation, the use of waste, and the right to divide common lands. For an account that gives undue emphasis to the royal administration's ability to gain control over seigneurialism, see Hilton L. Root, *Peasants and King in Burgundy: Agrarian Foundations of French Absolutism* (Berkeley, 1987).

17. Saint Jacob, *Paysans*, 382–85. *Parlement* did not register the edict until 1782.

18. Swann, *Provincial Power*, 409.

19. Ibid., 409–11.

20. This law greatly simplified the procedures for adjudicating the ever so numerous cases of damage to crops and fields by animals, providing for swift and fair settlements between the

vingtième taxes. Finally, by securing royal letters patent in 1788 the Estates at last brought the plan into existence, shifting more of the tax burden to privileged proprietors. *Parlement* rushed to denounce the scheme loudly, seeing in the reform an attack on privilege and the virtual abolition of the seigneurial courts' authority over fiscal issues.[21]

In sum, seigneurialism in Burgundy was hardly in decline when Louis XVI authorized the meeting of the Estates-General in 1788. It was strong and well entrenched. In judicial aspects it was functioning more effectively than ever before. Notable Burgundian seigneurs occupied the highest positions of *président* and *conseiller* in the sovereign court that governed the local justices on which seigneurial rule partly rested. These *parlementaires* and their colleagues limited or defeated initiatives by the royal administration or the Provincial Estates that appeared to undermine seigneurial authority. Ties of kinship and mutual interest made *parlementaires* and seigneurs solid and formidable allies. Still, most seigneurs were not themselves members of the sovereign court. Although they would look to the high court for aid when needed, they had confidence in their own capacity to maintain their rights, manage their estates, and augment their authority and wealth. Looking over the shoulders of two such lords will help us understand this outlook clearly.

Burgundian Lordship and the Mairetet of Minot

The power, profit, and honor of lordship formed a possession eagerly sought by commoners moving into the ranks of the provincial nobility. Indeed, it was the possession of a fief that was the critical step that led next to the purchase of an ennobling office.[22] In northern Burgundy, the Mairetet of Minot offers an interesting example of a local dynasty on the rise. The founder, Jean Mairetet (1605–81), married a notary's daughter and shortly thereafter

---

parties through the assessment of damage by village experts (*prudhommes*) whose decisions were formalized in the seigneurial courts. See *Réglemens généraux pour Les justices seigneuriales, corrigés & augmentés par Avocat de cette Ville, en l'année 1779.* Also, *Grands jours: Règlement du 26 mars 1776,* tome 14 des *Edits & Declarations, Parlement de Bourgogne,* Milsand Collection, 763, Bibliothèque Municipale of Dijon. Thanks also to Jeremy Hayhoe who helped clarify points about the new procedures for adjudication of *mesus.*

21. Saint Jacob, *Paysans,* 514. See also Swann, *Provincial Power,* 411, for a discussion of the *parlement*'s success in courting popularity as opposed to the public view of the Estates and its permanent administrative council, the *élus,* as a "despotic regime."

22. Roupnel, *Ville et campagne,* 187–89.

purchased a royal notarial office for himself. When his reputation as a capable man of the law became known in the *bailliage* of Châtillon, first one and then other seigneurs appointed him judge in their seigneurial courts. To his first appointment in 1644 he added eight others in the course of two decades, the last one being that of judge in the lordships of Minot and Thorey. As he accumulated judgeships, he also accumulated land, including a substantial farm in Minot.[23]

After his death in 1681, his son Denis Mairetet (1656–1743) carried the family into the ranks of noble seigneurs. The first and decisive steps up the ladder came in 1694. After ceding to his younger brother the notarial office that passed down from his father, he purchased the post of *conseiller secrétaire* in the *parlement* of Burgundy, a dignity for which he paid the handsome sum of 21,000 *livres*. Later that year, on 20 December 1694, he purchased the seigneuries of Minot and Thorey. When the royal *intendant* announced his intention to impose the *franc-fief* tax on the new but non-noble seigneur, Mairetet countered by buying the higher ennobling office of *conseiller* in the *parlement,* with its guarantee that transmissible nobility could be achieved in two generations. With that, Minot was once again classified as fief in noble hands, continuing a status in force from its inception. As lord of Minot, Denis turned next to expanding his lands, purchasing first the seigneurial farm of Minot and then a number of other domains in the village.[24]

To help pay for his rising status and new acquisitions, he soon set about exploiting his pecuniary rights of lordship. In his first major demand of Minot's inhabitants he laid claim to his *droit de triage*—the right, as he chose to interpreted it, to appropriate one-third of the community's woodlands. Not surprisingly, Minot's villagers were dismayed. Here was a man who until recently was living among them—a wealthy, principal inhabitant, but little more. Now their seigneur, he was suddenly demanding too much. To give over a third of the community's woodland was a threatening prospect. True, their woodlands were extensive, even vast in comparison to what many villages had. And yet their woodlands needed to be large. They not only supported the livelihoods of woodcutter families, they were the treasured source of communal revenues needed to meet their many collective obligations. After much protest and negotiation, a settlement was reached in

23. ADCO, 1F 169, George Potey, "Monographie de Minot" (1884–92), 2:1–2, 22. According to Roupnel, *Ville et compagne*, 248–49, the majority of acquisitions by Denis came through judicial sales of properties belonging to indebted nobles and commoners, suggesting that he used his position of judge and *notaire* to his good advantage.

24. Potey, "Monographie de Minot," 2:22.

1697. By its terms, Mairetet withdrew his claim of *triage* in exchange for an annual allocation of wood (*affouage*) equal to the amount enjoyed by Minot's two wealthiest inhabitants.[25] Although the crisis passed, villagers with foresight realized that Mairetet's right of *triage* had not been annulled but only deflected.

Under Denis Mairetet's successor, his son Alexandre (1693–1777), potential conflicts over *triage* failed to materialize, perhaps because Alexandre spent much of his time in Dijon attending to his rising career in the *parlement*. Accorded a dignity in 1771 typically reserved for judges in their waning years, he succeeded at the age of eighty-three to the deanship of the body, a sinecure that brought him an additional 7,000 *livres* per year in income.[26] Often occupied in Dijon, he left the routine management of the Minot estate to his wife Catherine Quirot.

After his death in 1777 his wife took a page out Catherine de Medici's book and became the unpopular regent of Minot. Acting on behalf of her son and heir, Denis (1726–1805), she revived old rights, including that of *triage*. The recent policy (1771) giving seigneurs thirty years to exercise the right no doubt entered into her decision; after all, the thirty-year rule was a virtual invitation that few lords were likely to refuse. After weighing her options, the dame de Minot invoked *triage* to back an alternative demand: that the seigneur be given one-third of the profits from the village's pending sale of wood valued at some 8,000 *livres*. Faced with the threat of a lawsuit it probably could not win, the village assembly struck a bargain. After shrewd negotiations by the village delegates, the community got a favorable settlement by presenting an ingenious argument: if the village gave her one-third of the proceeds from the pending sale, now earmarked for financing repairs to the church and rectory, then she would have to bear one-third of the cost for the church repairs herself. Consequently, the village paid madame 5 percent

25. Ibid., 4:21–23.

26. The timing of this elevation suggest that he may have received the deanship as an inducement to go along with the judicial reorganization of the *parlement* that Maupeou launched by the royal edicts of 3–4 March and 1 May 1771. The Burgundian judges were formally removed in November 1771, and the most prominent members were ordered into exile. Alexandre Mairetet was not among the judges exiled, and he joined the new court, as did about half of his colleagues. Interestingly, among the new judges recruited was his son and namesake, who was known as Alexandre Mairetet de Thorey, having added the name of the fief (Thorey) he received from his father. After the *parlement* was restored in 1775, Mairetet de Thorey would return as *conseiller* in 1780, presumably via the inheritance of his father's office after the latter's death in 1777. See La Cuisine, *Parlement de Bourgogne,* 3:267–68, 418. In certain Dijon circles, Alexandre *père* was known as a miser without equal. Colombet, *Parlementaires,* 277.

of the sale's proceeds, with the provision that this payment be accepted as a one-time-only concession and not as a precedent-setting agreement.[27]

Although Alexandre Mairetet was often occupied in Dijon, he was not an absentee or inattentive landlord. While his wife Catherine busied herself with the day-to-day details of estate management, Alexandre kept the books—indeed he kept them well. Begun in 1746 and continued by his wife and son after his death, his *livres de raison* were detailed account books that seigneurs of *parlementaire* standing or ancestry typically kept.[28] As with all such records, Mairetet's personal accountings offer a revealing view of Burgundian lordship in operation. In the notebooks, he carefully recorded each and all of the seigneurial rights he found in old *terriers,* together with a running list of payments and the precise terms of leases made with tenant farmers.

Following the payments owed for *cens* (quitrent), *corvées,* and harvest dues came the accounts on his *Droits de Noces,* the tribute owed to the lord of Minot upon a subject's marriage. Reading these entries calls to the mind's eye the contemporary print images that depicted peasant weddings in the courtyard of the lord's château. Designed to shed warm, sentimental light on paternal relations between the lord and his subjects, they picture bride and groom surrounded by smartly dressed and cheery dancers, while the *bon seigneur* looks on, presiding. Reading further in Mairetet's accounts shows that such prints were not whole-cloth fabrications but rites of paternalism, deference, and tribute that were still in practice. His entry for 7 February 1747 reads: "Nicolas Giraudot . . . who had married the servant of Coutinoires, the *fermier* of Saint Brion, came to the château following the mass, accompanied by his bride and many relatives; and to the sound of the oboe and drum; he presented to my servants a capon, a side of pork, a piece of beef, a leg of mutton, a *miche* of white bread, and a pint of wine."[29] Successive grooms appear to have continued this rite until Mairitet's death in 1777, when the reenactments became infrequent, reflecting no doubt the growing tensions between the new seigneur (Denis de Mairetet) and Minot's inhabitants.[30]

27. Potey, "Monographie de Minot," 4:26–27; ADCO, E Dépot 414 /2, Deliberations of the Village Assembly, 11 October and 8 November 1778.

28. In his study of the magistrates at the end of the Old Regime, Colombet claimed that they were excellent estate managers who were interested in agrarian improvement as well as increasing their incomes. For these reasons, "all *parlementaires* kept *livres de raisons*" so they could know at a glance the composition of their holdings, the terms of their leases, the *cens* and *lods* owed, and so forth. See *Parlementaires,* 118.

29. ADCO, E 1245 ter, *livre de raison* of Alexandre Mairetet, p. 116.

30. Ibid., p. 133 suggests at least one reason for intensifying grievances. Conflict over the *triage* in 1778, the seigneur's continuing encroachment in the community's woodlands and waste,

Alexandre and his wife were shrewd landlords.[31] To balance profit against risk, Alexandre engaged a number of farmers and adjusted the terms of contracts for payment in money or in kind according to prevailing market conditions. As prices edged upward at midcentury he realized that share-cropping leases tended to favor the tenant, so he added money payments to those due in kind. As prices rose dramatically after 1760, he put more of his land into his direct exploitation, using hired workers from the village as well as the labor that he commanded through the reactivated seigneurial *corvée* for some of the plowing and carting. After her husband's death, Catherine applied similarly flexible techniques such as shifting the *corvée* to payments in kind when advantageous.

Another seigneurial asset that the Mairetet put to good and varied use was the *lods*. A tax due on the sale or transfer of land within the seigneurie, in Minot the fee was substantial, amounting to one-sixth of the purchase price.[32] Like the *corvée* in labor or in kind, the *lods,* too, was an appreciating asset. As the price of arable land rose and that of meadow even more so, the *lods* rose as well, reaching amounts that ordinary peasants could not meet or could meet only by going into debt. As Minot's inhabitants complained in their *cahier* of 1789, so heavy were the *lods* that few could afford to acquire

---

and his failure to observe customary rights of pasture in his own woodlands all sharpened village resentments. Dwindling numbers of grooms continued to perform the traditional duty, but others simply refused to pay respect and tribute. The last groom to present himself appeared at the château door in April 1789, in what was perhaps a hollow gesture. A month earlier, in the parish *cahier* for the forthcoming Estates-General, villagers had given voice to a long list of grievances against their seigneur. Included was the testimony of some of Minot's *anciens* (oldest men) that the current seigneur's ancestor had long ago exacted the *triage* and thus any further claim of this kind was unjust and should be opposed with vigor. For the parish cahier, see ADCO, B2 209 bis.

31. This paragraph is based partly on Roupnel's discussion in *Ville et campagne,* 286–89, and on leases recorded in E 1245ter, Alexandre's *livre de raison* which was continued by his wife after her husband's death. A major lease by Catherine Mairetet to Nicolas Deschamps, dated 8 November 1782, on pp. 17–19, is revealing. It concerned the farming of the seigneurial domain. Its typical terms included the standard length of the contract (nine years), the timing of biannual payments in *livres*— 450 at Christmas and 450 on Saint Jean (21 June)—and the numerous rights reserved by the landlord. With buoyant grain prices holding and the coming slump still dim on the horizon, Deschamps must have been trying to get the lease before the price of such contracts rose further. Betting on the future, he took the contract that would replace the current leaseholder, Laurent Boileau, in two years' time. Nonetheless, the landlord still had the upper hand, so Deschamps would have to make due with less than Boileau. Madame reserved for her benefit certain buildings, portions of the orchards, and the hemp field; Deschamps was to farm the reserved portions but on new terms that blended sharecropping and the seigneurial *corvée*. Accordingly, she would receive one-third of the production—vegetables, fruit, hay, straw, and hemp—plus all the manure she wanted from the stables—and all this was to serve as payment of the *corvée*.

32. ADCO, E 1338, livre de raison, pp. 162 and 181.

land in the village. Consequently the seigneur came to possess more and more of the arable land and meadows, and always the best portions of each kind.[33] This was not an exaggeration. As early as 1750 Alexandre Mairetet had amassed a domain of 1,000 *journaux* (350 hectares) in arable and pasture, and he continued to add to this thereafter.[34] Here the *lods* were even more useful. Although the revenues might be comparatively small from the seigneur's point of view, this right enabled the seigneur to purchase the property via *rétrait féodale* should the seller be unable to pay the tax. In sum, the *lods* was a potent tool for rounding out a seigneur's landed estate.

Nicolas Philippe Berbis, Marquis of Longecourt

An even fuller history of enterprising lordship unfolds when we examine the papers and career of Nicolas Philippe Berbis de Longecourt. The Berbis family proudly traced their noble ancestry to 1435. The branch from which Nicolas Philippe descended came to prominence through service in the royal courts in Dijon and was founded by Jean Berbis, "*écuyer,* seigneur of Cromey, Grangey, and other places."[35] His son, Jacques Berbis, a judge in the Dijon *parlement,* purchased the seigneurie of Longecourt in 1681. Two decades later (1701), he acquired the adjoining lordships of Tart-le-Bas, Tart-le-Haut, and Tart l'Abbaye. So began the reconstruction, from previously fragmented fiefs, of a unified set of estates and the ascent of the Berbis de Longecourt. In the years following his accession in 1753, Nicolas Philippe, the great-grandson of Jean, the founder, proved a worthy heir. With diligent work, he brought the family fortune to its height in the 1780s and then largely preserved it during the Revolution. He died in 1807 under the reign of Napoleon, honored by the imperial title of *grand notable.*[36]

33. ADCO, B2 209, cahier of 14 March 1789, article 13.

34. Minot was an unusually large village, about a third of which was in woodlands. In 1844 the commune's surface was roughly three times larger than the average for villages in the Côte-d'Or and stood at 3,617 hectares. Of this, the arable land made up 2,255 hectares, pasture, 164 hectares, and woodlands, 997 hectares. ADCO, SM 2802. If the size of the village was about the same around 1750, then Mairetet's domain at that time amounted to about 15 percent of the arable and pasture.

35. J. d'Arbaumont, *Armorial de la Chambre des Comptes de Dijon, d'après le manuscrit inédit du Père Gautier avec un chapitre supplémentaire pour les officiers du Bureau des Finances* (Dijon, 1881), 90–92.

36. As a *grand notable* of the empire, he was one of sixty men so designated who resided in the Department of Côte d'Or. Anne-Marie Paris, *Côte-d'Or,* vol. 19 of *Grands notables du premier Empire,* ed. Louis Bergeron and Guy Chaussinand-Nogaret (Paris, 1992), 48–49.

Born in 1727, Nicolas Philippe Berbis was a twenty-one-year-old captain of cavalry when he and his father, Philippe, took their seats in the Burgundian Estates in 1748, an occasion that formally recognized the Berbis de Longecourt as old nobility of the province.[37] Five years later (1753), while still a serving officer in the Gramont regiment, he took control of his inherited lordships.[38] Young and energetic, Nicolas Philippe took his elevation to seigneur seriously and soon made himself known through bold initiatives aimed at bolstering his authority and settling matters that his father had let slip. Tightening the policing of unauthorized wine sales, stepping up punishment for trespass offenses and other violations, securing the collection of the *dîme*, and recovering seigneurial dues that had long remained unpaid—these were his decisive, initial steps.

As for the policing of wine, the seigneurial right to regulate the sale of wine (*banvin*) interested the young Berbis less as a means of raising revenue from the sale of licenses than as a way of maintaining discipline among his subjects. Because gatherings at a wine seller's premises led, in his view, to rowdiness, fights, and the spending of *sous* better reserved for other things, the young seigneur launched a long campaign to control drinking and impose good order. The first indication of this came in Tart-le-Bas: at the annual assizes of the seigneurial court (*grands jours*) in 1754, a number of residents were called before the court, sentenced, and fined for illicit drinking at a local cabaret. The seigneurial courts for Longecourt and for Tart-le-Haut imposed similar punishments in the 1760s.[39]

The tightening up of policing was reflected also in the increased number and nature of fines that the seigneurial justice of Longecourt imposed for other, more routine offenses. As always, the most frequent offense cited was damage to fields and crops by livestock that got loose, an offense known in

---

37. ADCO, C ★ 3044, *Carnot de la chambre de la noblesse aux Etats de Bourgogne,* 1748, p. 158. In the eighteenth century, entry into the Provincial Estates of Burgundy required that the candidate possess a fief and three to four generations of nobility. See Swann, *Provincial Power,* 69.

38. ADCO, C 8940, Registre de fiefs, 1740–84; copies of the *dénombrements* are in Archives de Longecourt, Longecourt-en-Plaine (hereafter ALCT), 5, and ADCO, B 11033, Chambre des Comptes, Reprise de fief, 30 Juillet 1753, Longecourt, Tart-le-Bas.

39. ADCO, 41 F 164 TLB, justice, 1694–1757, inventaire des minutes de greff. ALCT, 117, for complaints of 1762 in Tart-le-Haut and 1766 in Longecourt. The most aggressive assault on wine sellers and drinking that I've discovered came in the 1780s. In 1783, Jean Mairet of Longecourt, found guilty of illicit wine sales and fined 50 *livres,* was subject to public humiliation when, having refused to pay the fine, belongings he owned were seized and sold on two separate occasions to cover the fine. Two years later in 1785 two residents of Tart-le-Haut and one from Tart-le-Bas were similarly fined and made responsible for the fines that were meted out to more than a dozen other men charged as habitual drinkers.

Burgundy as *mesus*. In contrast to the 1730s under Berbis's father Philippe, a broader range of fineable offenses was being brought to justice, and the average number of punished offenses was higher as well. Field wardens (*messiers*) responsible for reporting *mesus* were also reporting residents whose gates were left open, while the elected village officers known as *prudhommes* were citing people for unkempt chimneys that could lead to fires.[40]

For Nicolas Philippe, securing the collection of the *dîme* was an urgent matter because it made up between 20 and 40 percent of the income from his lordships—a common pattern in Burgundy where privileged laymen possessed much of the substantial harvest duty that had originally belonged to the church. Because of its value for the lord and its onerousness for peasants, the *dîme* was a contentious matter. In the Tart villages, it was even more contentious because Berbis shared the right with two other nonresident owners. What perturbed the young seigneur was an unauthorized practice that had come to his attention in 1758. Rather than bringing all grain collected for *dîme* payments to the seigneurial barn in Tart-le-Haut as custom dictated, the shares due to other owners were being taken directly to their own barns. Citing the title deed (*terrier*) of 1551, Berbis promptly secured a court order reinstituting the customary practice. Once again, his authority was duly and visibly affirmed.[41]

In Longecourt, a matter left unresolved by Nicolas Philippe's father was a long-running dispute over the seigneurial *taille*. Inserted into the *terrier* of 1630, it entailed an annual imposition of 80 *livres* owed collectively by the village.[42] In 1748, his father's demand for payment had gone unpaid, and the villagers may have hoped that the matter would be forgotten in the years ahead. This was a vain hope, for in 1753 the young seigneur had his *fermier*, Toussaint Thomas, present the outstanding bill anew, complete with

40. ALCT, 110, registrès des causes et grands jours, 1731–36; 114, registres des causes et grands jours, 1753–56; ADCO, B II, 692 registre 5, amendes prononcés aux grands jours, 1770–85. The average number of offenses reported in the period 1729–31 was 72; for 1755–56, 108. To judge from the records for 1770 and 1785, this upward trend continued into the early 1770s. After that, fines reflected the change in procedures governing the settlement of *mesus*. In the 1785 accounting, only the fines for *mesus* were recorded: they numbered only 67 but yielded a total of 169 *livres*, slightly more than the 1770 total of 155 *livres* in fines for trespass as well as for defective gating, unkempt chimneys, and encroachments on another's field.

41. ALCT, 87, procès sur les conditions de levée la dîme, 1758.

42. ALCT, 30, copy of the *terrier* drawn up ca. 1630 for the Marquis de Varennes, seigneur of Longecourt at the time. The introduction of a *taille abonné* was typical of the more extensive seigneurial offensive of the seventeenth century. Communities accepted the new levy to settle debts, to avoid suit, or to forestall a more substantial loss of common lands, rights to shared woodlands, and the like.

interest and arrears. Villagers were no doubt shocked to learn what Berbis claimed they owed: 1,700 *livres*. Two years later, the inhabitants' foot-dragging prompted Thomas to bring suit in the seigneurial court. Nonetheless, village resistance stiffened and the contest continued into the 1780s.[43]

Seeing progress here and obstacles there, Berbis turned to review his titles, much as his grandfather and father had done before him. But by the 1760s it was clear that the heir was determined to surpass their achievements. Investing more time and treasure than they had, he would apply modern management techniques to rationalize his seigneuries and increase their value.

His first project rationalized the management of all properties falling within the *prairie* of Tart-le-Bas. A major undertaking, the comprehensive survey of all titles and parcels there surely seemed a timely step in the right direction. Over time, grasslands were more likely than arable to escape the seigneurial fisc through a lord's inattention and landholder fraud. Second, the value of meadowland, used for grazing and fodder, was greater than that of arable, especially in the Plain of Dijon where meadow was in short supply and eagerly sought. Economic conditions already in place pointed to higher returns in the future. With such considerations in mind, Berbis petitioned *parlement*. By the court's *arrêt* (ruling) of 25 May 1761, he was authorized to verify the titles to all properties, a legal proceeding known as *reconnaissance*. Well before the surveyor's first stake was in the ground in June, Berbis understood the importance of securing *parlement*'s backing: empowered by an *arrêt,* he could require every proprietor not only to present the deeds to his holding but to bear a proportional part of the survey's cost as well.[44] Berbis's expenses would thus be minimized.

Such surveys were long and complicated affairs, sometimes aimed chiefly at squeezing more from tenants, and sometimes undertaken to reassemble formerly fragmented fiefs, as was the case at hand.[45] On the *prairie*, extensive work on site was necessary to establish correct parcel boundaries. This

---

43. ALCT, 44, procedures: *taille abonné*. After incurring further fines for failing to make court appearances, a worried village assembly successfully petitioned the royal *intendant* for the authority to defend itself in a higher court. On advice from a lawyer, the village resolved to compel non-resident owners (*forains*), who owned more land than all the inhabitants combined, to pay a proportional share of the outstanding debt. Summoned by writ in 1760, the *forains* failed to attend the scheduled meeting. Intent on a proper defense, the assembly entrusted to the prosecutor of the seigneurial justice, Antoine Finot, the task of securing for it further legal advice.

44. ADCO, E 79, Arpentage général de la prairie de Tart-le-Bas includes a copy of the original petition and the *reconnaissance* that followed the survey. 41 F 172 contains a more legible copy of the survey, made all the more useful because of the marginal notes that Berbis made there.

45. Saint Jacob, *Paysans,* 73.

required the cooperation of the principal residents of Tart-le-Bas and entailed more than a hundred interviews of nonresident landowners or their representatives. In all, 464 parcels were carefully surveyed and mapped. Having required 180 working days to complete, the map and register were finally completed in 1764.[46]

Even before the register was complete, Berbis had begun a painstaking review of each and every title. To aid his work he engaged a feudist to make legible transcriptions of the medieval and sixteenth-century *terriers,* the earliest of which was a charter of 1275. Copious notes in Berbis's own hand show that he did much of the verification himself over the course of three or four years. As the examination went forward, he successfully challenged titles of numerous parcels, and as early as 1763 he had launched the first of two major lawsuits to recover sizable properties he had found in violation of seigneurial law.

These attempts did not always go according to plan. A notable setback occurred early on when the inhabitants of the neighboring village of Varanges successfully defeated Berbis's appropriation of a pasture called the *paquier* Foreux. At the advice of his surveyor, Berbis had claimed the land as his by seigneurial law: having been vacant and abandoned, it reverted to the lord. Moreover, the surveyor had turned up a map of 1688 on which the parcel was labeled as belonging to the seigneur. Confident of his claim, Berbis enclosed the parcel with hedges. Soon thereafter, however, Varanges residents repossessed the *paquier* and broke down the hedges, invoking a legally accepted custom to justify their actions: having pastured cattle there for a thirty-year period without incident or opposition, the land, they contended, now legally belonged to them. Undeterred, Berbis brought suit in the *bailliage* court, only to see it affirm the thirty-year custom and decide in favor of Varanges. Persistent, Berbis appealed the case to the *parlement.* Arbitrators appointed by the sovereign court not only upheld the verdict but assigned all legal costs to Berbis, including those incurred by Varanges. Admonished, he paid promptly.[47]

After this setback, he returned to his titles with a more vigilant eye, the better to meet further challenges to come. In June 1768 the formal verification of titles—the *reconnaissance* of *cens*—got underway. Proprietors or their representatives signed notarial acts, each act attesting that the property in question was held from the seigneur as a *censive* and was *not* freehold.

46. ADCO, E 79, Arpentage général de la prairie de Tart-le-Bas.
47. ADCO, 41F 146, Tart-le Bas: procedures: paquier du Foreux. The costs ran to 260 *livres.*

The *Prairie* of Tart-le-Bas, detail of survey map, 1764. ADCO, Plan 41 F 17306.

Through these verifications, Berbis acquired any holdings that lacked secure title, either by purchase or by confiscation via feudal retrocession when fraud was involved (*retrait féodal*). And so it went: a quarter of a hectare here, a half hectare there, a confiscated parcel here, and a forced sale there (see table 1). More important, Berbis confirmed his suzerainty over all parcels in the *prairie;* all were duly recognized as being held by seigneurial tenure. None were freehold.

The confiscations, forced sales, and recovery of *censives* deserve further attention because they suggest that the major assaults of the seigneurial

Table 1   Results of the Reconnaissance of the *Prairie* of Tart-le-Bas, 1761–1768

Results of Reconnaissance	Number of Parcels	Sum in Hectares	Mean Size of Parcels in Hectares
Acquired by purchase or confiscation	21	8.3	.4
Recovered for *cens*	73	36.7	.5
Total	94	45	
Total for the whole *prairie*	464	265	.58

SOURCE: ADCO, E 79, 41 F 172.

offensive in Burgundy were directed less at vulnerable villagers than at non-resident proprietors of the privileged classes. As shown in table 2, next to the seigneur himself, nonresident owners held the lion's share of the property in the meadowland of Tart-le-Bas. Some 37 percent of the *prairie* grasslands were owned by bourgeois, nobles, or ecclesiastics, all residents of Dijon. Ownership by residents of Tart-le-Bas amounted to a tiny fraction of the whole, and if all nonprivileged owners were counted, the proportion owned by ordinary residents amounted to less than 20 percent. Moreover, the bulk of that proportion was owned by one family in Tart-le-Haut, the Renaudot, the sole family of *laboureurs* (substantial, landowing farmers) who had survived the seventeenth century's sharp decline in peasant property.

The situation on the *prairie* of Tart-le-Bas was not uncommon, for in most northern Burgundian villages, peasant ownership ranged from insignificant to quite modest. With few exceptions the proportion of land held by villagers was a good deal less than the 30 percent figure customarily cited from the work of Georges Lefebvre. In short, what studies of the eighteenth-century lordship have often missed is that key conflicts in the seigneurial offensive after 1750 were likely to be those between seigneurs and *non*resident landowners, all of whom were more or less privileged. A review of two pertinent law suits illustrates the point. At issue in both suits were the rights that permitted a lord to repossess lands designated as *censives,* that is, lands held by seigneurial tenure that carried annual fees owed to the lord.

Possession of a *censive* gave its holder a permanent claim to the parcel as well as the right to transfer or sell it in exchange for a small annual payment to the lord, known as the *cens*. A *censive* however, was not freehold property in the modern sense. A parcel charged with *cens* meant that it had once belonged

Table 2 *Prairie* of Tart-le-Bas: Distribution of Property Ownership by Residence of Owner, 1768

Residence of Owner	Mean Size of Parcels, in Hectares	Number of Parcels	Sum of Parcels, in Hectares	Percent of Hectares Owned	Standard Deviation
Dijon	0.55	175	97	37	0.50
Longecourt (Berbis)	1.11	84	93	36	1.71
Tart-le-Haut	0.34	95	32	12	0.35
Nearby communities	0.43	46	20	8	0.33
Other communities in the Sâone Plaine	0.37	22	8	3	0.19
Tart-le-Bas	0.39	19	7	3	0.70
Bordering villages (seigneur of Marliens)	0.26	8	2	1	0.13
Total	0.58	449	259	100	0.88

SOURCE: ADCO, E 79, 41 F 172.

to the seigneurial domain (*domaine utile* or *directe*), and for this reason the seigneur continued to retain certain rights over its disposition. As we saw earlier in Minot, the most important right was that of collecting a transfer fee (*lods*) when the parcel was sold—typically at a rate of 5 to 18 percent of the purchase price—and the right to repossess the holding (*retenue*) if the required payment or other conditions were not met. It was upon sale that a parcel was particularly vulnerable to seigneurial attack. A sale required the lord's permission, and although usually a mere formality, his review of titles prior to sale sometimes produced grounds for repossession. Or, if titles were found to be in order, the lord could refuse the *lods,* thereby preventing the sale, and purchase the property himself. In short, the seigneurial right of repossession was an intimidating weapon. Depending on the circumstances, it was used to exact the payment of outstanding dues, to seize a parcel outright, or to impose some other form of settlement favorable to the lord's interest, such as an exchange of parcels that would help consolidate hitherto fragmented lands of the seigneurial estate.

Among the first of the wealthy proprietors Berbis attacked in court was the widow and minor children of Jean-Baptiste Engerant, a Dijon magistrate. At the death of her husband, the widow administered for the children a substantial domain of sixty-two hectares of land and meadow spread among the fields of Tart-le-Haut and Tart-le-Bas. Notified in 1767 that parts of the estate were for sale, Berbis reviewed the relevant titles and discovered that previous owners had fraudulently converted several parcels from *censives* into freehold. One after the other, the former owners had sold small parcels onto which they had shifted all of the *cens* payments that were due on the whole of their properties. Freed of the servile dues, the parcels they retained rose in value over *censives* and were sold as allodial land at a handsome profit. This was the kind of fraud that vigilant seigneurs had to guard against both because it diminished seigneurial control over the land and seigneurial revenues and because the peasant purchasers would have difficulty paying the exorbitant *cens* attached to them. After bringing suit, Berbis settled out of court in September 1768. By the terms of the settlement, the annual quitrents (*cens*) were restored, and the defendants, in addition to their cash payments for outstanding charges (*lods* and *cens*), ceded to the seigneur a choice portion of meadow of his choosing at a price determined by experts.[48]

---

48. ADCO, papers of the suit and negotiations in 41 F 54, and the feudal retrocession of 2 September 1768 in 4 E8 24. The amount of the payments for *lods* and *cens* was not mentioned in these records. The seven and two-thirds *soitures* of meadow was ceded to Berbis for 2,259 *livres*.

While this was a victory that Berbis could savor, the defeat in another suit taught him a costly lesson. The details are worth reviewing because they reveal much about the historical origins of seigneurial rights as well as their limits when contested by good lawyers of the day. Indeed, as the case unfolded it proved a veritable cause célèbre in Dijon legal circles, for at issue was a claim with potentially serious ramifications for nonresident proprietors throughout the province. Nicolas Philippe Berbis held that nonresidents possessing land in Tart-le-Haut and Tart-le-Bas were bound by seigneurial law to reside there within a year and a day of acquiring the property. Failing that, a charter of 1275 and subsequent *terriers* entitled the seigneur to seize the properties in question. The defendants in the case included the Engerant heirs once again, three bourgeois women, and the wife of a noble. At least three of the defendants had connections with the middle or upper ranks of the judicial world in Dijon, so Berbis prepared himself for a major battle. The defendants, one legal publicist warned, must spare no expense to carry the day.

> In an affair so important as this nothing must be neglected [by the defendants] because the case is of essential interest to the fortunes of a very large number of persons from different regions and of all the orders; it attempts to strip legitimate proprietors of property transmitted to them by their forbearers after the longest and most peaceable possession. The suit brought by M. de Longecourt strikes at the heart of many families who have possessed properties for twenty generations, of those who have sold them later, and of those who find themselves exposed to making good on guarantees of secure title after the properties were sold in good faith centuries ago. The nonresident proprietors [*forains*] deserve the most preferential treatment: the claims brought against some of them have no merit.[49]

In August 1763, the seigneurial judge for the Tarts had found in favor of the seigneur, and in 1768, the *parlement* of Dijon upheld the judgment. But when the defendants brought an appeal, the *parlement* reconsidered

---

The widow retained other holdings and the large house for her farmer (*maison de maitre*) in Tart-le-Haut under two provisions: that the arrears in *lods* would be paid and that other charges on her estate would remain subject to seigneurial rights, including a right of residence, which led to the much larger suit described in the text.

49. *Observations sur le proces intenté par Messire Nicolas-Philippes Berbis, Seigneur de Longecourt, de Thar-la-Ville, de Thar-le-chateau & Thar-l'Abbaye, à quelques Propriétaires-Forains de plusieurs fonds, situés dans le territoire de ces derniers Villages* (Dijon, 1769), Milsand Collection, 6520, Bibliothèque

the evidence and studied the new pleadings. In July 1771, before the *parlement* was reorganized by Chancellor Maupeou, the court overturned the earlier verdict and ordered Berbis to pay all legal expense. It was a very costly defeat: his own legal expenses alone came to 6,000 *livres*. More disturbing, he realized, was the legal precedent now established. In effect, the court's ruling rendered feudal repossession a weak instrument against anyone who could afford a good attorney. A day after the verdict, as his regrets stirred up doubts, he confided to a trusted friend and adviser, "I cannot escape the thought that I was wrong."[50]

This recognition was based partly on the pleadings by the lawyers representing the appellants. In a *factum* of ninety-nine printed pages, six lawyers developed a minute refutation of Berbis's claim and evidence.[51] The thrust of the argument alleged a long history of chicanery by lords who had successively concocted new levies and seigneurial powers. Underneath the tone of moral indignation running throughout the pleading was a detailed history of seigneurial offensives of the sixteenth and seventeenth centuries in this part of the Dijonnais plain. The 1550 *terrier* was but one of many examples the lawyers brought to light. New seigneurial rights, absent in previous documents, were here as numerous as they were onerous. In addition, previously existing fines were raised. For trespass offenses, fines were raised tenfold. Moreover, new fineable violations were "invented," such as failing to assemble when the lord so ordered or making an accusation that lacked sufficient proof. New levies appeared also. One was the lord's wine tax (*droit de banvin*), the pleading decried, that virtually prevented villagers from selling even their own wine without paying the seigneur a heavy fee. To these injustices, so the document continued, were added the obligation to use the lord's oven (*banalité du four*) with its attendant fees, and, heavier still, the right of *lods et retenue*. The final indignity was the phase redefining the inhabitants as *gens de poëte,* as men of servile status. Regrettably, the lawyers

---

Municipal de Dijon. In addition to this publication, a number of other commentaries were published in the run-up to the appeal. See *Réponse à l'écrit intitulé, Précis, signifié par M. de Longecourt, le 16 Juin 1769, à Anne Roche & aux mineurs Engurerrand, Propriétaires Forains à Tart* (Dijon, 1770), Milsand Collection, 6518; *Notes pour les Dlles. Petitjean & autres Propriétaires-Forains des terres de Thar* (Dijon, 1770), Milsand Collection, 6519.

50. ADCO, 41 F 250, letter to Devenet, *auditeur* at the Dijon *Chambre des Comptes,* 23 July 1771.

51. *Mémoire pour Dlle. Anne Petitjean, fille majeur, à Dijon & le Notaire Boiteux, en qualité de Tuteur aux Enfans mineurs du Sieur Engurerrand, Appellans de Sentence rendue aux Requetes du Palais à Dijon, le 7 Mars 1770.* The copy I consulted was in ADCO, E 77, papers of Berbis de Longecourt that were seized during the Revolution.

continued, this pattern of connivance grew worse in the 1650s under Sieur Sigismund Bernard and in the 1690s under Etienne Maleteste.[52]

Turning to address Berbis, the text bowed respectfully, entreating Monsieur de Longecourt to follow the honorable practice "of Monsieur Berbis his father, the memory of whom is still dear to his subjects." As his father before him, he should "set aside the bad idea of removal and confiscation." The appellants, after all, were willing to pay any dues and charges legitimately owed. But "it is a bit much to want to despoil them of a patrimony they possess in free hold by their own hands and their forbears for five or six centuries."[53]

This reasoning and the chagrin of a major defeat were not forgotten by Berbis. In the 1770s and 1780s prudence and an increased degree of paternalism tempered his ambitions, and only one major controversy arose. At issue was the *indire,* the right to double the *dîme* and other dues upon the marriage of the lord's eldest daughter. Not surprisingly, notification of the expected payment in 1775 was awful news for the members of the affected communities—Longecourt, Potengey, and the three Tarts—because each had to raise up to 1,200 *livres* to satisfy the extraordinary obligation. In Longecourt, resistance, mainly in the form of delays, ended when Berbis granted the village a small reduction in the amount owed. Soon thereafter all four communities agreed to pay their share of the *indire,* which totaled 2,911 *livres.*[54]

By the time Berbis had these payments in hand, an era of agrarian prosperity was in full bloom for landlords and shrewd tenant farmers. Acting on favorable circumstances, Berbis adopted improved methods of estate management to help secure higher prices for his leases. In 1777 he experimented with a practice many seigneurs were adopting: he let out all his estates to a single farmer, or *fermier général,* and at a far better price than before (see table 3). Compared to previous leases, this one was remarkable for its rigorous specification of terms. Not only were the rights and revenues described

---

52. Ibid., 51–63 treat the details for Tart-le-Bas and Tart l'Abbaye. Bernard and Maleteste, both members of Burgundy's *parlement,* were fairly typical of the bourgeois and new nobles of Dijon who in the seventeenth century came to own most of the land and seigneuries within the three *bailliages* that made up the Dijonnais region. Bernard's maneuverings extended beyond the Tart villages, and his attempt to acquire common lands in nearby Champdôtre in 1646 prompted a village protest. This protest led to the crown's intervention—and a short-term victory—through an *arrêt* of the Royal Council that restored the commons to the village. Sixteen years later, however, Bernard prevailed when his repurchase of the lands met with no successful challenge from the village or the state. See Roupnel, *Ville et campagne,* 224–25.

53. Ibid., 66.

54. ALCT, 33, *droit d'indire,* 1710–79.

with greater care than previously, but the responsibilities of the *fermier* were both more numerous and more exacting, leaving no doubt about the leaseholder's duty to keep and present scrupulous accounts. To be included in the accounts were reports of any and all changes in the holdings within the lordships. As was common during the bidding-up of leases in the 1770s, the contract required the lessee to pay a surcharge (*pot-de-vin*) in addition to the cost of the nine-year lease. The fortunate lessee in this case was Berbis's trusted steward, François Prudent. In paying 18,000 *livres* (plus 1,600 *livres* as *pot-de-vin*) Prudent perhaps got a lower price from his employer than the open market might have brought. In any event, like other *fermiers* who were amalgamating seigneurial leases, Prudent was granted the right, with a few exceptions, to sublet any of the rights and lands. This he did in short order at a good annual profit.[55] As for Berbis, to judge from the figures for Tart-le-Bas, his yearly return on the three lordships was no less than 50 percent higher than from the previous nine-year leases.

A few years later Berbis launched the ambitious undertaking of completing cadastral surveys begun in the 1760s for the *prairie* of Tart-le-Bas. The survey of Longecourt, the seat of his lordship and the site of his elegantly remodeled château, was finished in 1782. Three years later those for Tart-le-Bas and Tart-le-Haut were also complete. As in the 1760s, much of this work he oversaw personally, and his remarkable identification of *censives* from the fifteenth century onward attests to his abiding concern that none be allowed to slip into freehold.[56]

55. ADCO, 4 E 2 2688, 8 November 1777, "bail à ferme des terres et seigneurie de Tart-le-Haut, Tart-le-Bas, et Tart l'Abbaye par Mre Nicolas Philippe Berbis, seigneur de Longecourt, à Sieur François Prudent marchand d'Longecourt et agent dud sgr. et Dlle. Anne Barquand sa femme." After covering all costs and expenses of the lease, Prudent realized an annual profit of at least 730 *livres* in cash, in addition to the use of 13 *soitures* of meadow, 7 *journaux* of arable land, the château in Tart-le-Bas with its attached vineyards, and the exploitation of 3 *journaux* of woodland each year.

56. Berbis's devotion to his work as seigneur can be readily seen in his papers and account books, the latter carrying notes in his own hand, as to whether the title of a property was in order or not. For the Tart villages, see ADCO, 41 F 109, *reconnaissance,* ca. 1786; 41 F 166, état des amodiations et *cens,* ca. 1786. For Longecourt, ALCT, 17 *Cens: reconnaissances, procédures,* 1680–1784; ALCT, 18: *reconnaissances,* 1784–87. As for Berbis's expenses, it is unclear whether landowners were, as in the 1760s, obliged to pay a proportional share of the survey costs. Because his own properties were extensive in the three lordships, his share alone must have been substantial. The surveys and his interest in consolidating his lands occasionally led to further conflicts over seigneurial rights. Wary of court battles with parties capable of contesting his claims, Berbis sometimes fixed his attention on pliant peasants. When dealing with them, the threat of a lawsuit was usually sufficient to bring compliance. Numerous other cases are in ADCO, 41 F 5, and AL 17 and 18. In Tart-le-Bas, to cite an extreme example, a small farmer gave Berbis four pieces of pasture worth

Table 3   The Size (in Hectares) and Value of Berbis Lordships, 1682–1792

Lordship	Year						
	1682	1713	1753	1770	1777	1782	1789–91
Longecourt	1682	1713	1753	1770	1777	1782	1789–91
Arable	171		105			126	
Meadow	68		51			50	
Total	239		156			176	
Lease	1670 *l.*			8000 *l.*		13000 *l.*	13300 *l.*
(year)	(1685)			(1770)		(1781)	(1791)
Woodland	8		220				
Tart-le-Haut	1701	1713	1753			1785	
Arable	135	115	151			119	
Meadow	26	24	27			27	
Total	161	139	178			146	
Lease	1300 *l.*	1200 *l.*	2300 *l.*		5000 *l.*	7000 *l.*	9847 *l.*
(year)	(1693)	(1703)	(1744)		(1777)	(1786).	(1792)
Woodland	261	270	216				
Tart-le-Bas	1701		1753			1785	
Arable	100		104			110	
Meadow	95		107			120	
Total	195		211			230	
Lease			6200 *l.*	7000 *l.*	10600 *l.*	11750 *l.*	7215 *l.*
(year)			(1760)	(1767)	(1777)	(1784, 1787)	(1792)

SOURCES: ADCO, B10849, Reprise de fief et dénombrement, Longecourt, Potangey, Thorey, fief Gemeaux, 2 mars 1682 par Jacques Berbis; ALCT, 5, minutes de dénombrements de Longecourt, Potangey, Tart et Molaise, 1713 and 1753; ALCT, 12, Arpentage Général des Meix, Terres-Labourables & Prés, situés sur les Finages de Longecourt, Potangey, et Thorey . . . dressés par l'Arpenteur Noirot en 1782; ADCO, B10837, Reprise de fiefs et dénombrements de Tart le Chatel, Tard L'Abbeye, et Tard le Haut, 1677–1701; ADCO, 41 F 46, Arpentage des Tarts, fait par l'arpenteur Noirot en 1785; 41 F 252 18 décembre 1703: acte sous seing privé entre Malteste et Anatoire Renodot, Marchand, Tart-le-Haut; Q897 15 prairial an 7: ventilation du Bail du émigre Berbis a TLH (which summarizes the lease of 1786). Figures for the leases come from the relevant contracts in 41F 52; 41F 63; 4E 82–50; 4E 2 2452; 4 E 2 2472; 4E 2688; C 5829.

NOTES: Leases did not include woodlands, which were let out separately. Arable and woodland are given in *journaux* and meadow in *soitures,* converted to hectares and rounded to the nearest hectare (1 *journal* = 1 *soiture* in area = .34284 hectare).

The lease figures for 1789–91 are comparable with the earlier figures because they do not reflect the adjustments made later for the loss of revenues owing to the suppression of feudal rights and the *dîme*. The reduced amount for the Tart-le-Bas lease in 1792 probably reflects Berbis's loss of lands to Varanges, Marlien, and Tart-le-Bas itself, which reappropriated a large field in 1791 as authorized by legislation for lands that could be shown to have been appropriated by "feudal means."

Berbis's investment of time and money bore fruit. In the 1780s, when conditions favoring landlords began to weaken and *fermiers* increasingly felt the pinch of costly leases as grain prices crested and ebbed, Berbis managed to keep his revenues rising (see table 3). The improved management and accounting systems that the surveys brought to completion eliminated conflicts and guesswork that the seigneur and his *fermiers* had to contend with in the past. With a well-documented record for every parcel and every record in its place, the complicated task of consolidating holdings was easier, as the exchange of 1786 between the seigneur and the inhabitants of Longecourt made evident.[57] Foreclosures and forced sales for indebtedness were perhaps easier, too. And yet his improved accounting system seemed to go hand in hand with a more pragmatic, paternal approach to indebted subjects, for year after year he carried many on the books, some with as much as 800 *livres* in arrears.[58]

The substantial improvements realized in the 1780s probably made the seigneuries more attractive to current and prospective *fermiers*. Better records made it easier to meet the more exacting terms of the leases—just as it enhanced a *fermier*'s ability to hold small tenants to account. In 1784, three years before the leases for the seigneuries of Tart-le-Haut and Tart-le-Bas were to come up for renewal, Berbis changed course, seeing advantages in leasing various parts of his estates to a number of local men rather than engaging a *fermier général* as he had done in 1777. François Prudent having died, his son and widow took on major parts of the Tart-le-Bas lordship. Two men shared the lordship of Tart-le-Haut, while two other men leased the remaining parts of the Tart-le-Bas estate. Amid signs of declining prospects, the new arrangement yielded a 16 percent annual increase over the 18,000 *livres* per year Berbis received via his 1777 contract (see table 3).

In 1786 an aging Berbis took up his pen and copied out in full an *aveu et dénombrement* (title deed) of 1753. Thirty-three years before, it was this

500 *livres* to prevent the seigneur from exercising his right of recovery over lands the farmer was in the process of buying. Another case in 1782 was more typical. Then a Longecourt resident was caught attempting to sell a *censive* as freehold and ceded the parcel to Berbis to stay out of court and avoid risking greater losses. See also Saint Jacob, *Paysans,* 420.

57. ADCO, 4E 2 2472, notarial act of 21 November 1786. The terms of the act reveal that the dispute over the seigneurial *taille* begun in the 1750s was still unresolved. That Berbis did not press his claims in court suggests that he may have used the debt as a bargaining chip and he preferred to keep on good terms with his villagers.

58. ALCT, 22. Edme Lavot, for example, recognized a debt of 800 *livres* for arrears in 1779, for which he constituted a *rente* payable to the seigneur in annual installments of 35 *livres* 12 *sols.*

document, addressed to the king, that had formally marked his possession of the fief and seigneurie of Longecourt. Now a rich man, he could easily have employed a scribe for such work—as he usually had. But writing out the *aveu*, much of whose content he probably knew by heart, must have been satisfying. The act affirmed his life's work and his professional identity as seigneur. With devotion he had maintained the family tradition and estates entrusted to his care, and his lordships had doubled or more in value. He had added the distinction of *marquisate* to the family titles, and his remodeling of the old château of Longecourt had created a residence commensurate with the new dignity. *Marquis, bon et loyal seigneur,* he was also a good patriarch who turned his thoughts now to passing on the estates to his heirs—two married daughters. Writing out the *aveu* was part of his preparation for the eventual succession—still some twenty years in the future. So once again he reviewed his well-ordered papers and produced for his heirs and their husbands orderly dossiers containing all pertinent deeds and documents as well as his memoranda on their seigneurial duties in the future.[59]

Berbis's engagement and skill in accumulating and managing assets— typically attributed to the bourgeoisie—were not untypical but characteristic of his peers, substantial provincial nobles who were neither down-at-the-heels *hobereaux* or courtiers at Versailles like the Tavanes. For these nobles, a key element of individual and group identity was managing the seigneurie. In their eyes, working to do this well was a profession and noble calling.[60] The Mairetet of Minot also absorbed this outlook as the family passed from its *roturier* (commoner) origins into the ranks of noble seigneurs and *parlementaires* in the eighteenth century.

Debtors got a big break during the Revolution because they could pay their debts using the face value of deeply depreciating *assignats*.

59. ALCT, 5 minutes de dénombrements de Longecourt, Potangey, Tart et Molaise, 1713 and 1753. Dossiers drawn up by Nicolas Philippe Berbis in 1786; ADCO, 41 F 64, leases and other memoirs that passed to the daughter, Claudine Bernarde Agate Berbis, who inherited the Tart-le-Bas estate, which was administered by her husband, Jacquot d'Andalarre. A third daughter had entered religious orders and was living in a convent.

60. Berbis's remarkable vigilance was not unique. As Mlle Vignier, the former director of the archives of Côte d'Or told me, the Burgundian jurist Jean Bouhier kept an eagle eye on his more scattered estates and Sieur de Grosbois's reorganization of his seigneurie of Marigny showed the same kind of painstaking effort. Personnel communication from Mlle Françoise Vignier, 2 June 1993. See also Saint Jacob, *Les Paysans,* 73–74, for other examples. Colombet, *Parlementaires,* claims that all the magistrates were similarly attentive, but his confidence appears to come mainly from the account books kept by Benigne Alexandre Legouz de Saint-Seine, who took his seat in *parlement* in 1784.

Whether from Dijon or from the château in situ, Mairetet and Berbis made their presence felt in the countryside. Neither resembled the absentee, impoverished, and politically impotent nobles whom Tocqueville held to be typical of the Old Regime provincial nobility. In the communities under their lordship they were neither strangers nor remote figures like the royal *intendant*. Rather, they were superiors whose presence and faces were known. Given his fastidiousness, one can surmise that Alexandre Mairetet met often with more villagers than just the grooms who came to pay tribute. Similarly, one can readily imagine the former cavalry officer, Nicolas Philippe Berbis, riding out from his château to oversee things in person, be it the tithe barn in Tart-le-Haut in 1758, the *reconnaissance* of all properties in the prairie of Tart-le-Bas in the early 1760s, or the great cadastral surveys he commissioned in the 1780s in Longecourt and the Tart villages.

A lord's presence, authority, and economic clout made themselves known in other ways, of course, and often through the functioning of seigneurial justice. Although that functioning is not addressed in these pages, the close examination here shows that the well-run lordship was geared to making a profit under changing market conditions. This is not to claim that the Marquis de Longecourt was a full-fledged capitalist entrepreneur—an unwarranted conclusion that would fail to capture the complexity of his thinking and situation. Concerns for privileged rank and honor, the esteem of his noble peers, family lineage and its continuation, deferent compliance from his villagers—all this joined and legitimated his striving to accumulate wealth and what would later be called "capital." His close oversight, the costly cadastral surveys that greatly enhanced the management of his income-producing assets, the more exacting terms of leases—all stimulated *fermiers* and major tenants to look for improved ways of keeping accounts, marketing their production, and profiting from the lands and rights they leased. In this way the seigneurie became a vehicle for rural capitalism, and the growing benefits of the seigneurial enterprise accrued both to lords and to astute *fermiers* and major tenants.[61] In the Tart villages, chief beneficiaries of the enterprise were François Prudent, *père et fils*. The wealth the family accumulated was later reinvested by Prudent *fils* to purchase national lands during the Revolution.

61. Saint Jacob credited the "physiocratic seigneurs" and their remarkable cadastral surveys as having stimulated agrarian capitalism and an enterprising mentality among the peasant elite; see p. 434. In his study of the Norman barony of Pont-Saint-Pierre, Jonathan Dewald concluded that seigneurialism hindered capitalist development and that steps in that direction were those taken by large leaseholders, the Norman counterparts of the Prudent. He also shows that the last

In this partnership of lord and *fermier,* the conduct of either party could prove decisive. According to Saint Jacob, the rise of speculative merchant *fermiers* was responsible for a growing rural crisis and for intensifying peasant resentments toward the seigneur and his agents. The insertion of the *fermier général* between lord and peasants brought to power men possessed of keener knowledge and a greater will to exploit seigneurial property more aggressively than the lord himself was inclined to do. It was thus the *fermier général* of the later eighteenth century who was the true antihero of Saint Jacob's masterful study. "In certain parts of the countryside," he wrote, "the *fermier* became the terror of the population."[62]

In the villages studied here *fermiers* did not earn such a reputation, and the resentments and conflicts that surely arose between leaseholders and villagers were evidently limited. Arguably, the close supervision of their estates by both Nicolas Philippe Berbis and the Mairetet served as a critical constraint. Furthermore, enlisting the material interests and loyalties of some principal local residents meant that the functioning of the Berbis lordships—and of the Mairetet seigneurie to a lesser degree—diffused, in the short term, antagonisms and reduced the possibility of open, collective resistance that went beyond the lawsuits and negotiations that from at least the early seventeenth century characterized the Burgundian seigneurial regime. In time and under certain circumstances, of course, the engagement of principal villagers in lordship could accentuate antagonisms, further aggravating the popular resentments provoked by a Burgundian lord's right of *triage,* his monopoly over wine or milling, the *indire,* or other powers at his disposal.[63] Paradoxically, such aggravations made the strong and evolving seigneurial system vulnerable to eventual attack and collapse, but only when the Revolution created the opportunity for its abolition from above and below.

Of course, in 1787 no one clearly foresaw the Revolution or knew that seigneurialism would be swept away within the next few years. So in 1787, when Berbis leased his estates to François Prudent the younger and a half

---

of the barons, Caillot de Conquéraumont, who was cut from the same "robe cloth" as Mairetet and Berbis and took charge in the late 1760s, increased his income through a program of expansion and reorganization that resembled that of Berbis. See Dewald, *Pont-St-Pierre,* 231–38. For the attentive and improved management by robe nobles in the Toulouse region, see Forster's *Nobility of Toulouse.*

62. Saint Jacob, *Paysans,* 431

63. As mentioned above, in Burgundy the *indire* was a heavy levy owed by subjects at the marriage of his eldest daughter. Both Berbis and the Mairetet made use of it.

dozen other local men, they all believed they would continue to share in the profits of lordship in the future. Due in no small measure to Berbis's thorough reorganization of his estates, these profits were greater than before. Such was the evident result of his noble entrepreneurship.

4

POLITICAL ECONOMY AND THE FRENCH NOBILITY,
1750−1789

John Shovlin

The second half of the eighteenth century was a period when a new consciousness of, and attention to, economic affairs spread across Enlightenment Europe. France was no exception to the trend. Between 1750 and 1789 the French public showed a striking and sustained interest in economic matters, an appetite fed by hundreds of writers who penned works on agriculture, commerce, finance, taxation, banking, and public credit. According to Jean-Claude Perrot, who has inventoried this publishing boom, a total of 2,869 new political economic titles were published in France between the middle of the seventeenth century and the Revolution, about 80 percent of them between 1750 and 1789.[1] A second estimate, elaborated by Christine Théré, yields even larger aggregates. According to Théré, 391 political economic titles were produced for the French market in the 1750s, 613 in the 1760s, 668 in the 1770s, and 756 between 1780 and 1788.[2] Both sets of figures suggest that the 1750s constituted a significant turning point, with production of new titles more than quadrupling from the previous decade.

---

1. Jean-Claude Perrot, *Une histoire intellectuelle de l'économie politique: XVIIe−XVIIIe siècle* (Paris, 1992), 75.

2. Christine Théré, "Economic Publishing and Authors, 1566−1789," *Studies in the History of French Political Economy: From Bodin to Walras,* ed. Gilbert Faccarello (New York, 1998). Théré and Perrot use different criteria in classifying political economic texts. Perrot counts all texts that include in their titles such terms as *richesses, commerce, finances, impôts, crédit,* and *population.* Such an approach is open to error and especially to undercounting. Théré models her conception of political economy on the classification elaborated by the abbé André Morellet in his "Catalogue

By the 1760s, new works of an economic character were being produced at the rate of more than one title per week, outpacing the production of new novels.[3] Some of the great best sellers of the eighteenth century, moreover, were works of political economy. The marquis de Mirabeau's *L'ami des hommes, ou traité de la population* (1756) went through forty editions before the end of the century. The former controller general, Jacques Necker, published *De l'administration des finances de la France* (1784), a three-volume account of his economic philosophy and an implicit defense of his record as minister of finance; it is reputed to have sold 80,000 copies, making it one of the great best sellers of the age.[4]

Several factors converged in eighteenth-century France to stimulate public interest in political economy. The eighteenth century was a period when, across Europe, writers and intellectuals were elaborating new languages for the description of large human communities. Organizing concepts, such as *patrie* (fatherland), society, manners, civilization, people, public, and public opinion, were all emerging in eighteenth-century France as new ways to apprehend human relations.[5] Political economy, then, was just one of several new social vocabularies that emerged to prominence in this period. The need for an idiom to make sense of changes in the material realm was pressing, given the increase in the relative importance of commerce and manufactures in

d'une bibliothèque d'économie politique," an appendix to his *Prospectus d'un nouveau dictionnaire de commerce* (1769). She bases her enumeration on an annotated bibliography of approximately 5,000 works dealing with "economy and population" compiled by Jacqueline Hecht and Claude Lévy at the Institut National d'Etudes Démographiques in the 1950s. (*Economie et population: les doctrines françaises avant 1800,* ed. Alfred Sauvy [Paris, 1956].) This bibliography is based on a reading of content rather than titles, and Théré supplements it by drawing on major British and American catalogues of economic literature.

3. Based on a comparison with the figures in Angus Martin, Vivienne G. Mylne, and Richard Frautschi, *Bibliographie du genre romanesque français, 1751–1800* (London, 1977). Economic publishing expanded much faster than publishing in general in the 1750s and 1760s. The increase in the total number of new titles produced for the French market from the 1740s to the 1750s was of the order of 30 percent. See, Pierre M. Conlon, *Le siècle des lumières: bibliographie chronologique,* 18 vols. (Paris, 1983–98).

4. Kenneth E. Carpenter, *The Economic Bestsellers Before 1850: A Catalogue of an Exhibition Prepared for the History of Economics Society Meeting, May 21–24, 1975, at Baker Library,* bulletin no. 11 of the Kress Library of Business and Economics (Cambridge, Mass., 1975).

5. Keith Michael Baker, "Enlightenment and the Institution of Society: Notes for a Conceptual History," in *Main Trends in Cultural History: Ten Essays,* ed. Willem Melching and Wyger Velema (Amsterdam, 1994); David A. Bell, *The Cult of the Nation in France: Inventing Nationalism, 1680–1800* (Cambridge, Mass., 2001); Daniel Gordon, *Citizens Without Sovereignty: Equality and Sociability in French Thought, 1670–1789* (Princeton, 1994); Robert Romani, "All Montesquieu's Sons: The Place of *esprit général, caractère national,* and *moeurs* in French Political Philosophy, 1748–1789," *Studies on Voltaire and the Eighteenth Century* 362 (1998): 189–235.

national life, along with marked changes in consumption in the eighteenth century. Between 1730 and the late 1770s French foreign trade expanded between 400 and 500 percent. Colonial trade may have increased up to 1000 percent in the same period.[6] The expansion of the commercial economy was accompanied by something of a consumer revolution in urban France.[7] More directly, however, than any of these general factors, the rise of public interest in political economy was a response to the French military struggle with an economically and militarily successful Great Britain. The entire century was marked by conflict between Britain and France, a struggle renewed in the War of Austrian Succession (1741–48) and continued—disastrously for France— during the Seven Years' War (1756–63). As a body of texts that claimed to guide the statesman in increasing the wealth and power of states, political economy was of obvious value and interest in an age of international diplomatic and military conflict.

Any presupposition that political economy was a characteristically bourgeois idiom must be abandoned in face of the statistics on economic authorship offered by Théré and Perrot. The political economic debates of the second half of the eighteenth century engaged the French nobility deeply. Between one-third and two-fifths of the identifiable authors of eighteenth-century political economic tracts were nobles (nobles, by contrast, made up only 15 percent of authors writing in the genre of belles lettres).[8] Only 7–8 percent of the identifiable political economic authors were merchants or entrepreneurs.[9] Moreover, the proportion of noble authors of economic works was increasing in the second half of the century. Nobles were drawn into economic debate, I suggest, because, from the 1750s, the language of political economy became a critical site for debate on the place of the Second Estate in national life.

In the early 1750s, the dominant perspective within French political economy was antagonistic toward traditional noble values. Writers associated

6. Fernand Braudel and Ernest Labrousse, eds., *Histoire économique et sociale de la France* (Paris, 1970–82), 2:503.

7. Cissie Fairchilds, "The Production and Marketing of Populuxe Goods in Eighteenth-Century Paris," in *Consumption and the World of Goods,* ed. John Brewer and Roy Porter (London, 1993); Annik Pardailhé-Galabrun, *La naissance de l'intime: 3000 foyers parisien, XVIIe–XVIIIe siècles* (Paris, 1988); Daniel Roche, *The People of Paris: An Essay in Popular Culture in the Eighteenth Century* (Berkeley and Los Angeles, 1987); Roche, *La culture des apparences: une histoire du vêtement (XVIIe–XVIIIe siècle)* (Paris, 1989); Roche, "Between a 'Moral Economy' and a 'Consumer Economy': Clothes and Their Function in the 17th and 18th Centuries," *Luxury Trades and Consumerism in Ancien Régime Paris,* ed. Robert Fox and Anthony Turner (Aldershot, Hampshire, 1998).

8. Perrot, *Histoire intellectuelle de l'économie politique,* 78.

9. Théré, "Economic Publishing and Authors."

with the reforming *intendant* of commerce, J.-C.-M. Vincent de Gournay, argued that nobles made little contribution to the prosperity and power of the state and that aristocratic honor, in particular, was an impediment to economic development. In the late 1750s and 1760s, however, the marquis de Mirabeau initiated a countertendency in political economy calculated to forge for the nobility a new place in the life of the nation. Mirabeau's impassioned attack on luxury and his claim that agriculture rather than commerce was the foundation of long-term prosperity and power resonated with the ethic of the provincial nobility of which the marquis was himself a representative. Mirabeau's political economy equated the economic interests of provincial nobles with the national interest and elevated their economic values to the status of a patriotic ethic. Mirabeau carried a preoccupation with renovating the nobility into physiocracy, which he and François Quesnay founded in the late 1750s. Ultimately, however, physiocracy offered the nobility the prospect of renewal not as a distinctive class with its own corporate ethos but only as owners of land. Ironically, in the 1770s and 1780s, the political economic critique of luxury became a stick that critics used to beat the nobility; this was particularly the case during the prerevolutionary crisis. I suggest that antipathy to the court nobility, and especially the charge that *les grands* were guilty of luxury, spilled over into criticism of the nobility as a whole.

Much recent work on the nobility has emphasized the ways in which nobles might have unwittingly hastened the demise of their own order by adopting ideological perspectives that could readily be used against them. David Bien and his students have demonstrated that military nobles adopted a language advocating merit as the basis for professional advancement.[10] Nobles appear to have been blind to the possibility that this language might ultimately be used against them. Jay Smith has discerned a similar pattern in the noble engagement with the language of patriotism.[11] The noble adoption of patriotism as a value promised the nobility an avenue to regenerate the whole order by claiming love of country rather than hereditary privilege as

---

10. David D. Bien, "La réaction aristocratique avant 1789: l'exemple de l'armée," *Annales: E.S.C.* 29 (1974): 23–48, 505–34; Bien, "The Army in the French Enlightenment: Reform, Reaction and Revolution," *Past and Present* 85 (1979): 68–98; Jay M. Smith, *The Culture of Merit: Nobility, Royal Service, and the Making of Absolute Monarchy in France, 1600–1789* (Ann Arbor, 1996); Rafe Blaufarb, *The French Army, 1750–1820: Careers, Talent, Merit* (Manchester, 2002).

11. Jay M. Smith, "Social Categories, the Language of Patriotism, and the Origins of the French Revolution: The Debate over *Noblesse Commerçante*," *Journal of Modern History* 72 (2000): 339–74.

the defining feature of the Second Estate. But the paradigm of patriotism also problematized the whole social order of separate estates. The relation of the nobility to political economy seems to have worked in a similar fashion. Nobles perceived in the idiom a way to make a new place for themselves in national life and to identify some of their characteristic values with the welfare of the state. But political economy ultimately proved a rich resource for critics of the nobility. The noble engagement with political economy bears similarities to these other idioms but suggests that, in this case at least, nobles were quite conscious of the negative possibilities inherent in the new language and quite deliberately produced a counteridiom to try to "turn" the new discourse—and they did this with considerable success over several decades.

Political Economists Problematize Nobility

The lackluster French performance in the War of the Austrian Succession, together with the conviction that further war with Great Britain could not be long averted, prompted renewed attention after 1748 to the sources of Britain's economic and military success. Political economic works taking the measure of the English enemy proliferated in the early 1750s. A furor was created in 1754 by the *Remarques sur les avantages et les désavantages de la France et de la Grande Bretagne,* the anonymous work of a thirty-two-year-old official in the Chambre des comptes, Louis-Joseph Plumard de Dangeul.[12] Dangeul was one of a group of young publicists associated with the progressive *intendant* of commerce, Jacques-Claude-Marie Vincent de Gournay, who were interested in initiating the French public into the mysteries of political economy.[13] Assuming the identity of an English gentleman, Dangeul drew up a balance sheet of relative British and French strengths and weaknesses. The *Remarques* quickly became the talk of Paris, went into a second edition within a fortnight and two more editions before the end of the year.[14] The

12. Louis-Joseph Plumard de Dangeul, *Remarques sur les avantages et les désavantages de la France et de la Grande Bretagne, par rapport au commerce, & aux autres sources de la puissance des etats. Traduction de l'anglois du Chevalier John Nickolls* (Leiden, 1754).

13. On Vincent de Gournay and the intellectual circle associated with him, see Simone Meyssonnier, *La balance et l'horloge: la genèse de la pensée libérale en France au XVIIIe siècle* (Montreuil, 1989); Antoin E. Murphy, "Le développement des idées économiques en France (1750–1756)," *Revue d'Histoire Moderne et Contemporaine* 33 (1986): 521–41; Gustave Schelle, *Vincent de Gournay* (Geneva and Paris, 1984; orig. pub. 1897).

14. David T. Pottinger, *The French Book Trade in the Ancien Régime, 1500–1791* (Cambridge, Mass., 1958), 204.

press excerpted and commented extensively on the book, and even the king claimed to be reading it.[15]

The *Remarques sur les avantages et les désavantages de la France et de la Grande Bretagne* was very critical of the French nobility. Dangeul argued that France was handicapped by an excessive number of unproductive citizens who contributed to society neither through their industry, nor their consumption. He pointed out that the French nobility was numerous and poor, that noble families condemned their daughters to the convent and their sons to the church or the army for want of resources to perpetuate more than a single branch of the family. This destructive trend spread to other families through ennoblement.[16] He argued that commerce and agriculture were languishing in France because of the contempt in which merchants and farmers were held. "In a Nation where everything operates by honor or vanity," he claimed, "the most useful professions to the state: artisans, manufacturers, entrepreneurs, shopkeepers, sea-going merchants, all those classes comprised under the name of traders, are neither distinguished nor considered."[17] England, by contrast, honored merchants, and commerce prospered there.

A critical paradigm that shaped the attitude of Dangeul, and the rest of Vincent de Gournay's circle, toward the nobility was the Enlightenment discourse on commerce exemplified in Voltaire's representation of England in the *Lettres philosophiques* (1734). In the *Lettres*, Voltaire implicitly contrasted English institutions with French ones and identified the vestiges of feudal attitudes and structures in French society as a hindrance to the development of commerce and thus national power. In England, commerce was honorable, Voltaire argued—"the younger brother of a peer of the realm does not scorn to enter into trade"—and this superior prestige of commerce was one of the keys to English success. Voltaire drew an invidious contrast between the useful English merchant and the parasitic French courtier. A merchant "who enriches his country . . . and contributes to the well-being of the world," Voltaire declared, is more useful to his country than a "well-powdered lord . . . who gives himself airs of grandeur while playing the role of a slave in a minister's antechamber."[18]

The perception that aristocratic conceptions of honor were a hindrance to the development of commerce was quite widespread in eighteenth-century

15. Antoin E. Murphy, *Richard Cantillon: Entrepreneur and Economist* (Oxford, 1986), 310.
16. Plumard de Dangeul, *Remarques sur les avantages et les désavantages*, 16–17.
17. Ibid., 31.
18. Voltaire, *Philosophical Letters*, trans. Ernest Dilworth (Indianapolis, 1961), 39–40.

Europe. David Hume made the same argument in his essay "Of Liberty and Despotism," first published in 1741. Hume concurred with Voltaire, suggesting that the aristocratic character of French society made France less congenial to commercial activity. "In my opinion," Hume wrote, commerce "is apt to decay in absolute governments, not because it is there less secure, but because it is less honourable. A subordination of ranks is absolutely necessary to the support of monarchy. Births, titles, and place, must be honoured above industry and riches. And while these notions prevail, all the considerable traders will be tempted to throw up their commerce, in order to purchase some of these employments, to which privileges and honours are annexed."[19]

The full implications of this perspective were spelled out in Gabriel-François Coyer's *La noblesse commerçante* (1756).[20] Coyer implied that France ought to become a commercial society. The culture and corporate identity of the nobility was an obstacle to this development; therefore the nobility ought to abandon this identity and merge itself into the body of the commercial nation. Ostensibly, in *La noblesse commerçante,* Coyer was offering an impoverished element of the nobility a means to regenerate itself, but this intention is belied by the hostile remarks Coyer makes about the nobility throughout the text. In the barbaric era of feudal government, he argues, nobles held half of France in servitude, and this domineering spirit could still be found among the impoverished provincial nobility, leading country nobles to be quarrelsome, abusive to peasants, and to confuse might with right.[21] In fact, Coyer's principal concern was to destroy the last vestiges of "Gothic" attitudes toward trade by borrowing the luster of the nobility for commerce.[22] Coyer mobilized Plumard de Dangeul's argument that commerce in France was retarded by the dishonor under which it labored. Like Dangeul, he drew upon Voltaire's account of England to suggest that commerce

19. David Hume, *Essays: Moral, Political, and Literary,* ed. Eugene F. Miller (Indianapolis, 1985), 93. Hume changed the title of the essay to "Of Civil Liberty" in 1758.

20. Gabriel-François Coyer, *La noblesse commerçante* (London, 1756). The best account of the *Noblesse commerçante* controversy is Smith's "Social Categories, the Language of Patriotism, and the Origins of the French Revolution." Also useful are J. Q. C. Mackrell, *The Attack on "Feudalism" in Eighteenth-Century France* (London, 1973), chap. 4; and Leonard Adams, *Coyer and the Enlightenment, Studies on Voltaire and the Eighteenth Century* 123 (1974): 60ff.

21. Coyer, *La noblesse commerçante,* 7, 14–15. A number of the writers who supported Coyer in the subsequent controversy took positions critical of the nobility. See, for instance, J. H. Marchand, *La noblesse commerçable ou ubiquiste* (Amsterdam, 1756); M. A. Rochon de Chabannes, *La noblesse oisive* (n.p., 1756).

22. Coyer sees the perspective he is struggling against—that commerce is dishonorable—as a vestige of the "Gothic spirit," a cultural remnant as irrational and baneful as trial by ordeal. Coyer, *La noblesse commerçante,* 7–8, 112–13, 168.

flourished there because it was honored.[23] According to Coyer, it is essential that the French prejudice against trade be destroyed because, while other nations may be contented with enriching themselves, "the Frenchman wants glory."[24] The essence of his argument was that the very existence of the nobility as a corporate body with its own distinct pride and sense of self was inimical to the national welfare in an age when commercial wealth was the linchpin of power in the international system.

The hostile response that Coyer's *Noblesse commerçante* provoked in some quarters, and especially the chevalier d'Arcq's riposte to Coyer—*La noblesse militaire*—mark the origins of a counter idiom to the claims of the Gournay circle.[25] D'Arcq's position was that although commerce may be a good thing in itself, commercial *society*—which he represents as a venal order in which money has replaced honor and merit—would be disastrous. According to d'Arcq, the mischievous consequences of an order dominated by money are already apparent in the army, where wealth rather than merit attracts consideration and ensures promotion.[26] D'Arcq rejected commercial society because, he argued, if the "spirit of commerce" were infused into all social institutions, the results would be disastrous. The first casualty of such a com-mercialization would be the country's military prowess. Brave officers are animated by a sense of honor, a passion for glory, d'Arcq argues. Once a soldier begins to calculate and weigh his interest against his desire for glory he will become incapable of the kind of valor and self-sacrifice required on the battlefield. Without a group in society fiercely conscious of personal and familial honor and willing to make sacrifices to maintain it, he suggests, the country cannot remain well defended.

According to d'Arcq, the spread of mercantile values would also be disas-trous in the political realm. Drawing on Montesquieu's analytical framework, the chevalier argues that the noble pride criticized by Coyer was crucial in preventing the political degeneration of the French monarchy. According to Montesquieu, honor not only animates monarchies but acts as a brake preventing monarchy from degenerating into despotism. "In monarchical and moderate states," Montesquieu argues, "power is limited by that which

23. In what is almost a direct quotation from the *Lettres philosophiques,* Coyer notes that while Lord Oxford governed England he had a brother who was a merchant in Aleppo. Coyer, *La noblesse commerçante,* 3.

24. Ibid., 192.

25. Philippe Auguste de Sainte-Foix, chevalier d'Arcq, *La noblesse militaire, ou le patriote françois* (n.p., 1756).

26. Ibid., 89.

is its spring; I mean honor, which reigns like a monarch over the prince and the people."[27] The same sense of honor that makes nobles effective military officers also makes them a powerful bulwark against despotism. Montesquieu denounced the idea of a commercial nobility unequivocally in *De l'esprit des lois,* arguing that it is contrary to the "spirit of monarchy" for nobles to engage in trade.[28] According to d'Arcq, the problem with allowing nobles to enter into trade is that this sense of honor would be jeopardized—nobles would become "calculators" who would no longer care enough about their honor to resist a despot. D'Arcq insinuated that Coyer's scheme of effacing the distinctions between the nobility and the trading classes would precipitate a "revolution" that would threaten the existing form of government and allow France to drift toward despotism.[29] In the chevalier's view, a healthy monarchy could be preserved only within the confines of a social order where there was minimal movement between estates, because only in such a society was it likely that nobles would preserve their sense of honor. "The state does not begin . . . to falter," d'Arcq held, "until the moment when ranks cease to be distinct one from another, until they are mixed, until they are confounded, until they mutually absorb one another."[30] D'Arcq's *La noblesse militaire* was an assertion of the continuing relevance of the nobility and of a social order defined on the basis of distinctions of rank.

Political Economy and the Regeneration of the Nobility

A perspective strikingly similar to d'Arcq's was offered by the marquis de Mirabeau in his *L'ami des hommes, ou traité de la population* (1756).[31] Mirabeau did not publish *L'ami des hommes* as a direct riposte to Coyer—the marquis had been working on his lengthy opus for several years before the appearance

27. Charles de Secondat, baron de Montesquieu, *The Spirit of the Laws,* trans. Anne M. Cohler, Basia Carolyn Miller, and Harold Samuel Stone (Cambridge, 1989; orig. pub. 1748), 30 [bk. 3, chap. 10].

28. Ibid., 350 [bk. 20, chap. 21]. A trading nobility, he observes, would be "the means to destroy the nobility, without being of any utility to commerce." For Montesquieu, the fact that in England nobles are permitted to engage in commerce is a factor that has contributed to weakening monarchical government there (p. 350).

29. D'Arcq, *La noblesse militaire,* iii, 6, 45.

30. Ibid., 31.

31. Victor de Riqueti, marquis de Mirabeau, *L'ami des hommes, ou traité de la population* (Avignon, 1756). Although the first edition carries a 1756 date of imprint, the work was almost certainly not published until 1757 and did not become a subject of conversation until the late spring or early summer of that year.

of *La noblesse commerçante*. But some of Mirabeau's themes resonated closely with the chevalier d'Arcq's perspective, and at points in the book Mirabeau alluded directly to the debate on the commercial nobility. Like d'Arcq, Mirabeau argued that patriotic virtue could be fostered only in a revivified society of orders with the nobility dominating its upper reaches. According to Mirabeau, the class of Frenchmen preeminently animated by honor—the nobility—must be reinvigorated: "The prejudices that constitute honor make up a real part of the treasure of the state," he argued. "It is thus important to preserve . . . to the greatest extent possible that portion of the people among whom this money has the greatest currency, that is, the nobility."[32] Like d'Arcq, Mirabeau rejected a social order in which status was determined by wealth. If men were valued according to how much money they possessed, he pointed out, the lackey might well be prized over the soldier and the *valet de chambre* over the officer.[33] In such a world, men would be diverted systematically from public service toward corrupt and slavish activities.

Mirabeau had been preoccupied for at least a decade by problems of noble decline. He grappled with the issue in his first written work, a *Testament politique,* produced in 1747 for an as yet unborn heir. The primary theme of the *Testament,* as Gino Longhitano points out, is the emphasis it placed on regenerating seigneurial power via-à-vis the administrative monarchy.[34] In the *Testament,* Mirabeau described the representatives of the absolute monarchy in the provinces, the *intendants,* as "a sort of magistracy, shapeless and monstrous . . . against which it would be useless and harmful to struggle [*se raidir*] directly." Instead, he advises his heir to bolster his seigneurial authority in the local community and to try to neutralize appeals to higher tribunals of justice. Mirabeau pursued this theme further in his first public foray into the literary world, his *Mémoire concernant l'utilité des états provinciaux* (1750), where he called for the establishment of provincial estates in the *pays d'élections,* claiming that administration by estates was less fiscally oppressive than rule by *intendants,* and that the estates were better stewards of rural prosperity.[35] He also argued that the fundamental law of the French

32. Ibid., 3:180.
33. Ibid., 2:84.
34. Gino Longhitano, "La monarchie française entre société d'ordres et marché: Mirabeau, Quesnay et le *Traité de la monarchie, 1757–1759,*" in *Marquis de Mirabeau & François Quesnay, Traité de la monarchie (1757–1759),* ed. Gino Longhitano (Paris, 1999), x.
35. Victor de Riqueti, marquis de Mirabeau, *Mémoire concernant l'utilité des états provinciaux* (Rome, 1750).

monarchy called on the king to respect the privileges of the nobility and other traditional *corps.*

In *L'ami des hommes,* Mirabeau framed his call for the reinvigoration of a society of orders within a political economy denouncing "luxury" and representing agriculture as the linchpin of national prosperity. Countering Coyer, Mirabeau noted that the nobility must be prevented from degenerating not by asking them to enter another estate, but by giving them the means to thrive in their own.[36] A regenerated agriculture might offer such a means, creating the economic basis for a reinvigorated nobility. The marquis argued that it was not primarily commerce—and certainly not luxury—that was the basis of the prosperity and power of states. As he stated in the foreword, "I am going to finally prove, yes, demonstrate that luxury is . . . the ruin of a large state even more so than of a small one."[37] The central economic program advanced in *L'ami des hommes* was for the renewal of small-scale peasant cultivation and estate management by noble proprietors rather than agents or farmers. Mirabeau criticized the fact that land was engrossed into great estates where it was poorly cultivated by agents. He complained that land was misused for luxurious display; parks, avenues, and gardens, which produced nothing, had been substituted for productive land use. Agriculture was neglected also because there was too much greed for quick and easy wealth. False ideas of urbanity and politeness had made agriculture seem contemptible. As a result, the villager migrated to the town and the townsman gravitated toward the capital.

In making the claim that "luxury is . . . the ruin of a large state even more so than of a small one," Mirabeau was drawing upon a critique of luxury that had flourished in the ancient world and that enjoyed considerable popularity in seventeenth- and eighteenth-century Europe also.[38] Luxury was the ailment that classical moralists and historians claimed had destroyed the Roman Republic and subsequently also undermined the Roman Empire. A state of luxury was supposed to exist when the taste for wealth, or indulgence in consumption, diverted the rulers, or the citizens, of a state from the public good or sapped their capacity to defend their liberty. In the seventeenth century, French moralists used the anti-luxury tradition to try to preserve,

36. Mirabeau, *L'ami des hommes,* 3:179–80.

37. Ibid., 1:iv.

38. The fullest accounts of the development of the concept from classical antiquity to the eighteenth century are to be found in John Sekora, *Luxury: The Concept in Western Thought, Eden to Smollett* (Baltimore, 1977), and Christopher J. Berry, *The Idea of Luxury: A Conceptual and Historical Investigation* (Cambridge, 1994).

or restore, a noble monopoly on office or honor and to criticize the upward social mobility conferred by money.[39] They denounced as luxury the usurpation by non-nobles of clothing or other commodities appropriate only to their betters, a usurpation that "confounded ranks" and dissolved the symbolic boundaries that ought to distinguish one order from another. Under conditions of luxury, authority was vested in men of no merit or virtue whose only title to power was money. Moralists sympathetic to the nobility reserved their sharpest criticism for financiers, entrepreneurs who handled most of the financial business of the royal administration—from collecting taxes, to paying troops, to managing public services—in return for an opportunity to make a profit. Financiers, preeminently, had the money to buy venal offices or to vie with the nobility in the magnificence of their clothing and houses.

In addition to its continuing moral and political significance, in the eighteenth century luxury increasingly took on economic connotations. There was little agreement among political economists on precisely what luxury was in economic terms, and depending on the writer's conception of luxury, the category might be given either a positive or a negative slant. There was an important current within French political economy running from Boisguilbert in the 1690s to Vincent de Gournay in the 1750s that identified high consumption by the mass of the population as a critical factor in generating prosperity.[40] Some political economic writers—notably Jean-François Melon and members of Gournay's circle—used the term "luxury" to describe such consumption, conferring a positive connotation on *luxe*. The writers around Gournay, however, also used the term in a second and negative sense. Plumard de Dangeul identified as a destructive luxury an inequality of wealth so great that it decreased the capacity of ordinary people to consume. "Well-ordered luxury consumes," Dangeul remarked, while "excessive luxury abuses and destroys."[41] He attributed the second variety of luxury to fiscal institutions that enriched the few while impoverishing the many. François Véron de

39. Renato Galliani, for instance, sees the early modern anti-luxury discourse as the expression of a "noble ideology" aimed at reversing the process whereby a class of parvenus had come to compete with the ancient nobility for office and honor. Renato Galliani, *Rousseau, le luxe et l'idéologie nobiliaire: étude socio-historique, Studies on Voltaire and the Eighteenth Century* 268 (1989). The critics of luxury that Carolyn Lougee analyzes in her study of seventeenth-century polite culture and its detractors also sought to keep the merely wealthy out of the governing class. Carolyn C. Lougee, *Le Paradis des Femmes: Women, Salons, and Social Stratification in Seventeenth-Century France* (Princeton, 1976).
40. The key study of this current is Meyssonnier's *La balance et l'horloge*.
41. Plumard de Dangeul, *Remarques sur les avantages et les désavantages*, 65.

Forbonnais also noted the existence of a pernicious variety of luxury. "If luxury is not general, if it is not the fruit of national affluence," he observes, "one will see arise at the same time as it disorders capable of destroying the political body."[42] A different, but also negative, connotation was given to the word "luxury" by François Quesnay in his economic writings of the 1750s. In the articles he published for the *Encyclopédie,* particularly "Grains," Quesnay highlighted the role of Colbertist policies in generating "luxury." "For a long time luxury manufactures have seduced the nation," Quesnay argued. "We have given ourselves over to an industry that was alien to us; and a multitude of men have been employed in it at a time when the kingdom was being depopulated and the countryside was becoming a desert." "These manufactures," he warned, "have plunged us into a disordered luxury."[43]

The economic perspective most influential for Mirabeau when he wrote *L'ami des hommes* was that articulated by Richard Cantillon in his *Essay de la nature du commerce en général.* The first draft of *L'ami des hommes* preserved among Mirabeau's papers constitute a paragraph by paragraph commentary on Cantillon's *Essay.*[44] Cantillon argued that the successful pursuit of commercial prosperity initially had very positive effects on the power of states, but that in the long run, pursuing commercial development could leave a state weak and vulnerable. The increase in the money supply brought by trade would cause prices and wages to rise, Cantillon argued, undercutting the competitiveness of the affected country in the international marketplace. Eventually it would be undersold by neighboring lands where a shortage of money limited both wages and prices. At a certain point, the nation previously rich and powerful would decline into poverty and weakness. As Cantillon put it, "The too great abundance of money which, while it lasts, makes states powerful, throws them insensibly, but naturally, into poverty."[45] According to Cantillon, the Roman Empire was destroyed as a consequence of the specie-flow mechanism he analyzed. Cantillon's theory of history also explained the decadence of Spanish power since its apogee in the sixteenth century and the more recent decline of the Dutch Republic.

42. François Véron de Forbonnais, *Elémens du commerce* (Leiden, 1754), 2:308.

43. François Quesnay, "Grains," in *François Quesnay et la physiocratie,* 2 vols. (Paris, 1958), 2:459–60.

44. Georges Weulersse, ed., *Les manuscrits économiques de François Quesnay et du marquis de Mirabeau aux Archives Nationales (M. 778 à M. 785)* (Paris, 1910).

45. Richard Cantillon, *Essay de la nature du commerce en général,* ed. Takumi Tsuda (Tokyo, 1979), 231.

Mirabeau's conception of luxury confounded economic meanings of the term with older political and moral senses. There are at least three different meanings of luxury in play in *L'ami des hommes*. Mirabeau condemned luxury as an "ambitious" kind of consumption adopted by the consumer in order to attract the attention and respect due only to members of a more exalted social class. He also used the term in the classical sense of a corrupting venality inimical to patriotism and public virtue, commenting that France would go the same way as ancient Rome if it allowed luxury to continue to flourish. Finally, for Mirabeau, luxury was an economic order in which there was excessive attention to commerce and to the acquisition of mobile wealth and not enough attention to agriculture, which he regarded as the true basis of national prosperity and power.

This celebration of agriculture, and attack on luxury as the wellspring of corruption and national decline, resonated powerfully with the life experiences and prejudices of provincial nobles. In his pioneering study of the nobility of Toulouse, Robert Forster showed noble landowners to have been active and able estate managers.[46] An economic philosophy that identified the success of agriculture with the well-being of the state exalted their role as stewards of rural prosperity. Mirabeau's criticisms of luxury also echoed the values of provincial nobles. The provincial nobility lived according to an ethic of economic discipline and antipathy to frivolous expenditure. As Forster has shown, they engaged in consumption necessary to mark their status in provincial society but eschewed the prodigal expenditure on clothing and equipages in which the court nobility and financiers indulged. "Family and friends usually intervened as a corrective to the dangerous spending habits of a wayward squire," Forster notes; "sobriety, not profligacy, was the dominant note in the provincial noble family."[47] The use of wealth by non-nobles to acquire prestige and access to honors represented a profound threat to the social status and identity of middling nobles. It seemed to many nobles that such "luxury" was the principal obstacle preventing them from serving the king in the army or the magistracy. Within the military itself, noble officers complained that wealth rather than virtue was the principal channel to promotion, and they castigated this state of affairs as luxury also.[48]

---

46. Robert Forster, *The Nobility of Toulouse in the Eighteenth Century* (Baltimore, 1960), esp. 61–63.

47. Robert Forster, "The Provincial Noble: A Reappraisal," *American Historical Review* 68:3 (1963): 689.

48. Bien, "Army in the French Enlightenment."

Mirabeau's political economy offered the nobility a very modern language in which to condemn luxury, a language that appeared to align their interests with the national interest. Provincial nobles adopted political economy as a language of noble regeneration because it equated their values, values emphasizing careful estate management and a relatively ascetic attitude toward consumption, with the national welfare while condemning the luxury that made the maintenance of their social position so difficult. These powerful ideological implications of Mirabeau's *L'ami des hommes* explain, perhaps, why it was such an extraordinarily successful work. In the three years following its initial publication, the book appeared in twenty editions, and over the rest of the century seems to have enjoyed twenty more.[49] It appeared in nearly one in four of the five hundred private libraries from the period between 1750 and 1780 inventoried by Daniel Mornet, suggesting that it was among the most widely disseminated books of the century.[50] At court it was rumored that the dauphin wanted Mirabeau appointed preceptor to his son, while from St-Malo in Brittany, Mirabeau's brother reported that he was basking in the reflected glory of the "friend of mankind."[51]

The principal themes of Mirabeau's political economy were widely echoed and indeed amplified in the vigorous literature on agriculture that blossomed in the 1760s. The keynotes of this literature were the centrality of agriculture to the wealth, power, and stability of states, and the destructive effects of luxury on agriculture. Exemplary in this respect is Jean-Baptiste Dupuy Demportes's *Le gentilhomme cultivateur* (1761–63), one of the most widely read works of the 1760s advocating agricultural improvement.[52] In language charged with references to patriotism, Dupuy Demportes calls for the regeneration of agriculture in order to bolster the power of the state and the virtue of its population. He invokes the history of Rome as a cautionary example for France. "How can it be," he asks, "that the example of Rome

49. Gilles Henry, *Mirabeau père: 5 octobre 1715–11 juillet 1789* (Paris, 1989), 8; Carpenter, *Economic Bestsellers Before 1850*. Mirabeau later remarked to his confidant the marquis de Longo that the book had, by their own account, made its publishers a clear profit of 86,000 *livres*. Louis de Loménie, *Les Mirabeau: nouvelles études sur la société française au XVIIIe siècle*, 3 vols. (Paris, 1889), 2:141.

50. Daniel Mornet, "Les enseignements des bibliothèques privées, 1750–1780," *Revue d'Histoire Littéraire de la France* 17 (1910): 449–96.

51. Humbert de Montlaur, *Mirabeau: L'ami des hommes* (Paris, 1992), 183–84; Loménie, *Les Mirabeau,* 2:169.

52. Jean-Baptiste Dupuy Demportes, *Le gentilhomme cultivateur, ou corps complet d'agriculture, traduit de l'anglois de M. Hale* (Paris, 1761–63). On the popularity and wide dissemination of *Le Gentilhomme cultivateur*, see André Bourde, *The Influence of England on the French Agronomes, 1750–1789* (Cambridge, 1953), 65–66.

has had so little ascendancy over enlightened minds?" The military power of Rome was based on the land, he argues: "Nobody is unaware that in its rustic but happy simplicity it owed the extent and the solidity of its power only to agriculture." Rome's troubles began, Dupuy Demportes argues, when it exchanged a form of wealth that was healthy and solid for a form that was corrupting and illusory. "The Citizen, led on by love of an imaginary good, refused his care and attention to the land." Dupuy Demportes moves from this discussion of luxury in the abstract to a contemplation of contemporary France. He implies that great military exploits are not to be expected in a polity in which agriculture has been systematically neglected and disdained—a pointed comment in light of the military disasters of the ongoing Seven Years' War. Dupuy Demportes places the blame for this state of affairs on Colbert, complaining that Colbert gave too much attention to "luxury arts" at the expense of agriculture.[53]

Physiocracy: A Language of Noble Regeneration?

In the 1760s and 1770s, the most prominent version of a political economy that criticized luxury and founded national prosperity on agriculture was physiocracy. Mirabeau himself was one of the founders of this new school of political economy. In the summer of 1757, at the height of his literary fame, he met François Quesnay, the author of two obscure political economic articles in the *Encyclopédie*. Quesnay persuaded Mirabeau that the political economy he had articulated in *L'ami des hommes* was untenable, and an intellectual relationship began between the two men that eventually led Mirabeau to abandon or modify some of his original commitments. Mirabeau, however, did not forsake his interest in the welfare of the nobility, an interest that Quesnay was willing to accommodate. Physiocracy offered to nobles a means to reinsert themselves into the life of the modern nation in their capacity as landowners and custodians of rural prosperity. But physiocracy diverged sharply from Mirabeau's initial convictions in its refusal to countenance the reinvigoration of a society of orders. In this respect at least, Quesnay's views came to predominate over Mirabeau's.

Traditional scholarship on physiocracy assumes that the relationship between Quesnay and Mirabeau was a one-way street, with the doctor acting as theorist and the marquis as popularizer and publicist. But Elizabeth Fox-

---

53. Dupuy Demportes, *Le gentilhomme cultivateur*, i–v.

Genovese's work on the origins of physiocracy suggests that Mirabeau played a more active role.[54] One of his contributions to physiocracy, at least in its initial stages, was a concern to offer the nobility a way to restore its relevance in national life. The central argument of the physiocrats—that agriculture is the sole true source of wealth and, as such, the basis of national prosperity and power—offered a critical role in national life to the owners of land. The physiocratic call for provincial assemblies made up of landed proprietors to replace the administrative apparatus of royal *intendants* is reminiscent of Mirabeau's scheme of 1750 to reinvigorate provincial estates. It has been argued that this positive relationship to the nobility certainly could not have come from Quesnay's social thought, which derives from the Enlightenment, antifeudal tradition within which Coyer framed his *Noblesse commerçante*.[55]

But Quesnay may not have been so completely outside the current of thought represented by the pre-physiocratic Mirabeau or the chevalier d'Arcq. The central thrust of his advice to Mirabeau on how to present the nobility in the *Traité de la monarchie,* which the latter was writing in the late 1750s, was to play down noble privileges and redefine the noble as a patriot. "Do you wish to render [the nobility] honorable?" Quesnay writes. "Speak only of its duties, not of its status and its rights. . . . The general virtue of the noble is patriotic zeal of every sort."[56] The doctor was also sympathetic to the traditional noble critique of the luxury of financiers: he condemned such wealth as "base" and complained that it blurred social distinctions and eclipsed the nobility. Moreover, he argued that the fortunes of the nobility, those of agriculture, and those of morals were fundamentally linked, the enemy of all three being finance. He describes financiers as "those who form an order of base rich people, whose riches obscure by themselves and by misalliances all the luster of the nobility itself." "You cannot seriously talk of the nobility and of its dignity vis-à-vis a monarchical government," he warns Mirabeau, "where the destructive *état* of the *traitants* [financiers] becomes dominant. There nobility will be a chimera. The nobility as well as monarchy and *moeurs* can subsist only by plowing."[57]

54. Elizabeth Fox-Genovese, *The Origins of Physiocracy: Economic Revolution and Social Order in Eighteenth-Century France* (Ithaca, 1976).

55. Gino Longhitano argues that, in his basic intellectual sensibility, Quesnay was hostile to the pretensions of the nobility and strongly favored a commercial society. For Quesnay, Longhitano maintains, nobles were nothing but Franks who had usurped regalian rights and transformed monarchical government into a "confederation of despotic states." Longhitano, "La monarchie française entre société d'ordres et marché," lix.

56. Weulersse, ed., *Manuscrits économiques, 25.*

57. Ibid., 28.

One might argue that Quesnay takes such positions in deference to Mirabeau's feelings. But as early as 1756, Quesnay seems to have been aware that the political economy he was elaborating had regenerative implications for the nobility. If Quesnay favored a commercial and defeudalized society, he certainly did not want one on the model of the abbé Coyer's *Noblesse commerçante*. He was critical of Coyer's scheme to involve nobles in commercial activities, suggesting a route to noble regeneration through commercial agriculture instead. In his 1756 *Encyclopédie* essay "Grains," he noted that it would be far better, both for the nobility and for the country, if gentlemen were to lease farms of land rather than going into trade (assuming they would pay tax like anyone else on the profits of those farms). "This occupation is more appropriate to their condition," according to Quesnay, "than the *état* of retail trader in the towns, that some wish to assign to them."[58] Here, perhaps, there is even a suggestion that Quesnay is concerned with maintaining the dignity of the nobility as a class, along with stimulating agriculture. The comment is brief and made only in passing, but it indicates that, in the context of the *Noblesse commerçante* debate, Quesnay had begun to link the idea of agricultural regeneration with the notion of a renewal of the nobility.

In their pronouncements on luxury, the physiocrats implicitly validated the value system of the provincial nobility. Quesnay insisted that a fundamental cleavage existed in the Second Estate, a division between court nobles, whom he despised, and the remainder of the nobility, whom he characterized in very positive terms. "The nobility is divided into two classes: into courtiers and citizens," Quesnay observed in comments on Mirabeau's *Traité de la monarchie*. "The former are amused with candies that they are made to purchase with much baseness."[59] The role of landed proprietors in the physiocratic system—and it was a critical role—was to practice appropriate consumption habits, not to spend too much of the rents they received on luxuries but to plow back a considerable portion of their income into agricultural improvements. The most explicit physiocratic treatment of luxury is to be found in the abbé Nicolas Baudeau's *Principes de la science morale et politique sur le luxe et les loix somptuaires* (1767). Here Baudeau explained that the key to agricultural prosperity was for the proprietor to spend his money wisely; if he wasted too much on unproductive luxury, then the land would yield less the following year.[60]

58. Quesnay, "Grains," 491.
59. Weulersse, ed., *Manuscrits économiques,* 26.
60. Nicolas Baudeau, *Principes de la science morale et politique sur le luxe et les loix somptuaires* (Paris, 1767).

Where physiocracy is significantly at odds with the perspective of d'Arcq or the Mirabeau of *L'ami des hommes* is in its rejection of the idea that regeneration of the nobility meant the reinvigoration of a caste separate in principle from the rest of society. The nobility might be the leader of national life, the guardian of national prosperity and power, perhaps even the linchpin of patriotic virtue, but they would be such not qua nobles, but simply as owners of land. Mature physiocratic works, such as Mirabeau and Quesnay's *Philosophie rurale* (1763), or Le Mercier de la Rivière's *L'ordre naturel et essentiel des sociétés politiques* (1767), are written in an abstract language that eschews the categories of the society of orders. Membership in the physiocratic provincial assemblies was to be based not on dignity but on land holding. Mirabeau deplored the assemblies established by Necker in Berry and the Haute Guyenne in 1778 and 1779, respectively, in part no doubt to spite Necker, but also because they were based on the categories of the society of privilege.[61] In the *Philosophie rurale*, Mirabeau jettisoned a vision of social order based on rank and estate, stating that "Persons, dignities, superiority, inferiority count for nothing . . . it is the physical essence of things which alone we will consider."[62] In his later *Lettres sur la législation* (1775), he asked his readers if they ought really object to the abolition of such categories "in order to recognize no constitution but property, unassailable and sacred property."[63] Instead of using a language of hereditary and honorific distinctions, Mirabeau referred to "classes" of individuals based on their economic function: landowners, farmers, manufacturers, merchants. These classes were the basic units of society, he maintained, and the person who did not fit into any of them could be regarded as an "extrasocial being."[64] Such statements seem to foreshadow the social order of the nineteenth century; physiocracy heralded the transformation of noble into *notable*.

Luxury and the Rise of Antipathy to the Court Nobility

The attack on luxury articulated in French political economy of the 1760s proved a double-edged sword for nobles. By the 1770s, criticisms of luxury

61. Henri Ripert, *Le marquis de Mirabeau (L'ami des hommes): ses théories politique et économiques* (thèse pour le doctorat, Université de Paris—Faculté de Droit, Paris, 1901), 438.

62. Victor de Riqueti, marquis de Mirabeau, *Philosophie rurale, ou economie générale et politique de l'agriculture* (Amsterdam, 1763), 1:193.

63. Victor de Riqueti, marquis de Mirabeau, *Lettres sur la législation, ou l'ordre légal, dépravé, rétabli et perpétué* (Berne, 1775), 1:202.

64. Ibid., xlvii.

were increasingly being directed against a part of the Second Estate itself:
the court nobility.[65] I have already noted François Quesnay's harsh censure
of court nobles for their frivolity and intrigue. Such criticisms became more
widespread and more public in the 1770s as competing cliques at court used
the gutter press to attack and vilify one another. The 1770s and 1780s saw
a tide of anti-aristocratic criticism, much of it originating from Versailles,
accusing court nobles of corruption, degeneration, and luxury. Even without this political infighting, however, it was probably inevitable that, in an
intellectual climate increasingly hostile to luxury, the court nobility would
eventually come in for criticism. More than any other social group they
were associated with spectacular consumption and luxurious self-indulgence.
Moreover, since the early decades of the eighteenth century, they had
established increasingly close links with financiers—the traditional butt of
the anti-luxury critique. So close had these links become by the last third of
the century, that one could legitimately speak of the emergence of a hybrid
plutocratic elite. Ultimately, the anti-aristocratic sentiment directed at the
court nobility, including accusations of luxury, seems to have smeared the
provincial nobility to some extent also.

Robert Darnton and Jeffrey Merrick have both pointed to the torrent
of anti-aristocratic writing that inundated the public sphere in the 1770s
and 1780s, much of it sexual in nature. In Darnton's words, "This sexual
sensationalism conveyed a social message: . . . the great nobles were either
impotent or deviant . . . everywhere among *les grands* incest and venereal
disease had extinguished the last sparks of humanity."[66] One reason that
courtiers were increasingly seen in such negative terms is that court politics
was spilling over into the public sphere to a new extent in the last decades
of the eighteenth century. As Jeremy Popkin has shown, cabals of courtiers
commissioned scurrilous attacks on one another from Grub Street journalists
and had these damaging representations hawked about the streets of Paris.[67]
Conflicts in the law courts also found their way into the public sphere through

65. The opening line of a short poem on the "inconveniences of luxury" published in
the *Mercure de France* in 1771 describes luxury as a "dazzling phantom, revered at the Court."
M. Symon, "Les inconvéniens du luxe," *Mercure de France* (June 1771), 39–43.
66. Robert Darnton, *The Literary Underground of the Old Regime* (Cambridge, Mass., 1982),
30. See also Jeffrey Merrick, "Sexual Politics and Public Order in Late Eighteenth-Century
France: The *Mémoires secrets* and the *Correspondance secrète*," *Journal of the History of Sexuality* 1:1
(1990): 68–84.
67. Jeremy Popkin, "Pamphlet Journalism at the End of the Old Regime," *Eighteenth-Century
Studies* 22:3 (1989): 351–67.

judicial briefs published by lawyers who sought to influence public opinion
in favor of their clients. Sarah Maza has traced a series of dramatic cases in
the 1770s and 1780s in which lawyers represented their clients as innocent
victims of oppression by arrogant grandees.[68] The accusation that aristocrats
were guilty of a luxury that enfeebled and impoverished the country was
easy to make. Durand Echeverria has identified a strain in patriot discourse
in the early 1770s critical of the luxury of the rich and their apparent indifference to the fate of the poor.[69] In his *Journal historique de la révolution opérée
dans la constitution de la monarchie françoise par M. de Maupeou,* Pidansat de
Mairobert complained that "on one hand the provinces are despoiled to
provide tribute to the luxury and ostentation of a few families, as contemptible in their origins as in their behavior, who cannot see anything
superfluous in their opulence; while in the other class millions of families,
earning scarcely enough from their miserable toil to stay alive, seem a living
reproach to providence for this humiliating inequality."[70]

Accusations of luxury against court nobles were especially plausible in the
late eighteenth century because the court nobility had, to a certain extent,
merged with *la finance* to form a single plutocratic elite. Since the latter part
of the previous century, the sons and daughters of financiers had been inter-
marrying with *les grands,* a trend that continued and augmented in the
eighteenth century.[71] As Charles Pinot Duclos noted, as early as 1750, "people
of condition have already lost the right to despise finance, since there are
few who are not allied to it by blood."[72] In addition to marriage ties, the
court nobility and financiers were increasingly linked by common investments in tax farms and in monopoly trading and manufacturing companies.
For example, in the second half of the eighteenth century, the court nobility
began to figure among the stakeholders of the great Saint-Gobain glass
manufacture, a firm traditionally dominated by financier capital. Between

68. Sarah Maza, *Private Lives and Public Affairs: The Causes Célèbres of Prerevolutionary France* (Berkeley and Los Angeles, 1993).

69. Durand Echeverria, *The Maupeou Revolution: A Study in the History of Libertarianism. France, 1770–1774* (Baton Rouge, 1985), 51.

70. *Journal historique de la révolution opérée dans la constitution de la monarchie françoise par M. de Maupeou, Chancellier de France,* 6 (20 September 1774), 207–8.

71. Guy Chaussinand-Nogaret, *The French Nobility in the Eighteenth Century: From Feudalism to Enlightenment,* trans. William Doyle (Cambridge, 1985), 115; Guy Chaussinand-Nogaret, *Les financiers de Languedoc au XVIIIe siècle* (Paris, 1970), 250.

72. Charles Pinot-Duclos, *Considérations sur les moeurs de ce siècle,* ed. F. C. Green (Cambridge, 1939), 125.

1750 and the 1780s, board members included Anne de Montmorency, the vicomte de Ségur, the comte de Jaucourt, and the marquis de la Ferté-Imbault.[73] In addition, a portion of the revenues of tax farming passed into a complex network of aristocratic creditors and courtly pensioners. Most tax farmers owed a share of their profits to *croupiers,* sleeping partners who put up a portion of the purchase capital of a share. In 1774, nearly two-thirds of the places in the Company of the Farmers General were so divided, and often the *croupiers* were members of the court nobility.[74] Courtly investment in tax farming, it was widely believed, was an impediment to reform of the fiscal system. In October 1775, the Italian *Gazetta universale* reported that the controller general, Turgot, had presented the king with a plan to abolish the tax farms, a program that would not be easy to implement because "the greatest lords have interests in the finances."[75] The benefits the court nobility derived from tax farming were publicized in 1776 when, in the context of an attack on the administration of the abbé Terray, a list of the *croupes* attached to the General Farm was published.[76]

The claim was made increasingly in the 1770s that aristocracy was the principal source of luxury. This was one of the theses of Alexandre Deleyre's *Tableau de l'Europe* (1774), an assessment of the effects of colonial commerce on European life since the discovery of the New World. Deleyre offers a powerful defense of the benefits of commerce while suggesting that luxury is a consequence not of economic modernity but of social institutions that siphon the profits of commerce into the hands of a rent-seeking aristocracy. For Deleyre, the luxury that comes of commerce and manufactures is unambiguously a social good. The taste for luxury and comforts, he argues, creates an appetite for work that constitutes the principal strength of European states. The influx of money from international trade is a stimulus

73. Chaussinand-Nogaret, *French Nobility in the Eighteenth Century,* 102–3; Warren C. Scoville, *Capitalism and French Glassmaking, 1640–1789* (Berkeley and Los Angeles, 1950).

74. George T. Matthews, *The Royal General Farms in Eighteenth-Century France* (New York, 1958), 235–37.

75. *Gazetta universale,* no. 82 (14 October 1775), 650. Quoted in Franco Venturi, *The End of the Old Regime in Europe, 1768–1776: The First Crisis,* trans. R. Burr Litchfield (Princeton, 1989), 371.

76. Jean-Baptiste-Louis Coquereau, *Mémoires concernant l'administration des finances sous le ministère de M. l'abbé Terrai, contrôleur général* (London, 1776), 233–40; another edition of the same work also published in 1776 carries the title *Mémoires de l'abbé Terrai, contrôleur général, concernant sa vie, son administration, ses intrigues & sa chute; avec une relation de l'émeutte arrivée à Paris en 1775* (London, 1776). Robert Darnton lists it among the top ten illegal best-sellers of the eighteenth century. Robert Darnton, *The Forbidden Best-Sellers of Pre-Revolutionary France* (New York, 1995), 138.

to agriculture and domestic manufactures, and these manufactures lead to a more even distribution of wealth.[77] Often, however, when a nation grows rich through trade, Deleyre argues, those who hold the reigns of power manage to appropriate a considerable share of the benefits for themselves. It was not the economically active who were corrupted by the influx of mobile wealth from the New World, but the idle classes. Deleyre had the court nobility particularly in mind, observing that the idle rich gave themselves over to "luxury," "intrigue," and a "baseness that is called grandeur."[78] He condemned nobility when it served no useful social function: "Nobility is nothing but an odious distinction, when it is not founded on real services, truly useful to the state, such as defending the nation against invasions and conquest, and against the undertakings of despotism. It is only a precarious and often ruinous assistance when, after leading a soft and licentious life in the cities, it goes to lend a feeble defense to the country in the fleet or in the army, and returns to the court to beg for recompense for its cowardliness, places and honors outrageous and onerous for the People."[79]

Although it is clear that Deleyre has the court nobility in mind here, at other points in his argument his antipathy appears to extend toward the nobility in general. He makes some pointedly critical comments about provincial nobles in the course of his defense of manufactures and commerce. "A rich manufactory brings more comfort to a village," he observes, "than twenty chateâux of old hunting or fighting barons bring to a province."[80] Here Deleyre seems to echo the anti-noble remarks of Coyer or Plumard de Dangeul. But Deleyre could also sound like the marquis de Mirabeau. He insists on the primacy of agriculture in the national economy and demands a reform of the tax system to favor agriculture, along with the establishment of complete freedom of the grain trade.[81]

Deleyre's *Tableau de l'Europe* was not the only instance of anticourt sentiment spilling over into a criticism of the nobility as a whole. In an extended poem titled *Le luxe,* published in 1773, the chevalier Du Coudray, a minor man of letters, denounced the institution of nobility as an instrument of luxury:

77. Alexandre Deleyre, *Tableau de l'Europe, pour servir de supplément à l'Histoire philosophique & politique des établissements & du commerce des Européens dans les deux Indes* (Maastricht, 1774), 80, 89, 99.
78. Ibid., 80.
79. Ibid., 92.
80. Ibid., 101.
81. Ibid., 88, 93–94.

> La Noblesse est un mal par le Luxe introduit,
> Afin de mieux servir l'erreur qui la conduit.
> Hélas! que ne sont point les mortels téméraires,
> Pour usurper des noms souvent imaginaires.[82]

Du Coudray claims that he would esteem the nobility if they were "generous," "sublime," or "great"—that is, if they were really noble—but most nobles have nothing to offer in place of these virtues but "brilliant chimeras." His fundamental social dichotomy opposes useful and industrious citizens to the idle aristocratic rich:

> Nous naissons tous égaux, l'homme à l'homme est utile;
> Ce guerrier, ce Bourgeois, cet Artisan habile:
> L'un à l'autre engagés par de communs liens,
> S'entre-aidant tour à tour, sont les vrais citoyens,
> Et non pas ces frélons qui, dans leur indolence,
> De la soigneuse abeille usurpent la substance.[83]

What distinguishes the parasitic group most clearly from the true citizens is pomp—or as Du Coudray says in the following lines, "*éclat*":

> C'est chez l'Agriculteur, chez le Bourgeois tranquille,
> Le noble Campagnard, & l'artisan habile,
> Vivant presque ignorés, existans sans éclat,
> Qu'on trouve un citoyen colonne de l'Etat.[84]

I suggest that Du Coudray's text is more anti-aristocratic than anti-noble. He claims to hail from a provincial, military, noble family. He notes with pride that his father is the "Chevalier Seigneur du Coudray, du Plessis, & autres lieux."[85] His antipathy is directed not principally at the provincial nobility, who can be fitted without much difficulty into the categories "noble campagnard" or "guerrier" of which he heartily approves. It is those nobles whose nobility is a sign of wealth rather than a token of "virtue," or "merit,"

---

82. Alexandre-Jacques, chevalier Du Coudray, *Le luxe, poëme en six chants; orné de gravures, avec des notes historiques et critiques, suivi de poësies diverses* (Paris, 1773), 29–30.

83. Ibid., 30.

84. Ibid., 21.

85. Ibid., 132.

that he condemns. He singles out the marquis de Mirabeau as an example of the kind of noble he wishes was more typical of the order as a whole:

> ILLUSTRE MIRABEAU, citoyen vertueux,
> Toi, dont le sang répond au sang de tes aïeux;
> Politique éclairé, calculateur habile,
> Organe de Cérès, économiste utile.[86]

It is nevertheless significant that Du Coudray extends his criticisms to the nobility as a whole. In this respect, *Le luxe* was a harbinger of things to come.

Luxury, Political Economy, and the Prerevolutionary Crisis

In the course of the prerevolutionary crisis, the language of political economy proved an important resource for critics of the nobility. The abbé Sieyès and other champions of the political rights of the Third Estate found in political economic categories a ready and potent means to characterize the nobility as an alien and parasitic excrescence on society. In so doing, these critics drew upon both the anti-noble strain of political economy articulated by the Gournay circle in the 1750s and the idiom which flourished in the 1770s identifying court nobles as vectors of luxury. The attack on aristocracy unleashed in 1789 made little distinction between the thrifty provincial noble living on his estate and the courtly grandee wallowing in luxury. The old language of orders and estates lumped all nobles together as the Second Estate, and this idiom acquired renewed relevance when it came to be used to apportion political representation in 1788.[87] Moreover, when pamphleteers projected a rigid noble/non-noble distinction onto the language of political economy, a language in which luxury/agriculture had become a central duality, they inevitably mapped noble onto luxury and non-noble onto agriculture. One could hardly deny that agriculture was principally the business of peasants. The anonymous author of *Le dernier mot du tiers-état à la noblesse de France*, dated 23 December 1788, identified the Third Estate with the "farmers" and the "merchants" who created all the wealth of the kingdom, and counterposed them to nobles who did no work but nevertheless reaped the

86. Ibid., 35. The third part of the poem is dedicated to Mirabeau.
87. Colin Lucas, "Nobles, Bourgeois and the Origins of the French Revolution," *Past and Present* 60 (1973): 84–126.

treasure of the state.[88] The provincial nobility was pushed back into the same category as the court nobility—all parts of a group that consumed but did not work.

The same contrast was central to the comte de Volney's *Sentinelle du peuple,* a radical newspaper that pioneered criticism of nobles in the stormy waters of Breton politics. Volney used the traditional contrast between nobles who fight and commoners who work to establish an invidious distinction between the two estates. All of the arts useful and necessary for life are concentrated among the Third Estate while the nobles know nothing of them, Volney argued; nobles fight, but to defend their own privileges rather than for the sake of the *patrie.* He blamed the nobility for exclusive economic privileges and intrusive industrial regulations: is it not the gentlemen, by exclusions of all kinds, who chain our industry, he asked? He went on in the following issue to attack the "vicious inequality of wealth," blaming wealth for the intolerable pride of the nobility. He also turned his pen against financiers, advising his readers to "attack those rich commoners who aspire only to betray their Order: dismiss those corrupted men, who make of honor a price of finance." Volney turned traditional pro-noble ideology on its head, accusing nobles of excessive interest in money and insufficient attachment to honor: "Those French gentlemen, so jealous of honor, so free with their blood, we thought them avid for glory, [but] they were [avid] only for money: and for a little of that vile metal, they have set fire to their *patrie,* and preferred the loss of their Nation to the loss of their tyranny." [89]

The claim that the nobility was interested in money rather than honor—that is, that they were corrupted by luxury—was a central feature of the attack on the privileged late in 1788 and early in 1789. Jean-Baptiste Rougier de la Bergerie, a rising star of the Royal Agricultural Society in Paris, reverses some of the standard traits of the noble and the commoner, attributing to farmers qualities traditionally seen as noble traits, and attributing to nobles the excessive interest in money long considered a characteristic of the ignoble. The cultivator, he argues, is "always useful, always virtuous, always honest, always beneficent, always attached to his *patrie,* to his king."[90] He is always willing to spend his whole fortune and spill his blood for their glory and

---

88. Anon., *Le dernier mot du tiers-état à la noblesse de France* (n.p., 1788).

89. Constantin-Frédéric de Chasseboeuf, comte de Volney, *La sentinelle du peuple, aux gens de toutes professions, sciences, arts, commerce et métiers, composant le Tiers-Etat de la province de Bretagne,* nos. 1–5 (10 November–25 December 1788), 15, 18.

90. Jean-Baptiste Rougier de la Bergerie, *Recherches sur les principaux abus qui s'opposent aux progrès de l'agriculture* (Paris, 1788), 111.

interest. De la Bergerie implies that the modern nobility has been corrupted by an excessive interest in money: if you had proposed to a soldier that he become a tax farmer under the reign of Louis XIV, he would have been insulted, de la Bergerie claims, but today *chevaliers de Saint Louis* clamor for such positions.[91] Luxury was the critical failing of the nobility, according to Pierre-Laurent Berenger's *Les quatre états de la France.*[92] Calling for sumptuary legislation to reintroduce order and simplicity among nobles, Berenger argued that the nobility must be made to see that the way to win consideration was through virtue, not through dress.[93] Berenger leveled these charges within the context of a work that drew heavily on political economy: he attacked exclusive privileges and fiscalism as sources of rapid fortunes and destructive inequality; he warned about the poor state of the countryside and called for the encouragement of agriculture; and he condemned tax farmers, financiers, and the spending of the court.

Even more damning conclusions were drawn by the abbé Emmanuel-Joseph Sieyès, who emerged in 1789 as a leader of the Revolution. In his *Essai sur les privilèges* (1788), Sieyès suggested that, as a consequence of their luxury, nobles were more interested in money than non-nobles. According to Sieyès, "they are even more prone to give themselves over to that ardent passion, because the prejudice of their superiority inflames them ceaselessly to overdo their expenditure." While prejudice pushed nobles to spend, Sieyès argued, it cut them off from almost all honest ways to replenish their fortunes. Considerations of honor actually restrained nobles less than commoners, he suggested, because, being born with honor, it was difficult for them to lose it. As a consequence, "intrigue" and "beggary" had become the "industry" of the nobility.[94] Sieyès went on in his *Qu'est-ce que le tiers-état?* (1789) to define the nobility out of the nation altogether on the grounds of its economic uselessness.[95]

91. Ibid., 8. He suggests that the "zealous cultivator" ought to enjoy as much consideration as the "true gentleman." The nobility founded on the residence of a non-noble in a *seigneurie*, on the establishment of a manufacture, or on land reclamation, he argues, "ought without doubt to be preferable to the commonplace variety conferred by so many vain and useless offices" (109–10).

92. Pierre-Laurent Berenger, *Les quatre états de la France* (n.p., 1789).

93. For another example of the equation of luxury with nobility, see Pierre-Toussaint Durand de Maillane's diatribe against luxury, *La noblimanie,* published on 25 February 1789, which laid the blame for luxury squarely on nobles. Pierre Toussaint Durand de Maillane, *La noblimanie* (n.p., 1789).

94. Emmanuel-Joseph Sieyès, *Essai sur les privilèges* (Paris, 1788), 32–33.

95. Emmanuel-Joseph Sieyès, *Qu'est-ce que le tiers-état?* (Paris, 1789), chap. 1. On this point, see also William H. Sewell Jr., *A Rhetoric of Bourgeois Revolution: The Abbé Sieyes and 'What Is the Third Estate?'* (Durham, 1994), 66–108.

I hope it will be clear to the reader that it was not a foregone conclusion that political economy should be used to write the nobility out of the nation. This economic language was not inherently and essentially a framework that would exclude nobles from an important role in society. Certainly, since the 1750s, some French political economists had used political economy to criticize the role of the nobility in French society. Such writers as Véron de Forbonnais, Plumard de Dangeul, and Coyer outlined political economic positions suggesting that noble corporate distinctiveness, and the cultural attitudes associated with the nobility, were inimical to the national welfare. In response to such arguments, however, nobles, beginning with the marquis de Mirabeau, elaborated new political economic perspectives that were far more favorably disposed toward the nobility. These new political economies emphasized the centrality of agriculture, and thus of landowners, to national prosperity and power and gave powerful validation to the provincial nobility's anti-luxury ethic. Philo-agricultural political economists diverged on the precise role of the nobility. In the course of his own literary career, Mirabeau had argued in favor of reinvigorating a society of orders, whereas later, as a physiocrat, he offered nobles a chance to insert themselves into the commercial life of the nation only on the same basis as other large landowners. The Achilles' heel of the nobility proved to be its own topmost stratum, the court nobility. These grandees, distinguished from the rest of the nobility by their wealth, had formed an alliance with financiers over the course of the eighteenth century. This alliance left court nobles, and ultimately the whole of the Second Estate, vulnerable to the charge that *nobles* were the principal carriers and disseminators of luxury, a charge widely directed against the nobility in the late 1780s.

II

NOBILITY AND POLITICAL CULTURE

5

NOBLE TAX EXEMPTION AND THE LONG-TERM
ORIGINS OF THE FRENCH REVOLUTION:
THE EXAMPLE OF PROVENCE, 1530S TO 1789

Rafe Blaufarb

On the last day of 1787, a solemn procession filed into the Collège Royal Bourbon in Aix-en-Provence.[1] Composed of 19 high-ranking prelates, 128 fief-holding *gentilshommes* (nobles), and 58 municipal dignitaries representing the 36 privileged communities and 22 *vigueries* of the province, the gathering marked the first time since their suspension in 1639 that the estates of Provence had met. In reconvening the estates (or restoring the constitution of the province, as some local commentators put it), the royal government believed it was satisfying "the desire of all the Orders" of the "Provençal nation." In return, the king expected its grateful representatives to employ not merely their "zeal" and "*lumières*" on behalf of his financially ailing kingdom, but, more important, to place their not insubstantial "credit" at its disposal.[2] But hope that the assembly would settle down to work and expeditiously grant the crown's demands—especially the request for a three-million-*livre* loan expressed in the very first article of the royal *cahier*—faded as its sessions degenerated into a spate of squabbling over ancient rights and prerogatives. Many of these disputes were of the internecine variety, pitting aggrieved deputies against their own order. The marquis de Trans, for example,

---

1. A detailed account of the events described in the following paragraph may be found in Monique Cubells, *Les horizons de la liberté: naissance de la révolution en Provence, 1787–1789* (Aix-en-Provence, 1987).

2. Opening discourse of the comte de Caraman, the royal military governor of Provence, in *Procès-verbal de l'assemblée de nosseigneurs des états-généraux du pays et comté de Provence* (Aix, 1788), 7–8.

claimed precedence over the other deputies of the Second Estate on the grounds that his marquisate, erected in 1505, made him the "first marquis of France." Claims over rank also split the Third Estate, from which, for example, the deputies of Marseille withdrew in a huff when the estates placed them after the Arlesian deputation.[3]

But more ominous than the petty infighting was the increasingly determined opposition of the Third Estate to the composition of the estates, which by allowing every fief-holding *gentilhomme* to attend personally, gave the noble order an invincible majority. When its appeals for reform along Dauphinois lines failed to sway the nobility, the Third Estate resolved to take more forceful action. When the still unreformed estates were reconvened in January 1789 to designate the Provençal delegation to the Estates-General, the Third Estate deputies paralyzed the proceedings by denouncing their illegitimacy, refusing to constitute themselves as an order, and declining to participate. They also began to voice more sweeping calls for change. Their demands included allowing members of the lower clergy and non-fief-holding nobility to represent their respective orders in the estates of Provence, composing the Third Estate delegation more democratically, abolishing clerical and noble fiscal privilege, and convoking the Estates-General. Little in this would have struck contemporaries as unorthodox or terribly original. As it was unfolding in Provence, the political crisis known as the "prerevolution" seemed to be following a familiar pattern.

Yet the familiar elements in this drama were accompanied by unfamiliar ones whose importance has been overlooked. One of these was the Third Estate's demand for authorization to appoint a syndic. Although historians have largely ignored it, this issue was as crucial to politically engaged Provençaux in 1787–89 as the better-known ones of fiscal equality, the Estates-General, and political representation. The Third Estate had first called for a syndic on 2 January 1788, even before the provincial estates had verified deputies' credentials and resolved the precedence disputes. The commission that finally considered the request split along social lines, with all of its ecclesiastical and seigneurial members recommending that the full assembly refuse to deliberate on it. The Third Estate did not give up. For the next sixteen months, its leaders took every opportunity (in further sessions of the estates, meetings of the provincial executive council, assemblies of the *vigueries* and town councils, petitions to the royal government, and even protests registered

3. These incidents may be found in ibid., 29–31 and 34–35.

with notaries) to call for a syndic.[4] When the royal government's *bureau des états* (the bureau charged with dealing with the provincial estates) considered the troubles of Provence on 26 December 1788, the first item on its agenda was the syndic.[5] And in spite of their weighty occupations, even the parish and *bailliage* assemblies that met at the end of the following March to prepare for the Estates-General continued to press the issue. Of 187 surviving cahiers, 102 demanded a syndic.[6] This issue was surpassed in frequency only by fiscal equality (163), legal reform (137), internal customs frontiers (125), meritocracy (121), the salt tax (120), venality (113), and *lettres de cachet* (107). It appeared more frequently than such classic issues of national import as periodic meetings of the Estates-General (84), vote by head in that body (61), and liberty of the press (55). Finally, it seems to have surpassed all other specifically provincial demands, including equal representation between the Third Estate and privileged orders in the estates of Provence (100), reform of the Provençal constitution (79), and representation in their respective orders for the lower clergy and non-fief-holding nobles (78). In spite of this evidence, however, the most recent history of the prerevolution in Provence devotes it less than one line of analysis, describing it vaguely as a manifestation of the Third Estate's desire for "participation in the affairs of the province."[7] It is difficult to integrate the Third-Estate's archaic-sounding call for a syndic into the accepted narrative of the political crisis of 1787–89, as it is dominated by the more forward-looking, familiar themes of liberty, equality, and representation. But rather than cast it aside because it does not fit into the standard account, we should recognize that for this very reason the call for a syndic is a clue that can lead us to new ways of understanding the period and assessing its significance. Indeed, it may even raise such fundamental questions about the very notion of a prerevolution that it forces us to place the French monarchy's terminal crisis in a different analytical and narrative frame.

At the time, the royal government certainly felt that the issue of the syndic was central to the troubles of the province. From a series of reports it commissioned in 1788, it learned that the Third Estate wanted a syndic

---

4. For a typical example, see "Motifs et raisons pour obtenir la permission de nommer un syndic des communautés," in *Procès-verbal de l'assemblée générale des gens du Tiers-état, mai 1788* (Aix, 1788), 55–63.

5. Archives Nationales, Paris (henceforth A.N.), H^1 1240, "Precis de la conférence tenue chez M. Coster le vendredi 26 Xbre 1788."

6. This analysis is based on that furnished by Cubells, *Horizons,* 136–39.

7. Ibid., 20.

so badly because this official would have the authority to litigate on its behalf without first receiving the approval of the noble-dominated estates of Provence.[8] The Third Estate was so concerned with retaining a capacity for independent legal action, the government was told, because it was determined to resist recent attempts by the seigneurial nobility to revoke the royal declaration of 24 May 1783, which had confirmed the right of communities to buy back a certain type of tax-exempt property from their seigneurs. Finally, the government was informed that the current clash over the declaration of 1783 was just the latest battle in a war the Third Estate had been waging against the seigneurial nobility's fiscal privileges for 250 years. Known to contemporaries as the *Procès des Tailles,* this succession of distinct but interconnected legal battles raised fundamental questions about the nature, extent, and workings of noble tax exemption. From the outset, royal rulings tended to favor the Third Estate by restricting the growth and undermining the legal foundations of the nobility's exemptions. Over the course of the eighteenth century, the crown and Third Estate forged an alliance to bring more and more noble land into the tax pool. Despite the occasional minor victory, the general trend had become all too clear to the nobles of Provence by the middle of the century. Particularly unfavorable royal interventions in the 1770s and 1780s—a period when the state's appetite for noble taxes reached new heights—drove them to a state of desperation. It was at this juncture that the final crisis of absolutism, misleadingly termed the "prerevolution", gave them an opportunity to alter the balance of power in the province and salvage their battered privileges. Situated in this historical context, the one the royal government believed to be pertinent, the prerevolution in Provence appears not as a new departure, but rather as the latest act in a long-running political drama.

The *réalité* of the *taille*—the practice of assigning tax liability and exemption to property rather than persons—was not a timeless feature of the Provençal constitution, but an innovation imposed on the province in the mid-sixteenth

8. These reports, too numerous to cite individually, can be found in A.N., H[1] 1240. For a particularly succinct one, which explicitly situates the call for a syndic in the long-term historical context of the Third Estate's struggle against seigneurial tax exemption, see the anonymous report entitled "De la demande d'un syndic des communautés." This particular document warned that, if appointed, the syndic "will have no interest but to sow discord between the two orders, revive all suspended legal actions, and initiate new lawsuits at the slightest pretext." For an explicit statement linking the Third's demand for a syndic with the nobility's attempt to revoke the declaration of 1783, see A.N., H[1] 1240, "Lettre de M. de la Tour [to an unnamed bureaucrat, probably in the *bureau des états*]" (Versailles, 11 décembre 1788).

century by its sovereign count, the king of France. Before this time, the rationale of tax exemption in the province had been murky. Seigneurs generally claimed immunity for their lands, although usually only within the confines of their fiefs, in consideration of the public service they were required to provide. The municipal elites of the province did not always accept these claims, especially when applied to land a seigneur had recently acquired from a *roturier* (non-noble) who had until then paid taxes on it. To stop this practice and halt the erosion of the tax base, the commissioners responsible for carrying out the provincewide estimation of taxable property (*affouagement*) in 1471 issued an ordinance directing seigneurs to pay the *taille* on *roturier* land they acquired, even if such land lay in their fief.[9] Although the anti-seigneurial thrust of the ordinance suggests that the burden of taxation was already beginning to make itself felt in the province, it was not yet heavy enough to prompt the communities to make serious attempts to compel their lords to pay. It was simply less costly and acrimonious for a community to absorb its lord's quota than to pursue legal action against him. But as the rate of taxation rose during the first half of the sixteenth century, communities began to find it in their financial interest to press the issue.[10] Instead of prompting unified provincial resistance, growing royal fiscal demands underlined the contrast between lordly and bourgeois views of tax exemption and set the two groups on a collision course.

The 1530s and 1540s saw the proliferation of litigation—reportedly resulting in more than 300 pending lawsuits—in which communities challenged the tax exemptions claimed by their lords.[11] In 1548 the king consolidated the lawsuits pending between Provençal communities and their lords and evoked the whole matter to the *parlement* of Paris for "sovereign decision" to determine the underlying principles of noble tax exemption in Provence.[12] This marked the beginning of the legal war that was still raging in 1789 to form the *longue durée* historical backdrop to the political crisis of 1787–89. To defend their interests, the fief-holding *gentilshommes* of the

---

9. Bibliothèque Méjanes, Aix-en-Provence (henceforth B.M.), MS 729 (825), "Ordonnance des commissaires du réaffouagement général de toutes les villes et lieux de la province, portant entre autres que les seigneurs de fief avec juridiction payeroient la taille des biens roturiers qu'ils acquereront, quoique dans l'étendu de leur fief, si ce n'est que tels biens leur fussent obtenus par leur droit de fief, conformément à l'ordonnance du Roi René de 1448" (1471).

10. B.M., MS 723 (610), "Administration du pays de Provence," vol. 3, "Compensation des biens nobles avec les biens roturiers."

11. This figure is from Jean Papon, *Nouvelle et cinquième édition du recueil d'arrests notables de cours souveraines de France* (Lyon, 1569), 391.

12. Ibid., 329.

province obtained *lettres patentes* in October 1548 allowing them to incorporate under the misleadingly broad name *corps de la noblesse*.[13] For its part, the Third Estate already enjoyed corporate existence through the *corps des communautés,* an ancient body in which a handful of urban elites represented the thirty-six privileged communities of the province in periodic *assemblées générales des communautés.* It nonetheless deemed it necessary to appoint a syndic to lead its legal team. One can thus say that the Second and Third Estate of Provence both acquired their distinctive corporate identities in the course of a bitter legal fight over taxation.[14] Although the clergy and magistracy took part in the proceedings too, the first securing exemption for the lands it had possessed since 1471 and the second failing to win its case, the trial crystallized into a direct confrontation between the *noblesse* and the *communautés.*

In 1549 the *parlement* of Paris began to hear arguments.[15] The *noblesse* claimed tax exemption for all the land lords acquired in their seigneuries, while the communities asserted that lords had no right to transmit their exemption to formerly tax-paying lands they acquired, even if those lands lay within their fiefs. Following the recommendation of the royal advocate, Marillac, the *parlement* ruled in favor of the communities, declaring Provence

13. B.M., MS 726 (822), "Précis des registres de la noblesse de Provence, dont le premier commence en l'année 1549 et finit en 1624, et le second suit en l'année 1625 jusqu'à la présente année 1731." The fief-holding nobility's choice of this name for its *corps* is significant. By appropriating the name of a recognized order of society, the seigneurs sought to lend an imposing air of legitimacy to their self-interested agenda. Similarly, its opponent, the *assemblée générale des communautés,* which represented only a handful of privileged towns, used various names—the Third Estate, the province, the estates, the *gens des trois états,* or simply the *pays*—to cloak the fact that it too represented a narrow, self-serving cause. In related moves, both the *noblesse* and *communautés* sought to discredit their respective opponents by refusing to use their self-appointed names and instead addressing them in ways that made explicit their circumscribed social composition and narrow material interests. The *communautés* routinely dismissed the *noblesse* as nothing more than the "corps of Messieurs the fief-holders." The *noblesse* responded in kind, calling the *communautés* the "administrators of taxable property." This Provençal name game illustrates James Collins's observation that classes in early modern France frequently employed the rhetoric of order to defend their class interests. See James B. Collins, *Classes, Estates, and Orders in Early Modern Brittany* (Cambridge, 1994), 11–12. For the citations, see Archives départementales des Bouches-du-Rhône, Marseille (henceforth B.d.R.), C 110, "Registre des délibérations de la noblesse de Provence," "Assemblée particulière" (4 juillet 1759); and B.d.R., C 949, "Mémoire et consulation pour la noblesse" (6 novembre 1769).

14. Law, particularly tax law, was no mere reflection of the material interests of dominant groups. It was also constitutive of those groups. To take the example above, the *corps de la noblesse* acquired its distinctive social contours—notably the exclusion from its ranks of all members of the Second Estate who did not possess fiefs—from the evolving legal framework of taxation and tax exemption.

15. For a detailed account of the pleadings, see Papon, *Nouvelle et cinquième édition du recueil,* 329–92.

to be a *pays de taille réelle* in which land that had once paid taxes was to be considered as having contracted an ineffaceable stain of *roture*.[16] Explicitly linking the nobility of land to seigneurial authority, the *parlement* ruled on 6 March 1549 that only land held by lords with jurisdiction attached would be considered noble and exempt. All other land would be considered *roturier* and taxable. Confirmed by a subsequent ruling of the *parlement* in 1552, this decision was enshrined as the basis of Provençal fiscal jurisprudence by the royal *arrêt* of 15 December 1556. In addition, this law defined as noble all property possessed with jurisdiction by seigneurs on 15 December 1556, and it defined all other land as *roturier*.[17]

This legislation established Provence as a *pays de taille réelle*. Praised by contemporaries as the most equitable of all fiscal regimes because, in fixing immunity to specific parcels of land, it halted the spread of exemptions and thus resulted in lighter taxes for all property, this system also won the praise of later observers. One of these, Alexis de Tocqueville, even suggested that, had it been generalized throughout France, the bitterness generated by the better-known northern system of personal exemption for nobles might have been defused and the Revolution avoided.[18] In the case of Provence, however, the laws of 1549, 1552, and 1556 instituted two distinctive features which made its specific variant of the *taille réelle* an unparalleled source of division for the next 240 years. The first of these peculiarities, evidently unique in France, concerned the conditions under which noble land could retain its tax exemption. In Provence noble land had to be possessed with

16. The *parlement*'s "provisional decision" of 6 March 1549 was confirmed by a definitive ruling of 5 September 1552. This ruling, in turn, was confirmed by a ruling of the royal council that served as the fundamental law in matters of Provençal taxation until 1789. See *Arrest du conseil privé, donné entre le syndic du commun peuple et Tiers Estat du pays de Provence et le syndic delegué par les nobles, vassaux, et sujets de Sa Majesté audit pays, le 15 décembre 1556.*

17. B.M., MS 729 (825), "Arrest du parlement de Paris du 5 septembre 1552, entre le clergé, la noblesse, les officiers, et le tiers état de Provence, touchant la compensation des biens nobles"; *Arrest du conseil privé, donné entre le syndic du commun peuple et Tiers Estat du pays de Provence et le syndic delgué par les nobles, vassaux, et sujets de Sa Majesté audit pays, le 15 décembre 1556.*

18. Alexis de Tocqueville, "Appendix: The *pays d'états,* with special reference to Languedoc," in *The Old Regime and the French Revolution,* trans. Stuart Gilbert (New York, 1955), 212–21. In his monumental work on Languedoc, Georges Frêche echoes Tocqueville's glowing assessment. He mentions in passing, however, a "struggle against noble lands" waged by Languedocien communities throughout the seventeenth and eighteenth centuries, but devotes only one page to it. Georges Frêche, *Toulouse et la région Midi-Pyrénées au siècle des lumières (vers 1670–1789)* (Paris, 1976), 405–6. Robert Forster does not mention the issue in his book *The Nobility of Toulouse in the Eighteenth Century: A Social and Economic Study* (Baltimore, 1960). Nor does William Beik's more recent book, *Absolutism and Society in Seventeenth-Century France: State Power and Provincial Aristocracy in Languedoc* (Cambridge, 1985).

jurisdiction to sustain its exemption. If anyone other than its seigneur—
even a lord with jurisdiction over a different fief—acquired a parcel of
noble land, it would become liable to taxation. This restriction negated
the benefits Tocqueville perceived in the *taille réelle* by making personal
status critical to tax exemptions and associating those exemptions with a
distinct social group, the *corps de la noblesse.*

The second peculiarity, also unique in France, was known as the right of
compensation. This allowed lords who alienated a parcel of noble land—
thus making it taxable—to indemnify themselves by removing from the
cadastre an equivalent parcel of *roturier* land they already possessed or would
later acquire within the confines of their fiefs. First broached at the close of
the 1549 trial in Paris and subsequently agreed upon by noble and Third
Estate negotiators at a conference held in Aix in January 1553, compensation offered what seemed at the time to be a mutually acceptable solution
to their sharp differences over the question of exemption.[19] Confirmed by
the royal *arrêt* of 1556, this compromise not only promised an end to the
contestations agitating the province, but also had the great advantage of
keeping the tax base intact. All parties would be satisfied—the lords because
they could exempt coveted *roturier* lands they acquired within their fief, the
communities because the resulting loss would be made up by the insertion
of an equivalent parcel of noble land into the *cadastre,* the province because
the tax base from which it had to meet expenses would suffer no further
erosion, and the king because he would henceforth receive regular payments
from a tranquil province. In practice, however, compensation reintroduced
a destabilizing element of mobility to seigneurial tax exemptions, opened the
door to fraud, and drew lords and communities into new conflicts.

Even without the right of compensation, it is likely that tax-related conflict
was inevitable in the province. In contrast to Tocqueville, I would argue
that in *pays d'états,* where *tailles* were *réelles* and paid by *abonnement* (annual
lump-sum payments), there existed greater potential for internecine conflict
than in the *pays d'élections,* where older, collective imposts were being
supplanted by direct taxes that only struck individuals.[20] By demarcating
two distinct pools of land, one exempt and the other responsible for the
entire provincial *abonnement,* the *réelle/état* combination established a structural

19. B.M., MS 732 (828), "Recueil des délibérations des états depuis l'année 1523 jusques en
1554," "Assemblée des quelques gentilshommes et communautés à Aix" (janvier 1553).
20. Michael Kwass discusses the gradual shift in one *pays d'élection,* Normandy, from the
older, *solidaire* taxes like the *taille* to direct taxes like the *dixième* and *vingtième.* Michael Kwass,
Privilege and the Politics of Taxation in Eighteenth-Century France (Cambridge, 2000).

opposition between the tax-immune and tax-liable. In Provence this fiscal regime drew the *communautés* into a vicious tug-of-war with the *noblesse*. From the perspective of the *communautés,* the more land made exempt and removed from the tax pool, the more each remaining parcel would have to contribute to the lump sum demanded annually by the king. Conversely, the more land stripped of its exemption and subjected to taxation, the less each parcel would have to pay. It was this zero-sum logic that drove the *communautés* to take legal action to prevent the growth of the pool of exempt land and, if possible, find ways of diminishing this pool to their own profit.[21]

For their part, the *noblesse* had an obvious interest in combating any legal decision that might establish a precedent fatal to their exemptions. But in addition to this, they had a strong financial motive to mount a collective defense of their exemptions. Noble land had always been subjected to a variety of fiscal obligations, not least of which was the cost of defending against Third Estate lawsuits.[22] Other, even heavier charges began to multiply during the reign of Louis XIV. For the first time in French history, this monarch imposed taxes that even the nobility (and noble land) were required to pay. Of course, as Provence was a *pays d'état,* these charges did not strike

21. The attempts of the *communautés* to restrict the spread of tax exemption were unceasing; preserving the integrity of the tax base was their principal raison d'être and primary occupation. Increases in the tax burden, particularly those which resulted from the imposition of new direct taxes in the eighteenth century, tended to provoke both new efforts on the part of individuals and *corps* to claim exemptions and greater determination on the part of the *communautés* to block these claims. In the 1750s, a turbulent time that saw the introduction of the *vingtième,* as well as menacing moves by the *contrôleur-général* Machault to collect it directly in the province, legal conflict over tax exemption reached a new high. During this decade, the *communautés* undertook legal action to nullify the claims to exemption advanced by a procession of individuals and *corps*: the military officers in garrison at Toulon, the *curé* of Cassis, the *nobles verriers,* the *compagnie des Indes,* the engineers enlarging the port of Antibes, and the Princes of the Blood for the *roturier* land they possessed in the province. In each instance, the *communautés* prevailed. Over the course of the preceding century, other powerful groups had also been thwarted in their claims to exemption: ecclesiastics, religious houses, and the Knights of Malta (1661), secretaries and officers of the provincial chancelleries (1707), employees of the *Fermes* (1713), and army troops on the march or in garrison (1719). B.d.R., C 76, 78, and 80, "Registres des délibérations de la province" (1744–62).

22. These fiscal obligations were too numerous, varied, and complicated to discuss at any great length here. Suffice it to say that, even before the creation of the new direct taxes from which noble land was not exempted, the *corps de la noblesse* had to pay a range of *abonnements* to protect the integrity of its fiefs. By using some of the same techniques it employed to extract money from the *corps* of venal office holders—the creation of new offices (in the courts of the *seigneuries*), the imposition of various surtaxes on transfers of feudal property, and *recherches de fief* similar to the infamous *recherches de noblesse*—the royal government was able to derive substantial revenue from the institution of feudalism. And, as with venal office holding, its financial usefulness to the crown helps explain its continuing vigor.

the seigneurs directly, but were converted into a lump-sum payment the *noblesse* was required to furnish. To meet all these expenses, the *noblesse* levied annual taxes on the pool of noble land by an internal assessment procedure (*afflorinement*) similar to the province's *affouagement*. By the late seventeenth century, therefore, the province's fiscal landscape was dominated by two great masses of land, each associated with a distinct social group, each encumbered with a specific set of tax liabilities, and each with a direct financial interest in expanding at the other's expense.[23] When injected into this inherently conflictual structure, the right of compensation produced a series of sharp legal clashes—the *Procès des Tailles*.

Although the right of compensation was intended to maintain an exact balance between noble and non-noble land in the province, it opened the door to fraud by permitting tax exemption to be transferred from one parcel of land to another. The *arrêt* of 1556, it is true, carefully defined the conditions under which this right could be invoked, but seigneurs found that they could abuse it to increase their exempt holdings. The varieties of subterfuge they employed are too numerous—and by nature too covert—to detail fully. Several examples will suffice to give an idea of how these power-ful local figures could turn compensation to their own advantage.[24] With the compliance of allied or intimidated municipal officials, lords could give worthless noble lands such as rocky hilltops or shifting fluvial sand bars in compensation for rich *roturier* farmland and vineyards. They could also connive with estimators to overstate the value of a parcel of alienated noble land and understate that of the non-noble land exempted from taxes in compensa-tion for it. Or a lord could grant noble land in his fief to a front man (thus making it taxable) who would then deliberately default on his obligations. This permitted the lord to exempt an equivalent parcel of *roturier* land in his

23. Here I am deliberately overstating the social homogeneity of the two groups in order to underline my point about the potential for conflict inherent in the structure of the *taille réelle* regime of Provence. In fact, most *gentilshommes seigneurs* owned *roturier* land on which they paid taxes. Indeed, some possessed more *roturier* than noble land; these lords would have found their financial interests better served by the *communautés* than the *noblesse*. In addition, there were a number of *roturier seigneurs*, but it is unlikely that they would have identified closely with the *corps de la noblesse* since it denied them a voice in the collective affairs of the *corps*, even while taxing them for their fiefs.

24. These examples are taken from a report submitted to the royal council by the *intendant*, Cardin Lebret, around 1700. B.M., MS 729 (825), "Extrait du verbal de contestation dressé par le sieur Le Bret sur l'article du droit de compensation, entre les syndics de la noblesse et le Tiers Etat, avec la réponse des syndics de la noblesse."

possession in compensation for the original alienation, as well as reclaim the abandoned parcel of alienated noble land and reunite it nobly to his fief through the feudal right of *déguerpissement*.[25] Even when conducted legally, compensation could wreak havoc on municipal financial planning. Since the *arrêt* of 1556 did not stipulate a statute of limitations for compensation claims, it was not uncommon to find seigneurs in the eighteenth century scouring ancient records to discover noble lands that had been alienated without compensation in the second half of the sixteenth. This uniquely Provençal variant on the feudal reaction allowed lords to exempt from taxation lands on which communities had long depended to contribute to the common fiscal burden. To believe the reiterated complaints of the *communautés,* fraudulent and delayed compensations had been rampant in the century following the 1549 ruling by the Paris *parlement*. If not checked, they warned, these practices would so diminish the pool of taxable land that individual proprietors would be ruined and the province would no longer be able to pay its annual sum to the king.

Until the middle of the seventeenth century, the *communautés* had no effective way of defending their collective interests. When not in league with or cowed by their lords, the municipal councils of the communities of Provence had to stand alone against feudal usurpations. While many were dissuaded, some did bring legal action to overturn fraudulent compensations. But these lawsuits were costly and might have to be repeated generation after generation. Even when successful, legal victories obtained by isolated communities over their lords rarely had a provincewide impact and thus did little to check the erosion of the overall tax base through fraudulent compensations. In 1639 this situation changed dramatically. In that year, after threats to establish *élections* in the province, Richelieu instead suspended indefinitely the estates of Provence and transferred its authority to the *assemblée générale des communautés*.[26] Richelieu's reform radically altered the local balance of power. Now able to take legal action in the name of the entire province, the municipal elites who dominated the *assembleé générale* were henceforth

---

25. Although unfamiliar territory to most present-day historians of early modern France, the feudal procedure of *déguerpissement* was considered important enough in the seventeenth and eighteenth centuries to merit extensive treatment by jurists. Of these, the best known was Charles Loyseau, who devoted one of his five celebrated law books to it. See his, *Oeuvres de Maistre Charles Loyseau, avocat en Parlement, contenant les cinq livres du droit des offices, les traitez des seigneuries, des ordres et simples dignitez, du déguerpissement et delaissement par hypothèque, de la garantie des rentes, et des abus des justices de village* (Lyon, 1701).

26. B.M., F 733, "Mémoire sur le projet de rétablir les anciens états de Provence" (juillet 1787).

able to mount a concerted campaign against the right of compensation and ultimately seigneurial tax exemption itself.

The timing of the major provincial efforts in this regard—on the eve of *réaffouagements*—suggests one motive for the assault on seigneurial exemptions: to divert attention from the inequitable distribution of taxes *within* the pool of *roturier* property.[27] Some towns, particularly Aix, were more favored than others, but all towns were less heavily taxed than the countryside. In the course of the surveying operations ordered by the royal government in the 1660s, the *affouageurs* (exclusively municipal elites from the most privileged towns) claimed to have discovered widespread evidence of fraudulent compensations executed by seigneurs to the detriment of their communities.[28] In submitting the results of the survey to the king for approval, the *assemblée générale* of January 1666 requested in return that he aid the overcharged taxpayers of the province by abolishing the right of compensation.[29] The king responded with rare alacrity. The following month he issued a declaration not only forbidding future compensations but also imposing on Provence a system of tax exemption similar to that observed in neighboring Languedoc.[30] Henceforth, noble land would retain its tax exemption even if detached from seigneurial jurisdiction. With the respective pools of *roturier* and noble land fixed forever, there would be no more erosion of the tax base, no more fraudulent compensations, and no more costly lawsuits.

27. The *noblesse* had made this charge as early as 1549, in the initial trial before the *parlement* of Paris. Papon, *Nouvelle et cinquième édition du recueil,* 373.

28. Because the municipal elites who now controlled the provincial administration benefited from the existing repartition, they had little interest in updating the old *affouagement* of 1471— still in force when Louis XIV assumed personal rule in 1661. The king was convinced that a new survey would allow him to squeeze more revenue out of the province. The complaints of several less-favored towns about inequalities in the distribution of the tax burden furnished him with an ideal pretext to force the issue. By threatening to transform Provence into a *pays d'élection,* station unprecedented numbers of troops in the province, impose a new salt tax by armed force, and conduct the survey with its own officials, the royal government finally forced the *assemblée générale* to undertake a new *affouagement.* On the tense negotiations between crown and province over the *affouagement,* see the deliberations of the *assemblée générale des communautés* from 1660 through 1665. B.d.R., C 39, "Registre des délibérations de la province" (juillet 1658–octobre 1661) and C 41, "Registre des délibérations de la province" (3 novembre 1661–décembre 1665).

29. B.d.R., C 2071, "Cahier des remontrances" (1666), article 2.

30. *Déclaration du roi, sur la fixation des biens nobles et roturiers, sur l'établissement des dixains ou douzains des fruits, droits de bouvage, fourage et autres; et sur l'affranchissement des biens roturiers du payement des tailles* (Saint-Germain, février 1666). The *taille réelle* regime of Languedoc remained ill-defined until 1684, when the royal government finally issued a definitive ruling on it. See the *Déclaration du Roi du 9 octobre 1684, portant règlement sur la nobilité des fonds et heritages en la province de Languedoc.*

The *noblesse* wasted no time in opposing the declaration. In October 1666 it ordered its syndics to block its registration by the *cour des comptes* of Aix and named commissioners to reach "a reasonable accommodation" with the provincial administrators.[31] When negotiations broke down, the *noblesse* readied itself for a new clash with the *communautés*. It levied extraordinary taxes upon the fiefs to amass a war chest and appointed a skilled lawyer, Gaillard, to take charge of the case. A pragmatist, Gaillard realized that legal argument alone was unlikely to convince the royal government to revoke a law that furthered its own fiscal interests. Only by presenting the king with a more alluring prospect of financial gain could the seigneurs restore the socially exclusive, seigneurial basis of noble land and recover the right of compensation that allowed them to structure more profitable tax-exempt domaines—if not actually increase the mass of exempt land in their possession by fraud or otherwise. To this end, Gaillard persuaded the plenary meeting of the *corps de la noblesse* held in January 1668 to offer Louis XIV 300,000 *livres* to revoke the declaration. To end once and for all the abuse of power by the openly partisan *assemblée générale des communautés,* the *noblesse* also demanded the restoration of the old estates of Provence, a theoretically neutral body that was in fact dominated by the fief-holding nobility.[32] Accepting the bribe later that year, the king issued an *arrêt* on 15 June 1668 restoring the former fiscal regime, including the right of compensation, albeit with new safeguards to prevent abuses.[33] He did not, however, agree to reconvene the estates.

The *assemblée générale des communautés* did not regard this defeat as definitive but continued to press for the declaration of 1666.[34] In January 1680 it finally extracted from the royal council an *arrêt* directing the *intendant* of Provence, Rouillé, to look into the matter and report back with his findings.[35] He neither

31. B.d.R., C 108, "Registre des délibérations de la noblesse de Provence," "Conférence tenue à Aix dans la maison de M. maitre Scipion du Perrier, advocat de la Cour, l'un des sieurs syndics de la noblesse" (22 octobre 1666), and "Conférence tenue dans la maison de M. du Perrier, syndic de la noblesse, touchant les trois procès que le corps de ladite noblesse a contre les lieutenants, procureurs du pays, et le clergé, portant imposition d'un cote pour subvenir à la poursuite d'iceux" (26 mars 1667).

32. Ibid., "Assemblée générale de la noblesse" (26 janvier 1668); and B.M., MS 815 (838), "Mémoires dressés par MM. de la noblesse ensuite des déclarations du Roi contre eux" (1668).

33. *Arrest du Conseil qui maintient la noblesse du pays de Provence aux droits de compensation et aux exemptions des forains* (15 juin 1668). This *arrêt* was rendered on the report of Colbert. A.N., H¹1240, "Rapport pour le Roi fait en 1783 par M. Fortin touchant le Droit de Compensation en Provence et sur lequel est intervenu la Déclaration du 24 Mai 1783."

34. B.d.R., C 2072, "Cahier des remontrances" (1675).

35. *Extrait des régistres du Conseil d'Estat* (27 janvier 1680).

acted on this charge nor, apparently, came under pressure to do so. But in 1699, with another contentious *affouagement* under way, the embattled Aixois elites who dominated the provincial administration once again played the anti-seigneurial card to deflect criticism of their own fiscal privileges.[36] This attack on compensation received powerful backing from the new *intendant,* Cardin Lebret, who believed that seigneurial fraud was depriving the king of badly needed revenue. If not "promptly corrected," he warned *contrôleur-général* Pontchartrain, these abuses would so "diminish the property subject to taxation" that it would "force the abandonment of cultivation."[37] Royally mandated attempts by the provincial administration and *corps de la noblesse* to settle their differences amicably ended in acrimony, with allegations that seigneurial fraud was depriving the province of 100,000 *livres* each year and complaints about Lebret's "manifest penchant" for the Third Estate.[38] With the collapse of these negotiations in the summer of 1700, the question of compensation once again came before the royal council.[39]

On 7 February 1702 the council issued an *Arrest du conseil d'état du roy, servant de règlement entre le corps de la noblesse et celuy du tiers-état de Provence au sujet des tailles* intended to resolve the question of compensation once and for all. Exhaustively summarized in the forty-four-page document, the respective arguments of the two parties need not be inventoried here.[40] Although the *noblesse* initially viewed the ruling as a victory because it confirmed the legality of compensation, over the course of the century it would

36. A.N., G⁷464, "Lebret au contrôleur-général Pontchartrain" (Aix, 5 mars 1698). Once again, the *noblesse* claimed that the anti-seigneurial agitation of the *communautés* was a ploy to "appease the many communities" angry about the lack of "exact equality" in the new repartition. B.M., MS 729 (825), "Requête au Roi, du Syndic de la Noblesse, sur la Compensation et Qualité de Forain" (approximately 1698–1701).

37. A.N., G⁷464, "Lebret au contrôleur-général Pontchartrain" (4 décembre 1698).

38. Both figures and citation are from B.M., MS 729 (825), loose and untitled *mémoire* of the *noblesse* at the end of this register.

39. For accounts of these negotiations, see B.M., MS 729 (825), "Mémoire de ce qui s'est passé dans l'affaire qui est entre MM. de la noblesse et les sieurs procureurs du pays de Provence sur le fait de la compensation des biens nobles avec les roturiers, sur le droit de forain, etc., avec trois projets de règlement par la noblesse, par le tiers état, par les ministres" (1700); and B.d.R., 1 G 489, "Brière relation de ce qui s'est passé dans le traitté d'accommodement de l'affaire de la province contre Mᵣˢ les sindics de la noblesse." See also the relevant correspondence of Lebret and the comte de Grignan in A.N., G⁷464,

40. Many of the pleadings submitted to the royal council by the two parties can be found in B.M., MS 729 (825). A concise summary of their respective arguments is provided by the abbé de Coriolis, *Traité sur l'administration du comté de Provence* (Aix, 1786–88), vol. 3, pp. 326–37.

revise its opinion.[41] First, the regulation of 1702 established a notification procedure that seigneurs had to follow under pain of seeing their compensations nullified. Any lord desiring to carry out a compensation first had to inform the provincial administrators of his intention and furnish them with exact details of the exchange he wanted to make. If they found grounds to oppose the proposed compensation, the administrators could pursue legal action against the lord on behalf of and with the full might of the province.[42] Second, the regulation declared illegal all tax exemptions obtained by means other than a legal compensation. Thus encouraged, individual communities and even the province itself began to comb through old records looking for evidence of fraudulent compensations to contest. The prospect of having to engage in lengthy legal battles was enough to dissuade most lords from abusing the right of compensation and offered the province a powerful means of intimidation with which to cow the *noblesse*.

Finally, in its defense of the right of compensation, the *noblesse* invoked arguments that would ultimately be turned against their tax exemptions by sharp-minded lawyers of the Third Estate. So intent were they on combating the declaration of 1666 and any permanent fixation of the tax status of property that the lawyers of the *noblesse* failed to see the fatal implications of their principles.[43] According to the "jurisprudence invariably observed in Provence," they claimed, a parcel of noble land "alienated by the seigneur falls into *roture* and remains subject to the *taille*" even if only momentarily detached from "jurisdiction which is alone capable of upholding the exemption." By fixing the noble status of land and allowing non-seigneurs to enjoy its exemption, the declaration of 1666 had introduced a perverse

41. B.d.R., C 108, "Registre des délibérations de la noblesse de Provence," "Conférence" (25 février 1702).

42. To believe the complaints of the *noblesse,* the province deliberately used its authority to initiate lawsuits in the name of the collectivity to harass seigneurs and wear them down financially. Only an exhaustive study of tax-related legal actions in Provence could allow us to judge the validity of this charge. It was certainly true, however, that the province was determined to coordinate the formerly scattered efforts of the communities to oppose seigneurial usurpations and prevent complacent municipal councils from turning a blind eye to such abuses in their own neighborhood. On the *noblesse*'s accusations of harassment, see B.d.R., C 110, "Registre des délibérations de la noblesse de Provence," "Assemblée particulière" (9 janvier 1761). On the province's determination to coordinate the anti-seigneurial litigation of all the communities, see B.d.R., C 78, "Registre des délibérations de la province, 1752–1758," "Assemblée particulière" (5 août 1755).

43. Unless otherwise noted, all citations in this paragraph are from the "Moyens des Sindics de la Noblesse sur le droit de compensation" in the *Arrest du conseil d'état du roy, du septième février*

type of property—perverse because it enjoyed exemption from the *taille* without having to furnish personal service to the king. Perhaps property of this kind existed in other provinces, the lawyers of the *noblesse* observed, but this was irrelevant, "each *pays* having its own laws and customs which His Majesty and his Predecessor Kings have always had the goodness to maintain." In Provence, tax exemption had always been the privilege of land subjected to the obligation of feudal service. To sever this link would overthrow the "order established from time immemorial" in the province and sow the seeds of dangerous social confusion. "The unique advantage enjoyed today by the nobility is to possess *en franchise* these noble and feudal properties, in view of the jurisdiction which is attached to them."[44]

As the eighteenth century progressed, it dawned upon the provincial administrators—invariably lawyers themselves—that the *noblesse*'s refusal to countenance the existence of tax exemption apart from seigneurial jurisdiction actually worked in their favor.[45] Compensation certainly allowed seigneurs to exempt from the *taille roturier* land equivalent in value to noble land they had alienated. But compensation did not ennoble the *roturier* property it exempted since, according to the nobility's own arguments, land separated even momentarily from jurisdiction "irrevocably contracted the vice of *roture*" and "remained perpetually subject to the *taille*."[46] Because of this, *roturier* land that had been exempted from taxes by compensation could

---

1702, servant de reglement, entre le corps de la noblesse et celuy du tiers-état de Provence au sujet des tailles (Aix, 1702), 16–28.

44. B.d.R., C 110, "Registre des délibérations de la noblesse de Provence," "Mémoire pour la noblesse de Provence" (8 avril 1750). A protest against the introduction of the *vingtième,* this document mobilizes patrimonial—and even matrimonial arguments—to defend the tax exemption of noble land.

45. It took some time for this realization to sink in. The first reaction of the province to the regulation of 1702 was to issue strong protests and renew its calls for the declaration of 1666. For these initial remonstrations, see B.d.R., 1 G 489, "Remontrances des procureurs des gens des trois états de Provence contre les seigneurs féodataires de la dite province," and "Très humble remontrance faite au Roy pour les procureurs des gens des trois états de Provence contre les seigneurs de fiefs du mesme pais, au sujet de l'arrest rendu au Conseil d'Estat au mois de février 1702, non encore signiffié."

46. Jean-Joseph Julien, *Nouveau commentaire sur les statuts de Provence* (Aix, 1778), vol. 2, p. 155. Similar statements found in Julien's work include: "the property thus exempted is not noble and feudal; it is only free from the *taille*" (187) and "property that has already operated a compensation cannot operate a second one" (208). This principle had first been advanced in the mid-seventeenth century by Jacques Morgues, *Les statuts et coustumes du pays de Provence* (Aix, 1658), 359. For a more extended treatment of this question, see B.M., MS 729 (825), "Dissertation sur la question de savoir si un fonds affranchi de tailles et réuni au fief par voye de compensation, venant à être aliéné par le seigneur, sans juridiction, et rentrant dans le cadastre, dont il avoit été tiré, peut être donné en compensation."

not serve as material for a subsequent compensation, a right that pertained only to noble land. In practice, this meant that if a lord sold a parcel of land that had previously been exempted through compensation, not only would its exemption instantly cease, but, more important, its alienation could not be used to effect a compensation. In other words, two land sales and the original exemption would be forever extinguished without replacement. The implications of this were far-reaching. Two centuries of land sales and compensation had permanently and dramatically diminished the pool of noble land in the province. If the non-noble jurists were correct, all the noble land in Provence was becoming taxable.[47]

As their own lawyers had formulated the arguments from which this radical reinterpretation of compensation had been fashioned, the *corps de la noblesse* thus found itself caught in a trap of its own making. Although Gassier, the last *syndic de robe* (chief legal advocate) of the *noblesse* before the Revolution, denounced this interpretation as "an empty subtlety," he nonetheless recognized its fatal effect on noble exemption. "By this means, the mass of feudal property diminishes every day and, with time, will fall entirely into *roture*."[48] "While there are a hundred ways of making land taxable, hardly any remain to us to ennoble *roturier* property."[49] When the *afflorinement* it conducted in 1778–79 revealed that many fiefs contained more exempt than noble land and that some held no noble property at all, the *noblesse* grew desperate.[50] In 1779 its syndics approached the provincial administration with a proposal to adopt the declaration of 1666 it had opposed so fiercely for over a century. Although the *communautés* had once seen the declaration's permanent fixation of the tax status of property as the solution to their problems, times had changed. Confident in their reinterpretation of the right of compensation, their negotiators rejected the *noblesse*'s last-ditch proposition.[51] As Portalis, chief administrator of the province as well as an

47. An essential impetus to the province's efforts to elaborate this reinterpretation of the right of compensation was the royal government's newfound determination—evidenced by the attempts in the middle of the eighteenth century to introduce a new tax, the *vingtième*—to squeeze even more revenue out of the kingdom. As royal fiscal demands rose, the importance of noble tax exemption to both taxpayers and the privileged mounted accordingly. On the new fiscal climate of the mid-eighteenth century, see Kwass, *Privilege and the Politics of Taxation*.

48. B.d.R., C 110, "Registre des délibérations de la noblesse de Provence," "Assemblée générale" (15 mai 1769).

49. Ibid., "Assemblée générale" (12 juillet 1767).

50. Ibid., "Assemblée particulière" (30 juillet 1780).

51. For firsthand accounts of these unsuccessful negotiations, see B.d.R., C 953, Alpheran, "Mémoire sur le droit de compensation dont jouit la noblesse" (14 avril 1781); B.M., MS 723 (610), "Administration du Pays de Provence," vol. 3, "Compensation des biens nobles avec les

accomplished lawyer, explained, "In time the mass of non-noble property can only increase while the quantity of noble land can only diminish." Of course the nobility could request a new law, but could one seriously imagine that the government would favor a "doctrine tending to diminish the mass of property destined to support the charges of the state?"[52] Portalis's successor at the head of the province, the jurist Alpheran, maintained his predecessor's policy. The "hope of the Third Estate," he wrote in 1781, was "to see the nobility sell and alienate the property it had rendered exempt from the *taille* by compensation," forever extinguishing its *franchise*.[53] Compensation was dying a natural death and taking with it the tax exemptions of the seigneurial nobility.

The *noblesse* was discouraged but did not admit defeat. Instead, the seigneurs turned their attention to a type of tax-exempt property many possessed, the so-called *biens aliénés avec franchise de tailles en département de dettes,* in the hope of reuniting it nobly to their fiefs. This type of property had come into existence on 26 March 1639, when the royal government ordered indebted communities in Provence to sell off their *biens communaux* (collectively held properties) in order to raise money to reimburse their creditors. To increase the revenue produced by these sales, the government further directed the communities to attach an internally generated tax exemption to these properties. Although each community would still have to furnish the same contingent of taxes to the province as before, the former *biens communaux* alienated with tax exemption would no longer contribute to meeting the collective burden. The result was that the remaining tax-liable properties in a given community would each have to bear a heavier tax burden than before. While the sale of the *biens aliénés avec franchise de tailles* permitted many communities to pay off their debts, the practice had grave repercussions in the long term, especially from the point of view of royal fiscality which was concerned with increasing, not decreasing, the mass of tax-liable property. Acting on these considerations, the royal government issued an *arrêt* on 15 June 1668 that authorized communities to recover these properties simply by reimbursing their owners the original purchase price. Article 4, however, excepted from repurchase *biens aliénés* owned by seigneurs who could prove

biens roturiers"; and B.M., MS 783 (541), "Portalis, assesseur d'Aix à Msgr. l'archévêque d'Aix, sur le droit de compensation" (1780).

52. B.M., MS 783 (541), "Portalis, assesseur d'Aix à Msgr. l'archévêque d'Aix, sur le droit de compensation" (1780).

53. B.d.R., C 953, Alpheran, "Mémoire sur le droit de compensation dont jouit la noblesse" (14 avril 1781).

that these properties had formerly been part of their fiefs.[54] The mounting fiscal pressures of the mid-eighteenth century, particularly after the Seven Years' War, drove the royal government to reopen the question of the *biens aliénés*. In 1771, the king issued *lettres patentes* that, while preserving the seigneurial exception, reaffirmed the right of communities to buy back all other *biens aliénés* and for the first time authorized the province to act—with its considerable organizational capacity and financial clout—in their stead.[55] To make matters worse, at least from the point of view of the seigneurial nobility, in early 1776 the *contrôleur-général* Turgot directed the provincial administration to launch a provincewide buy-back of the *biens aliénés*. No less eager than Turgot to expand the mass of tax-paying land in the province, the administrators responded eagerly and efficiently to his call. Within a few years, they had assembled a list of all the *biens aliénés* in the province, constituted a provincial repurchase fund, and had goaded even the most lethargic municipalities into action.[56]

One predictable result of the buy-back campaign was to provoke new legal squabbles between communities and seigneurs seeking refuge behind article 4 of the *arrêt* of 15 June 1668. When these local disputes raised underlying questions of legal principle, both the province and the *corps de la noblesse* intervened on behalf of their respective constituents (notably the cases of the dame de Puget vs. Puget-les-Toulon and the marquis de Montauroux vs. his community). By 1779 a full-blown juridical debate over the interpretation of the article on seigneurial exception had taken shape. When the marquis de Trans initiated legal action before the royal council to prevent the community of Tourrettes from buying back the banal ovens and mills it had alienated with *franchise de tailles*, the *communautés* and *noblesse* agreed upon it as the test case to resolve the differences of interpretation underlying the current wave of disputes. The government acknowledged the parties' desire and agreed to issue a definitive declaration on the matter after hearing arguments. Both sides enlisted their most brilliant legal minds, Gassier for the *noblesse* and Portalis for the *communautés*, to draft detailed *mémoires* presenting their respective positions.[57] There were two general

---

54. *Arrest du conseil d'état du Roi, du 15 juin 1668, qui maintient les Nobles au droit de compenser les biens roturiers par eux acquis depuis le 15 décembre 1556, avec les biens nobles par eux aliénés depuis ledit tems.*

55. *Lettres patentes du Roi , qui révoquent la Déclaration du 14 septembre 1728, concernant les Biens aliénés par les Communautés de Provence, & les rétablissent dans la faculté de rachat desdits Biens* (Versailles, 10 septembre 1771).

56. The provincial administration's working papers can be consulted in B.d.R., C 258 and 259.

57. Gassier, *Mémoire sur le rachat des biens roturiers vendus par les communautés de Provence en département de leurs dettes, & en exécution des Arrêts du Conseil, avec franchise de Taille* (Aix, 1781),

points of disagreement. The first had to do with whether a community's right to initiate a buy-back was restricted by a statute of limitations (Gassier) or perpetual and imprescriptible (Portalis). The second concerned the interpretation of the seigneurial exception granted by article 4. Arguing for the broadest possible application of the exception, Gassier claimed that it covered all *biens aliénés* that had ever been part of the fief and had been acquired, no matter how, by the seigneur. Portalis naturally opted for a narrower reading of the law. He argued that it applied only to *biens aliénés* that had been part of the fief on 15 December 1556 (the day when noble land was defined as such) and only if the seigneur had subsequently acquired them directly from the community *en département de dettes* by virtue of the *arrêt* of 26 March 1639.

Following its standard practice, the royal council referred the matter to Gallois de la Tour, the *intendant* of Provence and *premier président* of the *parlement* of Aix, for his opinion. In a lengthy *mémoire* of his own, the *intendant* analyzed the respective arguments of the two parties and, in the opinion that followed, came down squarely on the side of the *communautés*.[58] He dismissed out of hand the *noblesse*'s demand for a statute of limitations, noting that it had no justification in existing jurisprudence and characterizing it as opposed to "the principles of order and the public interest." The question of how to interpret the seigneurial exception was more problematic. Gallois de la Tour began by asking why the royal council had allowed the exception in the first place. It had not been done, as Gassier had argued, to favor the reconstitution of fiefs by allowing seigneurs to reintegrate formerly alienated property. The *biens aliénés* were no longer feudal since they had passed from the fief to the community and thereby "contracted the ineffaceable stain of *roture*" and tax liability. In practice, moreover, to extend the exception to all *biens aliénés* that had ever been part of the fief and were now in the seigneur's possession would effectively prevent communities from buying back any such property since "there are very few seigneurs who does not have the *directe universelle* (territorial overlordship of a fief) and cannot say that all property owned by their communities and inhabitants does not derive from their fiefs." It was thus not a feudal rationale, the *intendant* concluded, that had led the government in 1668 to grant an exception to *seigneurs*. Provençal

and Portalis, *Mémoire sur le rachat des biens roturiers aliénés par les communautés en département de leurs dettes, avec franchise de taille* (Aix, 1780)

58. B.M., 1025 (834), "Principales affaires traitées à l'intendance, par M. Heran, avocat," "Lettre de Gallois de la Tour à Joly de Fleury" (Aix, 14 janvier 1782), 77–88. All citations in this paragraph come from this letter.

fiscal jurisprudence had been consistent, he maintained, in recognizing the right of compensation as the only legitimate way of exempting a piece of *roturier* property from taxation. Article 4, he deduced, must flow from the same principles as this right, not from the vague feudal ones alleged by Gassier. To harmonize the exception it granted with the general principles of compensation, Gallois de la Tour advanced an ingenious interpretation of article 4: it was intended to compensate the *bien aliéné*—which had originally been part of the fief and whose initial alienation thus gave the seigneur the right to effect a compensation—with itself when it returned to the seigneurs' domain.[59] To clarify these matters, the *intendant* recommended that the government affirm the imprescriptibility of the communities' right to initiate a buy-back and limit the seigneurial exception to *biens aliénés* that had left the fief after 15 December 1556 and had passed directly from the community to the seigneur *en département de dettes* (in payment for debts). To the horror of the *noblesse*, the royal council adopted these recommendations and, with the promulgation of the declaration of 24 May 1783, they all passed into law.[60]

By 1780 the seigneurs believed they were facing an unprecedented threat. With the disastrous turn compensation had taken and the new declaration dashing their hopes of seeing their noble domains reconstituted from *biens aliénés avec franchise de tailles,* there would soon be little to distinguish them from their *roturier* compatriots. Provence, as they recognized all too clearly, was well on its way to becoming the first and only province of Old Regime France to abolish specifically noble fiscal privilege. All their efforts to halt this trend had been in vain. Local courts had proven unsympathetic, and far from defending the interests of the nobility, the royal government had abandoned all pretence of impartiality and openly made common cause

---

59. Here is the *intendant's* argument: "These domains had been exempted from the *taille* because [they were] noble, but had ceased to be so upon leaving the fief. But their exemption could be applied to other properties that the seigneur could have acquired. The tax exemption that the communities had accorded to these same domains was illegal, but in fact it amounted to that which the seigneurs had lost and whose loss could be compensated. [Rather than allow the seigneurs to effect a compensation for the alienation of these noble domains], it seemed simpler to compensate these properties with themselves and to leave intact the tax exemption stipulated by the communities to replace that which the seigneurs could have recovered through the benefit of compensation."

60. *Déclaration du Roi, portant que l'action en rachat ou en encadastrement des biens aliénés par les communautés avec franchise de taille, en département de dettes, est indépendante de toute prescription ou déchéance, et qui détermine les preuves et les justifications que les seigneurs des lieux doivent rapporter pour être maintenus dans la franchise des tailles desdits biens* (Versailles, 24 mai 1783). The *comité des finances's* deliberations on this matter can be found in A.N., 144 AP 131.

with the Third Estate. In the face of the implacable alliance of crown and commons, the extinction of noble tax exemption in Provence seemed certain. In desperation the *corps de la noblesse* asked the *assemblée générale des communautés* for a two-year legal truce in order to reassess its position. Flushed with its recent victory in the royal council, the *assemblée* graciously acceded. When the armistice expired at the end of 1786, the monarchy's crisis was on the point of dramatically altering this state of affairs by creating an opening for the *noblesse* to pursue the reestablishment of the estates of Provence and seizing political power in the province from the Third Estate.

The nobility's success in reviving the defunct estates owed much to the general mood of reformism nourished by the summoning of the Assembly of Notables in early 1787, but it would be a mistake to regard these efforts as a radical new departure in provincial politics. Rather, the successful campaign conducted by the *noblesse* in 1787 to resuscitate the provincial estates was an attempt to shift its losing battle with the *communautés* away from the field of law and onto the more promising terrain of politics. By wresting the provincial administration away from their adversaries and vesting it in an assembly they dominated, the seigneurs could scuttle the campaign against their tax exemptions.[61] They might even be able to use the financial leverage they would gain from control of the estates to force the insolvent royal government to revise the jurisprudence that had undermined seigneurial fiscal privilege since 1549.[62] It is true that the *noblesse* articulated its demands in a political idiom built around such key notions as nation, constitution, and liberty. But even as we acknowledge the relative novelty of this emerging discourse, we must also recognize that the *noblesse* was using it to achieve longstanding aims—victory in the centuries-old struggle over fiscal privilege that it felt it now risked losing.

Judging it unwise to oppose openly the revival of the estates after their 150-year hiatus, the *communautés* sought to outflank the *noblesse* by claiming that the composition of this hallowed body was unfair because it no longer represented what they were now calling the Provençal nation. But to demand veritable representation in a province which had long resented not only the fiscal privileges of the fief-holding nobility, but also the political monopoly

---

61. This is exactly what happened. In early 1788, shortly after the first meeting of the revived estates, the provincial campaign to buy back *biens aliénés avec franchise de taille* was suspended. See A.N., H¹ 1240, "Lettre de La Tour" (Versailles, 11 décembre 1788).

62. Throughout 1787 and 1788, they were certainly trying to obtain the revocation of the Declaration of 1783. See B.d.R., C 4061, "Au Roi."

of the municipal elites, was to open a Pandora's box. By the end of 1788, a cross-estate alliance of the disenfranchised—parish priests, nobles without fiefs, and non-nobles barred from the clannish municipal oligarchies—had coalesced to demand even more thoroughgoing reform of the administration.[63] The demands of these groups received powerful, if volatile, support from the urban and rural poor. In the spring of 1789, at the moment of the elections to the Estates-General, Provence was rocked by a wave of popular violence aimed mainly at the system of municipal entry tolls (known as *reves*) on which urban finances—and to a great extent, those of the entire province—had rested.[64] By the time the Estates-General convened in Paris, the foundations of both seigneurial and municipal power in Provence had already been destroyed. In their determination to prevent the *noblesse* from seizing political power, the municipal oligarchs at the head of the Third Estate sent the *Procès des Tailles* veering off in a new, potentially revolutionary direction by employing rhetoric that invited new claimants to public power to enter the debates about political representation. Thanks to the new vocabulary of nation and liberty and rights, the restricted register of the *Procès* began to intersect with a national political battle that the original participants viewed with mixed feelings, at best.[65]

In 1962, Jean Egret published what remains the only synthetic study of what he termed the "French prerevolution." By this he meant the period between the meeting of the first Assembly of Notables in February 1787 and the convocation of the *bailliages* (bailiwicks) in January 1789 to elect deputies to the Estates-General. He considered these turbulent two years as

---

63. Rafe Blaufarb, "Conflits autour de la représentation dans les états de Provence pendant la prérévolution française," *Combattre, gouverner, écrire: études réunies en l'honneur de Jean Chagniot,* ed. Agnès Tartié (Paris, 2003), 120–31.

64. By means of these taxes (notably on flour, oil, and wine), Provençal towns raised the money to furnish their annual contribution to the overall provincial tax contingent. Thus, by means of the *reves,* municipal elites were able to shift the burden of taxation from their own property to the urban poor. On the wave of rioting that swept over Provence between March and June 1789, see the excellent account by Cubells in *Les horizons de la liberté,* 92–100.

65. A glance at the destinies of some of the key Provençal political figures of 1787–89 suggests the ambiguity of their relationship with the Revolution. Pascalis, leader of the Third Estate's struggle against the reestablishment of the estates, was hung by a mob in 1790; Portalis, after a brief stint as a right-wing deputy during the Directory, maintained a low profile until Napoleon's seizure of power; and d'André, the leader of the non-fief-holding nobility, became one of Louis XVIII's most effective spymasters. Mirabeau's early death renders the question of what he would have done after the overthrow of the monarchy a matter for conjecture.

an "intermediate stage" distinct from both the Old Regime and Revolution but "announcing" the coming cataclysm.[66] His account focused on the attempts of the royal government to reform itself during this period and the opposition which ultimately thwarted those efforts, forcing the king to resort to the Estates-General. Although he acknowledged the participation of certain provincial estates in the opposition, Egret assigned to the *parlements* the leading role in the resistance movement. But by insisting upon the "forms of 1614," the Paris *parlement* revealed "its attachment to aristocratic interests," prompted the "*prise de conscience* by the bourgeoisie of its new ambitions," and thereby unleashed the social conflict that would define the coming revolution.[67] Recent works by such historians as William Doyle, Peter Jones, Michael Kwass, and Timothy Tackett have added nuance to Egret's account by expanding the chronology of the crisis to include the reforms of the 1770s and 1780s, shifting the focus of the action from Paris to the provinces, emphasizing sources of opposition other than the *parlements,* and providing more complex interpretations of the origins of revolutionary social conflict. Yet these recent accounts share with Egret's a forward-looking perspective that tends to reduce the political struggles which preceded 1789 to a mere prelude. Whether in Doyle's retention of the idea of a distinct prerevolution in 1787–88, Jones's notion of a "transition from 'administrative' to constitutional monarchy" that took place between 1774 and 1791, Kwass's metamorphosis of "taxpayers into citizens" during the 1780s, or Tackett's description of the experience of mobilization after 1770 as a "political apprenticeship," all posit the existence of a liminal period of accelerated political change which prepared France for the great events to come.[68] Whatever its precise chronological limits, this phase is clearly demarcated in these accounts from the long stretch of mature absolutism which preceded it and the great revolution toward which it strained.

It is clear that great changes in the French state were underway by 1789. And it is also clear that a heightened sense of political possibility—reflected not merely in the monarchy's reform initiatives and the opposition to them, but in other areas as well—was already palpable in France by 1787, if not earlier. And finally, there is much evidence to suggest that the growing

66. Jean Egret, *La pré-Révolution française, 1787–1788* (Paris, 1962), 1. Egret credited Pierre Caron's *Manuel pratique pour l'étude de la Révolution française* with actually coining the term.

67. Ibid., 350 and 353.

68. Doyle, *Origins of the French Revolution,* 99; Peter M. Jones, *Reform and Revolution in France: The Politics of Transition, 1774–1791* (Cambridge, 1995), 1; Kwass, *The Politics of Privilege,* chap. 6; and Tackett, *Becoming a Revolutionary,* chap. 3.

perception that change, whether for good or for ill, was possible or even inevitable fed a climate of expectation, optimism, and unease that sharpened existing social tensions. If the new universal taxes of midcentury, the military defeats of the 1760s, or the reforms of the 1770s had not already convinced people that the French state was entering uncharted waters, certainly the appearance in 1787 of institutions resurrected from the early seventeenth century and the invention of new ones without precedent in French history made it clear to even the most obtuse that dramatic transformations were afoot. But we cannot fully grasp how people understood and sought to cope with these changes if we restrict our search for the political origins of the Revolution to a supercharged prerevolution detached from the mundane, long-term political history of the Old Regime. As a conceptual tool, the notion of a distinct prerevolutionary crisis has the grave defect of leading us to interpret the words and deeds of historical actors in the light of a revolution they did not know was coming and to discard evidence that does not lead to the foreordained destination of 1789. As the case of Provence illustrates, older concerns did not evaporate in the glare of the beckoning revolutionary future, but rather shaped the aims and assumptions political actors brought with them into the Revolution. Indeed, far from casting a blanket of irrelevance over the ancient quarrels, the political crisis of 1787–88 offered an unparalleled opportunity to reopen closed questions, renegotiate old settlements, and overthrow existing arrangements. Rather than rendering obsolete the political struggles of the Old Regime, the crisis inflamed them by creating a sense that everything was up for grabs. Seen from this perspective, Egret's classic prerevolution appears not so much as a prelude but rather as an abrupt, surprise finale.

6

WOMEN, GENDER, AND THE IMAGE OF THE EIGHTEENTH-CENTURY ARISTOCRACY

Mita Choudhury

After thirty years of revisionist attacks on the Marxist orthodoxy pitting the nobility against the bourgeoisie, and more recent reconsideration of that revisionism, French historians continue to uncover the complex and multifaceted nature of the Old Regime's most prominent and notorious social group, the nobility. Revisionists famously argued that the eighteenth-century nobility could hardly be described as a class, given the divisions within the order based on wealth, education, occupation, and lineage.[1] Still, the findings of David Bien, Timothy Tackett, and others also challenge the notion that urban nobles and bourgeois elites belonged to a socially unified and dynamic elite, one riven by tensions only at the onset of the French Revolution.[2] The nobility, however diverse and changing, remained a legally defined group within Old Regime society, and membership in the nobility conferred important privileges and advantages, including greater access to the channels of social promotion.

The separation of the nobility from the rest of society became a charged issue by the mid-eighteenth century, when notions of personal merit and social utility were gaining ground and traditional concepts, such as honor

---

1. The most "classic" example of the revisionist perspective remains Guy Chaussinand-Nogaret, *La noblesse au XVIIIe siècle: de la féodalité aux lumières* (Paris, 1976). For a recent study of the Parisian nobility, see Mathieu Marraud, *La noblesse de Paris au XVIIIe siècle* (Paris, 2000).

2. David D. Bien, "Manufacturing Nobles: The Chancelleries in France to 1789," *Journal of Modern History* 61 (1989): 445–86; Timothy Tackett, "Nobles and Third Estate in the

and virtue, were being reconstituted along more inclusive lines. As a result, nobles and non-nobles alike shared a rising anxiety over the definition of the social elite and over the nobility's place within the nation. The concerns about the nobility's status in an unsettled commercial and political world were reflected in the debates on the nobility, its attributes, and its function in society. As Jay Smith and other contributors to this volume have persuasively demonstrated, discursive exchanges surrounding these issues pointed to seismic shifts in the eighteenth-century understanding of the principles governing society. Social critics and political economists argued for ways to reform the nobility in order to fit into a hierarchical society based not on heredity alone, but on merit and social contributions as well.[3]

In this essay I consider one aspect of the reconceptualization of nobility in the eighteenth century, namely, the cultural construction of "aristocracy," the nobility's distorted mirror image. Sarah Maza has argued, in her work on the "myth" of the French bourgeoisie, that an integral part of the social world is something that can be profitably called the "social imaginary," a reflective but creative imaginative realm that involves "understandings of, and polemics and fantasies about, the social world."[4] My investigation of aristocracy adopts an approach similar to that of Maza, as it considers, through the example of abbesses, how the terms "aristocracy" and "aristocratic" increasingly expressed characteristics antithetical to the values associated with the worthy citizen. Long before the revolution, royal ministers, philosophes, novelists, members of *le monde* and the demimonde, bourgeois and noble, all targeted the aristocrat as the embodiment of unbridled vice, especially the evils of luxury and libertinism. Instead of contributing to society, this monstrous figure exercised unrestrained power and privilege while feeding off the labor of others. Beaumarchais's Count Almaviva stands as one well-known humorous representation of this figure, but the count of Morangiès featured in the trial briefs of the Veron-Morangiès scandal was a much more sinister personality. According to Maza, "the count's displays of wealth, his

---

    3. For example, see John Shovlin, "Toward a Reinterpretation of Revolutionary Antinobilism: The Political Economy of Honor in the Old Regime," *Journal of Modern History* 72 (2000): 35–66; Jay M. Smith, "Social Categories, the Language of Patriotism, and the Origins of the French Revolution: The Debate over *Noblesse Commerçante*," *Journal of Modern History* 72 (2000): 339–74.

    4. Sarah Maza, *The Myth of the French Bourgeoisie: An Essay on the Social Imaginary, 1750–1850* (Cambridge, Mass., 2003), 11.

charm and polished manners, are a veneer that conceals the reality of power based on intimidation and the threat of violence."[5]

For critics of the aristocracy, aristocratic women in particular encapsulated the misuse of power and wanton extravagance associated with the order as whole. For example, both *The Spirit of Laws* and *The Persian Letters* indicate that Montesquieu was of two minds about the influential place of women within his own elite circles. Although he attributed female weaknesses to their social displacement and called for gender parity, Montesquieu noted disapprovingly in *The Persian Letters* that "for every man who has any post at court, in Paris, or in the country, there is a woman through whose hands pass all the favors and sometimes injustices that he does."[6] Montesquieu's observations on court women resounded over the course of the century. Rousseau repeated similar arguments with added vitriol in the *Letter to d'Alembert* when he attacked the salon women (the *salonnières*), and Mercier picked up the drumbeat in the *Tableau de Paris*. These writers believed that they inhabited an inverted world in which women of the court and, to some extent, salon women worked behind the scenes and controlled appointments and favors. Moreover, these women reinforced an inequitable institutional structure that sometimes excluded deserving individuals, including members of the nobility.

In their studies of eighteenth-century political culture, historians such as Sarah Maza and Thomas E. Kaiser have used gender methodology and convincingly demonstrated that the anxieties about court women, such as Louis XV's mistress Madame de Pompadour and Louis XVI's queen Marie-Antoinette, reflected and fed the larger concerns about the uses or, more appropriately, misuses of power in the body politic.[7] The presence of high-profile women at court signaled "feminine" ways of wielding power that had spread throughout the body politic. Thus, like the women who

5. On the count of Morangiès, see Sarah Maza, *Private Lives and Public Affairs: the Causes Célèbres of Prerevolutionary France* (Berkeley and Los Angeles, 1993), 43.

6. Translation taken from Montesquieu, *The Persian Letters,* trans. C. J. Betts (London, 1973), 197. For a brief and generous overview of Montesquieu's overarching view of women, see Pauline Kra, "Montesquieu and Women," in *French Women and the Age of Enlightenment,* ed. Samia I. Spencer (Bloomington, Ind., 1984), 272–84.

7. On the various attacks against Pompadour, see Thomas E. Kaiser, "Madame de Pompadour and the Theaters of Power," *French Historical Studies* 14 (1996): 1025–44; Madelyn Gutwirth, *The Twilight of the Goddesses: Women and Representations in the French Revolutionary Era* (New Brunswick, N.J., 1992), 79–84. On Marie-Antoinette, see Dena Goodman, ed., *Marie-Antoinette: Writings on the Body of a Queen* (New York, 2003); Chantal Thomas, *The Wicked Queen: The Origins of the Myth of Marie-Antoinette,* trans. Julie Rose (New York, 1999).

governed them, men such as Louis XV dominated others using under-handed and hidden means to satisfy their passions. These paradoxical images of powerless yet tyrannical men contributed to the gradual erosion or "desacralization" of legitimate power.

While this research has broken new ground in our thinking about power and its meaning in the prerevolutionary era, eighteenth-century historians have not used gender as a tool for a sustained examination of nobility in this period. Although some attention has been given to court women and to the salon women of the Enlightenment, few scholars have used the category of gender to rethink the nobility and its place in the larger critique of power.[8] We may speculate that the virtual absence of such scholarship is an indirect result of revisionism. The jettisoning of the "social interpretation" of the French Revolution may have fostered a reluctance to study the nobility as such and therefore deterred in-depth explorations of how attitudes toward noblewomen, like those associated with the court, contributed to the public image of the despotic aristocrat. However, Montesquieu's words and recent studies by Maza, Kaiser, and others on the hostility toward court women strongly suggest that, in the public mind, images of women and aristocracy intersected, to the detriment of both.

With the full acknowledgment of the necessarily speculative nature of this endeavor, in this essay I will wade into these uncharted waters and examine mother superiors as a kind of case study through which we may consider how contemporaries might have drawn connections between an apparently decadent nobility and illegitimate female power. The criticism of superiors and nuns most often originated from the growing anticlerical sentiment that came from various segments of the eighteenth-century public. But for many opponents of monasticism, there was also a social dimension to their hostility. For them, the convent was an aristocratic enclave, a clearing house for unwanted

---

8. For the most part, the topic of eighteenth-century noblewomen has been subsumed by larger studies that encompass the early modern period, often emphasizing the sixteenth and seventeenth centuries, or those that cover a range of early modern women. See, for example, Sharon Kettering, "The Household Service of Early Modern French Noblewomen, *French Historical Studies* 20 (1997): 55–85; Sara Chapman, "Patronage as Family Economy: The Role of Women in the Patron-Client Network of the Phélypeaux de Pontchatrain Family, 1670–1815," *French Historical Studies* 24 (2001): 11–35. Another noteworthy area in women's history that has received a great deal of attention has been the early modern legal process. See Sarah Hanley, "Social Sites of Political Practice in France: Lawsuits, Civil Rights, and the Separation of Powers in Domestic and State Government, 1500–1800," *American Historical Review* 102 (1997): 27–52; Zoë A. Schneider, "Women Before the Bench: Female Litigants in Early Modern Normandy," *French Historical Studies* 23 (2000): 1–32.

girls from titled families. Within elite society, the most visible convent woman was the abbess, who traditionally came from a noble family. In keeping with her family's status, she possessed a great deal of influence within the convent as well as enjoying privileges beyond the cloistered walls.

From the 1760s onward, the power and rank of abbesses aroused suspicion, thanks in part to the efforts of lawyers involved in trials concerning convent governance. In such court cases as the trial revolving around the prioress Madame de Sesmaisons of the *hotel-dieu* in Pontoise (1769), lawyers claimed that abbesses exceeded their authority, thereby upsetting the spiritual serenity of the cloister. Unruly and impassioned women—haughty aristocrats—they subverted legal channels to satisfy personal whims and desires. I would suggest that abbesses like Madame de Sesmaisons were a discursive nexus in which concerns about the following merged: outmoded religious authority, feminine power, and aristocratic degeneracy. The essay below focuses on the intersection of the latter two in order to open up discussion of the place of gender in the debate about nobility.

As the Sesmaisons case and other such trials indicate, popular caricatures of mother superiors represented social expressions of privilege abused and used for private purposes.[9] As a scion of the nobility, the abbess in particular introduced aristocratic vice into the sacred space of the convent. These images of abbesses sketched in various *mémoires judiciaires,* or legal briefs, blended fears of female passion and aristocratic decadence. Lawyers repeatedly demonstrated that the result of this mixture was tyranny and disorder. This critique of personalized power was often coded in gendered terms, situated between normative standards of femininity and masculinity, in which the former denoted passion and the latter reason. These polar characteristics came to symbolize the difference between illegitimate and legitimate power, and the trials involving mother superiors would indicate that critics increasingly placed women and aristocrats in the former category. In essence, this essay represents an invitation to readers to consider how these two groups came to signify illegitimate power in tandem. Moreover, through it I hope to raise new questions about the eighteenth-century nobility by connecting the dominant perceptions of aristocracy with the escalating critique of the Old Regime's absolutist structures.

Within the patriarchal structure of absolutist France, the power and influence of the mother superior had been legitimated by law and custom. While the

9. Maza, *Private Live and Public Affairs,* 59.

scope of her authority depended on the structure and rules of a particular order and establishment, the superior exercised authority as the head of a corporate entity with legal privileges.[10] A superior was either selected by her peers through an election process or appointed by the king, procedures validated by the church hierarchy. On one level, the superior resembled other women who possessed genuine powers, such as the wife of an absent nobleman who acted as seigneur or the widow of a master printer who assumed the responsibilities of the print shop.[11] But unlike these women who acquired authority by default, the mother superior held an irreplaceable position since the cloister had to be governed by a woman who could live amongst the nuns.

The superior's leadership derived its legitimacy from its links to the masculine power of fathers, priests, and kings, guaranteed by the rules and constitutions of that community. A *mémoire judiciaire* written in 1769 outlined the full scope of the mother superior's authority: "Canon law gives them [mother superiors] the title of spiritual Mother, in the same sense that abbots have the quality of father. They [mother superiors] are in charge of souls . . . their jurisdiction is spiritual like abbots, they have the same right to order, punish, correct matters that concern monastic discipline." The nuns of the community must "obey them . . . like a mother, and like a superior invested with the episcopacy."[12] As this statement suggests, the power of the mother superior brought together the authority of parents, the monarchy, and the upper clergy. In effect, the superior asserted a "paternal" presence in the all-female environment of the cloister.[13] A good mother superior overcame the weaknesses of her sex and assumed the characteristics of a reasonable masculine figure able to command the willing obedience of her subordinates. But in the eighteenth century, a superior was increasingly a problematic figure because she possessed "masculine" authority, which social theorists and political critics alike considered an "unnatural" position for a woman.

10. For a schematic discussion, Geneviève Reynes, *Couvents de femmes: la vie des religieuses cloîtrées dans la France des XVIIe et XVIIIe siècles* (Paris, 1987), 9–13. For a more detailed overview, see Robert Lemoine, *Le Monde des religieux: l'époque moderne, 1563–1789*, vol. 15, pt. 2, *Histoire du droit des institutions de l'église en occident,* ed. Gabriel Le Bras (Paris, 1976).

11. See Natalie Zemon Davis, *Society and Culture in Early Modern France: Eight Essays* (Stanford, 1975), 70–71.

12. Gillet, Cellier, De Lambon, D'Outrement, Aubry, Mey, Vulpian, Leon, *Mémoire à consulter* (Paris, 1769), 11–12.

13. Reynes, *Couvents de femmes,* 77–78.

In their opposition to such female authority, polemicists singled out a certain category of superiors: the abbess who generally headed large and well-established institutions that had traditionally been associated with the nobility and the monarchy. That contemporaries made a distinction between such women and other superiors is suggested by a revolutionary pamphlet on the suppression of convents. In her treatise, the pedagogue Madame de Genlis described the abbess as a product of her rank, "a kind of queen [who] . . . lives with ostentation . . . governing her sisters and her equals despotically."[14] Genlis's prejudices reflect the ancient traditions surrounding abbesses. Going back to the Merovingian era, abbeys often had strong links to high-ranking noble families that donated vast sums of money and large tracts of land; these families generally maintained control over the convent by establishing a kinswoman as its superior.[15] Significantly, unlike mother superiors who were generally elected triennially by their peers, abbesses were appointed for life by the king, and only the king had the power to remove them.[16] After the Concordat of Bologne in 1516, which enabled the monarchy to appoint abbesses directly, the crown used convents as "benefices" to reward noble families. Thus, in the early years of the eighteenth century, the duc d'Orléans took advantage of his position as regent to remove Guyonne-Marguerite de Cossé-Brissac from the abbey of Chelles and installed his daughter Louise-Adélaïde in her place. In this manner, such institutions were an extension of the political and social structure founded on privilege and hierarchy.

In principle, abbesses may have renounced their noble rank when they pronounced their religious vows, but in practice, many continued to enjoy their worldly status. Since the Middle Ages, many abbesses were, in fact, large landlords possessing feudal rights, which included receiving homage from the

14. Stéphanie-Félicité de Genlis, *Discours sur la suppression des couvens de religieuses et sur l'éducation publique de femmes* (Paris, 1790), 2.

15. Jane T. Schulenberg, "Women's Monastic Communities, 500–1100: Patterns of Expansion and Decline," in *Sisters and Workers in the Middles Ages,* ed. Judith M. Bennett, Elizabeth A. Clark, et al. (Chicago, 1989), 217.

16. For example, the violent behavior of Marie-Anne-Gabrielle de Bourbon Condé, abbess of Saint-Antoine, forced Louis XV to place her in the abbey of Saussay in 1742. On the Sainte-Antoine affair, see "Avis de l'abbé générale de Cisteaux," Bibliothèque de l'Arsenal, Archives de la Bastille, 10183. See also Charles-Philippe d'Albert, duc de Luynes, *Mémoires du duc de Luynes sur la cour de Louis XV (1735–1758),* 17 vols. (Paris, 1862), 4:129; 10:249. E.-J. F. Barbier, *Chronique de la régence et du règne de Louis XV; ou, Journal de Barbier,* 8 vols. (Paris, 1866), 7:297, 299.

nearby population.[17] Indeed, the installation of an abbess was accompanied by the "sound of drums, violins and other musical instruments" heard throughout the vicinity of the abbey as the abbess, like a sovereign, assumed her position.[18] Abbesses' lifestyles sometimes matched their social status. They often resided in lavish abbatial apartments indistinguishable from a boudoir, and some of them welcomed guests from court and high society.[19] As a result of these various privileges and connections, the abbess was a powerful figure. Moreover, her social connections made her visible and therefore vulnerable in the critical political climate of the eighteenth century.

Abbesses came under attack from political and social critics who became increasingly willing to contest authority during the last decades of the Old Regime. The battles over Jansenism and the church's reluctance to assist the state financially had tarnished the church's public image. Political watchdogs thus came to regard all figures of clerical authority as potential threats to the rights of citizens and the well-being of the realm. By the mid-eighteenth century, Jansenist polemicists, parlementary magistrates, lawyers, and Enlightenment adherents cast a suspicious eye on the central authority figure associated with the convent, sometimes regarding her as an arm of bishops and the power-hungry Jesuits. In 1777, for example, the Jansenist periodical *Nouvelles Ecclésiastiques* did not complain about mother superiors in general but targeted abbesses in particular, noting that they often attempted "to reign in the most absolute and most arbitrary manner . . . requiring the most blind obedience."[20] Between 1740 and 1775, the *parlement* of Paris heard a cluster of court cases in which nuns brought their superiors to task for overstepping their authority. Sensational stories involving the Paris's work house the *Hôpital-général* (1749), the abbey of Malnoue and priory of Bonsecours (1746), the abbey of Beaumont in Auvergne (1764), and the *hôtel-dieu* in Paris (1769) demonstrated that the convent was rife with problems of abuse and insubordination.

While drawing from these trials, in the following discussion I will focus on an especially revealing conflict between the nuns and prioress of the *hôtel-dieu* of Saint-Nicolas in Pontoise that took place in 1769. Despite its

17. Lemoine, *Le Monde des religieux*, 211–12.

18. *Nouvelles Ecclésiastiques, ou mémoires pour servir à l'histoire de la bulle Unigénitus* (hereafter *NE*) (12 June 1783), 93.

19. For discussion of the links between the female convent and the larger world in the seventeenth century, see Barbara B. Diefendorf, "Contradictions of the Century of Saints: Aristocratic Patronage and the Convents of Counter-Reformation Paris," *French Historical Studies* 24 (2001): 469–500.

20. *NE* (16 October 1777), 167.

particularity, the anxieties that found expression in this case paralleled those brought to light in many others. Because of its paradigmatic nature, the Saint-Nicolas case suggests the outlines of a gathering anti-aristocratic critique of established authorities in the second half of the eighteenth century. The affair of Saint-Nicolas especially sheds light on how the denunciation of abbesses reflected an intertwined critique of feminine and aristocratic power. In this trial the lawyer Jean-Baptiste Faré sought to prove how the prioress Madame de Sesmaisons had failed both as a superior and as a "mother." He caricatured Sesmaisons as a figure of aristocratic vice, luxury-loving and decadent, arguing that such penchants directly resulted in despotic behavior, in unruly, feminine tyranny. Thus, Faré wove together the critique of aristocratic and feminine rule to produce a scathing indictment of despotism.[21]

In January 1768 one Marie-Anne Le Coq became a novice at the convent of Saint-Nicolas, which, as a *hôtel-dieu,* also functioned as a charitable hospital. Her novitiate coincided with the appointment of a new prioress, Françoise-Julie de Sesmaisons, by the prince de Conti.[22] Unlike the new mother superior, Le Coq, the daughter of a Parisian merchant, was no stranger to the convent where she had prepared for her first communion. A great favorite with the nuns, Le Coq earned a reputation for her religiosity and relentless hard work at the hospital. Despite Le Coq's piety and exertions, Madame de Sesmaisons declared her to be unfit for religious life. Subsequently, in the summer of 1768, the superior returned the novice home to her astounded parents. Outraged, Le Coq's father brought the case before the *parlement* of Paris in 1769. This trial became doubly charged because it contained a Jansenist component. In a separate suit, the nuns of the *hôtel-dieu* claimed that the superior had, in fact, broken the 1754 Law of Silence forbidding any discussion of *Unigenitus* or related subjects. The affair ended in May 1769 when the sovereign courts ruled in favor of Le Coq and the nuns, and the novice was received back into the convent.[23]

---

21. The most famous parlementary attack on clerical "despotism" was the campaign against the Jesuits in the early 1760s. The most detailed account of the expulsion of the Jesuits remains Dale K. Van Kley, *The Jansenists and the Expulsion of the Jesuits from France 1757–1765* (New Haven, 1975). On other opposition to the clergy's "despotism," see also Mita Choudhury, *Convents and Nuns in Eighteenth-Century French Politics and Culture* (Ithaca, N.Y., 2004), chaps. 2–3.

22. The account of this trial is taken from Bibliothèque Nationale de France, Fonds Joly de Fleury (hereafter BNF, JF), 602 and 159. The *Nouvelles Ecclésiastiques* also included detailed accounts of the affair, printing articles on 6 December 1768, 14 February 1769, and 18 July 1769.

23. Le Coq did not return to Saint-Nicolas without some resistance from Sesmaisons. See *NE* (18 July 1769), 113–15. Sesmaisons also complained to Joly de Fleury that the nuns continued to disobey her. BNF, JF, 1597, fols. 289–90.

Le Coq's triumphant return to Saint-Nicolas may, in large part, be credited to her lawyer Jean-Baptiste Faré whose demonization of Sesmaisons blended anti-aristocratic rhetoric with suspicions of feminine authority. In Faré's legal briefs for Le Coq, Sesmaisons's despotic tendencies were clearly tied to aristocratic inclinations that corrupted the sacred world of the convent. Moreover, she betrayed an emerging normative ideal of femininity that emphasized nurturing. Sesmaisons had betrayed her responsibilities as a "mother" and the head of an institution important to society. Faré politicized the threat this unruly aristocratic superior represented by demonstrating how Sesmaisons's rule was, in effect, a despotic regime.

In the first *mémoire judiciaire* for Marie-Anne Le Coq, Faré began his crusade by referring to Sesmaisons not as prioress, but as "abbess." On the surface, the lawyer's choice of title was an allusion to the prioress's previous status as abbess of Bival. I would argue that the title of "abbess," with its associations of rank and power, signified much more. In this context, it signaled aristocratic pretensions and autocratic leanings. Such associations with the title "abbess" had been made apparent nearly twenty-five years earlier when the lawyers Cochin and Gandouard had charged Madame de Rossignol, abbess of Malnoue, with seeking to merge the communities of Malnoue and the priory of Bon Secours so that she could live in Paris, the hub of high society, and retain the prestigious title of abbess.[24] The insinuations behind Faré's reference to Sesmaisons's previous title become clearer when read in conjunction with a pamphlet defending the Saint-Nicolas *hospitalières*. This anonymous polemic described how Sesmaisons detached herself from her fellow nuns. Residing in apartments isolated from the rest of the community, she lived like "a lady of the first rank," creating "a kind of court."[25] More to the point, "she lived like an abbess [*en abbesse*], although she was a simple prioress of a hospital, and without any income except that belonging to the poor and the nuns."[26] Faré's choice of appellation then was an accusation intimating that the aristocratic Sesmaisons was almost destined to create disorder in the convent because she clung to society's hierarchical values and the inequities inherent in that structure.

---

24. Henri Cochin and Gandouard, *Mémoire à consulter pour les dames religieuses de l'abbaye royale de Malnoue, opposantes à l'enregistrement des lettres patentes obtenue sur le décret d'union* (Paris, 1746), 21–22. For more on the affair, see Archives Nationales (hereafter A.N.), G⁹ 80, no. 13; G⁹ 81, no. 9; S 4590.

25. Anon., *Lettres concernant Madame de Sesmaisons, prieure de l'Hostel-Dieu de Pontoise* (n.p., 1769), 14.

26. Ibid., 11.

The negative connotations surrounding the title of abbess reflected the larger dissension over titles in French society. Increasingly, political economists and other social critics argued that titles were hollow because they were, in and of themselves, devoid of any merit. For example, Beaumarchais identified the growing skepticism regarding the relation between status and birth in Figaro's bitter words directed at Count Almaviva: "Because you are a great nobleman you think you are a great genius. . . . Nobility, rank position! . . . What have *you* done to deserve such advantages? Put yourself to the trouble of being born—nothing more!"[27] Of course, Beaumarchais's own career exemplified how merit and cunning could enable a man to achieve status and renown. For other writers, the discrepancies between talent and birth did not just represent an injustice but violated the state of nature. According to the abbé Guillaume-Thomas-François Raynal, savages, closer to a state of nature, abhorred the social distinctions created through titles: "The respect that we have for titles, dignities, and above all for hereditary nobility, they [savages] call an insult, an outrage to humankind." What made the man were not superficial labels but the ability "to guide a canoe, battle an enemy, build a cabin . . . without any other guide but the wind and the sun."[28] Thus, the "natural" leader of a society was defined by his accomplishments and efforts, and the adherence to birth and title were "unnatural" advantages that had the potential to create dissension.

These assertions that nature observed an equality that could only be corrupted through the application of rank were echoed by lawyers who charged abbesses with going against the essential spirit of convent life. Ideally, a superior was a member of the community like any other nun, and her rank entailed responsibility rather than privilege. Some individuals, however, treated their religious rank as an extension of their social status and thus betrayed the monastic vows that made nuns equal before God. A pamphlet in the 1764 trial involving Madame de Lantilhac, abbess of Beaumont in Clermont-Ferrand, described how worldly pretensions went against the spirit of the cloister: "There are in all communities these haughty nuns; believing they have honored the convent in which they have professed, [they] imagine that their birth precedes their duties and [claustral] regularity."[29]

27. Beaumarchais, *The Marriage of Figaro* in *The Barber of Seville and The Marriage of Figaro,* trans. John Wood (London, 1964), 199.
28. Guillaume-Thomas-François Raynal, *Histoire Philosophique et Politique* (La Haye, 1776), 22–23.
29. *A monsieur le lieutenant-général en la sénéchaussée d'Auvergne à Clermont* (n.p., n.d.), 2. For a more complete discussion of this trial, see Choudhury, *Convents and Nuns,* 73–87.

Failing to understand that they were a part of a community, these abbesses and superiors aspiring to abbess-like status, interpreted their responsibilities as personal power. In 1770 lawyers made arguments comparable to Faré's charges against Sesmaisons in their allegations against Madame de Saillant, the newly installed prioress of Bonsecours and coadjutor of Malnoue. Like Sesmaisons, Saillant was once an abbess of the convent of Nevers. Similarly, she sought to maintain the appearance of abbess through luxurious apartments, despite the distance from the cloister, despite the expense to a financially troubled convent, and despite an outside door that violated the rule of enclosure. The lawyers for the Bonsecours and Malnoue nuns trenchantly reminded the superior that "an abbess or prioress, unable [to own] personal property because of her vow of poverty, possesses nothing in general . . . and if her title gives her management over revenues, she is only a simple administrator of the goods over which the Monastery maintains ownership."[30] In other words, the position of abbess was one of duty, not of personal prestige and power. In cases such as these, these barristers put forth an idealized image of the convent as an arena untainted by the superficialities of social hierarchy, but which was threatened by aristocratic tendencies for pleasure and domination.

In his arguments against Sesmaisons, Faré intimated that the prioress's aristocratic posturing led to self-indulgence and corruption. The prioress, Faré argued, represented one of those women so "acutely attached to a society they miss that they busy themselves only with bringing in luxury and pleasures into the convent."[31] For readers, his remark may have invoked the scandalous activities of Madame de Lantilhac and her sister Madame de Sedières from the above-mentioned abbey of Beaumont. According to

---

30. Claude Mey, Nicolas de Lambon, Jacques-François Cellier, Jean-Baptiste Vulpian, *Mémoire à consulter* (n.p., [1770]), 13. This legal brief pertains to a high-profile case involving the priory of Bon Secours. In 1768 Madame de Saillant became prioress through a papal bull, a controversial appointment violating the terms of Louis XIV's 1695 Edict of Blois, which stated that an individual could not take possession of a benefice without presenting herself before the diocesan bishop. Although Louis XV supported this appointment, the nuns opposed it and brought their grievance before the *parlement* of Paris, represented by an army of lawyers including the four who wrote the *mémoire judiciaire*. Two years later, the nuns sought to undermine their new superior's authority by contesting the building of these apartments, a position supported by the archbishop of Paris, Christophe de Beaumont. BNF, JF, 469, fols. 259–304; BNF, JF, 1604, fols. 9–60; A.N., S 4590. The bookseller Siméon-Prosper Hardy's diary contain several entries noting both trials. Bibliothèque Nationale de France, Manuscrits français (hereafter BNF, MS Fr.) 6680, 14–15 April 1768, 21–22 April 1768, and 29 April 1768.

31. Jean-Baptiste Faré, *Plaidoyer pour le sieur Le Coq, marchand à Paris, Marie Louise Wantin, son épouse, et Marie-Anne Le Coq, leur fille* (n.p., 1769), 25.

Auvergnat lawyer Duclosel and the Parisian barrister Pierre-Daniel-Jean Le Roy de Fontenelle, these two nuns had pursued a lifestyle that was a veritable catalogue of aristocratic depravity. Their libertine extravaganzas violated the monastic vows of poverty and chastity. Duclosel declared that the abbess Madame de Lantilhac had converted her apartments into a "theater of fêtes and pleasures" and the convent itself into a "theater of licentiousness," so that it was "no more than a House of Pleasure."[32] Writing six years after Rousseau's contentious debate with d'Alembert over the theater, Duclosel's words suggested a critique of the aristocratic world in which Lantilhac and Sedières had been born and the deleterious effects of that world on society as a whole.[33] Although Faré only offered hints of Sesmaisons's aristocratic dissipation, his readers could easily imagine the rest based on real and fictional stories they encountered in novels like the *Histoire de dom Bougre* (1740), pamphlets, and *mémoires judiciaires* detailing aristocratic profligacy and claustral promiscuity.

Sesmaisons's flaws became magnified when compared to the virtues of Le Coq and her family. Although a conflict between an aristocrat and a bourgeoise was not the central drama of the Pontoise affair, the differences in social rank between the two parties underscored differences in temperament and character. Faré never detailed Sesmaisons's actual background, although it is probable that she came from a noble family given her selection by the prince de Conti. The prioress's own lawyer Henri Racine suggested as much when he questioned whether Marie-Anne Le Coq, "alone and without quality," had the right to bring charges against Sesmaisons.[34] But Faré glorified his client's social origins: "her [Le Coq's] parents are not puffed by wealth and birth; they pride themselves on their attachment to their duties and their love for their religion and virtue."[35] Their daughter replicated these virtues with her marked preference for seclusion and hard work. Social rank then was about character not status. Where Faré's client was "a timid and virtuous novice," the superior was "impassioned."[36] And where Le Coq's upbringing exhibited itself in obedience and piety, Sesmaisons's background revealed an unsteady character that made her regime unpredictable.

32. Duclosel, *Requête présentée à monsieur l'officiel par les dames ALBANEL, BRUNEL et GASCHIER, religieuses de l'abbaye royale de Beaumont contre LA dame de LANTILLAC [sic] leur abbesse, et la Dame de SEDIERES* (Clermont-Ferrand, 1764), 3, 8, 30.

33. Jean-Jacques Rousseau, *Lettre à M. d'Alembert sur son article "Genève"* (Paris, 1967).

34. Henri Racine, *Mémoire pour la dame de Sesmaisons, ancienne abbesse de Bival, et prieuré de Saint-Nicolas de Pontoise et la mère de Saint-Clement, religieuse au même prieuré* (Paris, n.d.),18.

35. Faré, *Plaidoyer pour le sieur Le Coq,* 5.

36. Ibid., 2.

As a result of these unruly emotions, Sesmaisons, her opponents contended, did not behave as a good "mother," which by the 1760s had deep cultural resonance. Authors of innumerable novels, pedagogical works, and social treatises all argued that a woman's virtue was derived in her ability to love her children and husband and to create an ideal domestic space for them.[37] Sesmaisons was implicitly held up to these standards of domesticity. According to the *Nouvelles Ecclésiastiques,* while the prioress was railing against the supposed disobedience of the community, "they [the nuns] for their part said not a word, and continued to fulfill their duties with new fervor. They prayed to God to open the eyes of the Mother, so that she recognized them for her true daughters."[38] Faré also drew attention to Sesmaisons's behavior as a bad mother by putting forth as a positive image of motherhood, Marie-Anne Le Coq's own mother. According to Faré, when Le Coq's parents heard the distressing news of their daughter's eviction from Saint-Nicolas, Madame Le Coq acted with all the instincts of an exemplary mother. Despite being seven months pregnant, Madame Le Coq impulsively traveled from Paris to the Pontoise convent to learn more about her daughter's fate. Her encounters with Sesmaisons and the nuns of Saint-Nicolas so upset Madame Le Coq that she gave birth before term, nearly dying in the process.[39]

By drawing attention to the contrast between the "two mothers," Faré judged Sesmaisons by familial values that accented nurturing over discipline, affection over authority. The constructions of motherhood and morality as "natural" rendered them universal and therefore relevant to all women, elite and nonelite, wealthy and poor, lay and clerical. The discourse on domesticity, however, often functioned as an ill-disguised critique aimed at aristocratic women, especially those who dominated the salons and the court. Their supposed preoccupation with their social life and political intrigue distracted them from their "natural" duties.[40] For example, in the *Tableau de Paris,* Louis-Sébastien Mercier begins his entry "Des femmes" with a diatribe against women who publicly played "the role of mediator" by writing to ministers in order to request favors. In contrast to these women who failed to know

37. Lieselotte Steinbrügge, *The Moral Sex: Woman's Nature in the French Enlightenment,* trans. Pamela E. Selwyn (New York, 1995), 30–34; Gutwirth, *Twilight of the Goddesses,* 51–66.

38. *NE* (14 February 1769), 27.

39. Jean-Baptiste Faré, *Mémoire pour le sieur le Cocq, marchand à Paris, Marie-Louise Wantin, son épouse, et Marie-Anne Le Cocque, leur fille* (n.p., 1769), 4.

40. Joan Landes, *Women in the Public Sphere in the Age of the French Revolution* (Ithaca, 1988), chaps. 1–3.

their place, bourgeois women were paragons of domesticity, "a model of wisdom and work (travail)" who held the family together.[41] With this model of maternity at its center, such rhetoric created an ideal of the family reconstituted around displays of affection and not power and rank, which muted parental authority. The political rhetoric of the mid-eighteenth century indicates that any misuse of such authority by parental figures was construed as despotism, the scourge of political and social order.[42] Indeed, Faré's assertions that Sesmaisons failed to be a good "mother" quickly devolved into accusations that she ruled in a capricious and harsh fashion, into a charge of despotism.

The lawyer's indictment of the prioress was more than a litany of grievances but encompassed a more systemic analysis of "monastic governments."[43] The second, more vitriolic brief, the *Plaidoyer pour le sieur Le Coq,* a response to Sesmaisons's own *mémoire judiciaire,* devoted considerable space to a sometimes convoluted discussion of this government, one that appears to have incorporated elements from Montesquieu's *L'Esprit des lois* (1748) and Le Paige's *Lettres historiques sur les fonctions essentielles* (1753–54), the period's most influential treatises on government. In the *Plaidoyer* Faré constructed a history of monasticism that followed a narrative of disintegration and renewal. Because of an absence of effective laws, early medieval monastic governments had tended to degenerate into "absolute monarchies" or despotic regimes. Consequently, secular and ecclesiastic authorities had joined forces and given monastic governments "a democratic and aristocratic form all at the same time."[44] According to Faré, the convent was a "democratic institution" because its constitutions stipulated that all important decisions be made through a plurality of votes. At the same time, since a mother superior took charge of minor day-to-day affairs, the cloister had an "aristocratic" structure. In effect, Faré's ideal of monastic government echoed Montesquieu's appeal to a balanced government based on checks and balances.

Despite these safeguards guaranteed by monastic constitutions, scandals like those involving the Pontoise *hôtel-dieu* indicated that the delicate fusion of aristocratic and democratic government had collapsed, and the convent had disintegrated into a nightmare of tyranny and injustice. In his diagnosis Faré attributed the problems of the convent to its cloistered structure.

41. Louis-Sébastien Mericer, *Tableau de Paris,* 8 vols. (Amsterdam, 1782–83), 3:151, 155.
42. Jeffrey Merrick, "Patriarchalism and Constitutionalism in Eighteenth-Century Parlementary Discourse," *Studies in Eighteenth-Century Culture* 20 (1990): 317–30.
43. Faré, *Mémoire pour le sieur le Cocq,* 5.
44. Faré, *Plaidoyer pour le sieur le Cocq,* 20–21.

Within the closed world of the cloister, superiors justified their rule by responding with "'I want it,'" a "revolting maxim that was the motto of the absolute monarchs of unhappy countries in the Orient."[45] Faré was, of course, evoking oriental despotism, which placed all government in the hands of one person without any laws or regulations to restrain his personal inclination. The convent closely resembled the harem, the feminized space central in the metaphor of oriental despotism. Like the seraglio, the convent was populated by celibate men and women secluded from the world. Like the seraglio, the convent's inhabitants were often at the mercy of their passions and fears. And just as significantly, like the seraglio, the convent was a hidden space.

The convent's enclosed spaces, the same elements that made the convent a sacred space, enabled and, indeed, encouraged superiors to misuse their authority and therefore necessitated intervention. Unlike even "the most absolute civil governments" in which "public opinion" stayed certain brutal acts, the cloister had no parallel means of hindering abuses of power. Why? Because "it is in the shadows that they [superiors] exercise their power, that they find the hope of immunity; it is with the sacred arms that they execute their blows . . . the screams barely pierce through the enclosure, where they are stifled and powerless."[46] According to Faré, the solution was parlementary intervention, and he appealed to the magistrates to reform the cloisters: "Fix, Messieurs, fix the authority of Superiors with precision; curb the despotism of their regime."[47] The lawyer made the magistrates the guardians of monastic constitutions as well as the "constitution" of France itself.[48] It was essentially the role of the *parlements* to make Sesmaisons understand that the *hôtel-dieu*'s constitutions had as much authority over her as they did the other nuns.

Through his references to the *parlement* and his allusions to the seraglio, Faré essentially pitted legitimate power against illegitimate power, tyranny

45. Faré, *Mémoire pour le sieur le Cocq*, 11.

46. Faré, *Plaidoyer pour le sieur le Cocq*, 43.

47. Ibid.

48. Treatises such as Le Paige's *Lettres historiques* made historical claims about France's "fundamental laws" and its ancient constitutions. Moreover, according to Le Paige, the *parlements* had responsibility to protect the constitutions of religious communities. Le Paige himself fought against ultramontane clerics who tampered with the constitutions of the Religieuses Hospitalières of the Rue Mouffetard (1756) or the Paris *Hôtel-Dieu* (1769). Keith Michael Baker, *Inventing the French Revolution: Essays on French Political Culture in the Eighteenth Century* (Cambridge, 1990), 33–37. See also Dale K. Van Kley, *The Religious Origins of the French Revolution: From Calvin to the Civil Constitution* (New Haven, 1996), 191–218.

against justice, and it was a contest coded in gendered terms. Like his legal counterparts, Faré invalidated Sesmaisons's rule while justifying the *parlement*'s authority by contrasting "feminine" arbitrariness with "masculine" justice. Feminine power within these legal briefs was configured as self-serving, dangerously irrational, and highly emotional. Faré did not necessarily negate the superior's authority because she was a woman, but because she used her authority in "feminine" ways. According to Faré, Sesmaisons disregarded the laws of the convent and preferred to establish a regime based on her whims and passions that exceeded the powers prescribed by Saint-Nicolas's constitutions.

In contrast, the magistrates of the *parlements* were very much masculine emblems of authority, their masculinity emphasized by their role as reasonable moderators who upheld the law and operated openly with the public's interests in mind. They operated in a world of transparency that contrasted sharply with the secrecy of the cloister. Indeed, Faré asserted his own masculine legitimacy by repeatedly claiming to unveil Sesmaisons's abuses before the magistrates and the public: "I must explain to you with candor the obscure and hidden motives [of Sesmaisons]."[49] In this manner, Faré's characterization of the prioress on the one side, and of the magistrates and himself on the other, were given meaning in the context of a cultural balance sheet that understood power in gendered terms. Sesmaisons represented "feminine" power, impassioned, secretive, selfish, and therefore, inherently illegitimate. The lawyer and the magistrates embodied "masculine" authority, reasonable, law-abiding, selfless, and transparent, all that was legitimate in government.

The gendered power structure embedded in the various arguments against abbesses and abbess-like superiors reveal the ways in which social imagery was an important element in the critique of monastic authority. As we have seen, Faré attributed Sesmaisons's behavior to her aristocratic background. Moreover, her "feminine" capriciousness ran parallel to her aristocratic sense of entitlement and her aristocratic appetites. The abbess, as a beneficiary of undeserved privilege, and as a weak moral character too easily tempted by the enticements of luxury and domination, became an illegitimate figure of authority in the legal and literary imagination of the mid-eighteenth century. What the Sesmaisons and similar cases involving mother superiors suggest is that the growing concern to define legitimate authority facilitated the fusion of the woman and the aristocrat in the political culture of the period.

49. Faré, *Plaidoyer pour le sieur Le Coq*, 3.

In the discussion below I briefly examine how some of the gendered criticisms against Sesmaisons recurred in a larger context. As such, it is a speculation on how gendered discourse shaped the more general assaults aimed at the aristocracy. In her work on Mary Wollstonecraft's feminism, Barbara Taylor provides a clue as to how we may consider politics, gender, and aristocracy together. Arguing that Wollstonecraft expressed misogynistic views against aristocratic women, Taylor notes that these attitudes extended toward the entire English aristocracy. According to Taylor, "throughout the late eighteenth century, political reformers had equated elite culture with what was dubbed 'effeminacy,' a polysemous term whose meanings all circulated around a feminized sexual subjectivity . . . to be found in women and the sexually incontinent, foppish, Francophile, and possibly homosexual men of the ruling class."[50] Wollstonecraft was repeating English hostility toward French aristocratic style and manners, but these sentiments did not recognize national boundaries. French social critics expressed very similar views about their own aristocracy, thus articulating an anxiety about failed leadership.

Literary authors provided vivid representations of effete, male aristocrats. Not only did aristocratic men become effeminized, but even the more masculine figures resorted to deception, motivated by their personal agendas. They failed to adhere to the standards of moderation that, according to Montesquieu, constituted "the very soul of this [aristocratic] government; a moderation, I mean, founded on virtue, not that which proceeds from indolence and pusillanimity."[51] When restraint and virtue were ignored, power became distorted. Instead of conforming to certain norms of masculinity, the aristocrat embodied the negative traits associated with women, thus creating a social and gendered crisis.

The urban nobility, or specifically the subset of the nobility most often labeled aristocracy, inhabited what Madelyn Gutwirth has described as a world replete with "cultural femaleness."[52] Aristocratic men and women shared an opulent lifestyle filled with gambling, extravagant fashion, amorous intrigues, and sumptuous surroundings, all of which made them easy targets in an environment where utility, citizenship, and public welfare were issues of debate. The *petit-maître* or fop epitomized the aristocrat who relinquished

50. Barbara Taylor, "Misogyny and Feminism: The Case of Mary Wollstonecraft," in *The Age of Cultural Revolutions: Britain and France, 1759–1820,* ed. Colin Jones and Dror Wahrman (Berkeley and Los Angeles, 2002), 208.

51. Montesquieu, *The Spirit of the Laws,* trans. Thomas Nugent (New York, 1949), 23.

52. Stephen D. Kale, "Women, the Public Sphere, and the Persistence of Salons," *French Historical Studies* 25 (2002): 89.

his masculinity through his devotion to fashion and frivolity. For example, the abbé Coyer reported a private interview with a young judge that took place while the latter was being dressed: "I thought I'd fallen in with an assault upon a duchess's curlings and perfumes. . . . Let our surprise henceforth cease in seeing male persons wearing earrings, doing embroidery, receiving company in their beds at noon, interrupting a serious conversation with a dog . . . steal, in sum, all its charms from the other sex."[53] Coyer's words indicate that for social critics, the members of this aristocratic set had merged into one sex, gendered female. This immersion in feminine pursuits automatically denoted absorption with the trivial. According to Helvétius, "a nation too occupied with the coquetry of a woman or the fatuousness of a fop, is for sure a frivolous nation."[54]

Behind Coyer's and Helvétius's words lay the notion that this aristocratic world was an inversion of nature, one in which powerful females and emasculated men dominated more virile exemplars of citizenship, who suffered the multiple indignities of an inequitable social and political system.[55] "Natural" leadership qualities that Raynal, for example, had cast in masculine language had become subsumed in a world of self-indulgence where women dictated the rules. According to Louis-Sébastien Mercier, aristocratic women are "the queens of society and the arbiters of taste and pleasures," and noblemen "extend their grasping hands around the dispenser of favors and money."[56] Instead of being in charge, the nobleman renounces his responsibilities and transforms into an aristocratic courtesan, a pathetic figure who prostitutes himself for his livelihood. Moreover, he participates in the effeminization of authority by submitting to a female "ruler."

Some of the more scathing critiques of this weakened masculinity appeared in literature such as Laclos's *Les liaisons dangereuses*. In *Les liaisons dangereuses* we see the libertine vicomte de Valmont shuttling back and forth between two feminine spaces: the aristocratic milieu of Paris, dominated by the marquise de Merteuil, and the "natural" world of Valmont's aunt and her protégé Madame de Tourvel.[57] I would suggest that Valmont himself is, in

---

53. As cited in Gutwirth, *Twilight of the Goddesses,* 14f.

54. Helvétius, *De l'homme, de ses facultés intellectuelles et de son éducation, ouvrage posthume de M. Helvétius* (London, 1773), 72.

55. For a discussion of effeminacy and the body politic in another context, see Kathleen Wilson, *The Sense of the People: Politics, Culture, and Imperialism in England, 1715–1785* (Cambridge, 1995), 185–204.

56. Mercier, *Tableau de Paris,* 1:23f.

57. Christine Roulston, *Virtue, Gender, and the Authentic Self in Eighteenth-Century Fiction* (Gainesville, 1998), 173.

many ways, a feminized, if not effeminate, figure who follows Merteuil's lead. Valmont's complex machinations parallel the marquise's subterfuge, and it is her approval that dictates his pursuit and subsequent break with Tourvel. Valmont may employ military language, speaking of "conquest" and "glory," but in the end, his battlefield is restricted to the realm of the private, comparable to Merteuil's own campaigns. Valmont the libertine reigns as a romantic conqueror, but Laclos the soldier hints that his "glory" reflects misdirected masculine energies. Valmont compares himself to "Turenne or Fredrick [the Great]," but even in the midst of rejoicing in his conquest over Madame de Tourvel, he confesses that "at present, I am unmanned [*m'être amolli*] like Hannibal in the delights of Capoue."[58] Given the resentments within the army against those who regarded military rank as another title as opposed to actual service, debates undoubtedly familiar to the artillery officer Laclos, Valmont's careless military references represented a misappropriation of his noble heritage in the service of personal desires and female authority.[59]

Thus, the criticism aimed against mother superiors like Sesmaisons, Lantilhac, and others echoed the cultural anxieties surrounding the stereotypes of such aristocrats as the *petit-maître* or the tyrannical lord. Both sets of characters featured a critique of effeminized, despotic power, power that was driven by personal caprice and used in an arbitrary and high-handed fashion. Moreover, the denunciation of feminine and aristocratic power paralleled this criticism of monarchical authority as indicated by public perceptions of a weakened male authority overpowered by women. The relationship between Louis XV and his mistresses and, later, the perceived interference of Marie-Antoinette aroused deep anxiety because many regarded these women as having usurped the king's power for private purposes. The interlocking nature of such views and the hostile observations about aristocratic manners is revealed in the ubiquitous metaphor of the harem. Montesquieu himself had argued that the harem-like setting of the court led to the corruption of the nobility: "He [the king] likes to reward those who serve him, but he pays as generously for the attentions, or rather the indolence, of his courtiers, as for campaigns laboriously carried on by his

58. Choderlos de Laclos, *Les liaisons dangereuses,* in *Oevures Complètes,* ed. M. Allem (Paris, 1951), 326.
59. David D. Bien, "La Réaction aristocratique avant 1789: l'exemple de l'armée," *Annales: E.S.C.* 292 (1974): 23–48, 505–34.

officers."[60] No doubt borrowing from Montesquieu, the marquis d'Argenson bitingly described how Madame de Pompadour corrupted the French court by converting it into a pleasure palace or, in d'Argenson's words, "the interior of a seraglio" so that she could maintain her influence over the king and state policy.[61]

For eighteenth-century social and political critics, a world governed by whims and luxury and the concealed schemes of women denoted despotism. Thus, notorious for his love of secrecy, Louis XV sullied legitimate sovereignty by acting in "feminine," despotic ways and yet was powerless in his relations with women. The checks and balances theorized by Montesquieu had failed, allowing both king and aristocracy to rule in illegitimate ways, out of step with an emerging commercial society and a changing political arena that increasingly valued "reason" and "transparency."[62]

Through this brief examination of abbesses and the gendered rhetoric of despotism, which fused anxieties about aristocracy and women, my hope is to promote further discussion about how the gendered imagery of aristocracy factored into the eighteenth-century crisis of authority. As this essay has suggested, aristocracy then did not just signal a sociopolitical group but a set of values associated with a certain section of the nobility.[63] How can this conceptual framework be used to reassess the nobility's role in the long-term origins of the French Revolution? I would suggest that one way to consider how gendered discourse can be brought to bear on our thinking about social relations is in analysis of the formation of the nation, a subject recently addressed by David Bell, Jay Smith, and others.[64] We may also profit from the work of British historians of the eighteenth-century, most notably Linda Colley, who have examined more closely how issues of gender and class, especially with respect to the aristocracy, contributed to the emergence

60. Montesquieu, *Persian Letters,* 91. Montesquieu is, of course, referring to Louis XIV.

61. René de Voyer de Paulmy, marquis d'Argenson, *Journal et mémoires du marquis d'Argenson,* 9 vols., ed. E. J. B. Rathery (Paris, 1857–67), 6:342; 7:400.

62. Colin Jones, *The Great Nation: France from Louis XV to Napoleon, 1715–1799* (London, 2002), 128–29; 223.

63. On the changing understanding of aristocracy in the English context, see Dror Wahrman, *The Making of the Modern Self: Identity and Culture in Eighteenth-Century England* (New Haven, 2004), 151.

64. David A. Bell, *The Cult of the Nation in France: Inventing Nationalism, 1680–1800* (Cambridge, Mass., 2001); Jay M. Smith, *Nobility Reimagined: The Patriotic Nation in Eighteenth-Century France* (Ithaca, N.Y., 2005).

of British identity.[65] In the decades before the French Revolution, the images of a gendered "aristocracy" may be seen as a construction of a political and cultural "other," at odds with the emerging cultural, if not purely political, construction of the nation. Pulsing with concern for the interests of the *nation*, Rousseau, Montesquieu, and many others had specifically demonized women, blaming them for a process of degeneration.[66] Members of the nobility, especially those who espoused ideals of personal merit and public service, would seek to distance themselves from the decadent aristocrat and despotic monarchy by calling for a form of regeneration that also required the elimination of unwarranted privilege and power. Nevertheless, at the onset of the French Revolution, the effete aristocrat would return to haunt such reforming nobles, who had to contend with the conflated images of aristocracy and feminine corruption in the decisive political debates of 1789.[67] Within the volatile politics of the Revolution, this aristocrat would become an outsider, effete and ineffective, who had betrayed the nation.

65. See Linda Colley, *Britons: Forging the Nation 1701–1837* (New Haven, 1992), chaps. 4 and 6; Philip Carter, "An 'Effeminate' or 'Efficient' Nation? Masculinity and Eighteenth-Century Social Documentary," *Textual Practice* 11:3 (1997): 429–43. While Joan B. Landes's work on visual representations and gender suggests the possibility of such investigation, it is restricted to the French Revolution and iconography. See Joan Landes, *Visualizing the Nation: Gender, Representation, and Revolution in Eighteenth-Century France* (Ithaca, 2001)

66. Bell, *Cult of the Nation*, 149–50.

67. Landes, *Visualizing the Nation*, 45–54.

7

NOBLES INTO ARISTOCRATS, OR HOW AN
ORDER BECAME A CONSPIRACY

Thomas E. Kaiser

The sweeping success of the revisionist interpretation of the French Revolution
has been nowhere more evident than in the portrait of the eighteenth-century
French nobility painted by the last generation of historians. While Alfred
Cobban and George Taylor were reconfiguring the bourgeoisie, such historians
as Robert Forster, William Doyle, and Guy Chaussinand-Nogaret attacked
long-standing notions of nobles as economically parasitic, intellectually
unenlightened, and politically retrograde.[1] Returning to many of the themes
advanced by Alexis de Tocqueville more than a century earlier, revisionists
contended that except for its privileges, the nobility closely resembled the
middle classes out of which many noble families had only recently emerged.
Even with regard to such sensitive matters as their tax exemptions, nobles
were far less insistent on maintaining their special status than had been previously thought. In Chaussinand-Nogaret's scenario, intermarriage, overlapping
economic interests, and congruent political outlooks were leading to a
fusion of the Second and Third Estates, with the result that by 1789 they

I should like to thank David Bien and William Doyle for their many incisive comments and
helpful suggestions with regard to this article.

1. Alfred Cobban, *The Social Interpretation of the French Revolution* (Cambridge, 1964); George
V. Taylor, "Types of Capitalism in Eighteenth-Century France," *English Historical Review* 79
(1964): 478–97, and "Noncapitalist Wealth and the Origins of the French Revolution," *American
Historical Review* 72 (1967): 469–96; Robert Forster, *The Nobility of Toulouse in the Eighteenth Century*
(Baltimore, 1960); William Doyle, "Was There an Aristocratic Reaction in Pre-Revolutionary
France?" *Past and Present* 57 (1972): 97–122; Guy Chaussinand-Nogaret, *La noblesse au XVIIIème
siècle: de la féodalité aux lumières* ([Paris], 1976).

had arrived at a common general political program. The *cahiers de doléances* (lists of grievances drawn up by electors when voting for representatives to the Estates-General) and other evidence, he contended, pointed to the conclusion that both the Second and Third Estates were prepared to jettison the Old Regime in favor of a new, more rational and democratic political system. Once the unpleasantness of the Terror was over, the two former orders stood ready to assume their joint historic roles as custodians of the postrevolutionary French state—a finding that coincided well with François Furet's contention that the end of the Terror witnessed the end of Jacobin fanaticism, unrestrained by objective social interest.[2]

In shifting attention away from social conflict toward politics in general and political culture in particular, this new view of the nobility, along with other aspects of the revisionist critique, opened the door to fresh reinterpretations of many revolutionary phenomena. But its most evident point of vulnerability was immediately apparent to perceptive observers, such as Emmanuel Le Roy Ladurie, who noted in his review of Chaussinand-Nogaret's book that the Revolution did become radically anti-noble after all. How, he legitimately wondered, could the prerevolutionary fusion of orders theory be reconciled with the abolition of the nobility in 1790 and the anti-noble violence of the Terror?[3] One sophisticated response strongly marked by revisionism was put forward by Patrice Higonnet.[4] For Higonnet, hostility to the Second Order arose not because of what nobles themselves wanted, thought, or did, but rather in response to the rise of so-called bourgeois universalism (essentially, belief in natural equality) and to the political opportunism of the revolutionary middle class, who exploited anti-nobilism as a means of deflecting popular demands for the redistribution of property. What Higonnet's analysis did not explain was why anti-nobilism proved such an effective weapon in the hands of bourgeois politicians—that is, why denunciations of nobles as "aristocrats" proliferated from even before the Revolution, and why urban masses, who had not directly borne the weight of "feudal dues," found so much visceral satisfaction in the guillotining of former nobles during the Terror.[5]

2. François Furet, *Penser la Révolution française* 2nd ed. ([Paris], 1983), 108.

3. Review by Le Roy republished in Chaussinand-Nogaret, *La noblesse,* 2nd ed. (Brussels, 1984), v.

4. Patrice Higonnet, *Class, Ideology, and the Rights of Nobles during the French Revolution* (Oxford, 1981).

5. Ibid., 118–25. Higonnet argued that popular urban anti-nobilism was an echo of bourgeois anti-nobilism, which bourgeois politicians pandered to but ultimately had to restrain. I think there is much to be said on behalf of this view, but the motivations behind anti-nobilism still remained obscure.

Further research now makes it possible and worthwhile to reexamine the perplexing phenomenon of anti-nobilism in the prerevolutionary and early revolutionary periods, which is the central concern of this essay.[6] If there has been a common conclusion of this research, it is that Chaussinand-Nogaret's portrait of the nobility as fellow travelers of the bourgeoisie, similarly alienated from the Old Regime, was considerably overdrawn and significantly distorted a much more complicated picture. To be sure, the critics of revisionism recognized that the Second Estate felt profound disaffection with many aspects of the Old Regime and that a liberal wing of the nobility was prepared to endorse many bourgeois demands. But these phenomena, they argued, hardly prove the existence of an emerging, broad bourgeois-noble consensus at the end of the eighteenth century. Indeed, as further research demonstrated, the clash between them was rooted in opposing interests and agendas after all.

One of the most powerful cases for this position was made by John Markoff and Gilbert Shapiro in their reexamination of the *cahiers de doléances,* upon which Chaussinand-Nogaret had so heavily relied.[7] Utilizing a far more systematic and nuanced methodology than any used previously, Markoff and Shapiro revealed profound differences in political outlooks of the Second and Third Estates. Thus, for example, although the nobility was willing to make notable concessions to the Third Estate regarding tax and other fiscal privileges, they were far from willing to abandon the honorific symbols of their privileged status, which meant far more to them than earlier Marxist accounts had recognized. Similarly, Markoff and Shapiro found that most nobles—Chaussinand-Nogaret's assertions notwithstanding—differed markedly from the Third Estate in their demands regarding voting procedures at the upcoming Estates-General. However often they cited the works of Voltaire and Rousseau, most nobles refused to accept the new status of "citizen" proffered to them by the bourgeoisie if this meant eradicating the distinguishing privileges that many noble families had worked long and hard to obtain. In short, the conflict between the Third and Second Estates in 1789 and after was less the result of misunderstandings and missed signals, as some revisionists argued, than of endemic differences in goals and interests.

6. In this essay, I shall not be dealing with rural anti-seigneurialism, which, although intersecting with elite anti-nobilism at various points, had its own political trajectory. For excellent insight on their interaction, see John Markoff, *The Abolition of Feudalism: Peasants, Lords, and Legislators in the French Revolution* (University Park, 1996).

7. Gilbert Shapiro and John Markoff, *Revolutionary Demands: A Content Analysis of the Cahiers de Doléances of 1789* (Stanford, 1998), chaps. 15 and 16. See also Markoff, *Abolition,* passim.

Careful analysis of the events of 1789 by Michael Fitzsimmons and Timothy Tackett further supported this position.[8] In stressing the strong reservations held by many nobles about the attack on privilege in the summer of 1789, these historians found the nobility to be much less radical and accommodating than Chaussinand-Nogaret had claimed, and by implication they rejected Higonnet's argument that what the Second Estate thought or did mattered little in relation to the outbreak of revolutionary anti-nobilism. To the contrary, Fitzsimmons and Tackett contended, noble resistance to Third Estate demands for political equality was vigorous and public, and this resistance remained energetic long after the fall of the Bastille, with important political consequences for the revolutionary process.

What implications did these results have for anti-nobilism? Most important, bourgeois *ressentiment* of noble privileges and prerogatives could once again be pointed to as a motivating force behind the attack on the nobility during the Revolution. But many anomalies remained to be dealt with. Not the least of them was the conundrum posed by the Society of Thirty, the much-celebrated public lobby that between late 1788 and the middle of 1789 led the campaign to expand Third Estate representation in the upcoming Estates-General. As revisionists had observed from early on, the vast majority of the Society was of noble background, a fact that told against any clean division of the political public between enlightened bourgeoisie and traditionalist nobles.[9] Fresh inquiry into the Society of Thirty by Daniel Wick in the late 1980s—followed soon thereafter by further research on the politics of the court—offered a new explanation of this anomaly, which not only reconfigured the map of Second Estate politics but also suggested new ways of approaching the problem of revolutionary anti-nobilism.[10]

In his prosopographical analysis of the Society, Wick reconfirmed its overwhelmingly noble complexion: of its fifty-five members, no less than 90 percent were from the Second Estate, and nearly half of these were of the *noblesse d'épée* who had been granted honors of the court. Wick observed something else highly significant: out of more than a thousand pensions granted in the *maisons* of the king, queen, and the king's brothers, and in

8. Michael Fitzsimmons, *The Remaking of France: The National Assembly and the Constitution of 1791* (Cambridge, 1994); Timothy Tackett, *Becoming a Revolutionary: The Deputies of the French National Assembly and the Emergence of a Revolutionary Culture, 1789–1790* (Princeton, 1996).

9. Elizabeth L. Eisenstein, "Who Intervened in 1788?" *American Historical Review* 71 (1965): 77–103.

10. Daniel L. Wick, *A Conspiracy of Well-Intentioned Men: The Society of Thirty and the French Revolution* (New York, 1987).

the royal stables, not a single one had gone to the court noble families of the Society of Thirty. From this finding Wick drew the conclusion that what impelled so many nobles in the Society to support the radical demands of the Third Estate was not the progressive political outlook attributed to them by Chaussinand-Nogaret, but rather their exclusion from high offices and favors in the court of Louis XVI. Indeed, argued Wick, through its highly skewed distribution of favors, the monarchy had launched nothing less than "an unprecedented assault on the traditional power and preroga- tives of the Court nobility."[11] The beneficiaries of this "assault" were a corps of newly created nobles, to whom Louis looked for more professional service to the crown, and also a small clique of royal favorites, who used their influence with the queen to extract obscenely generous graces and appointments for themselves and their cronies. While granting that the antagonism of many court nobles to the monarchy eroded in the general storm over privilege in 1789, Wick maintained that it persisted long enough to subvert the reform programs of Calonne and Loménie de Brienne. In the end, the royal couple's rough handling of court nobles had proved "a fatal mistake."[12]

Wick's work has been criticized, particularly for its analysis of the Society of Thirty's political program,[13] but his general picture of distribution of court favors under Louis XVI has largely held up. Indirect confirmation of his claims regarding the distribution of court favors was provided by T. J. A. Le Goff's illuminating study of royal pensions.[14] More direct support of Wick's view came from an exhaustive study of space allocation at Versailles by William Ritchey Newton.[15] Newton showed that during the eighteenth century a number of factors—principally, the growth of the royal family and architectural transformations at the château—substantially reduced lodging room available to court nobles. As a result, many high nobles, including princes of the blood, were driven from the court for want of *Lebensraum*. Furthering this process of exclusion were the personal habits of the royal

11. Ibid., 136.

12. Ibid., 145.

13. Kenneth Margerison, *Pamphlets and Public Opinion: The Campaign for a Union of Orders in the Early French Revolution* (West Lafayette, 1998), chap. 3.

14. T. J. A. Le Goff, "Essai sur les pensions royales," in Martine Acerra, et al., eds., *État, marine et société* (Paris, 1995), 252–81.

15. William Ritchey Newton, *L'Espace du roi: La Cour de France au château de Versailles, 1682–1789* (n.p., 2000). For another view, see Philip Mansel, *The Court of France, 1789–1830* (Cambridge, 1988), chap. 1.

couple, particularly Marie-Antoinette. Her disdain for court etiquette, reluctance to hold court ceremonies, undiplomatic snubs of established court families, and retirement into a private sphere with her close favorites stripped Versailles of its role as a public theater where court nobles displayed and reaffirmed their rank and honor. Thus, well before the royal family abandoned Versailles on 6 October 1789, the court had largely lost its function as an agency of social validation for the court nobility.[16]

Wick's demonstration of a rising tide of noble *ressentiment* against the court suggests that although bourgeois and nobles had different long-range interests and agendas, they shared a growing hostility to Versailles. This shared hostility for a time cemented their common front against "despotism" during the prerevolution.[17] But once the debate on privilege and representation at the Estates-General erupted in late 1788 and noble resistance to bourgeois demands for greater political and civil equality intensified in May and June of 1789, the Third Estate became progressively convinced that the nobility as a whole was plotting to undermine the Revolution with the same court coterie that seemed to have plundered the state and generated the fiscal crisis.

What I intend to demonstrate in the balance of this chapter is the key role played by an alleged aristo-ministerial conspiracy in facilitating this process.[18] Already evident in the controversies over representation in the Estates-General the previous autumn, this conspiratorial notion metastasized in the early summer of 1789. At this juncture, noble resistance to the revolutionary process and impolitic fraternizing with court insiders lent

16. Although there is no room to analyze it here, other recent work that sheds light on court-noble relations includes John Hardman, *Louis XVI* (New Haven, 1993) and *French Politics, 1774–1789: From the Accession of Louis XVI to the Fall of the Bastille* (London, 1995); Munro Price, *Preserving the Monarchy: The Comte de Vergennes, 1774–1789* (Cambridge, 1995); Rory A. W. Browne, "Court and Crown: Rivalry at the Court of Louis XVI and Its Importance in the Formation of a Pre-Revolutionary Aristocratic Opposition" (D.Phil., Oxford University, 1991).

17. An early adumbration of this argument can be found in Henri Carré, *La noblesse et l'opinion publique au XVIIIe siècle* (Paris, 1920).

18. Timothy Tackett has argued that conspiratorial thinking was a relatively rare and fitful phenomenon among French elites in the later eighteenth century until 1791. "Conspiracy Obsession in a Time of Revolution: French Elites and the Origins of the Terror, 1789–1792," *American Historical Review* 105 (2000): 691–713. For a contrary view, see Peter Campbell, "Conspiracy and Political Practice from the Ancien Régime to the French Revolution," in *Conspiracies and Conspiracy Theory in Early Modern Europe from the Waldensians to the French Revolution,* ed. Barry Coward and Julian Swann (Hampshire, Eng., 2004), 197–212. See also, Peter Campbell, Thomas Kaiser, and Marisa Linton, eds., *Conspiracy in the French Revolution* (Manchester, Eng., forthcoming). On contemporary meanings of "conspiracy," see Jean-Claude Waquet, *La Conjuration des dictionnaires: vérités des mots et vérités de la politique dans la France moderne* (Strasburg, 2000).

credibility to the belief—eventually accepted even by the most sober and skeptical deputies of the Third Estate—that an aristo-ministerial plot was about to be sprung and had to be crushed in order to save the Revolution. Climaxing in the preemptive defense of Paris on 14 July, the counter-campaign against the "aristocracy" intensified again on the eve of the October days. By this time, belief in an aristo-ministerial plot, whose existence was thereafter officially confirmed by the Assembly's report on the July crisis and by other government inquiries, had hardened. To be sure, hopes persisted that members of the nobility might yet be persuaded to cast their lot with the Revolution rather than with the plotters and to accept the civil equality mandated by the abolition of noble titles in June 1790. But by then a shadow of suspicion had been cast over the whole former noble order; ex-nobles had become prima facie "aristocrats."

Anti-Nobilism and Conspiracy in Early Modern France

Over the history of the Old Regime, anti-noble sentiment took different forms calling for different responses. One of its early incarnations appeared during the chaotic sixteenth-century Wars of Religion, when a palpable wave of popular protest arose against seigneurial oppression and violence committed against *roturiers*. These protests seem to have dropped off pre-cipitously during the reign of Henry IV.[19] Much more enduring was a royalist strain of anti-nobilism. Although echoing popular complaints, royalist anti-nobilism entailed a far more learned and systematic attack on noble prerogatives and rights that cleared the way juridically for the asser-tion of the king's absolute sovereignty. In support of this cause, royal jurists, such as Charles Dumoulin, Charles Loyseau, and Louis Chantereau-Lefebvre, fashioned a national history that cast the medieval progenitors of the lords as villains in two guises: first, as usurpers of public powers originally granted as temporary royal concessions, and second as "tyrants" who had inflicted an "odious" servitude on their tenants through intimidation and force.[20] It was only with the growth of royal power at the end of the Middle Ages,

19. Davis Bitton, *The French Nobility in Crisis, 1569–1640* (Stanford, 1969), chap. 1; Ellery Schalk, *From Valor to Pedigree: Ideas of Nobility in France in the Sixteenth and Seventeenth Centuries* (Princeton, 1986), chap. 5.

20. The literature on these developments is vast. For a good brief synthesis, see Harold A. Ellis, *Boulainvilliers and the French Monarchy: Aristocratic Politics in Early Eighteenth-Century France* (Ithaca, 1988), 31–39.

went the royalist argument, that the French people was gradually liberated from feudal "tyranny," since it was only a reinvigorated royal state that effectively contained the malfeasance of the lords. With some significant changes, much the same case against the nobility was made again in the eighteenth century by a string of royalist historians, most notably the abbé Jean-Baptiste Dubos and Jacob-Nicolas Moreau.[21] Although these juridically minded historians painted a highly unflattering portrait of the nobility, their objective, it should be stressed, was not to strip nobles of their privileged status; indeed, this status, as William Beik and others have demonstrated, was made all the more secure by the consolidation of absolutism.[22] Rather, their intent was to throw the nobility and other privileged bodies on the ideological defensive in the constant, often bitter negotiations over the limits of royal power that inevitably arose in a polity without an articulated constitution. As the French Revolution amply demonstrated later, however, these arguments could be used to advance a much more radical agenda.

What gave further resonance to the juridical perspective of the royalist jurists was the history of noble revolt. It was one of the nobility's proudest claims under the Old Regime that the Second Estate had been historically the monarchy's strongest resource and could be counted on to rally to the king's side in times of trouble.[23] Whatever the truth of this self-serving commonplace, it was no less true that absolutism had developed partly in reaction to a series of noble military challenges to the crown, all of which failed but some of which proved highly destabilizing. During the Hundred Years' War, the War of the Public Good, the Wars of Religion, and the Fronde, French nobles pitted their armies against the king's, often in league with foreign powers. Arlette Jouanna has analyzed the structural similarities and variations among these noble revolts, many of which took

---

21. Thomas E. Kaiser, "The Abbé Dubos and the Historical Defense of Monarchy in Early Eighteenth-Century France," *Studies on Voltaire and the Eighteenth Century* 267 (1989): 77–102; Dieter Gembicki, *Histoire et politique à la fin de l'ancien régime: Jacob-Nicolas Moreau, 1717–1803* (Paris, 1976).

22. William Beik, *Absolutism and Society in Seventeenth-Century France: State Power and Provincial Aristocracy in Languedoc* (Cambridge, 1985).

23. See, for example, the "Mémoire des Princes" of 12 December 1788, in which the princes invoked the memory of "this brave, ancient, and respectable nobility, which has shed so much blood for the *patrie* and for its kings, which placed Hugh Capet on the throne, which took the scepter from the hands of the English so as to offer it to Charles VII and was able to secure the crown for the founder of the current dynasty." *Archives parlementaires de 1787 à 1860*, 1st ser., 2nd ed. (Paris, 1879), 1:487–89.

the form of so-called *ligues, conjurations, complots,* and *conspirations* (variations of conspiracy).[24] As Jouanna points out, the internal organization and animating spirit of these movements bore a striking similarity to certain elements of the royal state. For the monarchy, as we now know, was no monolithic bureaucracy but a polity riddled with clientage networks and other associations. Like the subversive revolts launched against it, these groups were bound together by ties of *fidélité* and motivated by a proto-nationalist ideology rivaling the king's.[25] Thus, one late sixteenth-century noble text invoked the subversive term *ligue* in conjunction with "the name of *français,*" which "is not the name of a province, city, or country but that of certain valorous personages recruited from all nations, *leagued* [italics mine] together" to oppose the alleged abuse of royal power.[26]

To be sure, the dismantling of noble armies in the face of overwhelming royal military supremacy during the seventeenth century tipped the balance of power in favor of the crown; indeed, nobles became progressively more dependent upon service in the king's army to sustain their prestige and fortunes.[27] By 1700 the threat of armed noble revolts had clearly receded, although it could not be altogether ignored, especially when domestic noble opposition attracted foreign support.[28] At the same time, the expansion of the royal court, whose "disciplining" of the nobility has been vastly over-emphasized by Norbert Elias and other historians, created new opportunities for subtler forms of noble mischief.[29] As Roger Mettam has shown for the reign of Louis XIV and Peter Campbell for the reign of Louis XV, the corridors and back alleys of Versailles became sites for endless scheming by nobles seeking honorific and material privileges and positions for their clans and clients, often to the detriment of the king, who struggled to keep their

24. Arlette Jouanna, *Le devoir de révolte: la noblesse française et la gestation de l'état moderne* ([Paris], 1989), chap. 13. See also Orest Ranum, *The Fronde: A French Revolution* (New York, 1993), 209–10; and Jonathan Dewald, *The European Nobility, 1400–1800* (Cambridge, 1996), 134–39.

25. Sharon Kettering, *Patrons, Brokers and Clients in Seventeenth-Century France* (New York, 1986).

26. Cited in Jouanna, *Devoir,* 373–74.

27. On the army and nobility, see André Corvisier, *L'Armée française de la fin du XVIIe siècle au ministère de Choiseul,* 2 vols. (Paris, 1964); David A. Bien, "La réaction aristocratique avant 1789; l'exemple de l'armée," *Annales: E.S.C.* 29 (1974): 23–48, 505–34, and "The Army in the French Enlightenment: Reform, Reaction, and Revolution," *Past and Present* 85 (1979): 68–98; Rafe Blaufarb, *The French Army, 1750–1820: Careers, Talent, Merit* (Manchester, 2002).

28. For one such instance, see John D. Woodbridge, *Revolt in Prerevolutionary France: The Prince de Conti's Conspiracy against Louis XV* (Baltimore, 1995).

29. Nobert Elias, *The Court Society,* trans. Edmund Jephcott (New York, 1983).

"cabals" steadily in view.[30] It was principally court nobles La Bruyère had in mind when, in a celebrated passage, he described the typical courtier as a man "deep, impenetrable . . . [who] misrepresents his favors, smiles at his enemies, represses his desires, disguises his passions, contradicts his heart, [and] speaks, acts against his [true] sentiments."[31]

That noble plotting became part of politics as usual during the Old Regime hardly meant it was universally well viewed. To be sure, in the flood tide of reaction to the Sun King's reign during the Orléans regency, readers thrilled to the memoirs of the Fronde leader Cardinal de Retz, and they retained a lively interest in escapades such as his.[32] But writers sympathetic to the crown projected a far darker counterimage of noble conspiracies, which drew upon the perennial royalist antifeudal themes of noble "usurpation" and "tyranny" while also reflecting more immediate concerns. Thus, the celebrated late sixteenth-century *Satyre Menippée* took devastating aim at noble rebellions, which it represented as a product of unrestrained ambition masked by religious hypocrisy.[33] During the eighteenth century, the rehabilitation of the historical role of the nobility by Boulainvilliers and Montesquieu elicited a powerful reaction among royalists like Voltaire, who struck back by deconstructing histories of noble rebellion justified as defenses of French liberty. Thus, in his *Essai sur les moeurs,* Voltaire ridiculed the feudal law requiring a liege vassal to join his lord's antiroyal insurgencies as an "ordinance for making civil war."[34] He likewise described the late Valois court—ravaged by noble factions—as the site of daily "conspiracies, real or supposed, duels, assassinations, imprisonments without form or reason, worse than the troubles that had caused them."[35] In his *Henriade,* he depicted the plots of the dissident Guises as the product of ambition allied with religious "fanaticism."

If the history of French noble revolts had a profound impact on Voltaire and his contemporaries, no plot left so deep a mark in this neoclassical age

30. Roger Mettam, *Power and Faction in Louis XIV's France* (Oxford, 1988); Peter R. Campbell, *Power and Politics in Old Regime France, 1720–1745* (London, 1996).

31. Jean de La Bruyère, *Les Caractères, ou les Moeurs de ce siècle* (Paris, 1962), 221.

32. On the reception of Retz's memoirs, see J. H. M. Salmon, *Cardinal de Retz: The Anatomy of a Conspirator* (London, 1969), 3–5.

33. In the words of the *Satyre,* to princes in revolt "religion is but a mask, with which they amuse the simple, just as foxes amuse magpies with their long tails to trap them and eat them at will." Anon., *Satyre Menippée de la vertu du catholicon d'espagne et de la tenue des Etats de Paris,* 3 vols. (Bonn, 1709), 1:159. The first edition of this frequently republished work appeared in 1594.

34. Voltaire, *Essai sur les moeurs et l'esprit des nations,* 2 vols. (Paris, 1963), 1:522.

35. Ibid., 2:514.

as did the Roman conspiracy of Lucius Sergius Catilina.[36] Transpiring at a time of growing threats to the Republic in the first century BCE, the Catiline conspiracy was a failed plot to seize power by noble malcontents, who were eventually hunted down and executed on the instigation of Cicero. This bloody tale was known to eighteenth-century readers primarily from the accounts of Cicero and Sallust, who presented the story less as a case study in statecraft than as a cautionary moral tale.[37] Catilina was represented as a vice-ridden monster, a master of sexual and pecuniary entrapment of accomplices, a dissembler and an arch-hypocrite hiding his raging personal ambition under a pretense of devotion to republican liberty. In the eighteenth-century retelling of this tale, including Voltaire's celebrated play *Catilina ou Rome sauvée,* the social origins of Catilina and his cronies were pointedly contrasted with those of the hero, Cicero. Whereas Catilina's gang descended from the dispossessed nobility and their vices were attributed specifically to their pedigree, Cicero was portrayed as the "new man," who, by dint of his bourgeois virtues, ascended the greasy, aristocratic pole of Roman politics and emerged on top just in time to save the Republic.[38] Little wonder that at the end of the Old Regime the patriot André Chénier perceived in the tale of Catilina a warning for his own and all future ages. "Patrician jealousy," he declaimed, "survives and crosses generations to all these noble families, who, although separated by century and country, always, so long as they have the same pretensions, the same spirit, the same language, seem to compose a single body that together advances on the heads of other men and maintains itself through force, always avid for empire and exclusive power."[39]

If the Catiline conspiracy provided the paradigm for noble subversion, government by the nobility was also viewed through a classical lens, namely, Aristotle's notion of "aristocracy."[40] A term that under the Old Regime was neither specific to the nobility nor necessarily pejorative, "aristocracy" meant simply "rule by the best." Thus, according to Aristotle and his

36. Among other works written on the subject, see Claude Prosper Jolyot de Crébillon, *Catalina* (1749); Séran de La Tour, *Histoire de Catilina* (1749); and Isaac Bellet, *Histoire de la conjuration de Catilina* (1752).

37. For modern English editions, see Cicero, "Against Lucius Sergius Catilina," in *Selected Political Speeches,* trans. Michael Grant (London, 1969), 71–145; Sallust, *The Conspiracy of Catiline,* trans. S. A. Hanford (London, 1963).

38. For a discussion, see Chantal Grell, *Le dix-huitième siècle et l'antiquité en France, 1680–1789,* in *Studies on Voltaire and the Eighteenth Century* (Oxford, 1995), 330–31: 1091–98.

39. Cited in ibid., 1097.

40. Aristotle, *The Politics,* trans. T. A. Sinclair (Baltimore, 1962), bks. 3, 5.

French epigones, it could be applied to a variety of constitutional arrangements, from regimes so inclusive they approached "democracy" to others so
exclusive they approached "oligarchy." Like Aristotle and for many of the
same reasons, some Old Regime political writers perceived advantages to
aristocracy as a form of government, whose benefits, they contended, were
exemplified by the benign regimes of Venice and Genoa.[41] Yet also like
Aristotle, most Old Regime writers were highly wary of the abuses of aristocracy, especially in its hereditary forms. Aristotle warned that aristocracies
tend naturally to degrade into oligarchies, wherein the privileged few misuse
their power and enrich themselves, and for this reason he favored aristocracies
leaning toward democracy.[42] French royalists, intent upon making the case
against noble pretensions and disorders, applied the term specifically to
noble designs in a manner that evoked these pejorative implications, hence
their reference to the French nobility as an "aristocracy of ambition."[43]
Even if he did not condemn all forms of aristocracy, it is scarcely surprising
that the radical democrat Jean-Jacques Rousseau followed suit, contending
that of all forms of government, hereditary aristocracy was absolutely the
worst.[44] It is more notable that Montesquieu—the great defender of noble
prerogatives—essentially concurred. Not only does "extreme corruption
occur when nobility becomes hereditary" in an aristocracy, Montesquieu
wrote, but in addition, "the more an aristocracy approaches democracy, the
more perfect it will be."[45] The critical point here is that for Montesquieu
the same privileges that made a hereditary nobility essential in a monarchy
as a constraint on its despotic tendencies also made them pernicious in an
aristocracy, since aristocracy—as one form of republic—depended upon
unsullied "virtue" as its motivating principle, whereas monarchy operated
upon "honor."

What this background demonstrates is that for all the considerable deference
paid to noble status under the Old Regime, sufficient ideological scaffolding
was in place to build a powerful indictment against the noble order given
the appropriate circumstances. The long tradition of royalist antifeudalism

41. Diderot and d'Alembert, *Encyclopédie, ou dictionnaire des sciences, des arts et des métiers,* 17
vols. (Paris, 1751–65), 1:651.

42. Aristotle, *The Politics,* bk. 5, chap. 7.

43. *Satyre,* 1: 280.

44. Jean-Jacques Rousseau, *Du contrat social* (Paris, 1962), bk. 3, chap 5.

45. Montesquieu, *De l'esprit des lois,* 2 vols. (Paris, 1961), pt. 1, bk. 8, chap. 5, and bk. 2,
chap. 3.

had laid the groundwork for charging nobles with the usurpation of power and privilege and the tyrannizing of other subjects. The long history of noble revolt and court cabals "proved" that nobles were liable to form conspiracies against the commonwealth. Even if some conspiracies acquired legitimacy because they had been directed against royal "despotism," it was not difficult to represent others as motivated by the private vices of a Catilina rather than the public virtues of a Cicero. Indeed, insisted the marquis d'Argenson, "a monarchy becomes a despotism almost solely by way of aristocracy; ministers and the grandees working for the monarch believe they are working for themselves; they suppress the people and elevate the throne because they have ties to it and disdain the vulgar."[46] From Montesquieu's perspective, the corruptibility of the noble order did not appear so threatening in a monarchy motivated by "honor." Yet by the same token, republican virtue was necessarily critical in a weak monarchy tending toward aristocracy, since an aristocracy dominated by a hereditary nobility and uninformed by virtue was likely to be as "despotic" as any monarchy. If revisionist historiography has explored in detail the ways in which the French monarchy made itself appear "despotic," it remains to be seen how the nobility did likewise.

The Making of an Aristo-Ministerial Plot in the Prerevolution

It would be impossible here to recapitulate the main developments that led to the crisis of 1787–89.[47] For the purposes of this essay, what is important to note above all is that anti-nobilism in various guises was promoted by the monarchy to discredit its opposition during the prerevolutionary period. In March 1787, Calonne tried to foment anti-nobilism as part of his effort to delegitimate the privileged orders in general during the Assembly of Notables.[48] Calonne's mudslinging campaign against "aristocracy" met with no better reception than the financial plan he proposed. But the monarchy reignited the campaign during its subsequent, bitter battle with the *parlement* of Paris, hoping to deflect the *parlement*'s sustained attack on its own alleged "despotism" by impugning the *parlement*'s alleged magisterial "aristocracy."

---

46. René de Voyer de Paulmy, marquis d'Argenson, *Considérations sur le gouvernement ancien et présent de la France* (Amsterdam, 1764), 183.

47. The standard but aging account is Jean Egret, *La pré-Révolution française, 1787–1788* (Paris, 1962).

48. William Doyle, *The Oxford History of the French Revolution* (Oxford, 1989), 73.

Although public opinion still strongly favored the *parlement,* the campaign threw the *parlement* sufficiently on the defensive for it to feel obliged to deny publicly on 11–13 April 1788 that it was ridden with "ambitious aristocrats."[49] In fall 1788, ministerial pamphleteers broadened the attack on "aristocracy" once again, indicting not only the magistracy, but the nobility in general, the high clergy, and occasionally the world of finance.[50] While it remains difficult to measure the impact of the crown's anti-aristocratic offensive, the offensive does seem to have gained further ground by this time. Clearly, the *parlement's* ratification of vote by order at the upcoming Estates-General on 25 September 1788—however innocently intended—could only have validated the anti-aristocratic charges made by the monarchy's defenders, especially in light of the precedents set by the provincial assemblies and the estates of Dauphiné, which had voted by head.

This background is important for a proper understanding of the Society of Thirty, which has often been identified as the single most important engine of revolutionary consciousness in the prerevolution. Wick's demonstration that the Society's membership was overwhelmingly noble—and included both alienated court nobles and *parlementaires*—should underscore the fact that this association was composed of the same sociological types the monarchy was denouncing as "aristocrats." Why did a predominantly noble organization advocate wider Third Estate representation at the Estates-General?[51] Kenneth Margerison argued persuasively that the Society did so because it was trying to scoop the monarchy in bidding for Third Estate support through strategic concessions. But he also showed that its support for vote by head was neither unanimous nor unequivocal, and, like Wick, he observed that a good many members jumped ship and became born-again defenders of noble privilege as the Revolution approached. All this suggests that far from being committed to a highly divisive, radical Third Estate agenda à la Sieyès, what the Society really advocated was a more consensual "union of orders" in the face of "ministerial despotism."[52] If so, then it was critical to the Society's success, especially given its overwhelmingly noble membership, for it to

49. Jules Flammermont and M. Tourneux, eds., *Remontrances du Parlement de Paris au XVIIIe siècle,* 3 vols. (Paris, 1888–98), 3:738.

50. See the discussion in Dale K. Van Kley, "The Estates General as Ecumenical Council: The Constitutionalism of Corporate Consensus and the *Parlement's* Ruling of September 25, 1788," *Journal of Modern History* 61 (1989): 45.

51. Margerison, *Pamphlets,* 57.

52. Ibid., chap. 3. For the Jansenist background to this notion, see Van Kley, "Estates General."

refute the standard monarchist accusation that all opposition to the crown was "aristocratic." Mirabeau's description of the Society as a "conspiracy of well-intentioned men" is one indicator of a will to preempt dismissal of the Society as yet another noble subversive league.

A second such sign was the Society's effort to drive an ideological wedge between court nobles close to the queen and the noble order in general. Given the substantial overlap in their social standing, this was not an easy goal to achieve. One of its most notable and influential iterations appeared in Emmanuel d'Antraigues's *Mémoire sur les Etats-Généraux* (1788), which was almost certainly sponsored by the Society and, in its fourteen editions, became the most widely read pamphlet of the prerevolution.[53] Cast in standard Jansenist-*parlement* rhetoric, the pamphlet was primarily directed against royal "despotism." But d'Antraigues also took aim at court favorites, whom he denounced as "natural enemies of public order" for corrupting princes and as a "crowd of debased slaves, both insolent and vile, whose education has mutilated the mind and heart."[54] Far from representing the entire noble order, these courtesans—"the invaders of all positions, of all dignities in the state"—were pointedly contrasted with the "true nobility," who "were reconciled with the people in the provinces, and stricken by despotism, have finally understood . . . the most pressing need to join itself forever with the people, with whom they will find solid, true support in every encounter."[55]

That d'Antraigues's views reflected sentiments felt outside the Society is evident from comparison of his work with a much less celebrated contemporary pamphlet composed by an anonymous marquis to deflect slights made against his order. Waxing particularly lyrical over "the honor, *delicatesse,* and generous bravura that has distinguished the French knight and characterizes the true gentlemen,"[56] the marquis insisted along strict Montesquieuian lines that the nobility had been born at the same historical moment as the monarchy and had always supported its glory. But like d'Antraigues, he openly admitted that some members of the Second Estate had been corrupted

---

53. Emmanuel-Henri-Louis-Alexandre de Launay, comte d'Antraigues, *Mémoires sur les Etats-généraux, leurs droits et la manière de les convoquer* (n.p., 1788). On its context and diffusion, see Margerison, *Pamphlets,* 63, and Dale Van Kley, "From the Lessons of French History to Truths for All Times and All People: The Historical Origins of an Anti-Historical Declaration," in *The French Idea of Freedom: The Old Regime and the Declaration of Rights of 1789,* ed. Dale K. Van Kley (Stanford, 1994), 81.

54. D'Antraigues, *Mémoire,* 26.

55. Ibid., 86.

56. M. le marquis d'Av★★★★★★, *Réflexions en faveur de la noblesse* (n.p., [c. 1789]), 13.

by the court; indeed, they "numbered among the oppressors of the *patrie,* of whom [they have] become an accomplice"—even if it was also true that the nobility as a whole had censured their conduct and was unsullied by their turpitude.[57]

What lay behind this distinction between "true" nobles and noble "oppressors"? In the case of d'Antraigues, a nobleman who would soon defect to the "ministerial" position, it is apparent that he was intent above all on protecting the "patriot" alliance against the monarchy's broad-based "aristocratic" charges. But he also sought to reverse these charges and pin them on the crown, just as the crown was seeking to dodge the "despotic" label and pin it on the Second Estate. Behind d'Antraigues's rhetorical maneuver lay an anti-courtier discourse dating from the sixteenth century,[58] which in the eighteenth century revived and blended with "republican" themes to produce a discourse that represented court extravagance as a sure sign of impending "despotism."[59]

Beyond discourse, what imparted strength and plausibility to d'Antraigues's tactic were the many years of court "corruption" recently illuminated by Wick and others, and it is at this point that one can begin to grasp the implications of their research for the complex politics of anti-nobilism. As they have shown in detail, the old court nobility had been alienated—not from the Old Regime in general, *pace* Chaussinand-Nogaret, but from the court in particular because of the disproportionate favoritism shown to insiders in the distribution of royal favors. As these historians have not sufficiently emphasized, what made such "corruption" of considerable interest and grievous concern to the public at large was not only its broadcast and amplification by the Grub Street writers beloved by Robert Darnton, but also the direct and threatening impact it had on the lives of ordinary citizens.[60]

57. Ibid., 14.

58. Pauline M. Smith, *The Anti-Courtier Trend in Sixteenth-Century French Literature* (Geneva, 1966).

59. Marisa Linton, *The Politics of Virtue in Enlightenment France* (New York, 2001), chaps. 5–6. In regard to popular views of the court, the "reign" of Madame de Pompadour proved to be a turning point, although many of the criticisms leveled at her had been made against earlier favorites. See Thomas E. Kaiser, "Madame de Pompadour and the Theaters of Power," *French Historical Studies* 19 (1996): 1025–44. On the refashioning of the image of nobles in relation to virtue, see Jay M. Smith, *Nobility Reimagined: The Patriotic Nation in Eighteenth-Century France* (Ithaca, 2005), chaps. 1–2.

60. Most recently in Robert Darnton, *The Forbidden Best-Sellers of Pre-Revolutionary France* (New York, 1995).

One case in point was the bankruptcy scandal surrounding the Rohan-Guéménée family.[61] A venerable dynasty near the top of the noble pyramid, the Rohans had acquired, among other concessions, the key posts of grand chamberlain and governess of the children of France, which gave them immediate access to the royal family and thereby powerful allies and a potentially unending stream of patronage. But when in October 1782 the news broke that this venerable family, known for its extravagance and heavy gambling, had fallen thirty-three million *livres* into debt, the Rohans rapidly became the object of popular outrage and for good reason. Unprecedented in its scale, according to one contemporary source, the bankruptcy had a domino effect on the fortunes of a reported three thousand small lenders to the Rohans, who stood to lose most or all of their meager assets.[62] Moreover, it was soon reported that the bankruptcy was fraudulent—that the Rohans had contracted loans borrowed even after they knew they were bankrupt—a report which so enraged their petty creditors that they took to assaulting the Rohans in the street and forced the Rohans to publish an apology.[63]

What made the bankruptcy dangerous for the crown was not simply its overall bad odor, but also the public knowledge that the king had authorized the family's debts.[64] The upshot was that Louis and Marie-Antoinette sought to cut their public relations losses by distancing themselves from the Rohans out of fear that the mud slung at their disgraced favorites would fall on them. They immediately "accepted" Mme. de Guéménée's resignation as royal governess; and although the crown did grant madame a pension of 60,000 *livres* and purchased property of the Rohans to enable them to repay their debts, this compensation hardly equaled the lost patronage the family might have obtained had madame kept her post.[65] Nor was it the end of the story. As Rory Browne has persuasively argued, the bankruptcy proved to be the prologue to the much messier, notorious Diamond Necklace Affair,

61. See Browne, *Court and Crown*, chap. 5, and Thomas E. Kaiser, "Scandal in the Royal Nursery: Marie-Antoinette and the *Gouvernantes des Enfants de France*," *Historical Reflections/ Réflexions Historiques*, forthcoming in 2006.

62. Louis Petit de Bachaumont, *Mémoires secrets pour servir à l'histoire de la république des lettres en France depuis MDCCLXII jusqu'à nos jours,* 36 vols. (London, 1777–89), 21:133.

63. Adolphe-Mathurin de Lescure, ed., *Correspondance secrète inédite sur Louis XVI, Marie-Antoinette, la cour et la ville de 1777 à 1792,* 2 vols. (Paris, 1866), 1:513–14; for further commentary on its impact, see, S.-P. Hardy, "Mes Loisirs ou journal d'événements tels qu'ils parviennent à ma connoissance," Bibliothèque Nationale (henceforth BN) MS Fr. 6684, ff. 218, 237. For the apology, see Prince de Guéménée, *Requête du prince de Guéménée au Roi* (n.p., [1782/3]).

64. Hardy, BN MS Fr. 6684, f. 218.

65. Marc-Marie, marquis de Bombelles, *Journal,* 5 vols. (Geneva, 1977–2002), 1:159–60.

which damaged the already fragile reputation of Marie-Antoinette, while it ironically restored some of the Rohans' lost public favor, since it turned the prosecuted cardinal into a victim of "despotism."[66] In a final coda, the king and queen were once again publicly embarrassed by their relations with the Rohans during the Assembly of Notables, when Lafayette assailed the monarchy's purchase of Rohan property for putting an unjustifiable additional burden on long-suffering taxpayers.[67]

Equally notorious was the rise of the Polignac syndicate, which, despite their more modest background, grabbed far greater favors than the Rohans. Indeed, the Polignacs managed to become something of a vetting lobby for administrative appointments and court largesse, much of which they claimed for themselves, including the charge of governess of the royal children relinquished by the Rohans in 1782. Exercising a leverage that derived from their connections to Maurepas, the favor of the queen, and, what has been frequently overlooked, their familiarity with the king, the Polignac syndicate made an enormously bad impression on the public, for their extravagant demands aroused, in the words of one contemporary, "continual complaints."[68] This impression is confirmed by many of the major sources from which one can track contemporary opinion—for example, Hardy, Mercy-Argenteau, and the anonymous correspondence edited by Lescure—as well as the hostile pamphlets written during the French Revolution.[69]

One—of many—instances of their notorious profiteering was the celebrated affair of the Bordeaux alluvions of 1786, recounted by William Doyle.[70] In this affair, the Polignacs sought to profit personally and covertly from royal efforts to strip owners of their riverbank property in the Bordelaise under the guise of reclaiming land allegedly usurped from the royal domain. Leading the resistance in which reportedly "all citizens are interested,"[71] the *parlement* of Bordeaux came to the rescue of the threatened proprietors in a dramatic encounter before the king. By the end of the noisy incident, the Polignacs had been publicly associated with "agents of despotism." They

66. Rory Browne, "The Diamond Necklace Affair Revisited: The Rohan Family and Court Politics," *Renaissance and Modern Studies* 33 (1989): 21–39.

67. Bachaumont, *Mémoires secrets,* 35:54–55.

68. Alfred d'Arneth and Auguste Geffroy, eds., *Correspondance secrète entre Marie-Thérèse et le comte de Mercy-Argenteau,* 3 vols. (Paris, 1874), 3:123.

69. For the anti-Polignac literature, see J. B. D. N., ed., *Facéties révolutionnaires sur madame de Polignac* (Neufchâtel, 1872).

70. William Doyle, *The Parlement of Bordeaux and the End of the Old Regime 1771–1790* (London, 1974), chap. 16.

71. Lescure, *Correspondance secrète,* 2:57.

were said to have so abused the queen's confidence that a "cabal" was launched to detach her from them, and their reputations were so tarnished that they felt obliged to wage a public campaign alleging they had never participated in the attempted expropriation.[72] It is unlikely that this campaign persuaded many observers, but more important, the affair, like the Rohan bankruptcy, helped discredit the monarchy and its circle of favorites. Beyond the queen, Calonne, in particular, was implicated because he had become a fixture of the Polignac circle and was known to have suppressed six thousand copies of the remonstrance of the Bordeaux *parlement* that denounced the crown's "despotic" alluvial initiative.[73]

In the period of the prerevolution, the association of court favorites—especially the Polignacs—with "despotism" of the ministerial variety made them vulnerable to charges of "aristocracy" as well. After the Paris *parlement's* ratification of vote by order in September 1788, the patriot party began drawing heavily on the monarchy's anti-aristocratic rhetoric and deployed it in areas of bitter constestation over representation at the Estates-General. A notable example was Brittany, where Volney denounced and demanded action against a "conspiracy of noble leaguers."[74] But far from abandoning the popular front against "despotism" to fight this cause, the patriots conflated "despotism" with "aristocracy," thereby engendering, in Dale Van Kley's felicitous phrase, "the twin *bêtes noires* of the apocalypse."[75] Although the abbé Sieyès's *Qu'est-ce que le Tiers-Etat?* is best known for its polemical indictment of the nobility, the pamphlet had resonance not merely because of its passionate ventilation of the usual anti-aristocratic charges, but also because of its elision of these *bêtes noires*. According to Sieyès, France had been the victim of both feudal "tyranny" and of "pure [i.e., monarchical] despotism." But in recent ages, he contended, neither had predominated. Instead, France had been governed primarily by an "aulic aristocracy," that is, by court favorites, who had used the resources of the crown to benefit their fellow travelers in the Second Estate. "It is the court that has reigned and not the monarch. It is the court that acts and counteracts, appoints and dismisses ministers, creates and distributes positions, etc." As a result, claimed Sieyès, although the court may have seemed altogether subject to the king's will, in reality it was the organizing agency of an "immense aristocracy that

72. Ibid., 2:56, 61; Hardy, BN MS Fr. 6685, f. 397.

73. Lescure, *Correspondance secrète,* 2:64.

74. Constantin François de Chasseboeuf Volney, *La Sentinelle du Peuple* 2 (20 November 1788): 7.

75. Van Kley, "From the Lessons," 91.

covers all parts of France, that through its members acquires everything and everywhere controls what is essential in all parts of the public sphere."[76] In short, "aristocracy" and "despotism" were not irreconcilable rivals; thanks to the institution of the court, they were, on this view, co-conspirators.

Sieyès's pamphlet was certainly incendiary and raised multiple specters—most notably the "aulic aristocracy"—that would soon return to haunt the Revolution, but as Margerison has shown, in going so far as to demand the disenfranchisement of the nobility, it did not have the overwhelming, immediate effect often attributed to it.[77] Indeed, Sieyès himself soon backed away from some of his more radical prescriptions. More typical of the patriot stance in early 1789 was the argument of Rabaut Saint-Etienne. In his *Question de droit politique,* Rabaut put forward the Third Estate's non-negotiable demand that the Estates-General meet as a single-chambered body on the grounds that the three estates had the same interests and that division into orders would prevent adequate expression of the national will. In hopes of persuading the nobility to act on their own and the nation's better interests, Rabaut, unlike Sieyès, extended an open hand in their direction. He praised the Second Estate for its willingness to surrender tax exemptions and expressed the belief that nobles would eventually rally to the patriot position since they had suffered from past "abuses" as much as the Third Estate.[78] With regard to recent conflicts, Rabaut refused to indict the nobility as such, preferring the less provocative path of blaming socio-logically indeterminate factions, so-called particular interests, which he charged with hypocrisy and secrecy.[79] Yet Rabaut's invitations to the privileged orders were tinged with strong admonitions that failure to accept Third Estate demands would have a devastating, boomerang effect upon them. Noncompliance would show that France had fallen into an "aristocracy" abhorrent to both the king and Third Estate. In response, Rabaut warned, the crown and the commoners would form a counteraristocratic "league" that would be "necessarily fatal" to the two first Estates.[80]

Ominous as it sounds, Rabaut's invocation of "fatality" needs to be understood in context and should not be construed as the harbinger of

76. Emmanuel Joseph Sieyès, *Qu'est-ce que le Tiers-Etat?* ed. Jean-Denis Bredin (Paris, 1988), 51–52.

77. See the important discussion in Margerison, *Pamphlets,* chap. 5.

78. Jean-Paul Rabaut Saint-Etienne, *Question de droit public: doit-on recueillir les voix, dans les Etats-Généraux, par ordres, ou par têtes des délibérants?* (Languedoc, 1789).

79. Ibid., 35.

80. Ibid., 96.

anything remotely like the Terror. Indeed, Rabaut did not even go so far as to demand the abolition of privilege, let alone call for violence against the nobility. At the same time, his argument makes it questionable whether one can distinguish as sharply as did Higonnet between anti-nobilism, which entailed hostility to the nobility as private persons, and anti-corporatism, which denoted hostility to the noble order as such.[81] As Sarah Maza and Marisa Linton have shown, the moral fiber of nobles both as an order and as individuals had been publicly called into question during the last decades of the Old Regime, and despite the efforts of nobles to associate themselves with virtue and social utility, the status of nobles as citizens was surely in doubt by September 1788.[82] Although it was expressed in juridical language, Rabaut's pamphlet, by denouncing "hypocrisy" and "secrecy," effectively moralized political status, such that any person whose deeds bore the telltale signs of these Catilinian vices could be plausibly identified as an anti-citizen. For the moment, Rabaut and most of his colleagues still had reason to think, or at least hope, that the nobility possessed the civic responsibility to choose the high road of collaboration with the Third Estate. After all, most nobles had suffered under the same aristo-ministerial condominium that had oppressed the king's other subjects, and some nobles had joined the Third Estate in publicly denouncing members of their order who had betrayed the nation to curry favor with the court. It remained to be seen what happened when the Second Estate as a whole refused to follow through on these early, promising initiatives.

The Crisis of July 1789 and After:
An Aristo-Ministerial Plot Confirmed

In light of the major differences that Shapiro and Markoff have discovered between the political views and agendas of the Second and Third Estates, it appears less shocking to us than it did to contemporaries that the opening of the Estates-General in May 1789 led to an immediate standoff over voting procedures, thereby disappointing high hopes for a "union of orders." As

81. Higonnet, *Class,* 66–72.
82. Sarah Maza, *Private Lives and Public Affairs: The Causes Célèbres of Prerevolutionary France* (Berkeley, 1993), 319; Linton, *Politics of Virtue,* 176–77. On the interpretation of merit and status, see Jay M. Smith, *The Culture of Merit: Nobility, Royal Service, and the Making of Absolute Monarchy in France, 1600–1789* (Ann Arbor, 1996). For the prerevolution, see Smith, *Nobility Reimagined,* chap. 6.

close analysis has shown, only a minority of nobles—some of them associated with the Society of Thirty—were willing to join with the Third Estate, and even fewer embraced vote by head. [83] To be sure, most nobles were willing to renounce their pecuniary privileges, but this concession only made them insist all the more upon retention of other rights. Some of these rights were "merely" ceremonial. Others, however, gave them access to leadership positions in the army, church, and magistracy and were bound up with noble perceptions of merit and the sound administration of society. Abandoning such rights, in their view, would have entailed not only severe personal sacrifice but also dereliction of duty. In addition, a goodly number of noble deputies felt sincere compunctions about abandoning the dictates of their electoral mandates, which pledged them to preserve the integrity of The Second Estate as a voting chamber. By the time the Estates-General convened in May 1789, there had already been sufficient attacks on noble goals and motives for many nobles to take a hard line against the Third Estate out of fear that concessions could lead only to further erosion of their status. After all, how much respect for their privileged position could they anticipate from the Third Estate when on 25 May the comte de Mirabeau declared he took no pride in his title and with undiluted sarcasm offered to donate it to anyone who cared to unburden him of it?[84] How much reassurance could they draw from the statements of another Third Estate deputy who, when denying there was any project to dissolve the noble order, added the slighting quip, "totally absurd as it [the nobility] is"?[85]

Noble intransigence, it hardly needs saying, only encouraged the Third Estate to imagine the worst of the Second Estate and to send the nonprivileged further down the twin paths of noble anti-corporatism and personal anti-nobilism. Thus, while some voices in the Palais-Royal recycled the argument that the nobility as a corporation lacked justification from the standpoint of natural justice and good sense,[86] others adopted a different line by dilating upon nobles personally as a source of social corruption. "I believe in the nobility," one deputy from Languedoc reportedly said in sorrow on May 18, "[and] I respect its ranks; but I do not believe that among the nobles there is one [single] citizen."[87] "The nobility," wrote another deputy,

83. See the analyses of Shapiro and Markoff, and of Tackett.
84. Jacques-Antoine Creuzé-Latouche, *Journal des Etats-Généraux et du début de l'Assemblée Nationale 18 mai-29 juillet 1789,* ed. Jean Marchand (Paris, 1947), 12.
85. Ibid., 13.
86. Ibid., 38.
87. Adrien Duquesnoy, *Journal d'Adrien Duquesnoy,* 2 vols. (Paris, 1894), 1:24.

"causes the corruption of the nation because it discourages virtue and talents, it stifles emulation, it corrupts justice, it disposes of positions and graces and has them distributed to the unworthy."[88]

Despite bitter sentiments and opposing agendas, common ground might have been found had the monarchy taken a stronger line from the start. But royal indecision—reflecting divisions within the ministry—wound up promoting anxiety on all sides.[89] Since both the privileged orders and the Third Estate had looked to the king to put pressure on their antagonists, this weak stance only further encouraged the contending parties to dig in their heels out of fear they might have to carry on without the king's wavering support—a development that the establishment of the National Assembly on 17–20 June could only accelerate. As one deputy reported as early as 22 May, "Within the Third, one speaks only of 'aristocrats,' within the nobility only of 'democrats.' These are the war cries! We have lost sight of the ministry only to tear each other to pieces."[90]

For the Third Estate, the apparent "loss" of the monarchy, as evidenced by Louis's refusal to recognize the National Assembly and his reaffirmation of separate orders on 23 June, was devastating, particularly since it undercut their strategy of threatening the nobility with Rabaut's counteraristocratic "league." Deploring the "abominable maneuvers of the aristocracy," the Third interpreted Louis's position as a sign that the king was "surrounded by mad and impious courtiers who mislead him, who use him, who alienate him from the hearts of his subjects, imperil his throne, and compromise his authority by forcing him to commit absurd and tyrannical acts."[91] Although they typically excluded the king himself from their nightmare scenarios, the Third Estate, after weeks of stalemate, rewarmed Sieyès's notion of an "aulic aristocracy" and blew it up into a vast conspiratorial plot between court favorites and the nobility to unite against the Third Estate. By the end of June, various accounts of the anatomy of this conspiracy were in circulation. According to the journalist Nicolas Ruault, Parisians were convinced that a "Polignac Committee" was meeting nightly with the king, queen, and the "heads of the aristocracy" to slander the intentions of the people

88. Creuzé-Latouche, *Journal,* 13.

89. The best and most recent analysis of the crown's maneuvering in this crisis is Munro Price, *The Road from Versailles: Louis XVI, Marie Antoinette, and the Fall of the French Monarchy* (New York, 2002), chap. 4. See also, Pierre Caron, "La Tentative de contre-révolution de juin-juillet 1789," *Revue d'histoire moderne et contemporaine* 8 (1906–7): 5–34, 649–78.

90. Duquesnoy, *Journal,* 1:38.

91. Creuzé-Latouche, *Journal,* 142–43.

and to undermine the Estates-General.[92] Marie-Joseph-Blaise Chénier, too, claimed that the plot was centered in the "ministerial aristocracy" of the court—that "enemy, always aroused, always indefatigable, which never lets its prey escape." But he went on to assert that it was associated with other "aristocracies"—those of the Sword, Robe, Clergy, and other corps, which were "equally tyrannical" and equally complicitous in a "ministerial aristocracy."[93] Such constructs bore all the marks of "conspiracy" as that notion had been elaborated over the centuries—secrecy, cruelty, corruption, elitism. Because of the Third Estate's stalwart opposition, the conspiracy "in its powerless rage, which it vainly tries to hide, resorts to all means imaginable."[94]

"Evidence" for the plot and its alleged collusion seemed hard to miss, especially since the nobility, often unwittingly, itself dropped so many "clues." Thus, from the very beginning of the Estates-General, it appeared to many in the Third Estate that "the nobility [had] sold out to the court."[95] As yet unaware of the political meaning of his actions, the marquis de Ferrières, as he reported to his wife with pride and a thrill in May and early June, attended with other noble deputies a special performance of the Comédie Française sponsored by the queen. Shortly thereafter, he and others were graciously and repeatedly received at social gatherings held by the Polignacs, where they rubbed shoulders with the king's notorious brother, the comte d'Artois.[96] Such "innocent" meetings could only have reenforced the impressions of one Third Estate deputy on 3 June that the Estates-General might soon be dissolved "through a series of maneuvers by the nobility and the ministers."[97]

Much as the Third Estate deputies were "all disposed to prevent themselves from being struck down by ministerial coups, last resource of the aristocratic cabal,"[98] they did not give up all hopes of reconciliation with the Second Estate. Erosion of noble intransigence on the voting issue at the end of June, increasing noble absenteeism in the Assembly, and the king's sudden, somewhat mysterious reversal of policy on 27 June allowed for a

92. Nicolas Ruault, *Gazette d'un Parisien sous la Révolution: lettres à son frère. 1783–1796* ([Paris], 1975), 138–39.

93. [Marie-Joseph-Blaise Chénier], *Lettre à M. le Comte de Mirabeau, l'un des représentans de l'Assemblée nationale. Sur les dispositions naturelles, nécessaires & indubitables des Officiers & des Soldats François & Etrangers* (n.p., [1789]), 4, 13.

94. Ibid., 4.

95. Duquesnoy, *Journal,* 1:2.

96. Charles-Elie, marquis de Ferrières-Marçay, *Correspondance inédite (1789, 1790, 1791),* ed. Henri Carré (Paris, 1932), 47–48, 51, 55.

97. Creuzé-Latouche, *Journal,* 44.

98. Ibid., 132.

brief era of better—if not exactly good—feeling in early July.[99] Yet the signs of happy reconciliation, such as the celebration of unity on 29 June, that followed in the wake of the fusion of orders should not be overinterpreted. For some members of the Third Estate viewed this fusion as a forced concession that was much less than a true victory. Indeed, just as revolutionary logic would construe other "gains" in many later instances, the belated creation of a single chamber could well lead to a more severe vengeance, which could easily be veiled by hypocritical gestures of good will until this vengeance was visited upon its victims. As one Third Estate deputy warned darkly on 29 June, reflective observers could not share the elation felt by some of his colleagues since it was scarcely credible that the nobility, who were resolved "to destroy the state rather than renounce their odious pretensions" and stood guilty of "contradiction, chicanery, low intrigue, flattery of and even servility to the government," were now "changed suddenly into zealous patriots well disposed to the reform of abuses and the liberty of the nation."[100] Indeed, the partial relaxation of tensions in early July might well have amplified the impact of the crisis of 12–15 July, which Tackett aptly described as the "most harrowing" moment in the Constituent career of most representatives.[101]

The ministerial maneuvering behind this crisis remains obscure even today. To many Third Estate deputies, signs began appearing by late June that the aristo-ministerial plot they had feared was about to be sprung. On 24 June, it was noted that the queen, who was closely linked to Artois and other hard-liners, had spent an entire evening with the princes of the blood, the duc de Luxembourg (a deserter from the Society of Thirty and now the fiercely partisan president of the noble chamber), and similar "ardent enemies of public liberty."[102] On June 30 the maréchal de Broglie was named supreme army commander. "Nothing," wrote one deputy, "indicates more clearly the hostile intentions of the court. The maréchal is one of the hardest of men . . . and certainly he will not hesitate to give and have executed the bloodiest orders."[103] Twenty-five thousand troops, it was reported, had been put under Broglie's command in the vicinity of Versailles, and over the next week the numbers continued to grow.[104]

99. Tackett, *Becoming*, 158–62.
100. Creuzé-Latouche, *Journal*, 165. Cf. Duquesnoy, *Journal*, 1:180.
101. Tackett, *Becoming*, 162.
102. Duquesnoy, *Journal*, 1:118.
103. Ibid., 1:144.
104. Ibid., 1:114.

The arrival of military force on the scene, which has been emphasized by all standard accounts of the July crisis, was bad enough; what made it all the more sinister—and what has been frequently underemphasized—was the "foreign," that is to say, "German" character of the regiments involved. For the French, who were Austrophobes of long standing, had been exposed for decades to fresh, virulent anti-Austrian propaganda generated by enemies of the 1756 Austrian alliance and Marie-Antoinette—propaganda alleging, among many other charges, that the queen was secretly draining the treasury and exporting large sums to the Habsburgs.[105] Many of these old fears were stirred up again in a new revolutionary context. What were these foreign troops doing here, demanded Mirabeau. With all the military installations in place, "one would think [we were in] an enemy location about to be besieged, and that feared location is the hall of the Estates-General. Public events, hidden facts, secret orders, orders suddenly countermanded, the most menacing preparation for war, strike us all and fill all our hearts with indignation." When on 8 July Mirabeau successfully moved that the Third send a delegation to remonstrate with the king about the crisis, the abbé Grégoire added an amendment—also approved—stipulating that the Third seek to unveil "the authors of these detestable maneuvers; that we denounce them to the nation as guilty of national *lèse-majesté* (treason), so that contemporary execration can precede the execration of posterity."[106]

It was thus after several weeks of apparent intimidation that the Third Estate got word of the change of ministry that would spark the events of 12–14 July. Fresh ministers could hardly have been found who were more likely to feed Third Estate trepidations.[107] Headed by Breteuil—a creature known to be close to the hated queen and a one-time associate of the Polignacs—the new ministry also included the maréchal de Broglie, whose harsh reputation has already been mentioned. In Versailles, it was duly noted that the Polignacs and other "aristocrats" were exhibiting an unusual gaiety, that they and Artois were commingling with the troops stationed there, and that the duchesse de Polignac had invited officers to her home and provided

105. Thomas E. Kaiser, "Who's Afraid of Marie-Antoinette? Diplomacy, Austrophobia, and the Queen," *French History* 14 (2000): 241–71, and Kaiser, "Ambiguous Identities: Marie-Antoinette and the House of Lorraine from the Affair of the Minuet to Lambesc's Charge," in *Marie Antoinette: Writings on the Body of the Queen,* ed. Dena Goodman (London, 2003), 171–98.

106. *Le Moniteur* 1 (4–6 July 1789), 122; *Archives parlementaires,* 8:211.

107. Creuzé-Latouche, *Journal,* 216.

them with refreshment and liqueurs.[108] Mirabeau's account of this fraternization, which also implicated the queen, reads now like a rehearsal of
the banquet which ignited the march to Versailles on 5/6 October. But to
Mirabeau the events he described recalled the blackest day to date in
French history. "All night these foreign satellites, gorged with gold and
wine, celebrated in their impious songs the subjection of France, . . . their
brutal wishes invoked the destruction of the National Assembly, . . . courtesans
joined their dances to the sound of barbaric music, . . . such was the prelude
of Saint-Bartholomew."[109] Indeed, a bloodbath was on the minds of people
other than just the Parisians during the critical days of 12–14 July, for the
deputies in Versailles believed that the "massacres" perpetrated by the
"German" regiment of the prince de Lambesc in the Tuileries might well
be duplicated in Versailles. As Bailly, president of the Third Estate, later
recalled, rumors rippled through the Assembly that the king was about to
abandon Versailles and that the Gardes-Françaises were to be dismissed. If
this happened, Third Estate deputies would be "at the mercy of several foreign
and German regiments camped in the Orangerie," which might mean the
springing of "some great plan, some disastrous project."[110]

When the rising of Paris put an end to the "ministry of the hundred
hours," the king recalled the troops and made a fence-mending visit to
Paris. Soon thereafter, the Third Estate breathed a collective sigh of relief.
"The aristocrats hoped to consummate their crimes militarily," noted
Grégoire succinctly, "but force united with justice."[111] As Tackett has
shown, another period of more relaxed tensions between the Second and
Third Estates ensued in the weeks following the crisis.[112] Yet the events of
12–14 July lived on, and not only in the multiple celebrations of the
Bastille's storming that turned the events surrounding it into a national
myth.[113] For all the new bouts of good feeling, these events also left behind
the disquieting impression that a deadly aristo-ministerial plot had only

108. Ibid.; Jean-Sylvain Bailly, *Mémoires d'un témoin de la Révolution, ou Journal des faits qui se
sont passés sous ses yeux, et qui ont préparé et fixé la Constitution française,* 3 vols. (Paris, 1804),
1:121–22.

109. *Archives parlementaires,* 8:236.

110. Bailly, *Mémoires,* 1:121.

111. *Archives parlementaires,* 8:232.

112. Tackett, *Becoming,* 163–75.

113. Hans-Jürgen Lüsebrink and Rolf Reichardt, *The Bastille: A History of a Symbol of Despotism and Freedom,* trans. Norbert Shürer (Durham, 1997).

barely been checked, a plot that even the taking of the Bastille had only attenuated, not eliminated.

Indeed, as time went on and further inquiries were made into the affair, the crisis took on a progressively blacker appearance. In an account published later in *Le Moniteur,* it was announced that the king had been the "puppet of an infamous cabal" and that his name had been used to cloak "one of the most odious conspiracies that history has transmitted to the memory of mankind." Although vague about the identity of the perpetrators, who were collectively denounced as "the court," the report invoked tropes that had traditionally been used to censure noble conspiracies, most notably referring to the conspirators as "Catilinas." To highlight the moral degeneracy that lay at the core of the plot, the Polignacs' fraternization with troops on the eve of the coup, which had caught the eye of Mirabeau, was now recounted with new details: the event was reconfigured as an orgy in which an insatiable blood thirst had been eroticized and the people's resistance had aroused a will for revenge. "Women of the court flattered [the soldiers], caressed them, lavished gold, wine, kindnesses on them, excited them to murder by the lure of rewards and booty. The courage of the people inspired in them only atrocious resolutions, which they took amidst the most disgusting excess of debauchery that crowned all their odious plots and made the delirium of crime succeed the delirium of inebriation." In addition, the "German" background of the troops was further highlighted; Mirabeau's "barbaric music" became "German music."[114]

Other newspaper reports and many pamphlets further embroidered upon these themes.[115] Several noted that the arch-aristocrats had fled abroad to Austrian-held territories immediately following the failure of their coup, thereby underlining the connection between the thwarted coup and foreign powers. Thus, the journal *Révolutions de Paris* reported that Brussels was hosting the so-called little court of France, including Artois, who was expected to move to the Viennese court, "where he will no doubt be very amply compensated."[116] Also located at her new Austrian base of operations was the notorious duchesse de Polignac, who inspired a large pamphlet

114. *Le Moniteur* 1 (17–20 July 1789), pp. 169–71. I am grateful to Ted Margadant for informing me that *Le Moniteur* began publication only on 24 November 1789 and that the issues of *Le Moniteur* dated before 24 November in its reimpression were in fact assembled after that date from various materials and published in issues predated to correspond to the events described. See the introduction to Duquesnoy, *Journal,* 1:xiii.

115. On Brissot's reportage of the event, see Barry Shapiro, *Revolutionary Justice in Paris, 1789–1790* (Cambridge, 1993), 40–42.

116. *Révolutions de Paris,* no. 2 (18–25 July 1789), p. 25.

literature all to herself that focused principally on her alleged moral decadence and ferocity. "I am at the home of the emperor, your ally," she is made to say in one pamphlet. Promising to return to wreak her vengeance, she utters the chilling words, "we will see each other again, French people, I do not bid you adieu."[117] The image of the "aristocrat" as *émigré* had now entered popular political demonology side by side Marie-Antoinette's representation as an Austrian agent.

Memories of the July "conspiracy" were further fixed by official efforts to deal with its consequences, which, as Barry Shapiro has shown, almost immediately became entangled in the new politics of the crowd.[118] Under considerable popular pressure to unmask and neutralize malefactors, revolutionary authorities also feared unleashing fresh rounds of disorders. Thus they sought, on the one hand, to protect themselves from accusations that they were covering up new threats and taking too little preventive action and, on the other, to avoid inciting further violence by accrediting the most lurid conspiracy claims. The result was a spotty policy of arrest and prosecution that permitted many alleged conspirators to emigrate or win acquittals but also documented and thereby validated at least the major outlines of the July conspiracy as it was popularly understood. The Assembly's Comité de Recherches published its long official report at the end of 1789, which in no uncertain terms affirmed the existence of the July plot, charged by name the usual suspects for their complicity (while exculpating the king), and juridically demonstrated its status as a crime of *lèse-majesté*.[119] Although Marat denounced the report as evidence of a cover-up, no less a radical—still in good standing—than Brissot praised it for its thoroughness.[120] Additional confirmation of the court's malfeasance and the aristocracy's parasitism came in November 1789 with the publication of the *Etat nominatif des pensions sur le trésor royal,* which showed that some of the major July criminals— the Polignacs, Breteuil, the duc de Broglie, the duc de Coigny—had been receiving enormous pensions of many tens of thousands of *livres* at state

---

117. J. B. D. N., *Facéties,* 84–85. The prince de Lambesc also emigrated; on his vilification, see Kaiser, "Ambiguous Identities."

118. Shapiro, *Revolutionary Justice.*

119. Jean-Philippe Garran de Coulon, *Rapport fait au comité de recherches des représentants de la commune, par M. Garran de Coulon, sur la conspiration des mois de mai, juin & juillet derniers, imprimé par ordre du comité* (Paris, 1789). This report was also published in installments in the *Le Moniteur* during the last week of December 1789.

120. Jean-Paul Marat, *Oeuvres politiques, 1789–1793,* ed. Jacques de Cock and Charlotte Goëtz, 10 vols. (Brussels, 1989–95), 1:519–20; *Le Patriote Français,* no. 138 suppl. (24 December 1789), pp. 5–6.

expense.[121] This document caused venom to flow from Brissot as well as from Carra, who denounced the so-called aristocratic cake. "It was thus," Carra fumed, "that finances were used; and it was thus that the intimates of the court were served in their golden cups the tears and blood of the people."[122] The following spring saw the publication of the *Livre rouge* with yet more revelations of fiscal profligacy and corruption. This time even the former hero of the people, Necker, was deeply implicated, just as more evidence came to light "proving" the transfer of enormous sums to the Austrians.[123]

How convincing was this recurring evidence of aristo-ministerial conspiracy? How much did it tarnish the image of the nobility as a whole? There is no way to answer these questions precisely, yet the evidence indicates that the July crisis and its sequelae at the very least put the nobility under suspicion as potential members of an "aristocratic" conspiracy. To be sure, Timothy Tackett, after having convincingly demonstrated the strength of noble resistance to the leftward drift of politics throughout 1789 and after allowing for an occasional brief outbreak of conspiratorial anxiety among the Third Estate just before 14 July, has recently contended that in general conspiratorial thinking played an unimportant role in elite French politics until Varennes.[124] He has also shown that there were limits to belief in aristocratic conspiracy among the peasantry during the Great Fear.[125] But in my view, these conclusions must be balanced against evidence pointing to the critical weight of conspiratorial thinking. This evidence includes not only the diatribes of such radical journalists as Brissot, who fulminated against claims that the "aristocracy" was a "chimera" and that the left was slandering the nobility by attributing to it certain "dark projects," but also testimonials of the very deputies Tackett has studied so sensitively and well.[126] Deputies certainly varied over time and among themselves in their inclination to

121. *Etat nominatif des pensions sur le trésor royal, imprimé par ordre de l'Assemblée nationale,* 4 vols. (Paris, 1789–91).

122. *Annales patriotiques,* no. 35 (26 December 1789), p. 3; Brissot fumed about these pensions in *Le Patriote Français,* no. 114 (30 November 1789), p. 3.

123. *Livre rouge* (Paris, 1848). For its impact on Austrophobia, see Kaiser, "Who's Afraid?"

124. Tackett, "Conspiracy Obsession."

125. Timothy Tackett, "Collective Panics in the Early French Revolution, 1789–1791: A Comparative Perspective," *French History* 17 (2003): 149–71. I thank the author for allowing me to read an advance copy of this article.

126. *Le Patriote Français,* no. 87 (3 November 1789), p. 3. Whether Brissot and his colleagues actually believed in the conspiracy plots they denounced, invented them for political purposes, or both, is an extremely difficult question to answer. Of course, the consequences of their rhetoric must be distinguished from the motivations behind it.

credit conspiracy accusations. Yet non-noble and even some noble deputies, while often critical and even dismissive of some charges, gradually came to believe—to an extent and in a manner conditioned by their own particular political considerations—that there was at least a nucleus of truth to allegations of aristocratic conspiracy.

This incremental tendency to credit reports of conspiracy is evident in the journal of the Third Estate deputy Adrien Duquesnoy. Duquesnoy's innate skepticism and political sobriety did not lead him into blindly accepting the charges of the left despite his commoner status, and for this reason the shifting nature of his views may well say more about the overall direction of Third Estate opinion than does the consistently hard line of the radicals. At the outset of the Estates-General, Duquesnoy bemoaned the weakening influence of the moderates, noting how anyone who tried to occupy the center was not only ignored but also excluded from effective participation. Far from subscribing to a Sieyèsian radicalism on the issue of the nobility, Duquesnoy pointedly identified the ministry—not the "aristocracy"—as the Third Estates's chief enemy, and he freely acknowledged how little the abolition of the Second Estate would help the rural masses.[127] Even after the July crisis, Duquesnoy continued to resist radical propaganda. He dismissed frequently alleged conspiracies as "vain and ridiculous scarecrow(s)" erected by demagogues, and he argued that the events of July, even if they had foiled a real plot, should calm fears of further conspiracies.[128] But after the attack on Versailles on 5/6 October—which some accounts represented as another preemptive strike against an aristo-ministerial conspiracy—Duquesnoy began to shift his stance, noting that although these accounts did not offer a coherent story, there was some strong evidence to support them.[129] By November, his credulity had hardened. Upon the presentation of a report by the Comité de Recherches to the Assembly, he noted that although there might be some exaggeration to its report of a court-based plot to kidnap the king, "it [is] impossible not to believe that some of their conjectures are founded . . . and difficult not to think they are following the thread of a criminal, a profoundly criminal project."[130] By February 1790 Duquesnoy's remaining doubts appeared to have largely melted away. "It would be impossible to describe the consternation, the furor of the aristocrats; there

127. Duquesnoy, *Journal,* 1:38.
128. Ibid., 1:252–53.
129. Ibid., 1:413.
130. Ibid., 2:72.

are few of them, no doubt, but they still exist and perhaps they would be only more dangerous if the Assembly lapsed into too great a complacency."[131] Laissez-faire skepticism had metamorphosed into activist faith.

A still more interesting case of conversion is that of a provincial nobleman, the marquis de Ferrières, who had been a proud guest at the Polignacs' infamous soirées of May–June 1789. His political itinerary is particularly noteworthy because he wound up following much the same political trajectory as the *roturier* Duquesnoy, but for somewhat different reasons. Flattered by the attention he had received from the Artois/Polignac syndicate, Ferrières was clearly shocked by allegations that the July crisis had been an "aristocratic" plot and by the application of the same smears generated by the crisis against the court to all titled individuals, himself included. "The insurrection against the nobility is universal," he wrote his wife in consternation on 29 July.[132] At first, simple "prudence" seemed an adequate remedy.[133] But Ferrières soon realized that an "infamous calumny" alleging he had joined the party of Artois and the queen could be refuted only by some strenuous assertions: first, that he had quickly abandoned their dubious "society," and second, that from the moment the Second Estate had joined the Third, he had boycotted the nobles' chamber and "clandestine meetings."[134] Most significantly, Ferrières began to criticize a certain "part of the nobility" for their "irregular and dangerous conduct,"[135] and after the 5/6 October march on Versailles, he agreed that the court similarly deserved some of the reproaches leveled against it for its "secret intrigues"—about which he personally could have only "vague suspicions," since he no longer belonged to "any party."[136]

In June 1790, Ferrières, like the rest of his order, faced the sad prospect of the Assembly's suppression of noble titles. The now former marquis blamed the legislation principally on radical journalists, who had allegedly convinced the majority of the nation that the nobility was universally hostile to the Revolution and hence that extreme measures were necessary. "The nobility is painted as the enemy of the Revolution; one hears it constantly said that it wants to reestablish the former feudal regime and put the nation under the yoke of ministerial despotism in order to restore the same abuses

131. Ibid., 2:352.
132. Ferrières-Marçay, *Correspondance inédite,* 99.
133. Ibid., 106.
134. Ibid., 112.
135. Ibid., 112.
136. Ibid., 173.

and share the profits."[137] But if journalists bore the main responsibility for the revocation of noble status, Ferrières made it clear that their unwitting accomplices had been court-favored nobles like the Polignacs and royal ministers, including Necker. In this limited sense, Ferrières, too, had become a believer in the existence of an aristo-ministerial conspiracy. To him, the freshly published evidence of the *Livre rouge* confirmed that these culprits had jointly pillaged the treasury. Bad enough in itself, this revelation was particularly egregious because it provided unscrupulous journalists with the tar to blacken the entire nobility—"as if the provincial nobility had ever participated in such abuses," which is to say, as if someone like him could ever possibly have been an "aristocrat" or "courtesan."[138]

To Ferrières, the only plausible solution to the nobility's quandary was quiet resignation and strategic patience, which might possibly incline the public ultimately to distinguish the mass of innocent nobles from the guilty few. Certainly if there were the least noble resistance to the new decree, Ferrières warned, "the odious name of 'aristocrat' . . . will be . . . a tocsin always sounding against the nobility, a plausible pretext for insults and violence."[139] Given the overwhelming popular sentiment against the nobility and his own order's self-destructive tendency to commit "follies in the name of courage," he could not hold out much hope, at least for the immediate future.[140] "The people," he despaired, "continue to cry out against the aristocrats," a cry that despite all his prudent advice would only grow louder over the course of the Revolution.[141]

To be sure, nobles had never been nor would they henceforth be represented as the sole members of the "aristocracy," a term used so loosely during the Revolution that it was applied to virtually anyone deemed to have set his/her face against the newly constituted nation and/or opposed the equality of rights.[142] Indeed, the term was elastic enough for nobles themselves to apply it to their enemies. One case in point was the marquis de Laqueuille, who in angry reaction to the abolition of titles in June 1790 accused the Assembly of erecting "the most dangerous aristocracy."[143] But none of this

137. Ibid., 207–8.
138. Ibid., 226.
139. Ibid., 208.
140. Ibid., 227.
141. Ibid., 245.
142. See, for example, the discussion of "aristocracy" in Carra's *Annales patriotiques,* no. 58 (29 November 1789), pp. 3–4.
143. *Archives parlementaires,* 16:386.

semantic elasticity meant that Ferrières lacked good reason to worry about the fate of his ex-order, for if by 1791 all those considered aristocrats had not been nobles, all former nobles were considered more or less "aristocrats."[144] As recalled in a pamphlet entitled *Antidote du poison aristocratique,* the events of the mid-1789 crisis had amply revealed the nobles' duplicity and moral bankruptcy. At a time when the country had sorely needed their sacrifice and virtue, the first acts of the majority of nobles had been "the reclamation of privileges, the announcement of a willingness to die rather than abandon them, the refusal to verify powers with the Third, [and] the criminal, shameful desire to see [the Third] degraded . . . to demand that it appear only on bended knee."[145]

This moral reindictment of nobles makes it questionable whether Higonnet's distinction between hostility to them as an order and hostility to them as individuals was as sharp as he claimed. Surely Higonnet was correct to argue that most legislation and bourgeois rhetoric between 1789 and 1791 left open the possibility of rehabilitating nobles as individuals once their privileged status was eradicated; surely the violence leveled against them—which made a deep impression on Ferrières and remained a concern—was far less systematic than it would become under the Terror. Still, as Ferrières sensed, the fact that most nobles had already spurned the hand extended to them by Rabaut and his colleagues in 1789 put all of them under a cloud of suspicion that the removal of their privileges did not dispel. As the bourgeois Charles Lambert observed following the abolition of titles, even if "as an order the nobles are no longer anything, . . . as individuals they could still be dangerous." Depriving them of their hereditary titles, he contended, would certainly go a long way to reducing their danger, but he clearly intimated that this did not mean they could be trusted. For they possessed an "esprit de corps that they will never be able to shed and will always make them a separate people among the people itself."[146] Ex-nobles had become presumptive "aristocrats."

144. Here I agree with Patrice Higonnet, in his "'Aristocrate,' 'Aristocratie': Language and Politics in the French Revolution," in *The French Revolution 1789–1989: Two Hundred Years of Rethinking,* ed. Sandy Petrey (Lubbock, 1989), 50.
145. Roussel, *Antidote du poison aristocratique* (Honfleur, [1790]), 9.
146. [Charles Lambert], *Abolition de la noblesse héréditaire en France proposée à l'Assemblée nationale; par un philanthrope, citoyen de Belan* (Paris, 1790), 27. Higonnet argued correctly (*Class,* 67–68) that the harsh indictment by J.-A. Dulaure in his *Histoire critique de la noblesse depuis le commencement de la monarchie jusqu'à nos jours* (Paris, 1790) targeted the "regime" of the nobility rather than its members. But Dulaure's noble readers were unlikely to take much comfort in such assertions as "the nobility, being a vicious institution, could generally produce only vicious men," and his argument that the legal abolition of the nobility hardly made his attack on it

Conclusion: A Tocsin Always Sounding Against the Nobility

In conclusion, I should like to draw several points together regarding revolutionary anti-nobilism. First, I maintain that however much revolutionary anti-nobilism arose in response to the immediate circumstances of 1789, its ideological pedigree went back at least to the sixteenth century, when noble revolt produced charges of "conspiracy" and "aristocracy" deriving principally from the crown. To be sure, the rise of the royal state and court fundamentally altered the nature of noble politicking, but in the end the negative images of noble revolt continued to prove useful in an age when noble armies were less likely to challenge the crown directly and national politics became centered on the play of court factions. Although the crisis of 1789 forced the crown and large elements of the nobility into a *mariage de convenance,* the anti-noble argument generated by the monarchy over the centuries handed the Third Estate an ideological weapon, refashioned with republican motifs, that the latter deployed with ultimately disastrous consequences for both the king and his noble cousins.

Second, the growth of anti-noble sentiment was, if not inevitable by 1789, highly probable, given fundamental and possibly irreconcilable differences between noble and bourgeois agendas on matters of honorific, if not fiscal, privilege. With relations between the two orders already tense as a result of disputes over representation in the provinces, the conflict over voting procedures at the Estates-General illuminated these differences in such conspicuous ways that compromise became virtually impossible. As Bailly noted in his memoirs, if the French nobility as a whole had accepted the union of orders instead of resisting it so fiercely, "the Revolution, which would have occurred nonetheless, would have taken another form."[147] But, of course, they had not, and at this crucial juncture how the nobles had thought and acted made an enormous difference to the bourgeois public and the crowd. Anti-nobilism did not spring alone from the ideology and opportunism of bourgeois politicians pandering to the people.

Third, in railing against the court, which had denied them the patronage to which they felt entitled, important elements of the court nobility fell into a trap partly of their own design. The unrestrained rapacity of the Polignacs

---

pointless, for even "if the body of the nobility has been destroyed, the alleged nobles are not." Dulaure, *Histoire critique,* v, vii. In other words, there was recurring slippage from condemnation of the noble order to condemnation of nobles individually.

147. Bailly, *Mémoires,* 1:31.

and other royal favorites went a long way to discrediting the court in public opinion all by itself, but reproaches coming from the highest reaches of the nobility among the Society of Thirty certainly furthered the process. The problem for the nobility arose when, to protect their status, a considerable number of them cast their lots with the same monarchy they had previously attacked and when they paraded openly with the likes of Marie-Antoinette, Artois, and the Polignacs. If there was a conspiracy to shut down the Revolution in July 1789, it is unlikely that many nobles were party to it, but in the end that did not matter. What did matter was the seeming semitransparent collusion between the nobles and the court, which allowed the public to believe an aristo-ministerial plot had just barely been foiled and could strike again. When evidence and confirmation of such a plot grew in later 1789 and early 1790, it became harder and harder to distinguish between the malefactors of the court and the nobility in general. Despite the fervent hopes of provincial nobles like the marquis de Ferrières, "the odious name of 'aristocrat'" had become, as he had feared, "a tocsin always sounding against the nobility, a plausible pretext for insults and violence."

Finally, it is evident from the evidence cited in this essay that conspiracy was a significant factor in defining elite political perceptions in 1789. Tackett was absolutely right to caution us against assuming that every development in this period was perceived or explained in conspiratorial terms. But, at a minimum, fear of conspiracy did play a major role in generating anti-nobilism during the opening act of the Revolution, which suggests that even when other psycho-political factors were on center stage, conspiracy anxiety was always waiting in the wings.

III

NOBILITY AND "ARISTOCRATIC REACTION"

8

A RHETORIC OF ARISTOCRATIC REACTION?
NOBILITY IN *DE L'ESPRIT DES LOIS*

Johnson Kent Wright

For all of the celebrity of *De l'esprit des lois*—commonly regarded as the most influential work of political thought of the French Enlightenment—the political stance of its author has always been a matter of dispute. The basic positions were established in a sharp exchange early in the last century, when Elie Carcassonne's portrait of Montesquieu as a liberal constitutionalist drew a blunt rejoinder from Albert Mathiez, who described him instead as a "feudal reactionary."[1] Mathiez seems to have won the argument in the short term. The claim that *De l'esprit des lois* was fundamentally a work of aristocratic apology found expression in a series of striking midcentury statements, starting with a famous chapter in Franklin Ford's *Robe and Sword,* published in 1953. For Ford, Montesquieu was in fact the foremost spokesman for the "noble reaction" against Bourbon absolutism that eventually helped launch the Revolution. Echoed six years later in a Marxist register by Louis Althusser, this view was then enshrined in one of the great monuments of postwar liberal scholarship, R. R. Palmer's *The Age of the Democratic Revolution,* which presented Montesquieu as the last and greatest theoretician of "aristocracy" itself, on the eve of its overthrow in the West. But what might thus be termed the "social interpretation of *De l'esprit des*

I would like to thank David Bien for helpful comments on an earlier draft of this essay, and Jay Smith, for his invitation to contribute to this volume and for his patience in waiting for the contribution.

1. A. Mathiez, "La place de Montesquieu dans l'histoire des doctrines politiques du XVIIIe siècle," *Annales Historiques de la Révolution Française* 7 (1930): 97–112; Elie Carcassonne, *Montesquieu et le problème de la constitution française au XVIIIe siècle* (Paris, 1927).

lois" was not destined to survive the subsequent revisionist assault on Jacobin-Marxist "orthodoxy." Since the sixties, the main current of interpretation of Montesquieu, in both French and Anglophone scholarship, has flowed very much in the opposite direction, toward the position staked out by Carcassonne. In fact, for some thirty years now, virtually every important study of *De l'esprit des lois* has minimized or disregarded altogether the elements of aristocratic apology once thought central to its interpretation and instead sought to secure its place among the canonical texts of early modern liberalism. Long seen as the first theorist of the liberal doctrine of the "separation of powers," Montesquieu today appears, in Catherine Larrère's attractive profile, as the eighteenth century's foremost advocate of cultural diversity and political pluralism.[2]

In the meantime, however, the passing of the revisionist ascendancy has brought a welcome renewal of interest in the role of social class in the history of both the Enlightenment and the Revolution. Indeed, the revolutionary bourgeoisie—considered alternately as "rhetoric," "myth," or manifest reality in the work of Sewell, Maza, and Jones—has returned to center stage in recent Anglophone historiography.[3] Can its traditional antagonist, the reactionary nobility, be far behind? There is a further reason why this might be an apt moment for reconsideration of the social interpretation of Montesquieu. Despite universal acknowledgment of its central impact on modern political thought, the actual volume of scholarship devoted to *De l'esprit des lois* is surprisingly slight, particularly in English. The sole intellectual biography of Montesquieu has now entered its fifth decade of service, with no successor in sight; it has since been joined by only a tiny handful of monographs, none really rising to the grandeur of their subject. Naturally, the literature on Montesquieu is far more abundant in French, and the new edition of *oeuvres complètes* forthcoming from the Voltaire Foundation is likely to arouse renewed interest in its author. Still, it is very telling that the only comprehensive effort to establish Montesquieu's place in the central ideological contest of the eighteenth century should remain Carcassonne's *Montesquieu et le problème de la constitution française au XVIIIe siècle,* published in 1927. This is a work of remarkable erudition, still indispensable for approaching the question of the intellectual origins of the Revolution. But it is also badly in need of

2. Catherine Larrère, *L'actualité de Montesquieu* (Paris, 1999).
3. William H. Sewell Jr., *A Rhetoric of Bourgeois Revolution: The Abbé Sieyes and What Is the Third Estate?* (Durham, N.C., 1994); Sarah C. Maza, *The Myth of the French Bourgeoisie: An Essay on the Social Imaginary* (Cambridge, Mass., 2003); Colin Jones, *The Great Nation: France from Louis XIV to Napoleon* (New York, 2003).

updating, in light of the complete transformation of the wider field of the history of French political thought, both empirically and methodologically, since Carcassonne wrote. In the landscape revealed in this newer scholarship, *De l'esprit des lois* remains an isolated peak—perpetually in view, yet seldom scaled today. Obviously, this is not the occasion for launching a major expedition. The most that will be attempted here is a brief consideration of the issue that is central to any judgment about the social interpretation of Montesquieu today: the handling of the topic of nobility in *De l'esprit des lois* itself.

The Social Interpretation of *De l'Esprit des Lois*

Before turning to the text, we might begin by looking back at the classic statements of the social interpretation, each of which had its distinctive themes. Franklin Ford's discussion of *De l'esprit des lois* came at the end of a major work of historical sociology, which sought to explain the "resurgent" power of the French nobility in the eighteenth century in terms of a "regrouping" of the class. Hitherto at loggerheads, the two main factions of the nobility, feudal "Sword" and judicial "Robe," joined forces under the economic, political, and intellectual leadership of the latter, who then steered the French nobility into the aristocratic revolt that precipitated the Revolution. On Ford's account, the economic and political reconfiguration of the French nobility was well underway by the first third of the eighteenth century. But ideas lagged behind. Not only did a chasm remain between the ideologists of Sword and Robe, but the intellectual offensive in the first part of the century had in fact passed decisively to the side of the monarchy. Boulainvilliers, major spokesman for the *thèse nobiliaire*—the interpretation of French history that accorded priority in it to the Frankish nobility of the sword—was long gone, leaving the crowd of creative apologists for the opposing *thèse royale*—Dubos, d'Argenson, the young Mably—without response. It was in this context, Ford argued, that Montesquieu's achievement should be seen. In *De l'esprit des lois,* the French nobility found the perfect expression of its contemporary "regroupment." In his theory of the "intermediate powers" that defined the very essence of monarchy, the former *président* of the *parlement* of Bordeaux provided a kind of *summa* of the entire parlementary tradition, which he then "fused" with a powerful restatement of the *thèse nobiliaire* in the closing books of *De l'esprit des lois.* Montesquieu's criticisms of both Boulainvilliers and the major proponent of the *thèse royale,* Dubos, should not deceive, Ford concluded: "the former is his man." For all of its "enlightened" trappings and seeming proto-liberalism, *De l'esprit des lois* became the charter for the "feudal reaction" that dominated relations between nobility and crown down to the Revolution that ended the rule of both.

The theoretical background to *Robe and Sword* was eclectic, with Ford appealing simultaneously to Pareto, Marx, and Weber. Althusser's *Montesquieu: La politique et l'histoire* was, by contrast, the work not merely of a Marxist philosopher, but of the author of one of the most distinctive theories of ideology of the entire Western Marxist canon. It was only a decade later that Althusser produced the formula that captured the full flavor of a theory mingling Spinoza, Freud, and Lacan: "Ideology is a 'representation' of the Imaginary relationship of individuals to their Real conditions of existence."[4] But the basic elements of this conception are there in his analysis of Montesquieu. The chapter on "Montesquieu's *parti pris*" came at the end of a reading of *De l'esprit des lois* extending across a hundred pages. "Do the categories in which the men of the eighteenth century thought the history they were living answer to historical reality?" Althusser asked in conclusion. For contemporaries, the fundamental political issue of the epoch was the struggle between nobility and monarchy. But this political and ideological contest, pitting partisans of the *thèse nobiliaire* against those of the *thèse royale,* was in effect an "imaginary" one, serving to conceal the "true relation of forces" in society. In reality, the interests of crown and nobility were at one in their common struggle against another social antagonist, all but invisible in the political writing of the time. This was not the bourgeoisie of the period, whose relations with the nobility in the Old Regime were not, contrary to legend, fundamentally antagonistic—the belief that they were was an anachronism bequeathed by the nineteenth century. Instead, appealing to Porshnev's study of Meslier, Althusser identified the "fourth power," from whose labors the material conditions of existence of crown, nobility, and bourgeoisie alike derived, as the French *peasantry.* It was their struggle against the other three—a struggle between "power and poverty"—that formed the "real" social antagonism of the Old Regime. As for Montesquieu, Althusser concluded, he was as blind to this struggle as any of his contemporaries. For all of the grandeur of *De l'esprit des lois,* whose conception of social "totalities" anticipated that of Marx, Montesquieu too fell prey to the illusion that the struggle between crown and nobility was what mattered

4. Louis Althusser, "Ideology and Ideological State Apparatuses," in *Lenin and Philosophy and Other Essays,* trans. Ben Brewster (New York, 2001), 109.

and took up arms on behalf of his own class. Paradoxically, this "reactionary" stance explains his preeminence in eighteenth century thought: "Montesquieu himself merely wanted to re-establish a threatened nobility in its outdated rights. But he thought the threat came from the king. In fact, taking sides against the king's absolute power, he lent his hand to the undermining of the State apparatus which was the nobility's only rampart."[5]

The same paradox was noted by Robert Palmer in the first volume of *The Age of the Democratic Revolution,* which also appeared in 1959. For Palmer, Montesquieu was "not a true conservative, because he was not satisfied with the way the Bourbon monarchy had developed and was developing in his time . . . in France, the aristocratic school was not conservative. In France, the aristocracy hoped for change. It became dissatisfied with the monarchy long before the middle class."[6] Like Althusser, Palmer believed that the friction between nobility and monarchy in France, if not quite "imaginary" in the technical sense of the term, was certainly secondary to the much more profound social upheaval that was about to shake both. For Palmer, taking his inspiration from Tocqueville rather than Marx, this was of course the "democratic revolution" against aristocracy that swept across the Atlantic world between 1760 and 1800, moving from the colonial periphery to the metropolitan center of European civilization. This chain of revolts had been unleashed essentially by ideas—the egalitarian doctrine of the "rights of man" propagated by the Enlightenment—and Palmer was accordingly less interested in the economic foundations of aristocratic power than in its most visible political projections. The great bulwarks of aristocratic privilege in old regime Europe were the "constituted bodies" that littered its political landscape—estates, parliaments, diets, assemblies, and councils of every kind. It was the achievement of Montesquieu, Palmer argued, to have provided the most rigorous theorization and most eloquent defense of these institutions: "The *Spirit of the Laws* set forth, in amplified and cogent form, what members of the constituted bodies of Europe had long been saying in more fragmentary ways." As for Ford, this achievement was largely a synthetic one: "The strength of Montesquieu's book . . . lay in his weaving together many diverse strands, each strand representing the position taken by actually existing institutions or groups of men. He combined the arguments of the

    5. Louis Althusser, "Montesquieu: Politics and History," in *Montesquieu, Rousseau, Marx,* trans. Ben Brewster (London, 1982), 106.
    6. R. R. Palmer, *The Age of the Democratic Revolution,* vol. 1, *The Challenge* (Princeton, 1959), 60, 62.

old feudal and the new parlementary nobility of France. He put together England and France, showing that each in their way had the institutions necessary for political liberty, England through its balance of kings, lords, and commons, France through the moderating influence of 'intermediate bodies' upon the crown." But the libertarian aspect of *De l'esprit des lois,* making possible legends about his "influence" on the American Revolution, should not mislead us: "Palatable or not, there is no disputing that for Montesquieu the preservation of political liberty presupposed a hierarchic form of society and an aristocratic code of personal honor."[7]

Such then were the major statements of the social interpretation of *De l'esprit des lois.* Neither Ford, nor Althusser, nor Palmer were willing to reduce Montesquieu to the status of "feudal reactionary" *tout court,* as had Mathiez. All three acknowledged the elements of proto-liberalism that had been stressed by Carcassonne, which were part and parcel of the wider aristocratic comeback in the eighteenth century. But none of the three had any doubt that *De l'esprit des lois* was a partisan intervention in the major ideological dispute of the age, nor left any question as to what side Montesquieu took in the contest. In any case, for all the apparent authority of *Robe and Sword, Montesquieu: la politique et l'histoire,* and *The Age of the Democratic Revolution,* these were also the *last* attempts to understand Montesquieu as a kind of aristocratic apologist. No doubt the tabling of the idea had a good deal to do with the subsequent domination of the field by a revisionist historiography hostile to social interpretations of any sort. But it also reflects a surprising falling off of interest in Montesquieu, at least in Anglophone scholarship. Two years after Palmer's first volume, there appeared Robert Shackleton's *Montesquieu,* which remains to this day the only intellectual biography in English based on primary research. A meticulous reconstruction of Montesquieu's life and the genesis of his works, Shackleton's study was almost entirely silent on the larger question of his political *parti pris,* concentrating instead on his intellectual relations to the early Enlightenment. It took more than a decade for further significant writing on Montesquieu to appear in English, and the dominant trend was announced in the title of Thomas Pangle's *Montesquieu's Philosophy of Liberalism* (1973)—the effort to secure a place for Montesquieu among the canon of great "liberal" founders of modern political thought. For Pangle, a Straussian philosopher reacting against the rise of a new left promoting the virtues of "participatory republicanism," this canon included Hobbes, Spinoza, and Locke; among these,

7. Ibid., 56–67, 59.

Montesquieu was perhaps "the most helpful and relevant for us" because of his defense of a rather more prudent "liberal republicanism" inspired by his admiration for the English constitution.[8] Judith Shklar's brief profile for the Oxford Past Masters series, published in 1987, also presented Montesquieu as a liberal constitutionalist, whose hatred of despotism expressed itself in—a memorable phrase—a "liberalism of fear."[9] Montesquieu appears in a similar guise in Catherine Larrère's still more recent portrait, though in current conditions of neoliberal triumph, the accent is no longer on fear but on the active promotion of cultural diversity and pluralism. The only significant dissent from this view has come from those who think that Montesquieu's heart belonged not to England but to Sparta, Athens, and Rome—that he was fundamentally a "classical republican" rather than a "liberal" thinker. This is the conclusion arrived at in the chapters on Montesquieu in Nannerl Keohane's sweeping survey of early modern French political thought, *Philosophy and the State in France*: "In his youth, Montesquieu cast in his lot with the Ancients against the Moderns; he never reversed himself. His most fundamental admiration was reserved for the classical polity, the site of true human virtue."[10] Mark Hulliung, however, had already found it possible to declare Montesquieu both "liberal" and "republican," blending Athenian, Roman, and English norms together in a single "radical" model. The result was one of the more amazing theses in the historiography of political thought: "[Montesquieu] was a foremost detractor of the old regime and the proponent of a radical alternative. When viewing England, Montesquieu dreamed of nothing less than a national republic and a democratic society in France which could displace a monarchical politics and an aristocratic society."[11]

As Hulliung's thesis—which, were it accurate, would place Montesquieu well to the left of Rousseau on the political spectrum—suggests, the portrait of Montesquieu as "liberal" and/or "republican" involves overturning the social interpretation of *De l'esprit des lois* altogether. Indeed, for some forty years now, nearly every major study of *De l'esprit des lois* has agreed in minimizing or simply disregarding the concerns that were uppermost to Ford,

---

8. The interest in Montesquieu from a Straussian standpoint has persisted, interestingly enough—the inspiration, roughly speaking, for *two* recent collections of essays in English: David W. Carrithers, Michael A. Mosher, and Paul A. Rahe, eds., *Montesquieu's Science of Politics: Essays on The Spirit of the Laws* (Lanham, Md., 2001), and David W. Carrithers and Patrick Coleman, eds., *Montesquieu and the Spirit of Modernity* (Oxford, 2002).

9. Judith N. Shklar, *Montesquieu* (Oxford University Press, 1987).

10. Nannerl O. Keohane, *Philosophy and the State in France: The Renaissance to the Enlightenment* (Princeton, 1980), 419.

11. Mark Hulliung, *Montesquieu and the Old Regime* (Berkeley, 1976), x, ix.

Althusser, or Palmer. At the same time, it is worth stressing that none of the writings just mentioned, most of them exercises in "political philosophy" and "presentist" in practical orientation, even remotely approximates the kind of careful historical work that is necessary to arbitrate such claims. The fact is that, after all these years, there has been not a single attempt to update Carcassonne—no comprehensive effort to restore *De l'esprit des lois* to its contemporary intellectual and ideological context and then to trace its impact in the succeeding decades, down to the Revolution. The lacuna is all the more surprising given the revolution in the methodology of the history of political thought that in the meantime overtook the discipline. For the central themes of Cambridge-school contextualism—contention over "ancient constitutions" and "feudal law," the recovery of the classical republican tradition, the evolution of "natural rights" theory—are precisely those that are most at stake in the interpretation of Montesquieu. There is no doubt that the comprehensive application of the methods and themes of Pocock and Skinner to the French zone has been slow in coming, for a variety of reasons. But a number of figures other than Montesquieu, including Boulainvilliers, Dubos, Mably, Rousseau, Saige, Sieyès, and Say, have benefited from attention inspired by Cambridge in the recent past.[12] The inhibition in regard to Montesquieu probably has to do with the sheer scale of the totalization involved in tackling *De l'esprit des lois* from this perspective, standing as it does at the crossroads of all the major political traditions of early modern France, and serving, as it also does, as the *fons et origo* of most of the major political ideologies of the Revolution itself. But there is no doubt that an enterprise of this kind, however daunting it may seem, is long overdue.

Nobility in *De l'esprit des lois*

In a short essay such as this, the most that we can do is to focus on a single issue, albeit one that is crucial to the larger question of Montesquieu's political *parti pris*: the treatment of nobility in *De l'esprit des lois*. The topic seems likely to be vast, given the notoriously sprawling and ramshackle

12. For examples, see Harold Ellis, *Boulainvilliers and the French Monarchy: Aristocratic Politics in Early Eighteenth-Century France* (Ithaca, N.Y., 1988); Thomas E. Kaiser, "The Abbé Dubos and the Historical Defence of Monarchy in Early Eighteenth-Century France," *Studies on Voltaire and the Eighteenth Century* 267 (1989): 77–102; Johnson Kent Wright, *A Classical Republican in Eighteenth-Century France: The Political Thought of Mably* (Stanford, 1997); Helena Rosenblatt, *Rousseau and Geneva* (Cambridge, 1997); Michael Sonenscher, introduction to Sieyès, *Political*

shape of the treatise. But if we ask ourselves a simple question—what is any open-minded reader, relatively familiar with the traditions of European political thought, bound to notice about the handling of the subject in *De l'esprit des lois?*—some preliminary points seem obvious. First, nobility for Montesquieu, as for his contemporaries, was not a "class" in the economic sense of the term, Marxist or otherwise (a concept and terminology that emerged only in the nineteenth century), but rather a social "order" or "estate." Second, neither the generic concept nor any of the traditional three orders or estates are ever analyzed as such in *De l'esprit des lois* in the fashion, say, of Loyseau's famous *Traité des ordres et simples dignitez*. Montesquieu clearly assumes that these categories are far too familiar to his readers to require that kind of scrutiny or explanation. Third, no reader will fail to recognize that the Second Estate is accorded very special treatment, from one end of *De l'esprit des lois* to the other. The first part of the treatise is devoted to the presentation of a basic typology of three forms of government, one of which—*monarchy*—turns out to be intimately related to nobility, in Montesquieu's view. Four hundred pages later, *De l'esprit des lois* concludes with a series of historical studies that take us back in time to the very moment when the nexus between nobility and monarchy in France was first established—the advent of "feudal government," the historical ancestor of the form of monarchy described in the typology. Whatever ultimate judgment we make about Montesquieu's politics, it is impossible to avoid the conclusion that this is one of the central abiding concerns of *De l'esprit des lois,* if not its principal one: not nobility in and of itself but the *relation,* theoretical and historical, between noble order and monarchical state.

The typology first, then. "There are three forms of government: republican, monarchical, and despotic," Montesquieu declares at the start of book 2: "republican government is that in which the people as a body, or only a part of the people, have sovereign power; monarchical government is that in which one governs alone, but by fixed and established laws; whereas, in despotic government, one alone, without law and without rule, draws everything along by his will and caprices."[13] The novelty of this schema as a whole is sometimes exaggerated. It was in fact born of a fusion between two distinct typological traditions, one focused on the *location* of sovereign power, the other on the *mode* of its exercise. On the one hand, there was

---

Writings (Indianapolis, 2003); Richard Whatmore, *Republicanism and the French Revolution: An Intellectual Biography of Jean-Baptiste Say's Political Economy* (Oxford, 2001).

13. Montesquieu, *The Spirit of the Laws,* trans. Cohler, Miller, and Stone (Cambridge, 1989), 10.

the classical typology of the One, the Few, and the Many, which the European republican tradition had long since streamlined by treating "aristocracy" and "democracy" as Montesquieu does, as variants of a single nonmonarchical form; Machiavelli's is only the most famous earlier example. On the other hand, there is that striking early modern innovation, the use of the neologism "despotism" to differentiate Muslim and Asian autocracies from European monarchies, chiefly by reference to the role of proto-constitutional law in the latter. The result was typically to hold up a critical mirror to the European states.[14] No doubt this was one of Montesquieu's purposes in soldering the two traditions together in this fashion, since it renders *monarchy,* the form of government that appears in both prior traditions, the pivot of his typology as a whole.

At the same time, there is no close counterpart anywhere in early modern political thought for the specific analysis of monarchy, internal to the typology, that follows in *De l'esprit des lois.* Its fundamental feature is the umbilical connection that Montesquieu establishes between monarchy and nobility. This was made possible by a crucial conceptual innovation, the distinction between the "nature" of governments (their objective structure) and their "principle" (the subjective motivation or "passion" setting the structure "in motion"). In purely formal terms, Montesquieu supplies monarchy with a definition that is more or less identical with that of the most intransigent absolutist apologist: "In a monarchy, the prince is the source of all political and civil power." But both the specific "nature" and the "principle" of monarchy lead us straight to nobility. For as every reader remembers, the "nature" of monarchy is first specified in terms of the "intermediate, subordinate, and dependent powers" on which "fundamental laws" depend—the "most natural" of which, the only one specified, in fact, then turns out to be the nobility itself. Indeed, nobility is revealed to be the very "essence" of monarchy, whose "fundamental maxim" is *"point de monarque, point de noblesse; point de noblesse, point de monarque."*[15] As for the "principle" that sets this structure in motion, the functional counterpart to the "virtue" or "fear" that animate republics and despotisms, respectively, this is, of course, aristocratic "honor" *tout court:* "Since honor is the principle of this government, laws should relate to it: in monarchy, they must work to sustain that nobility for whom honor is, so to speak, both child and father."[16] Now there clearly

14. See R. Koebner, "Despot and Despotism: Vicissitudes of a Political Term," *Journal of the Warburg and Courtauld Institutes* 14 (1951).

15. Montesquieu, *Spirit of the Laws,* 17–16.

16. Ibid., 55. The initial analysis of the "principles" of governments comes in bk. 3.

were precedents for each of the component parts of this amalgam. The idea of "fundamental laws" unalterable by the sovereign was a staple of absolutist ideology itself, the object of careful analysis by Bodin and Bossuet: for both, respect for inherited constitutional norms marked all the distance between legitimate absolute sovereignty and "arbitrary" rule. Montesquieu's notion of "intermediate and subordinate powers" descended directly from the alternate juridical or corporate tradition in which he was formed. The intimate relations in Europe between kings and the landed nobilities serried about them had long been the object of commentary in early modern political thought—the fourth chapter of Machiavelli's *The Prince,* with its contrast between France and the Ottoman state, is again a famous case in point. But there was no precedent at all for the hybrid *fusion* of these various elements into a single whole in *De l'esprit des lois.* No political theorist before or after Montesquieu ever insisted on so drastic an existential equation between monarchical state and noble order or expressed it with such lapidary force— "no monarch, no nobility; no nobility, no monarch."

Meanwhile, we can designate monarchy, thus understood, as "European" for reasons that are only hinted at in part 1 of *De l'esprit des lois.* It is left to the succeeding five sections of the treatise to make explicit the spatial and temporal dimensions of the schema, whose upshot is to render monarchy the most widespread and suitable form of government in modern Europe. Most famous of all is the theory of geography and climate introduced in part 3, which reveals despotism to be fundamentally an Eastern or "Asian" phenomenon, never other than alien to Europe. More pertinent to our concerns, however, are the more properly *historical* factors that account for what Montesquieu saw as the basic dynamism of "Western" history: the transition from the republican world of classical antiquity to the monarchical one of modern Europe. Fittingly, the fulcrum of Montesquieu's explanation for this is presented only at the very end of *De l'esprit des lois,* as the climax of part 6—the two long books that describe "an event which happened once in the world and which will perhaps never happen again," the advent of "feudal government." Before turning to those books, however, we need to consider a short chapter in part 2, which constitutes, in fact, the *only* glimpse we are given in all of *De l'esprit des lois* of Montesquieu's vision of European history as a whole. As it happens, part 2 is also the linchpin of every presentation of Montesquieu as a "liberal," since it includes the famous portrait of the English constitution in book 11, chapter 6, as uniquely designed for the promotion of "political liberty." Chapter 6, with its extended analysis of the three "powers" common to all governments ("legislative power, executive power over the things depending on the law of nations, and executive power over things depending on civil right") and warnings against concentrating all three in any one hand, is perhaps familiar enough not to need rehearsal—except to point out that there *is* a significant upshot here for the general theory of monarchy in *De l'esprit des lois*. At the start of book 11, Montesquieu highlights the extraordinary range of meanings given to the word "liberty" and supplies an enigmatic definition of his own: "having the power to do what one should want to do and in no way being constrained to do what one should not want to do." Then he asserts: "Democracy and aristocracy are not free states by their nature. Political liberty is found only in moderate governments. But it is not always in moderate states. It is present only when power is not abused."[17] A page later, once the theory of the "powers" is introduced at the start of chapter 6, Montesquieu is still more explicit about "moderation": "In most kingdoms of Europe, the government is moderate because the prince, who has the first two powers, leaves the exercise of the third to his subjects. Among the Turks, where the three powers are united in the person of the sultan, an atrocious despotism reigns."[18] Aside from the vindication of "judicial power," in line with the general theory of monarchy in part 1, what is perhaps most striking here is a startling shift in the terminology of "moderation." For this is not the first time the concept appears in *De l'esprit des lois*. In part 1, "moderation" plays an important role, identified as the specific form of "political virtue" that is the animating principle of one of the main forms of government—*aristocracy*.[19] Yet in book 11, aristocracy appears, with its counterpart democracy, as an "immoderate" form of government, while "moderation" has migrated decisively over to monarchy. Every reader senses how important the terminology of "moderation" is to Montesquieu's outlook as a whole: what is the meaning of this shift in its "place"?

The beginnings of an answer to this question lie in the two chapters that immediately follow chapter 6. The first, entitled "The Monarchies That We Know," extends the preceding analysis back across the Channel:

> The monarchies we know do not have liberty for their direct purpose
> as does the one we have just mentioned; they aim only for the glory

17. Ibid., 155.
18. Ibid., 157.
19. Ibid., 24–25.

of the citizens, the state, and the prince. But this glory results in a spirit of liberty that can, in these states, produce equally great things and can perhaps contribute as much to happiness as liberty itself.

The three powers are not distributed and cast on the model of the constitution which we have mentioned; each instance shows a particular distribution of them and each approximates political liberty accordingly; and if it did not approximate it, the monarchy would degenerate into despotism.[20]

No mention of "moderation" here, but it is clearly at work in the "spirit of liberty" that is "approximated" in modern European monarchies. From here, Montesquieu turns in chapter 8 to a historical problem: "Why the Ancients Had No Clear Idea of Monarchy." The answer is worth citing nearly whole:

The ancients did not at all know of the government founded on a body of nobility and even less the government founded on a leg-islative body formed of the representatives of a nation. . . . Here is how the plan for the monarchies that we know was formed. The Germanic nations who conquered the Roman Empire were very free, as is known. On the subject one has only to see Tacitus on the *Mores of the Germans*. The conquerors spread out across the country: they lived in the countryside, rarely in the towns. When they were in Germany, the whole nation could be assembled. When they dispersed during the conquest, they could no longer assemble. Nevertheless, the nation had to deliberate on its business as it had done before the conquest; it did so by representatives. Here is the origin of Gothic government among us. It was at first a mixture of aristocracy and monarchy. Its drawback was that the common people were slaves; it was a good government that had within itself the capacity to become better. Giving letters of emanci-pation became the custom, and soon the civil liberty of the people, the prerogatives of the nobility and of the clergy, and the power of the kings, were in such concert that there has never been, I believe, a government on earth as well tempered as that of each part of Europe during the time that this government continued to exist; and it is remarkable that the corruption of a government of a

20. Ibid., 166–67.

conquering people should have formed the best kind of government men have been able to devise.[21]

It seems evident that this brief chapter is a good deal more important
to the intellectual architecture of De l'esprit des lois than its more celebrated neighbor—the modern English constitution being the anomaly
par excellence in the text, resisting any simple categorization in terms of
Montesquieu's basic typology of governments.[22] That typology is initially
presented, in part 1, without any temporal specification, as if the forms of
government might appear at any given moment in history. Now, however,
we learn that one of them—candidly described here as "the government
founded on a body of nobility"—had a very punctual historical birth. Both
modern monarchy and its English variant (here, "the government founded
on a legislative body formed of the representatives of a nation," elsewhere
in De l'esprit des lois a "republic disguised as a monarchy") descend from
a common historical ancestor, the "Gothic government" established by
German invaders on the ruins of the Roman Empire. It is no accident that
Montesquieu cites the authority of Tacitus at this point. As Catherine
Volpilhac-Auger has shown in a marvelous study, Montesquieu was the
eighteenth century's foremost interpreter of the Roman historian.[23]
Indeed, as we shall see in a moment, Tacitus's Germania is the polestar for
Montesquieu's extended analysis, at the end of De l'esprit des lois, of the
origins of "feudal government"—the term substituted there for "Gothic
government," which here makes its one and only appearance in the text.
Before turning to that analysis, however, we need to emphasize the aston-
ishing vision of subsequent historical development in Europe that closes
chapter 8, the only passage of its kind in all of De l'esprit des lois. For not
only does Montesquieu, famous both for his sober realism and his refusal
of the problematic of political "legitimacy," here identify "the best kind of
government men have been able to devise." But this also turns out to be a
variant of the oldest figure of utopian political discourse in the West—the

21. Ibid., 167.
22. Space precludes a full discussion of the reasons why Montesquieu cannot be regarded as
a straightforward "admirer" of the English constitution, much less an advocate of it as a model
for emulation elsewhere in Europe, as is required in most interpretations of him as a "liberal"
thinker. For incisive remarks on the subject, see Keith Michael Baker, *Inventing the French Revolution* (Cambridge, 1990), 173–78.
23. Catherine Volpilhac-Auger, *Tacite et Montesquieu,* in *Studies on Voltaire and the Eighteenth
Century* 232 (1985).

"mixed government." In Montesquieu's view, the first incarnation of "Gothic government" was a mixture of monarchy and aristocracy, erected over an enserfed population. But the abolition of serfdom seems to have added the necessary democratic admixture, resulting in a uniquely harmonious balance between royal power, noble privilege, and civil liberty. When was this "concert" achieved, exactly? The temporal markers suggest that Montesquieu can only be referring to the early absolutist "estates monarchies" of the Renaissance—in France, the rule of the rejuvenated Valois monarchy of the later fifteenth and sixteenth centuries, after serfdom was over but while the Estates-General, descendant of the "representative" assemblies of the Champ-de-Mars, still met. If so, this text is remarkable indeed, for the Estates-General is otherwise, notoriously, never so much as mentioned by name in *De l'esprit des lois*. In any case, we can now grasp the logic of the transfer of the crucial normative terminology of "moderation" from aristocracy to monarchy in part 2 of the text. As Montesquieu's theory of its "essence" might have warned us, modern monarchy turns out to be a form of "mixed government" in all but name. Even—or especially?—after its recovery of legislative power, monarchy owes its "moderation" precisely to its aristocratic component, a nobility in firm possession of "judicial power": "In most kingdoms of Europe, the government is moderate because the prince, who has the first two powers, leaves the exercise of the third to his subjects."

At all events, this fleeting glimpse of European political history as a whole in part 2 is in a sense merely a preamble for the conclusion of *De l'esprit des lois* in part 6, when Montesquieu returns to analyze the founding moment of "the monarchies that we know" in exhaustive detail. More than any other section of the text, the five large books of part 6, describing the transition from Roman to feudal law at the end of antiquity, have tended to flummox interpreters. The standard view is to regard them as a bloated appendix, in which Montesquieu indulged antiquarian concerns incidental to the principal themes of his treatise. Nothing could be further from the truth, of course. For whatever else might be said about the concluding books of *De l'esprit des lois,* their concerns were anything but antiquarian in the ideological context in which Montesquieu wrote. As in every other absolute monarchy in Europe, the principal terrain for political dispute in France had long been a historical one: debate over the origins and nature of the "ancient constitution" of the monarchy forming the natural idiom of ideological contention, especially in periods of political and social stress. The epoch of the Wars of Religion, marking the tumultuous transition from early to mature absolutism, had thus seen the richest earlier intellectual episode of this kind. Not surprisingly, the end of the reign of Louis XIV, the moment of the passing of Bourbon ascendancy in Europe, unleashed a second great round of contention over the "ancient constitution," one that went on continuously down to the Revolution itself—precisely the fateful exchanges explored by Carcassonne in *Montesquieu et le problème de la constitution française*. Even if Montesquieu had omitted its final books, *De l'esprit des lois* would still have constituted an important, if oblique, intervention in these debates. But the very centerpiece of the text—the singular analysis of modern monarchy, whose fundamental maxim is "no monarch, no nobility; no nobility, no monarch"—pointed toward precisely the historical analysis of "feudal government" that Montesquieu attempted at the end. That is certainly how he saw it himself: "For my work to be complete," he explained in the midst of feverish composition in 1748, on the eve of the publication, "I need to finish the two books on feudal laws. I think I have made some discoveries in this, the most obscure matter we have, which is, all the same, a magnificent subject."[24]

What had Montesquieu discovered on this subject both obscure and magnificent? Books 30 and 31 form a set, the first addressing "The Theory of the Feudal Laws among the Franks in Their Relation to the Establishment of the Monarchy," and the second, "The Theory of the Feudal Laws among the Franks in Their Relation to the Revolutions of the Monarchy." Book 30 opens with a memorable statement of purpose: "I would believe that there was an imperfection in my work if I did not mention an event which happened once in the world and which will perhaps never happen again. . . . The spectacle of the feudal laws is a fine one. An old oak tree stands; from afar the eye sees its leaves; coming closer it sees the trunk; but it does not perceive the roots; to find them the ground must be dug up."[25] The ultimate origins of feudal law had, of course, been the object of fierce historical debate for centuries, with contestants having long since divided into "Romanist" and "Germanist" camps. Montesquieu's starting point in book 30 is to set forth an emphatically Germanist account of the roots of feudal law, with two overarching themes. First, Tacitus's *Germania* establishes

24. Montesquieu, *Oeuvres complètes,* ed. André Masson (Paris, 1950–55), vol. 3, pp. 1116–17. The citation is from a letter to his correspondent Ceruti, 28 March 1747; the translation is borrowed from Harold A. Ellis, "Montesquieu's Modern Politics: *The Spirit of the Laws* and the Problem of Modern Monarchy in Old Regime France," *History of Political Thought* 10, no. 4 (1989): 669. Ellis's insightful essay, it should be noted, is the only important recent attempt in English to reconstruct the ideological context in which Montesquieu wrote.

25. Montesquieu, *Spirit of the Laws,* 619.

beyond any doubt that the essence of feudal law is to be traced back to the unique phenomenon of *vassalage,* the paradoxical bonds of hierarchical submission and reciprocal loyalty that attached German warriors to their war leaders, "honorable" because freely chosen. Secondly, although vassalage only very gradually became connected with grants of lands—fiefs—from the very start vassals acquired certain kinds of political authority in exchange for their submission: "rights of jurisdiction." The wider meaning of this interpretation of the "Gothic" essence of feudal law is not hard to see: at its origins, in the forests of Germany, the Frankish aristocracy wore both Sword and Robe.

But this is in any case preliminary to Montesquieu's larger purpose in books 30 and 31, which is to trace the role of feudal law, thus understood, in the founding of the French monarchy, from its initial "establishment" to the series of "revolutions," stretching across four centuries, that completed the process. This task of course took Montesquieu straight into the thick of contemporary debate over the "ancient constitution." It is thus not surprising that not only are these two books (together with their pendant on "civil law," book 28) the longest in *De l'esprit des lois,* they are also by far the most polemical. Indeed, Montesquieu's account of the founding and early development of the monarchy is basically a critical one, which proceeds by means of attack on two preceding and opposed interpretations. One of these opponents is hardly surprising. By far the most important statement of the *thèse royale* in the first half of the eighteenth century was the abbé Dubos's *Histoire critique de l'établissement de la monarchie française dans les Gaules,* published in 1734, at the moment when Montesquieu launched work on *De l'esprit des lois.* For Dubos, the French monarchy was always-already absolutist, its Merovingian founders having inherited full sovereign authority, unencumbered by aristocratic advice or consent, from its Roman predecessor. In fact, there *was* no French nobility at the outset, the Second Estate emerging only gradually over time, entirely the creature of the monarchy itself. Famously declaring this thesis to be a "conspiracy against the nobility," Montesquieu of course subjects Dubos's *Histoire critique* to an extremely harsh demolition, which takes up nearly the last third of book 30. On the one hand, he argues, there is not the slightest evidence for any kind of Merovingian inheritance of Roman authority, political, fiscal, or military; on the other, a hereditary Frankish nobility, founded on "Gothic" vassalage and already exercising "rights of jurisdiction," was separated out from the rest of the population from the earliest history onwards. So much for the abbé Dubos. Rather more surprising, perhaps, are Montesquieu's criticisms of another historian—the comte de Boulainvilliers, whose account of the "ancient constitution" in a variety of historical works (above all, the posthumously published *Histoire de l'ancien gouvernement de la France* of 1727) had formed the main object of Dubos's own polemic. For Boulainvilliers, the founding moment of the French state lay in the *conquest* of Gaul by the Frankish nobility, which resulted in both the enserfment of the local Gallic population and the creation of what Boulainvilliers expressly termed "feudal government," in effect, an aristocratic republic with an elected king. The original and sole legitimate form of state in France, "feudal government," was subsequently overthrown, and the Frankish nobility stripped of both its political liberties and its economic rights by a series of usurper dynasties, culminating in the degraded "despotism" of the Bourbon monarchy. Here, then, was the *thèse nobiliaire* in its purest and most striking form. As we have seen, one of the central pillars of the social interpretation of *De l'esprit des lois* is the claim that its closing books amount to a restatement of Boulainvilliers—kinder and gentler, to be sure, but a version of the *thèse nobiliaire* nevertheless. It is thus very important to be clear about Montesquieu's criticisms of Boulainvilliers, which are indeed less harsh and pointed than those to which Dubos is treated—but emphatic all the same.

For Boulainvilliers's notion of a punctual Frankish "conquest," resulting in both the enserfment of the Gallic peasantry and the creation of "feudal government," is dismissed by Montesquieu as no less fictional than Dubos's notion of political continuity with Rome—a "conspiracy against the third estate," in fact. Both serfdom and "feudal government" were the result not of the original Frankish occupation of Gaul, but of the secular process of social development that is described in exhaustive detail in book 31: the gradual attachment of vassalage to grants of lands, or "fiefs," and then the evolution of fiefs from conditional to hereditary property. It was only in the tenth century that this process reached its climax, in the midst of the anarchy that followed the collapse of Carolingian political authority, at which point both serfdom and "feudal government" arrived more or less in tandem. One effect of this alternate account of the early history of the monarchy is, of course, to sever any connection between serfdom and a right of "conquest," which had been one of Boulainvilliers's chief ideological claims—not surprising, given what we have seen of Montesquieu's view of the *end* of serfdom. More important still, however, is what happens to the idea of "feudal government" in Montesquieu's hands. Boulainvilliers seems in fact to have been the inventor of the term, which was then ignored entirely by Dubos. Montesquieu embraced it, thereby marking a watershed in the development of the idea of "feudalism" as a category in European historiography. But he also altered its meaning dramatically. For on Montesquieu's account in book 31, "feudal government," too, was the effect of the evolution of fiefs from conditional to private property between the sixth and tenth centuries, a process that gradually eroded the political authority of the Merovingian and Carolingian dynasties, until the monarchy, in effect, surrendered—their Capetian successor assuming power as merely the highest feudal lord. At the very end of book 31 Montesquieu sums up the process thus: "The inheritance of fiefs and the general establishment of under-fiefs extinguished political government and formed feudal government," at which point, declaring, "*Italiam, Italiam* . . . I close the treatise on fiefs where most authors have begun it," Montesquieu ends *De l'esprit des lois*. It remains to suggest what these criticisms of the *thèse nobiliaire* à la Boulainvilliers mean for the larger question of Montesquieu's *parti pris*. But one thing is clear. "Feudal government" for Montesquieu was not the nobiliairy republic that Boulainvilliers had glimpsed in the sixth century and called "the masterpiece of the human mind;" it was instead at the moment of its birth in the tenth century, feudal *monarchy*.

De l'Esprit des Lois in Ideological Context

In any case, with our brief tour of the text complete, we can now try to draw some conclusions about the handling of the topic of nobility in *De l'esprit des lois*. As we have seen, neither the noble order nor any of the traditional three "estates" are ever the object of definition or scrutiny as such. Nobility is plainly not to be confused with "aristocracy," which Montesquieu theorizes as a variant of *republican* government, equivalent to the classical conception of rule by the Few. But nobility turns out to be absolutely central to rule by the One, at least in its modern European form. For Montesquieu's analysis of monarchy in the opening section of *De l'esprit des lois* declares nobility to be of its very "essence," to the point of existential equation—"no monarch, no nobility; no nobility, no monarch." This equation, in fact, appears to govern the larger typology of governments as well: nobility without a king, we may surmise, is precisely what "aristocracy" is; and Montesquieu is very explicit as to what a king without a nobility amounts to—"rather, one has a despot." At any rate, the rest of *De l'esprit des lois* supplies what is in effect a historical explanation for the intimate bond between monarchical state and noble order in modern Europe. The nexus between the two can be traced back, we learn, to an "event which happened once in the world"—the emergence of "feudal government" among the Gothic invaders who over-threw the Roman Empire, which provided the basic model for contempo-rary monarchy in Europe, "the government founded on a body of nobility." Originally a mixture of aristocracy and monarchy, the abolition of serfdom at the end of the Middle Ages then rendered "Gothic government" "the best kind of government men have been able to devise," so long as it lasted. The past tense at the end of chapter 8 of book 11 seems to point to the general suspension of "representative" assemblies by later absolutist monarchies, as in the abandonment of the Estates-General in Bourbon France. For Montesquieu, however, a royal monopoly of executive and legislative power did not prevent monarchy from being a reliably "moderate" form of govern-ment, so long as "executive power over things depending on civil right" was left to the monarchy's "subjects"—there being no ambiguity at all about the identity of the latter.

A rapid survey over a terrain as vast and variegated as *De l'esprit des lois* is, of course, liable to the distortions of simplification and foreshortening. Still, assuming that the above summary captures something accurate about Montesquieu's treatment of nobility in the text, we can now ask: what bearing does it have on the social interpretation of *De l'esprit des lois,* such as it was presented in the work of Ford, Althusser, or Palmer? First and perhaps foremost, their insistence that the proper ideological context for approaching Montesquieu's masterpiece is the great debate over the "ancient constitu-tion" of the Bourbon monarchy in the early eighteenth century is surely correct. To claim as much is, obviously, not to reduce *De l'esprit des lois* to mere political propaganda—as if it were not also by far the greatest work of social thought of the Enlightenment, the founding text of half a dozen modern social science disciplines. But due acknowledgment of those achieve-ments in no way precludes inquiry into its obvious normative and prescriptive dimensions; indeed, the latter may well have been the condition of the former. Bernard Manin has tried to capture these dimensions by insisting, against the persistent idea of Montesquieu as a detached "relativist," that for the author of *De l'esprit des lois,* "reason shows that there is one political evil (despotism) but several political goods (moderate monarchy, republican govern-ment—especially of the commercial variety—and the English regime)."[26]

---

26. Bernard Manin, "Montesquieu," in *A Critical Dictionary of the French Revolution,* ed. François Furet and Mona Ozouf, trans. Arthur Goldhammer (Cambridge, Mass., 1989), 730. See also Manin's brilliant rejoinder to Pangle's interpretation of Montesquieu: "Montesquieu et la politique moderne," *Cahiers de philosophie politique* 2–3 (1984–85).

This is indeed a happy formula for approaching the essential *pluralism* of Montesquieu's outlook; Manin is not the only commentator to suggest an affinity between Montesquieu and Aristotle in this regard.[27] But there is one respect in which it still might concede too much to "relativism." For monarchy is obviously not just one form of government among several possible choices: for precisely the geographical and historical reasons spelled out at length in *De l'esprit des lois,* it is the *only* possible form of government for the vast majority of Montesquieu's readers, his compatriots above all. There is no reason to doubt the sincerity of the famous lines from the Preface: "It is not a matter of indifference that the people be enlightened. . . . If I could make it so that everyone had new reasons for loving his duties, his prince, his homeland and his laws and that each could better feel his happiness in his own country, government, and position, I would consider myself the happiest of mortals."[28] This goal is precisely what made the historical inquiries of books 30 and 31—putting Montesquieu's intention to intervene in the debates over the "ancient constitution" beyond question—the logical conclusion to *De l'esprit des lois* as a whole.

Is there any doubt about which side Montesquieu took in the dispute between the partisans of the *thèse nobiliaire* and the *thèse royale?* At first glance, the case for seeing Montesquieu as the greatest spokesman for the "noble reaction" against Bourbon absolutism—asserted in their different ways by Mathiez, Ford, Althusser, and Palmer—would seem to be ironclad. Nothing in the scholarship of the last few decades has challenged the accuracy, in particular, of Ford's description of the ideological landscape in the first half of the eighteenth century. The final years of the reign of Louis XIV had indeed provoked an extremely lively aristocratic reaction, whose intellectual ornaments, in addition to Boulainvilliers, included figures as various as Jurieu, Saint-Simon, and Fénelon. But this aristocratic offensive was then answered, during the epoch of stable rule under Fleury in the 1730s and 1740s, by a remarkable royalist counterattack, now quickened by the rationalism of the early Enlightenment—not just in Dubos, but in Voltaire, Mably, d'Argenson. These were also the years in which *De l'esprit des lois* was written, and on Ford's account, seconded by Althusser and Palmer, Montesquieu now responded to this resurgent royalism by gathering together all the earlier elements of aristocratic resistance to Bourbon absolutism in a single synthetic statement of irresistible power. At the head of *De l'esprit des lois* Montesquieu

27. See, for example, Isaiah Berlin's essay, "Montesquieu" in *Against the Current* (Oxford, 1979).
28. Montesquieu, *Spirit of the Laws,* xliv.

presented a theory of monarchy that drew on the long traditions of "constitutional" resistance to absolutism associated with the judicial Robe: monarchy was defined by its respect for "fixed and established laws," whose guardians were the "intermediate, subordinate and dependent powers" that constituted its very "nature," and for which aristocratic "honor," finally, provided the animating "principle." At its other end, Montesquieu concluded *De l'esprit des lois* with a powerful restatement of the *thèse nobiliaire* associated with the martial Sword, rendered all the more forceful for being blunted by Montesquieu's circumspection about the "conquest." In fact, this entire construction was accompanied by a formidable negative assault on "despotism"—the menacing alternative to "moderate monarchy"—calculated to appeal well beyond any narrow class interests. In *De l'esprit des lois,* the *ressentiment* of noble Sword and Robe alike joined forces with the more diffuse libertarianism of the early Enlightenment to make an unanswerable indictment of the regime of Versailles.

If the general accuracy of this description of *De l'esprit des lois* seems incontrovertible, there nevertheless remains a dangling thread to account for: the upshot of Montesquieu's criticisms of Boulainvilliers in books 30 and 31. Ford noticed these but minimized their importance, treating them largely as a matter of residual chafing between Sword and Robe, if not a rhetorical ploy altogether. In fact, as the symmetry of his criticisms of Dubos and Boulainvilliers suggests—the one charged with "conspiracy against the nobility," the other with "conspiracy against the Third Estate"—we need to take seriously the possibility that Montesquieu really did intend to stake out a position different from that of either of his predecessors. As we have seen, Boulainvilliers assigned an absolute priority in French history to the Frankish nobility, to the point of severing any historical connection with monarchy: "feudal government" was not a form of monarchy at all, but rather an aristocratic republic erected over a subject laboring class by right of "conquest"; true monarchy arrived on French soil only with the Capetians, who duly set about the process, completed by their Bourbon successors, of stripping the French nobility of the dual fruits of the "conquest"—political liberty and the serfdom of the Gallic peasantry. Dubos's response to this provocation was to depict an "ancient constitution" that was its mirror opposite: a monarchy already absolute, ruling over a free population. For Dubos, it was nobility that came later, usurping the political authority rightfully exercised only by kings and reducing their formerly free subjects to serfdom. Faced with these diametrically opposed understandings of the national past, Montesquieu's first move, at the end of book 30, was to launch a destructive attack on Dubos—a Frankish nobility was on the historical stage well before a French monarchy, which, when it did arrive, owed nothing at all to Roman authority. But to demolish Dubos was not to vindicate Boulainvilliers. For Montesquieu, the first "feudal" government was not the aristocratic republic of the Frankish nobility, but the feudal *monarchy* of the Capetians, whose vocation was not to overthrow the rights and liberties of the nobility but to seal and *guarantee* them. Where Boulainvilliers had sought to drive a historical wedge between nobility and monarchy, the entire thrust of Montesquieu's account was in the opposite direction—using the common ground of feudal property to stress their *intimacy* rather than their conflict. In fact, we can already guess what the "fundamental maxim" of "feudal government" must have been—surely: "no monarch, no nobility; no nobility, no monarch." For what is most striking of all about Montesquieu's vision of the early history of the French monarchy in books 30 and 31 is its consonance with the general theory of modern monarchy presented at the start of *De l'esprit des lois,* affirming an organic connection *between* monarchy and nobility, state and class, through every historical vicissitude.

What does this theme suggest about Montesquieu's *parti pris* in the central ideological dispute of his time? There remains no question about his *basic* political orientation, of course: the assault on a leveling "despotism" in the opening parts of *De l'esprit des lois,* the violence of the attack on Dubos at the end (whose vituperation Boulainvilliers escapes), together with the cult of aristocratic "honor" that suffuses the text throughout—all point in one direction only. But we are certainly looking at two distinct variants of aristocratic ideology in Boulainvilliers and Montesquieu, two different versions of the *thèse nobiliaire,* with distinct strategic consequences for contemporary politics. Socially, there was less distance between the two than Boulainvilliers's apparent apology for serfdom might imply—that "apology" largely intended to provoke rather than persuade, of course. As Althusser argued, the French peasantry is indeed almost invisible in *De l'esprit des lois,* except for Montesquieu's consistent stamp of approval for the basic structure of absolutist taxation, in which the full weight of the main source of royal revenue, the *taille*—a "centralized feudal rent," as the Russian historian Porshnev aptly termed it—fell on the peasantry alone.[29] The divergence

---

29. For an acute recent discussion of Montesquieu's views on taxation, focusing on a neglected early text from the Regency, see David W. Carrithers, "Montesquieu and the Spirit of French Finance: an Analysis of his *Mémoire sur les dettes de l'état* (1715)," in *Montesquieu and the Spirit of Modernity,* ed. Carrithers and Coleman, 159–90.

between Boulainvilliers and Montesquieu was primarily *political*. The chief focus of the former's historical writing was always the succession of "representative" political assemblies that he held to have been the legitimate possessors of sovereign power in France, from the meetings of the Frankish nobility on the Champ-de-Mars to the Estates-General. It was the extinction of this line that constituted the tragedy of French history for Boulainvilliers. The dream at the core of his work was the recovery of noble political liberty by means of the restoration of an aristocratic legislative assembly. That dream was alien to Montesquieu. He certainly noticed the existence of "representative" assemblies in the distant past (and present, in England) but consistently showed little interest in them on French soil. His own account of the "ancient constitution" focuses not on a Frankish nobility assembled on the Champ-de-Mars, but on a French nobility fully integrated into the pyramidal structure of a feudal *monarchy*. At the other end of French history, nothing illustrates the nature of Montesquieu's ideological position so powerfully as his nearly complete repression of the memory of the Estates-General. There is perhaps the merest hint of nostalgia for it in chapter 8 of book 11, but otherwise its very name is erased from French history. By contrast with Boulainvilliers, Montesquieu seems to have spoken for a French nobility that had made its peace with the surrender of political autonomy to absolutism, content with the security of property—in ancestral land and venal office alike—that it had received in return, the exchange guaranteed, in fact, by its continuing grip on "judicial power."

It was this bifurcation within the aristocratic reaction of the first half of the eighteenth century that the social interpretation of *De l'esprit des lois* in the work of Ford, Althusser, or Palmer, for all of its general accuracy, probably underestimated. The divergence here was not so much a matter of Robe versus Sword as the difference between an apologetic that was genuinely *reactionary* and one that was merely *conservative,* in the ordinary sense of these terms. It was Boulainvilliers who dreamed of setting aside the compact between absolute monarchy and nobility, by returning to a status quo ante. It was Montesquieu who argued for the maintenance of that status quo— against both of its critics. For if the message of *De l'esprit des lois* for Dubos and other proponents of a modernizing, "Enlightened" absolutism was "no nobility, no monarch," Montesquieu's warning to Boulainvilliers and other nobles nostalgic for the recovery of a lost political liberty was surely "no monarch, no nobility." Was the advice heeded by either camp? The fate of Montesquieu's arguments about the nobiliary "essence" of modern monarchy in the decades after the publication of *De l'esprit des lois*—the badly needed updating of the second half of Carcassonne's study—are naturally beyond the scope of this essay, which has been confined to trying to assess his place in debates in his own time. There is space for only one brief remark. All the evidence suggests that *De l'esprit des lois* was far and away the most influential work of political thought of the Enlightenment. Montesquieu's intellectual authority went virtually unchallenged down to the Revolution, when it was finally surpassed by the revolutionary cult of Rousseau. In particular, there is no doubt about the contribution of *De l'esprit des lois* to both the "discourse of justice" of parlementary oppositionism and the "discourse of will" of emergent republicanism, such as they figure in Keith Baker's influential tripartite analysis of the ideological field in the last half of the eighteenth century. But intellectual authority is one thing, and political impact another. Montesquieu's practical advice seems to have been ignored, even where his influence might be expected to have been greatest. For within the fractious judicial politics that exploded in the 1750s, with such fateful consequences for the Bourbon monarchy, the inspiration of the conservative was almost immediately overtaken by that of the reactionary. By the end of the decade, the *parlements* and their apologists had declared themselves not merely the "depositories of the laws," the function ascribed to them in *De l'esprit des lois,* but also, according to the novel doctrine of the *union des classes,* the unitary and legitimate heirs of the original Frankish legislative assemblies cherished by Boulainvilliers.[30] A dozen years later, in the wake of the monarchy's counterattack, the reactionary chrysalis produced its radical butterfly, a "patriotic" movement for the restoration of the Estates-General. Few "patriots," of course, foresaw the consequences—that soon afterwards, a restored Estates-General, in command of what can very accurately be described as a "republic disguised as a monarchy," would proceed very swiftly to the formal abolition of nobility itself. But readers of *De l'esprit des lois* could not deny that they had been well warned: "no monarch, no nobility; no nobility, no monarch."

---

30. It is no accident that in their powerful essay on "historical legitimation," which in some measure traces the origins of the revolutionary mentality back to Boulainvilliers, François Furet and Mona Ozouf should have omitted any mention at all of Montesquieu: see "Deux légitimations historiques de la société française au XVIIIe siècle," *Annales: E.S.C.* 34 (1979): 438–50.

9

THE MAKING OF AN ARISTOCRATIC REACTIONARY:
THE COMTE D'ESCHERNY, NOBLE HONOR,
AND THE ABOLITION OF NOBILITY

Jay M. Smith

In the 1760s, the Swiss nobleman François-Louis d'Escherny moved to Paris and embarked on an intellectual and social itinerary that made him the prototype of the forward-thinking aristocrat, utterly seduced by the Enlightenment. He regularly attended the salon of Madame Geoffrin, he befriended Diderot, d'Alembert, and Helvétius, and by 1765 he had also become a close personal companion to Jean-Jacques Rousseau during the latter's temporary exile in Switzerland.[1] In a treatise on morals in 1783 he defended "modern philosophy" against the many "ingrates" who attacked it.[2] As the Old Regime passed into history, he condemned the "rapacity" and "depredations" of the court aristocracy in France, and he declared that the "career of honors" should be "opened to all individuals of the nation."[3] Marked by cosmopolitanism, open-mindedness, and faith in the progress of enlightenment, the activities and attitudes of the comte d'Escherny in the years before the Revolution seem to offer resounding proof of Guy Chaussinand-Nogaret's influential thesis about the modernity of the urban and well-to-do nobility of the later Old Regime and its gradual fusion with like-minded individuals from the upper reaches of the Third Estate.[4]

---

1. J.-F. Michaud, *Biographie universelle ancienne et moderne*, 45 vols. (Paris, 1854–65), 13:14–17.

2. [François Louis d'Escherny], *Les lacunes de la philosophie* (Amsterdam, 1783), 223–24.

3. Escherny, *Essai sur la noblesse* (Paris, 1814), 175, 265.

4. Guy Chaussinand-Nogaret, *La noblesse au dix-huitième siècle: de la féodalité aux lumières* (Paris, 1976).

Escherny's rhetoric in later years is not so easily reconciled with the happy image of liberal consensus. Several months after the National Assembly's abolition of titles of nobility in June 1790, the comte wrote an essay in which he denounced the "holocaust" carried out in the name of equality and lamented the measures of social reorganization that the Assembly had implemented in pursuit of its "principles." "I confess," he declared emphatically, "that I have the misfortune of not believing in these principles."[5] Escherny feared that all of France was now overrun with "philosophical maniacs."[6] Published first in 1791 as part of a set of reports on revolutionary events sent to various friends in England and Switzerland, Escherny's letter on "the *journée* of 19 June 1790," written in October of that year, was later published, essentially unchanged, as a stand-alone *Essai sur la noblesse* in 1814.[7] Sometime between 1783 and 1790, then, Escherny appears to have experienced a conservative awakening similar to the one that, in little more than a year's time, transformed the former Rousseauist comte d'Antraigues into an ardent counterrevolutionary.[8] Escherny evidently felt so strongly about the disastrous effects of the Revolution that he went to the trouble of restating his opposition to the National Assembly's controversial decree against nobility more than two decades after the actual event. What had happened? How can the discrepancy between the Old Regime liberal and the revolutionary reactionary be explained?

At first glance, the case of Escherny seems to fit neatly into two explanatory frameworks made available by revisionist scholarship in the 1970s and 1980s. First, Escherny's apparent conservative turn would seem to confirm the well-known argument that the nobility's self-consciousness of itself as a class, and as a conservative political force, was more a consequence than a cause of the revolutionary conflicts of 1789 and later. Only after experiencing the shock of popular violence and political demagoguery in 1789, and only after it had been identified as an enemy by those seeking ideological clarification, did the nobility, or at least some of the nobility, recognize a need for political solidarity. Until then, goes the argument, a loose liberal consensus had obscured or submerged the political differences between the various noble

---

5. Escherny, *Essai*, 171–72.

6. Ibid., 218.

7. *Correspondance d'un habitant de Paris avec ses amis de Suisse et d'Angleterre, sur les événements de 1789, 1790 et jusqu'au 4 avril 1791* (Paris, 1791). The only change made to the later edition involved the omission of potentially embarrassing paragraphs in which Escherny praised Robespierre, Barnave, and other Jacobins for asserting much needed leadership in 1790. His appeal to the Jacobins to "bring back the nobility" (447) would have looked terribly naïve in retrospect.

8. See Roger Barny, *Le Comte d'Antraigues: un disciple aristocrate de J.-J. Rousseau* (Oxford, 1991).

and non-noble segments of the nation's broad elite.[9] Second, Escherny's forthright defense of traditional institutions in 1791 can also be read as proof of the decisive impact of political events on the consciousness of individuals and groups. As Timothy Tackett has argued, in a manner consistent with the revisionist emphasis on the essentially "political" and contingent character of the Revolution, only the crucible of political debate in the spring and summer of 1789 produced mutually antagonistic groups of liberal and conservative deputies. Differences in outlook, experience, and relative wealth had certainly existed before 1789, but only the radicalization of ideas and rhetoric, forced by the pressure of unexpected events, led to the splintering of the Assembly into right- and left-wing factions in the summer of 1789.[10]

Although no one can dispute the notion that revolutionary events propelled French politics in new directions, the case of Escherny actually points, surprisingly enough, to the continuities of thought that bridged the rupture of 1789 and enabled participants and observers to assert meanings for the dramatic events that they witnessed. I argue in this essay that the conservative rhetoric in Escherny's text of 1791/1814 represented not a repudiation but an elaboration of his prerevolutionary ideas and attitudes, that the "event" of the abolition of nobility was probably less surprising than historians generally suppose, and that the antagonisms between the nobility's defenders and its critics in 1790 and after showed the intensification of an ideological division that had informed prerevolutionary political argument since the middle of the century. That ideological division had appeared, moreover, not because the cultural significance of the nobility had steadily declined in a modernizing eighteenth century, as some have argued.[11] Rather, feelings about nobility ran high in 1789 precisely because the reading and writing public in France had labored long and unsuccessfully to redefine the vital relationship between nation and nobility, even though (or indeed because)

9. The thesis that "the nobility"—as an ideal, as a social group, and as a political enemy—was largely an invention or product of the Revolution itself was developed most famously by François Furet, *Interpreting the French Revolution,* trans. Elborg Forster (Cambridge, 1981), 54, 100–111, but see also Patrice Higonnet, *Class, Ideology, and the Rights of Nobles in the French Revolution* (Oxford, 1981), and Chaussinand-Nogaret, *La noblesse au dix-huitième siècle.*

10. Timothy Tackett, *Becoming a Revolutionary: The Deputies to the French National Assembly and the Emergence of a Revolutionary Culture, 1789–90* (Princeton, 1996).

11. The supposedly declining significance of the legal distinction between noble and non-noble in the eighteenth century was central to Colin Lucas's influential argument in "Nobles, Bourgeois, and the Origins of the French Revolution," *Past and Present* 60 (1973): 84–126; echoes of Lucas's assertion are heard throughout revisionist and postrevisionist writing.

provocative and conflicting accounts of that relationship had been proffered by Montesquieu, Mirabeau, and other literary lights in the middle decades of the century.[12] Escherny's apparent conservative turn in or around 1790 was not proof of hypocrisy or earlier insincerity, but an expression of the reactionary possibilities built into the aristocratic embrace of various "enlightened" projects under the Old Regime. If Escherny's reflections in the fall of 1790 can be considered "reactionary" in spirit—and in some ways they certainly were—they actually belonged to a "reaction" whose roots went deep into the Old Regime.

Analysis of Escherny's *Essai sur la noblesse* suggests, however, that anyone inclined to remove the concept of a prerevolutionary "aristocratic reaction" from the revisionists' mothballs will have to proceed with maximum caution because the tattered blanket placed in storage in the 1970s scarcely functioned as a single blanket at all. The "aristocratic reaction" unceremoniously thrown aside amid the anti-Marxist housecleaning of a generation ago was in fact a patchwork quilt made up of clashing colors and misshapen squares connected by frayed threads. The quilt threatens to break into fragments at the slightest touch. Even after many years of exceedingly rough handling, however, the abandoned quilt still reveals an unmistakable pattern when set off at a distance. Densely textured, the pattern acquires its form through contemporaries' insistent articulation of the idea that nobility played a critical role in French society, and that the distinction between noble and commoner had therefore to be preserved, and even strengthened. Escherny, because of the starkly contrasting hues present in his own small corner of the quilt, helps to display the rich and vibrant context in which conservative and progressive ideas commingled in the 1770s and 1780s. By throwing into relief the nature of the conservative ideals retained even by avowedly "liberal" nobles like Escherny in 1789, I will suggest in this essay why the concept of aristocratic reaction captures a phenomenon the analysis of which remains indispensable for understanding the nature of the French Revolution.

In the summer or fall of 1789, when Escherny penned a long letter on "the causes of the Revolution," he proudly defined himself as "an idolater of liberty, a partisan of the revolution, an implacable enemy of tyranny, injustice,

---

12. For more thorough discussion of debates surrounding the idea of nobility in the eighteenth century, see my *Nobility Reimagined: The Patriotic Nation in Eighteenth-Century France* (Ithaca, N.Y., 2005).

and abuses, a zealous defender of the natural rights of man."[13] He regarded the Revolution as "the first success, the first triumph of reason . . . over passions, stupidity, and prejudice."[14] By 1790, Escherny struggled to represent himself as a sympathetic dissenter victimized by circumstances that had spiraled out of control. "The meaning of the words *aristocrat* and *democrat* has changed so much in the course of the revolution that no one knows what they signify, or what idea should be attached to them." The "democrats" of eighteen months ago, who had "rejoiced at the conquest of liberty and the fall of the old government" were now "astonished" to see themselves "metamorphosed into aristocrats in the eyes of the people."[15] "No one," Escherny insisted, "cherishes the benefits of the revolution more than I, and no one has more admiration for most of the assembly's laws," which had been directed at the whole "mass of abuses" engendered by the former government. The new laws represented the "progress of knowledge, and it is glorious for the assembly to have produced them at the height of a century of philosophy and enlightenment." "It is because I admire the new edifice," protested Escherny, "that I examine its foundations and desire to find others more solid."[16] In the rush to elaborate a new constitution, Escherny charged, the majority in the assembly had somehow become oblivious to the fact that the very form of government, whose spirit should be expressed by the constitution, still remained a matter of dispute. Sadly, the National Assembly had become a "battlefield, where each day one hears the triumphant cries of the victors, and the groans of the vanquished, the wounded, and the dying. Each law is preceded by a defeat, each decree is a prize of combat, and a new order of things is being constructed on top of ruins and cadavers."[17]

In the fall of 1790, the "cadaver" that Escherny had most in mind was noble status itself, and the nature of his mourning reveals much about the complex blend of values and ideas with which many nobles confronted the Revolution. In his agitated "reaction" against the abolition of noble status, Escherny looked not backwards in time toward some prerevolutionary golden age but forward to a period in which nobility would be free of abuses, legally reformed, and finally able to play its assigned role as moral exemplar of the nation. Even as he defended the principle of nobility, Escherny decried the reality of nobility under the Old Regime in bitter

13. Escherny, *Correspondance*, 134.
14. Ibid., 286.
15. Escherny, *Essai*, 258–59.
16. Ibid., 257, 260.
17. Ibid., 257.

terms. In fact, his "reactionary" ideas grew in part from a preexisting, and unmistakably radical, agenda for change.

That agenda had been informed by a particular reading of the French nobility's modern history. In the course of the reigns of Louis XIV and Louis XV, Escherny observed, the nobility had sacrificed its ancient power and independence to the pleasures of the antechamber and the thrill of intrigue. In place of armor and its old feudal strength, the nobility had found new strength in a political strategy suggested by the monarchy itself, with whom it worked in partnership. By the methods of this "completely new policy," the nobility had "imperceptibly spread its roots across the entire surface of the realm." The nobility's roots had become "interlaced" with men it had formerly disdained. "We see, on the one hand, [the nobility] allying itself with financiers and dividing its services between the army and the courts; we see, on the other hand, that it opens its bosom, in exchange for money, to a crowd of new men. Offices, positions of every kind, [and] frequent ennoblements form, in the heart of the nation, a whole new people of privileged nobles, who extend the order and add to its power."[18]

This unprecedented expansion of the nobility created new hierarchies within the corps, and honor soon came to be reserved "for the superior classes." In the new "noble system," four great corporations—"*the high clergy, the high magistracy, the high nobility* [of the army], *and high finance*"—dominated society and the state. Working together as a "formidable aristocracy," these four "principal branches" of the nobility soon deprived the monarch himself of his authority, and they ruled, tyrannically, in his name. "It is quite inappropriate to talk of the feudal colossus" supposedly vanquished by the National Assembly, asserted Escherny, because that colossus "had not existed since the time of Richelieu." Feudalism, in its day, had indeed shaken the throne and intimidated the people, "but this new system, far more dangerous, tended visibly to take over sovereignty itself. This was a new power far superior to, and of a completely different nature from, that which the nobility had supposedly usurped [in the feudal age]."[19] All the realm seemed to be exploited "for the profit of fifty illustrious families, who regarded themselves as a species apart, as a privileged class superior even to the provincial nobility, who were just as good and often better."[20]

Escherny's disgust and anger carried him toward a sweeping condemnation of "aristocracy" surprisingly reminiscent of the abbé Sieyès's *What Is*

18. Ibid., 184–85.
19. Ibid., 185–87.
20. Ibid., 175.

the Third Estate? Echoing Sieyès's claim that the ancient government of France had been commanded not by a monarch but by a court cabal, Escherny complained that the "noble system" that had come into being by the second half of the eighteenth century represented not a "feudal colossus" but a detestable "political machine" composed of "four monstrous wheels" that crushed everything in sight.[21] Indeed, Escherny reported that he spoke personally with Sieyès on the floor of the assembly in June, 1789, and that he had "complimented him on several of his works."[22] He also supported the so-called patriot position in the heated debate over voting procedures in the Estates-General, and he faulted the conservative noble deputies for their "obstinacy" and "arrogance" in refusing to proceed to a common verification of credentials in the opening weeks of the Assembly.[23] Like other liberals of all persuasions, Escherny reacted to the climactic days of late June—when the Estates-General reconstituted itself as a National Assembly and resistant nobles and clergy were forced to join the Third Estate in common deliberations—with great optimism about the prospects for national regeneration. He was certain that the time had come to repair the damage inflicted by a detestable aristocracy. "Who could doubt," asked Escherny, "that such a system was in need of reform, and what better time to implement such a reform than in a revolution!"[24]

Only in the wake of the heady days of June did Escherny and his erstwhile allies have to confront the reality that recognition of the "need of reform" implied no consensus on the precise shape of the reform to be implemented. In Escherny's eyes, the course of action called for in the wake of the Third Estate's procedural victory could not have been clearer. "All that was needed was to suspend the disastrous operation of the four wheels I have described, and to reconstitute the instrument of nobility—by composing it of similar elements from throughout the realm, by putting it in harmony with the fundamental and parallel instruments of the king and the represented people, and by insuring that all three act reciprocally, simultaneously, and indivisibly."[25] To perfect the ancient principle of nobility, Escherny wished to base noble status on sound moral rather than merely legal foundations, thus minimizing its formerly exclusionary and offensive connotations. "In the eyes of philosophy," after all, "the very best title of nobility is nothing

21. Ibid., 187.
22. Escherny, *Correspondance,* 14–15.
23. Ibid., 125.
24. Escherny, *Essai,* 188.
25. Ibid., 188.

other than a *birth certificate."* Proofs of nobility rested on mere "charters and written titles," and "we know all about the vice of tradition, the errors of history, . . . and the inaccuracies of documents." In any case, "the archives of nature" proved convincingly that "the [genealogical] origin of the first water carrier on the street is as grand and imposing as that of the greatest king in the universe."[26] Bloodlines would count for little, then, in Escherny's reconstituted "noble system." An excellent constitution, he wrote, "is that in which the plebeian acquires nobility through the exercise of grand offices, and the patrician can practice all the arts and all professions without fear of losing his nobility. The one does not derogate by practicing the lesser professions, and the other is ennobled by practicing the greater ones. Such is the kind of equality that can be reconciled with the monarchical form."[27]

Like the most committed reformers from the Third Estate, Escherny had entered the decisive summer of 1789 committed to the ideals of liberty, reason, and the rights of man, even including the right of equality—so long as that equality remained consistent with "the monarchical form." The first year of the Revolution would show, however, that it was precisely over the definition of equality that deep divisions persisted in the collective consciousness of the French citizenry; disagreement on this issue even divided those who had unflinchingly championed reform throughout the prerevolutionary years of 1787–89. In the initial debates over the constitution in the summer and early fall of 1789, the National Assembly's distinction between "passive" and "active" citizens, its failure to extend voting rights to women, its ambivalent stance on the issue of slavery, and its brief flirtation with the idea of an English-style legislature with a separate chamber reserved for the wealthy or well-born had already exposed the conflicting ambitions on which the revolutionary claim to equality rested.[28]

In the Assembly's renegotiation of the relationship between the nation and the nobility, different understandings of equality would likewise be brought to bear in the various projects entertained by the deputies and

---

26. Ibid., 225–26.

27. Ibid., 264–65.

28. On these issues, see, for example, Keith Michael Baker, *Inventing the French Revolution* (Cambridge, 1990), 252–305; William H. Sewell Jr., "Le citoyen/la citoyenne: Activity, Passivity and the Revolutionary Concept of Citizenship," in *Political Culture of the Revolution,* ed. Colin Lucas., vol. 2 of *The French Revolution and the Creation of Modern Political Culture* (Oxford, 1987–89), 105–23; Shanti Singham, "Betwixt Cattle and Men: Jews, Blacks, and Women, and the Declaration of the Rights of Man" in *The French Idea of Freedom,* ed. Dale K. Van Kley (Stanford, 1994), 114–53; Ran Halévi and François Furet, *La Monarchie Républicaine: La Constitution de 1791* (Paris, 1996), 100–170.

those who sought to influence them. For Escherny, the equality that deserved to be introduced into the French polity could be defined essentially as equality of opportunity. Tellingly, though, the opportunity that Escherny seemed most eager to extend to all citizens was the opportunity to earn distinction, public esteem, and exalted status. By granting to all citizens the prospect of acquiring "honors, renown, glory and nobility as the price of their efforts," and by also permitting the "noble" to exercise any and all professions, the new government would inspire a "vivid emulation between the people and the nobility" and thereby create a kind of moral equality consistent with French traditions and with a political system based on the monarchical principle.[29]

Escherny objected to the actions taken on 19 June 1790 not only because the decree abolishing nobility had been passed "precipitously, by surprise in an evening session, in contravention of one of the Assembly's rules," but, even more, because the destruction of nobility established a "kind of equality" that all subjects of the French crown would eventually find insulting.[30] The decree had "debased all Frenchmen; it declares that they are unable to become noble, that they are incapable of transmitting the quality [of nobility] to their descendants, and in doing so it degrades them. It breaks the most precious spring in the social mechanism, the spring of emulation, honor, and activity." Through "the greatest of evils," the "precious spring" of emulation would now be replaced by the spring of "cupidity, avarice, and corruption, by gold and by wealth."[31]

Escherny's remarks about the motives of social action provide important clues about the overall conceptual framework that guided his reading of the Revolution. Indeed, the connections between Escherny's reaction to the dramatic event of 19 June, his own prerevolutionary thinking, and the broader cultural context in which various agendas for social and political reform had taken shape in the years before the Revolution become most conspicuous in his lengthy discussion of honor and its functions. Since at least 1748, when Montesquieu had effectively defined honor and virtue as competing, if not antithetical, principles of politics, countless writers had debated the meaning and relative merits of the two qualities, and virtue had been rendered suspect, at least in socially conservative minds, because of its close association with civic equality. Both Montesquieu and Rousseau defined

29. Escherny, *Essai,* 265.
30. Ibid., 173, 177.
31. Ibid., 177.

virtue as a completely selfless form of patriotism that had been characteristic of ancient republics in Greece and Rome, where citizens had led frugal and simple lives and had borne the rights and responsibilities of citizenship equally. Both also maintained that patriotic virtue could not be sustained in large states and had little chance of being revived in a modern world largely defined by egoism, luxury, and vast inequalities of wealth.

Few accepted the pessimistic judgments of Montesquieu and Rousseau uncritically—after 1748 France saw concerted efforts both to inspire a new patriotism and to redefine virtue for the context of a complex modern world—but the concept of honor clearly received new scrutiny in the moralizing literature of the age, and many would-be French "patriots" promoted it energetically as a viable alternative to virtue in the moral constitution of the modern monarchy. Montesquieu had emphasized the political utility of having whole corporate bodies zealous to defend their particular rights, status, and prerogatives against over-reaching monarchs, and he especially defined honor as a self-centered consciousness of rank and standing. Others highlighted the selfless dimensions of honor, and they often insisted on the compatibility of pride in rank, on the one hand, and patriotic generosity, on the other hand. In his only prerevolutionary publication, *The Lacunae of Philosophy* (1783), Escherny complained that people now employed the word "virtue" indiscriminately, without knowing what it is, and without having a "distinct idea" of its meaning (hence the "lacunae" which his title promised to address).[32] Escherny argued, with less originality than he assumed, that virtue could not be separated from "love of self," that the aphorism "virtue is its own reward" was misleading at best, and that concern for the self was eminently "social" and therefore morally legitimate.[33] The authentic opposite of virtue was not innocent love of self but rather rank *egoism*, which stood as the "high priest" of "cupidity" and acquisitiveness.[34] Although the category of honor did not enter explicitly into his argument, one of the few clear purposes behind the inelegantly written *Lacunae of Philosophy* was Escherny's desire to lay claim to virtue on behalf of all those motivated in part by "love of self."

The theme reappeared in a more elaborated form in his letter of October 1790. Behind the "kind of equality" that had been enshrined in the decree of 19 June, Escherny detected the always seductive—but still inadequately

---

32. Escherny, *Lacunes,* xiii.
33. Ibid., 81, 206.
34. Ibid., lxxii.

examined—principle of virtue. To discredit the Assembly's maneuver, and to reassert the appropriateness and necessity of moral hierarchies in French politics, Escherny developed an elaborate analysis of "ancient" and "modern" history in which he compared the principles, and the hidden social and political implications, of honor and virtue. Placing emphasis on the fragility of the principle of virtue, which had proven historically to be a "violent" condition that "cannot last," Escherny explained that ancient virtue had sustained the political arrangements of the ancients only because it had been supplemented by religious "fanaticism."[35] Pure virtue required an utterly selfless form of sacrifice, and the ancients had shown themselves to be virtuous because they lived in a state of permanent euphoria. Echoing Mirabeau's *Friend of Man* (1756), Escherny asserted that ancient legislators had "understood well that the *patrie* and liberty, by themselves, would be weak and powerless mainsprings if their activity were not excited by the delirium of religious enthusiasm."[36] In vain would one search for a constitution, among the free peoples of the ancient world, "where fanaticism for the *patrie* and for liberty were separated from [fanaticism] of religion." One could say, in fact, that the *patrie* (fatherland), having been "imprinted with a sacred character, formed part of religion itself, and served as its extension."[37] This combination of religious and political devotion had been rendered impossible, of course, with the introduction of Christianity, whose "single God" taught that "this world is nothing other than a valley of misery" whose afflictions one should suffer patiently in hopes of earning a trip to paradise.[38]

Fortunately, however, the fall of the Roman Empire had brought to light another source of virtue, one that had been "unknown to the ancients." In paragraphs reminiscent of Boulainvilliers's *History of the Ancient Government of France* (1727), Escherny explained that this new source came from the "forests of Germany," and that it had been introduced among the Gauls "along with the morals and customs of their rustic conquerors, the Franks." And what was this new source of virtue? "The fanaticism of honor, which blends perfectly with love of the *patrie* and of liberty, and marvelously strengthens all of its foundations." It soon had become clear that the "motor" of honor would be naturalized in the kingdom of France, where it would spawn "virtues superior to those produced in its native land." Indeed, through

---

35. Escherny, *Essai*, 196.
36. Cf. Mirabeau, *L'Ami des hommes,* 2 vols. (Avignon, 1756), vol. 2, pt. 2, pp. 73–74.
37. Escherny, *Essai*, 199–200.
38. Ibid., 201–2.

its assimilation to the institutions of chivalry and feudalism, transplanted honor had acquired "a new degree of energy and activity," creating the impression that honor "was made for the French, just as the French were made for honor." In time, honor's "superb effects" had placed the French "almost at the level of the Greeks and the Romans."[39]

Because of the historical conditions in which honor had been introduced and developed in France, however, "honor and nobility had become synonyms for the French"; the two words expressed "the same idea." Consequently, to destroy the nobility in France would be "to renounce the one kind of fanaticism that can elevate sentiments of courage, [and] incline people toward sacrifice and magnanimous actions."[40] Escherny's argument for the centrality of rank and honor certainly reflected the influence of Mandeville, as mediated by Montesquieu, but his position also grew out of his own earlier ruminations on the ambiguous and surprising meanings of virtue. "Art," wrote Escherny, "sometimes consists in drawing from the motive of [personal interest] another motive that is diametrically opposed to it." Through the medium of honor, "art manages to extract from personal interest virtue itself. Happy are the men and the governments in whom these two motives are mixed and become one."[41] Honor had the capacity to satisfy personal interest, however, only because of the existence of ranks and distinctions. Escherny likened hierarchies of distinction to the various notes in a musical scale, as both kept all in their proper place and therefore insured "social and musical harmony."[42] Crowning all such hierarchies was the status of nobility, "a sublime tool, in the hands of a legislator, [useful] for directing pride toward the general good of the political association and turning vanity into virtue." Distinction of ranks had been considered "in all times, and by all legislators, as one of the firmest supports of civil society," and France, whose national character and morals harmonized perfectly with the institution of nobility, would suffer more than any other state from its "dangerous extirpat[ion]."[43]

Escherny's commitment to the principle of honor explains how he could simultaneously call for the destruction of the corrupt "noble system" that had dominated French politics for a century and insist that the "sublime tool" of nobility must be maintained in the reformed social system of revolutionary

39. Ibid., 203.
40. Ibid., 203–4.
41. Ibid., 194.
42. Ibid., 180.
43. Ibid., 177.

France. Indeed, this combination of hatred for the existing institution of nobility and yearning for a purified form of nobility rooted in genuine honor seems to have characterized the thinking of a great many nobles in the waning years of the Old Regime—including the enigmatic comte d'Antraigues, the secretive counterrevolutionary who is so often dismissed by historians of the Revolution as an unpredictable, contradictory, or vainly self-interested political operator. In fact, if one reconsiders the case of d'Antraigues in light of Escherny's own political trajectory, one detects important lines of continuity that go far toward mitigating the charges of intellectual dishonesty and craven self-interest so often leveled at the "secret agent" of counterrevolution.[44] Comparison of the two also underscores why the radical political aspirations of reform-minded aristocrats under the Old Regime often contained the seeds of future "reaction."

The general outlines of d'Antraigues's story are well known. A future noble deputy from the Bas-Vivarais of Languedoc in the Estates-General, d'Antraigues wrote a series of pamphlets from the summer of 1788 to early 1789 in which he called for national unity against the abuses of despotism, denounced both the court and the principle of hereditary nobility, championed the rights of the Third Estate, and evoked a Rousseau-inspired vision of the "sovereign will of the people" that made him one of the most progressive, and celebrated, writers of the early prerevolution.[45] By the time the Estates-General convened in May, however, d'Antraigues had become a featured spokesman for those who defended the principle of deliberation by order, and he insisted that although "the truth can be seen from different angles," custom had an authority that only new laws could override.[46] His contemporaries in 1789 accused d'Antraigues of hypocrisy, betrayal, and irresponsibility, and most historians have echoed the assessment ever since.[47]

---

44. Léonce Pingaud, *Un agent secret sous la révolution et l'empire: le comte d'Antraigues* (Paris, 1893).

45. D'Antraigues, *Mémoire sur les Etats Généraux, leurs droits, et la manière de les convoquer* (n.p., 1788); *Seconde mémoire sur les Etats-Généraux* (n.p., 1789).

46. D'Antraigues, *Discours prononcé par le comte d'Antraigues, député aux Etats-Généraux, dans la chambre de la noblesse, le 11 mai, 1789* (n.p., 1789), 8.

47. The author of *Un Plébéien à M. le comte d'Antraigues, sur son apostasie, sur le schisme de la noblesse, & sur son arrêté inconstitutionnel, du 28 mai 1789* (n.p., 1789) accused d'Antraigues of hypocrisy, cowardice, and the unforgivable sin of having sacrificed his "principles" for his "interests" (2–3). Historians have largely repeated these charges. Roger Barny, in an illuminating study that traces the influence of Rousseau on the prerevolutionary thinking of d'Antraigues, claimed that d'Antraigues was simply "unable to rise above the point of view of a condemned class." See

If one places d'Antraigues's radical writings of 1788 in the context of his entire literary career, his reformist agenda acquires new dimensions. In spite of the extreme rhetoric he employed in 1788, much evidence suggests that d'Antraigues envisioned not the destruction of nobility per se, but the restructuring and reinvigoration of a nobility whose moral autonomy and patriotism could counter the moral torpor and thoughtless egoism that had arisen in the wake of the usurpations of France's monarchs. "A Master, three hundred thousand soldiers, and twenty million slaves, that's what one finds in France," complained d'Antraigues in a manuscript of 1782. Anticipating Escherny's own argument about the insidious partnership formed between an ambitious monarchy and a quiescent aristocracy in the course of the eighteenth century, d'Antraigues asserted that this modern "slavery" had been created through the collaboration of monarchs and the nobles who were only too happy to accept privileges in exchange for docility.

> Nobility, they say in France, is the support of monarchy. Indeed, I believe it. That is the least that the nobles owe [the monarchy], since it elevates them at the expense of their equals. Consider the status of a noble in Switzerland, and guess whether the nobles of France would choose to support the tyranny that elevates them, [or rather,] a legitimate power that simply places them among the ranks of citizens. A great man [Montesquieu] has said that the intermediary ranks occupied by the nobility temper royal authority and separate it from despotism. With all due respect to a great genius, I must say that he is terribly mistaken. How do the satellites of a tyrant temper tyranny?[48]

In his "Voyage in Turkey" of 1778, D'Antraigues's righteous anger led him to denounce both honor and the hereditary principle. "These vain and barbarous prejudices . . . that M. de Montesquieu calls honor, what are they? What good do they do for the state, and by that I mean the People?

Barny, *Le Comte d'Antraigues*, 199; Timothy Tackett characterized d'Antraigues as "erratic" (*Becoming a Revolutionary*, 86); Ralph Leigh considered d'Antraigues a "counterfeit" and an "inveterate liar." See *Correspondance complète de Jean-Jacques Rousseau*, ed. R. A. Leigh, vol. 37 (Oxford, 1980), 367. An exception to the rule is Colin Duckworth (*The d'Antraigues Phenomenon: The Making and Breaking of a Revolutionary Royalist Espionage Agent* [Newcastle upon Tyne, 1986]), who makes some effort to explain the "irreconcilable inconsistencies" in d'Antraigues's behavior (see 16, 176).

48. As cited in Barny, *Le Comte d'Antraigues*, 57.

Honor arms [the nobles] against their *patrie* so that they can sustain the will of the despot. . . . What noble and generous sentiment inspires this barbarous honor that is so celebrated? None." Hereditary nobility could be considered "a scourge that devours the *patrie,*" an abuse that rendered the nobility "devoted to tyrants by their estate. Tyrants create and assure the existence of the nobility, and together they scorn and exploit the people who nourish them."[49]

D'Antraigues's hatred of tyranny and his concern for the well-being of the forgotten *patrie* produced strong words in his critical assessment of nobility, but many clues indicate that his condemnation of the nobility derived especially from his distaste for the high nobility of court and capital. The detested "satellites" of the despot congregated "at Versailles, where the highest nobility of the state assemble. There they exercise their empire and appear in their greatest force. . . . The court unites . . . these nobles, your eternal enemies, always ready to extinguish any virtuous sentiments in the tyrant's lair, avid for your property which the tyrant seizes in order to distribute to them."[50] Few nobles regarded courtiers as representatives of the nobility as a whole, however—in 1782 the vicomte Toustain de Richebourg lamented the tendency of outsiders to "judge the nobility in general on the basis of that of the court in particular"—and other semi-autobiographical reflections written by d'Antraigues in the early 1780s show his own longing for an idealized medieval past populated by virtuous and noble seigneurs.[51] "Never have I approached an ancient chateau without feeling a vivid sense of happiness that elicits both smiles and tears," he wrote in one fictionalized epistle. "A thousand times more sweet were my sensations on finding, amid abandoned ruins, an old manor in all its gothic beauty, well kept and inhabited by simple men not rich enough to have ruined it all by replacing tapestries admired by the nobility for centuries, or [by replacing] an armchair that, for three hundred years, was both cradle and death bed for the scion of the family. . . . When I enter these manors, with their long and dark halls, when I see these massive chimneys that gathered the entire family around a hot fire, I feel as though I'm leaving my century, escaping my age."[52] D'Antraigues's harsh words toward the nobility in the 1770s and

49. As cited in ibid., 58–59.
50. Ibid., 78.
51. Toustain de Richebourg, "Observations sur la noblesse, communiquées aux memes, par M. le comte de Toustain," *Journal Encyclopédique,* 1782, vol. 2, 489.
52. As cited in Barny, *Le Comte d'Antraigues,* 72–73.

early 1780s reflected his condemnation of a certain vision of nobility, one characterized by artificiality, arrogance, and civic irresponsibility. But that condemnation should not obscure his affinity for another vision of nobility, one rooted in long-lost chivalric virtues and a simplicity and selflessness that resembled the patriotism of the ancients.

Even the rhetoric of d'Antraigues's most read, and most radical, pamphlet, the *Essay on the Estates-General* (1788), provides evidence of the comte's continuing double vision with regard to the nobility. Hereditary nobility appears again as "the most awful scourge that the heavens in their anger can inflict on a free nation," and courtiers are said to have rendered the king incapable of producing just legislation, because "born in the den of corruption, from the beginning his gaze is fixed on the natural enemies of public order."[53] D'Antraigues had nothing but contempt for "these nobles who are as vain as they are weak, this nobility which is the enemy of the popular will [*popularité*], which lays siege to the throne and seizes everything by right of birth, and which seems to form around the king a new nation, enemy of the people."[54]

D'Antraigues's evocation of two nations—one constituted by the "people" and the other by its aristocratic enemies—anticipated the thinking of Sieyès (and of Escherny). But this first "enemy" nation described by d'Antraigues really comprised only part of the nobility, for while the enemies "multiply at court," invading all offices and dignities and nurturing their "bizarre" and "feudal" obsession with genealogy, "the true nobility," d'Antraigues declared, "comes to a meeting of minds with the people in the provinces; stricken by despotism, it has at last understood . . . that necessity requires that it unite with the people, so as to assure itself true and solid support in every circumstance."[55] D'Antraigues's "true nobility" of the provinces had little in common with the "satellites" of the despot, who eagerly exploited all of the unfortunate abuses inherited from feudal times but did nothing to perpetuate the admirable morals that had partly compensated for the nobility's usurpations in the distant Middle Ages.

To underscore the contrast between the two nobilities that occupied his mind, d'Antraigues conjured an image of a regretful courtier who evoked "past centuries of glory, virtue, and simplicity" while drawing his last

53. D'Antraigues, *Mémoire*, 61, 26.
54. Ibid., 85.
55. Ibid., 86.

breath. The nostalgia embodied in this mournful courier resembled that expressed years earlier by d'Antraigues himself.

> And so a courtier, raised in the ancient château of his fathers, deep in some poor province and far from the throne, leaves his Gothic manor when the prizes of ambition seduce him. [He] approaches the palace of a master in search of a lucrative servitude. If he still retains any of the virtues of his fathers, he senses soon enough at what price one obtains the favors of kings. He longs for the old hearth, he desires the tranquility of his home; but habit holds him, his heart bursts, and he dies as a slave. But his last breath, his last vision, takes him back to the peaceful place of his happy childhood. In the same way, in this time of oppression, a time nevertheless prepared for liberty, the Frenchman of this century . . . calls up memories of that short but precious era when his ancestors lived free.[56]

In this passage d'Antraigues identified the process of French regeneration with the nobility's figurative return to its moral home.

A clear sense of the moral atmosphere that d'Antraigues imagined enveloping the hearth of a reinvigorated nobility is communicated through his paean to the cult of honor that had supposedly prevailed before the coming of modernity. In a fascinating passage from his *Essay on the Estates-General,* he represents the moral resilience of the age of chivalry as a fore-shadowing of the patriotic revival now sweeping across France in a new time of change. "The birth of chivalry—its principles and heroism before its degeneration—offers a story as satisfying as it is useful. It is a bouquet of flowers in the middle of the desert of Libya."[57] In the postclassical age of barbarism, when people "could no longer adore their *patrie,*" the heart nevertheless remained "free" to express its affections. It therefore devoted itself entirely "to the service of love and friendship." In those uncertain times of violence, the commitment to serve the object of one's love required "acts of inconceivable courage and ceaseless peril." At the dawn of the feudal age "the heroism of the ancient republics germinated and flourished along with the most horrible servitude."[58] In the absence of a genuine *patrie,*

56. Ibid., 66–67.
57. Ibid., 89.
58. Ibid., 88.

ancient virtue had taken the form of medieval honor, and lovers and warriors thereby found new inspirations for self-sacrifice.

From a combination of sentiments and will "there was born a sort of grandeur, a kind of honor that preserved hearts from the abject state where slavery would have placed them, [an honor] that finally made possible a national resurrection when Philip the Fair's excesses made it necessary."[59] At the time of the first Estates-General in 1302, the nation managed once again, after three centuries of servitude, to articulate "the principles of public liberty." Unfortunately, the opportunity to effect lasting change was eventually squandered, largely because the representatives to this national assembly "saw everywhere the remnants of ancient feudalism; the remnants of these insane pretensions became the seeds of eternal discord, carefully cultivated by the kings and their ministers, who wished only to render these supreme assemblies impotent." Stymied by internal divisions and their inexperience in asserting their will, the estates allowed resurgent "despotism" to reabsorb most of their rights, leaving the unfinished project of national regeneration to be resumed at a later date.[60]

D'Antraigues's defense of the nobility's corporate rights in the spring of 1789 and after may indeed have seemed jarringly inconsistent with his earlier denunciation of hereditary nobility, feudalism, the prejudice of honor, and the pretensions of the privileged orders. His many critics in 1789 may also have failed to notice or appreciate, however, the many telltale signs of the comte's attachment to an alternative model of nobility that he and others deemed entirely compatible with patriotic regeneration and the promotion of the rights of the Third Estate. In his writings of the 1770s and early 1780s, d'Antraigues had seen the "true nobility" of the provinces as a foil to the corrupt nobility of city and court; to the scourge of "hereditary" privilege he had opposed the Swiss custom of granting personal nobility to urban notables; to a false modern honor unsustained by any "noble and generous sentiment" he had opposed the chivalric honor of the Middle Ages, an honor robust enough to have once inspired a "national resurrection." In a manner strikingly similar to that of Escherny—who also revealingly complained of the perversion of the modern "honor" monopolized by the "superior classes" of the nobility—d'Antraigues looked forward to the overthrow of courtiers and other superprivileged nobles who benefited from the "insane pretensions" attached to a corrupt institution. But d'Antraigues's conviction

59. Ibid., 89.
60. Ibid., 95–96.

that the current crisis demanded a moral solution, and his admiration for the simple virtues of those nobles either historically or geographically insulated from modern corruption, surely suggested certain advantages to retaining the corporate existence of the nobility, especially if that nobility bore the imprint of genuine sentiments of honor. His rhetorical assault on nobility in 1788, in other words, had not been incompatible with a vision of reform that incorporated a new and improved nobility into a regenerated social system.

Signs of misunderstanding, or misread intentions, can be found on all sides of the divisive debates of 1789–90. Just as readers of d'Antraigues or Escherny might have missed early indications of their continuing attachment to the idea of a corporate nobility, Escherny and others like him may also not have fully realized that the broad movement against despotism and privilege in the late 1780s had also harbored another nascent critique of nobility, one that challenged the entire principle of noble preeminence precisely on the grounds that the link between honor and nobility had been irreparably damaged. From the later 1760s, a great many writers had sought to make honor a "national" characteristic that inhered not in the corps of nobility but in the French people as a whole.[61] This effort, which involved rereading French history as a story of the unfolding of French "patriotism," rather than as a record of specifically noble heroism, coincided with and depended upon a redefinition of honor that brought its meaning ever closer to "virtue"—the very same virtue that Montesquieu had thought properly characteristic only of small republics and that Escherny regarded as a hopelessly unstable source of patriotic action. According to the new view, true honor was consistent with both virtue and equality. In fact, the "honoring" of deserving citizens implied an a priori basis in equality, both because the civic qualities that constituted true honor could only be properly recognized by one's fellow constituents within the community, and because the possession of civic spirit could not conceivably be limited to privileged groups whose own interests actually interfered with the patriotic sensibilities that true honor required.

Few of the proponents of "national" honor envisioned the elimination of nobility as a social or moral category, but well before 1789 many of them had begun to articulate a new definition of nobility, one that made noble

61. For examples, see C.-L.-M. de Sacy, *L'Honneur François* (Paris, 1769–84); Joseph Servan de Gerbey, *Le soldat citoyen* (Dans le Pays de la Liberté, 1780); Basset de La Marelle, *La différence du patriotisme national chez les François et chez les Anglois,* 2nd ed. (Paris, 1766). The phenomenon of the "nationalization" of honor is discussed in Smith, *Nobility Reimagined,* 143–81.

status a purely honorific sign of the esteem accorded by one's fellow citizens.[62] Disputes over the meaning, and social valence, of honor marked the debates over the composition of the Estates-General in 1788–89, and the appeal of the new ideal of the purely honorific nobility seems to have reached even such vigorous opponents of the Second Estate as Sieyès. In 1788, his *Essay on Privileges* dismissed the superstitious honor trumpeted by the descendants of the feudal seigneurs but praised "true" honor as the product of a "sublime commerce between the services rendered to the people by great men and the tribute of esteem offered to great men by the people."[63]

The debate about nobility in the early stages of the Revolution—the debate about its constitutional prerogatives, its rights and duties, its relation to the Third Estate, and its capacity for patriotism—was argued in large part over the contested terrain of honor. The abolition of nobility on 19 June 1790 surely surprised nobles because of its suddenness and its curious timing, but the idea that lay behind the abolition could not have come as a great surprise to anyone who had paid attention to the debates of the previous two years. The competing perspectives on nobility in 1789–90 happened to correspond to differing perceptions of honor, perceptions that had been articulated at length before and ever since the beginning of the revolutionary crisis.

One writer who clearly interpreted the abolition of nobility through the lens provided by earlier debates over honor and status was Jacques-Antoine Dulaure, a historian of eclectic interests who became a fervent opponent of aristocracy after 1789.[64] Dulaure's *Critical History of the Nobility,* written shortly after the abolition of noble titles, is a venomous diatribe against the nobility's historical claims to social preeminence, and Dulaure goes to great lengths to demonstrate that noble customs and beliefs had been so manifestly "stupid," "barbarous," and "superstitious" in the feudal age that the preeminence nobles acquired in that violent time could be attributed only to their unjust

62. See J.-M.-A. Servan, *Discours sur le progrés des connaissances humaines en général, de la morale, et de la législation en particulier; lu dans une Assemblée publique de l'Académie de Lyon* (n.p., 1781); Holbach, *Ethocratie* (Paris, 1776).

63. *Qu'est-ce que le tiers état? par Emmanuel Sieyès, précédé de l'Essai sur les privilèges,* ed. Edme Champion (Paris, 1982), 5–6.

64. Among the subjects of Dulaure's historical curiosity: beards, Paris, religion, art, and the "cult of the phallus" in the ancient world. See, for example, *Pogonologie, ou Histoire philosophique de la barbe* (Constantinople and Paris, 1786); *Nouvelle description des environs de Paris: contenant les détails historiques & descriptifs des maisons royales* (Paris, 1787); *Critique des quinze critiques du salon; ou, Notices faites pour donner une idée de ces brochures, suivie d'un résumé des opinions les plus impartiales sur les tableaux exposés au Louvre* (Rome, 1787); *Le culte du phallus chez les anciens et les modernes* (Puiseaux, 1997; first published 1805).

use of force against the useful but peaceful members of society.[65] Dulaure's broad rhetorical strategy, in laying out the "crimes" and "horrors" committed by the nobility in both the feudal and absolutist ages, consisted of shaming the nobles, which thereby would deprive them of the very quality that they had always claimed separated them from the rest of humanity, namely, honor.

In Dulaure's retelling of French history, the nobles' twisted logic had imposed itself, for example, on the will of medieval kings, who had permitted and even encouraged the custom of dueling. "These immoral laws," formed in a time when might made right, had been the source of "a thousand atrocities. Crime became a duty, an honor." Even later, when the laws were reformed, "the nobles retained their habits of honor;" indeed, they were still in operation during the century of *lumières*.[66] What made the survival of their customs so ironic was the ever-widening discrepancy between image and reality. After the nobles' domestication by Louis XIV, for example, they had sought "to please the monarch, and to serve him through shameful and criminal means." In quest of the king's favor, they had been fully willing "to humiliate themselves, to grovel, to plead." They filched honors and riches "that were not the king's to give."[67] But the honors had lost their meaning in any case. "For a long time it has been remarked that the majority of these honorable heroes were utterly without honor, without good faith, loaded down with debts, and absolutely defamed." The "chivalric virtue" on which they prided themselves would just as soon be found among the brigands and street urchins of the *quai de la féraille*, the Parisian recruiting grounds for the lowliest foot soldiers in the army. "The word honor," when used by the nobility, "expresses nothing but an old superstition."[68] The honor observed by *gentilshommes* was "immoral, destructive, opposed to the laws and to common sense, and completely different from true honor." In fact, a "survey of the content of this book must lead one to conclude that it is dishonorable to be a noble."[69]

As Dulaure explained it, nobility had paradoxically come to stand for the opposite of honor, which could really only be found among those whose productive work "forms the wealth of states."[70] This contradictory arrangement, which secured nobility for the dishonorable while denying nobility to those who possessed genuine honor, highlighted the inverted, and intolerable,

---

65. J.-A. Dulaure, *Histoire critique de la noblesse* (Paris, 1790), 247.
66. Ibid., 290.
67. Ibid., 161–62.
68. Ibid., 292.
69. Ibid., 314, 317.
70. Ibid., 199.

logic of the old social system. Hereditary distinction should be regarded as "the radical vice" of a government, since "equality of rights" established the only firm basis of a government's "strength and honor." Hereditary nobility constituted a "crime against the rights of that part of the nation deprived [of the status]."[71] The "true honor" that Dulaure proposed as the alternative to the nobles' fraudulent honor could be cultivated only in a nation of equal citizens, where all could be regarded as equally noble.

Escherny and Dulaure disagreed strongly over the abolition of nobility, but juxtaposition of their texts reveals fascinating points of contact between the perspectives of the opponents and supporters of the Assembly's action of 19 June 1790. Like Dulaure, Escherny recalled with disgust the domestication of the nobility by Louis XIV, and he held in contempt the sycophantic courtiers who, working in league with kings, had shamelessly siphoned off national resources to which they had no legitimate claim. Escherny denounced the "formidable aristocracy" that had perpetuated an unjust regime, and he supported the principle of equality of rights. Escherny indicated that all professions deserved equal respect, and he pointedly demanded that the "career of honors" should be "opened to all individuals of the nation." On all of these critical points Dulaure and Escherny—like many eager reformers from both the Second and Third Estates—would have had little trouble finding common ground in the months before the Estates-General meeting of May 1789.

Despite their similar discontents and their use of a common vocabulary, the impassioned reactions of Escherny and Dulaure to the abolition of nobility reveal the presence of a deep fault line in the reformist thought of the later Old Regime. That fault line divided contemporaries' perceptions of nobility, and its divisive power was expressed in the confrontation of conflicting attitudes toward the role of honor in a reformed French polity. Dulaure, like many moralists, educators, merchants, soldiers, and lawyers since the 1760s, rejected the deformed honor represented by corrupt "aristocrats" and sought to appropriate true honor on behalf of the nation at large. Identifying honor with the rights of citizenship itself, Dulaure imagined a nobility that encompassed every patriotic and useful citizen. In a genuinely reformed France, he was convinced, the borders of nobility would be so fluid that no "part of the nation" would be deprived of the

71. Ibid., iii–iv.

status. Titles of nobility could serve no purpose in such a polity since honor would inhere in every conscientious citizen, and this would render pointless and redundant the awarding of conspicuous markers of putative moral excellence.

For Escherny, by contrast, French honor ultimately could not be detached from the hierarchical and inegalitarian context in which it had first developed.[72] Honor's moral weight, its spiritual power, and its utility as a political tool all came from the differentiating function that it performed in society. Some foolishly expected, wrote Escherny, that "eminent posts, and the abilities of those who occupy them, can take the place of the prejudice of nobility" in the minds of the people, and that they can inspire "deference and respect" all by themselves. But "the people do not appreciate a merit that is purely intellectual." Having an innate "love of the marvelous," they respect only that which "strikes the senses and the imagination."[73] The operation of social institutions required "exaltation" and "enthusiasm," and these were never the products of "cold reason."[74] Prejudices are to the political body "as sails are to a ship; passions are the wind, and reason is the calm which sailors fear as much as the strongest storm."[75] Religious fanaticism could prove to be one of the motors of "movement and action" necessary to the social body, as Escherny had explained in his discussion of ancient virtue, but in its absence "the prejudice of rank, of nobility, and the fanaticism for honor which derives from it" served even better.[76] Honor's status as "the most precious spring in the social mechanism" arose precisely from its ability to establish gradations of rank, on the one hand, and to inspire emulation in all those impressed by splendid images of moral superiority, on the other hand. Escherny thus took for granted the value of the nobility's existence as a separate and distinct body, even within a regenerated society. Nobility, he was convinced, was "one of the wisest institutions ever conceived by man."[77]

Straddling their conceptual fault line in 1789, both Dulaure and Escherny welcomed the earthquake that toppled from power the formidable aristocracy

---

72. Perhaps the best expression of the conflicting attitudes about honor that drove divergent plans of reform in the last years of the Old Regime is the contrast between the spirit of Joseph Servan's *Le soldat citoyen* (1780) and that of Pierre Augustin de Varennes's *Réflexions morales, relatives au militaire françois* (Paris, 1779).

73. Escherny, *Essai*, 237, 239.

74. Ibid., 235.

75. Ibid., 228.

76. Ibid., 235–36.

77. Ibid., 224.

that consisted of courtiers, financiers, and the extravagantly advantaged. Escherny's apparent about-face after the abolition of nobility in 1790 did not signify the waning of his earlier reformist zeal, nor did it entail the repudiation of liberal assumptions he had harbored for decades. Escherny's shift of emphasis in 1790 simply testifies to the existence of two very different visions of the polity that revolutionaries had expected to emerge from the rubble of the Old Regime. Dulaure hoped that France's work of civic reconstruction would incorporate the materials of honor and public esteem, but without the compromised element of nobility to which those materials had once been bound. Escherny was eager to throw off the defective components of nobility, but he never doubted that some form of nobility would be central to the civic culture created by a regime that claimed to elevate reason over the base passions. Indeed, in 1790 Escherny charged that the National Assembly's abolition of nobility had been motivated by "vengeance, envy, ambition, the passions in short, even though no one would dare to own up to them"; in his eyes the event signaled the Assembly's own moral degradation.[78]

In articulating his vision of reform, Escherny hardly gave expression to "aristocratic reaction" in its classic sense, that is, an aggressive and self-conscious defense of the interests of the socioeconomic class to which he belonged. After all, he reacted not only against the presence of rich newcomers in the prerevolutionary nobility but also against a clique of parasites and usurpers that included the highest nobles in the land. He envisioned the creation of a nobility open to high achievers from all professions, one that would be characterized above all by a commitment to the common good. Nevertheless, Escherny's ideas and attitudes, shaped as they were by the historical and political analyses of Montesquieu and Boulainvilliers, and rooted as they were in a prerevolutionary program to cleanse, purify, and reform an order betrayed by the state and by its own gullibility, attest to the existence of a form of social conservatism destined to prove incompatible with the nation's general claim to honor in 1789. The elaboration of that more general claim had been made possible by a lengthy dialogue over the social and constitutional implications of honor's meaning, a dialogue that predated Dulaure's *Critical History* by decades. One of the interlocutors in that dialogue was a segment of the nobility whose own moral reaction against the corruption of the age had produced an ever more refined definition of honor, a definition centered on rank, hierarchy, and the necessity

78. Ibid., 263.

of inequality. When the question of noble status and its meaning became central to constitutional discussions in 1788, the clash between two over-lapping but irreconcilable programs for reform, two revolutionary agendas, and, in a sense, two forms of "reaction," became inevitable. Escherny and Dulaure rehearsed in a new context a debate that would have been familiar to all who had contemplated the need for political and moral reform under the Old Regime.

10

THE MEMOIRS OF LAMETH AND THE RECONCILIATION
OF NOBILITY AND REVOLUTION

Doina Pasca Harsanyi

"Almost all my contemporaries left memoirs recounting the story of their lives or at least that of a significant portion of their lives," wrote Madame de Genlis on the first page of her own memoirs. Indeed, the Revolution altered so much the status and life-style of the nobility that many nobles seemed to have felt a need to bear witness. The great number of aristocratic memoirs written in the two or three decades after the Revolution speaks to the desire to sort out and comprehend the nature of the events that so dramatically and irrevocably changed their lives.[1] At the same time, the memoirs do not represent the entire spectrum of the nobility. Impoverished rural nobles or staunch counterrevolutionaries picked up the pen less often than the urban salon-goers who could recall at least some mild flirtation with the "new ideas" before the Revolution. These individuals wrote in response to the anti-nobilism of the Revolution, in an attempt to produce a different narrative of the last years of the Old Regime and their own place in it, one that allowed individual nobles a voice capable of rescuing them from the abhorrent role of collective villain.[2]

"The decision to write memoirs," observed Georges Gusdorf, "expresses the desire of reappraising one's existence, responding to an intimate necessity, to a disaccord between the subject and his own life."[3] In the case of the

---

1. The critical bibliography by Alfred Fierro contains 1,502 titles, about half written by nobles. Alfred Fierro, *Bibliographie critique des mémoires sur la Révolution écrits ou traduits en français* (Paris, 1988).
2. See Henri Rossi, *Mémoires aristocratiques féminins, 1789–1848* (Paris, 1998), 269–85.
3. Georges Gusdorf, *Les écritures du moi: lignes de vie 1* (Paris, 1991), 257.

nobles, there was profound disaccord between the nobility's self-image as a benevolent and worthy elite and the revolutionary rhetoric that collapsed aristocracy and nobility into one repugnant class of privileged defenders of an unjust system. In the eyes of most nobles this was a grossly reductive indictment that obscured several decades of self-analysis, internal debate, and adjustment to new circumstances. No strangers to the ongoing discussions on merit and social utility, nobles often chastised the "abuses and vices" within their own ranks in an effort to reconcile the critical discourse of the Enlightenment with the prerogatives of their condition.[4] As David Bien put it, "In this climate of new ideas many members of the nobility felt impelled to take on new roles, to be active, and, by their own lights, useful in one way or another."[5] For this reason it is no accident that most memorialists portray the life of their families and close circle of friends as a stream of enlightened good works, intellectual pursuits, and charity enterprises, far from the images of contemptible idleness propagated in revolutionary writings. According to the vast majority of the memoirs, if there were indeed nobles who indulged in the much decried "abuses and vices" of the Old Regime, they were most often "the others," that is, sycophantic courtiers like the Polignacs.

The memoirs also bring to light the shared culture of the nobility, the feeling of belonging together, of understanding each other across deep political or ideological differences. In this sense, Henri Rossi is right to point out that the similar narrative patterns and the obvious goal of painting a positive image of the nobility allow us to consider all noble memoirs as a collective work, dedicated "to the continuous construction of a vanished universe; they constitute the swan song of a class which senses that it is progressively dispossessed."[6] On this level, recreating the famed *douceur de*

---

4. Many studies have examined the internal rifts within the nobility as well as the successive self-definitions that maintained the nobility at the top of the social order. Mathieu Marraud, *La noblesse de Paris au dix-huitième siècle* (Paris, 2000), 334–534. Jay M. Smith, *The Culture of Merit: Nobility, Royal Service and the Making of Absolute Monarchy in France, 1600–1789* (Ann Arbor, 1996), 11–56; Jean-Marie Constant, "Absolutisme et Modernité" in *Histoire des elites en France,* ed. Guy Chaussinand-Nogaret (Paris, 1991), 147–68; David Bien, "Aristocracy" in *A Critical Dictionary of the French Revolution,* ed. François Furet and Mona Ozouf (Cambridge, Mass., 1989), 616–28. For the self-critical discourse of the nobility to the point of self-denial, see Guy Chaussinand-Nogaret, "Un aspect de la pensée nobiliaire au XVIIIe siècle: l'anti-nobilisme," *Revue d'histoire moderne et contemporaine* 29 (1982): 441–52.

5. Bien, "Aristocracy," 624. There were, of course, nobles who made no apologies for enjoying their privileges at the expense of the low born. The majority of memoirs however insist on some form of utility.

6. Rossi, *Mémoires aristocratiques féminins,* 13.

vivre as a gentle, generous, and, in some respects, useful way of life also contained an implicit rebuttal of the leveling anti-aristocratic discourse of the Revolution. For if there was no connection between the art of living nobly (*vivre noblement*) and despotism, and if well-meaning nobles enlightened rather than oppressed their subjects, it followed that the anti-nobilism that fueled the revolutionary discourse was a misunderstanding of colossal proportions. Correcting this error of perspective is the driving force behind most aristocratic memoirs of the revolutionary era.

At the same time, there were subdivisions even among the "good" nobles, who, in the words of Madame de Chastenay, "wanted principles, wanted merit and consideration."[7] The question for them was: how far was too far? To what extent should nobles have engaged in a revolution meant to upset the entire social order as they knew it? Moreover, how could nobles participate in radical reforms without becoming traitors to their own order? Former prerevolutionary nobles answered these questions in their memoirs by attempting to define the appropriate line of conduct for enlightened, yet loyal members of their order. By replaying the events and pointing to the errors of certain members of the nobility such narratives imply that the nobility's downfall was a matter of accident and poor judgment unrelated to the success of the Revolution itself. The Revolution did not require the defeat of the nobility to accomplish its goals, and, symmetrically, the survival and even prosperity of the nobility did not depend on the failure of the Revolution. In the telling of most aristocratic memoirs the responsibility for the nobility's disgrace lay mostly with various nobles themselves. First, with those irresponsible and careless nobles who facilitated accusations of immorality, uselessness, and frivolity; and second, with those individuals amongst their ranks, no less irresponsible, who got carried away by the egalitarian language of the Revolution to the point of forgetting their obligations and abandoning the very qualities that made up the noble character. Those so designated were the Patriot nobles, who allegedly took too far their enthusiasm for the new ideas and not only joined the Revolution but contributed to its radicalization, which made them responsible for the Terror and its cortege of disasters.

The Patriot nobles themselves, a tiny minority to begin with, ended up trapped between two streams of accusations. Once the Revolution gathered steam, revolutionary writers and leaders rarely took the time to point to any differences between prerevolutionary nobles and the rest. Anti-aristocratic rhetoric designated all nobles, with no exception, as objects of contempt

7. *Mémoires de Madame de Chastenay, 1771–1815* (Paris, 1896), 1:57.

282 NOBILITY AND "ARISTOCRATIC REACTION"

and animosity. Many nobles, in contrast, regarded with equal contempt the efforts of a few *gentilshommes* to blend in with the common people or to become *peuple* as Robespierre would have put it. The Patriot nobles who left memoirs did so in part, then, to fend off accusations of treason to the Revolution, on one hand, and of treason to the nobility, on the other. This essay will examine the views on nobility, and on its relation to the Revolution, expressed by one of the most vocal and active Patriot nobles, Alexandre de Lameth. Lameth composed his detailed *Histoire de l'Assemblée Constituante* as a political memoir meant to shed light on his own prerevolutionary activism. As he retold the story of his own and other like-minded nobles' revolutionary activities, Lameth rejected the accusation of traitor to the nobility while maintaining full loyalty to his unambiguous political stands during the Revolution. His book is a double protestation of loyalty to revolutionary and noble ideals at the same time. It offers therefore a valuable entry into the political, ideological, and moral dilemma of a segment of the nobility that tried to bridge two worlds by reconciling revolutionary radicalism with noble dignity.

Alexandre de Lameth placed himself on the far left of the Patriot faction from the very beginning of the Revolution, although prior to the political effervescence of 1788–89 he did little to attract attention to himself. He had followed a rather commonplace path for young men of his order in the latter half of the century. Born and raised in Paris, he owed his relatively high standing within the Second Estate to his mother, a member of the illustrious and wealthy Broglie family. It was his mother who obtained for all four of her sons a generous royal pension after the death of her husband.[8] Alexandre became *garde de corps,* then *sous-lieutenant,* and finally captain in the Royal-Champagne regiment. With this rank he served in the American Revolutionary War, where he probably became concerned, like many French officers, with the new ideas of equality and freedom. Back in Paris he joined the Masonic lodge of "Bons Amis," frequented a few salons, and became part of the enlightened nobility described by Daniel Roche as consumer and occasional producer of the Enlightenment discourse critical of the absolutist status quo.[9]

---

8. Two payments of 20,000 *livres* each to the countess of Lameth are recorded in the famous "Livre rouge." The gratification was of 60,000 *livres* to be paid in three installments, but a third payment had not been recorded. For comparison, 200,000 *livres* had been spent as alms for the poor at the death of Louis XV. Cf. *Régistre de dépense depuis le 19 mai 1774 à 16 aout 1789. 122 feuillets reliés en maroquin rouge.*

9. See Daniel Roche, *Les Républicains des lettres: gens de culture et lumières au dix-huitième siècle* (Paris, 1998), passim. However, participation in the sociability and intellectual life of the

Lameth's life, and no doubt his ideas, found a clear structure and line of action in September 1788 when he and his brother Charles were admitted at the Society of Thirty, led by Adrien Duport. The friendship with Duport carried on during the Constituent Assembly, where the two Lameth brothers formed, together with Duport and Antoine Barnave, the famous "triumvirat." The Society outlined a clear agenda: transforming the corporate French society into a society of property-owning citizens equal before the law, enjoying individual rather than corporate freedoms under the rule of a written constitution.[10] The first point of strategy was to insure the election to the Estates-General of as many of their members as possible, in order to create a powerful pressure group that would mold an obsolete corps into a national assembly. Following this strategy, Lameth stood for election and was indeed elected as deputy of the nobility of Péronne. His brother Charles was elected by the nobility of Arras, the same *bailliage* (electoral district) that sent Robespierre to Versailles as deputy of the Third Estate.[11]

Lameth threw himself into political activism with great gusto. He was certainly involved in the decision of the electors of his *bailliage* of Péronne to send a common *cahier* for the nobility and the Third Estate. After being entrusted with the *cahier*, Lameth pronounced a passionate discourse where he affirmed his allegiance to the rights of men and to the "public spirit" that had changed hearts and minds for the better. His passion foreshadowed his future enthusiastic campaigns against private, as opposed to general, interests: "It [the public spirit] spread the light, warmed men's hearts, and replaced selfishness and personal interests with general views; finally, it is to this principle, so beneficial, that we owe the happy revolution which is under way."[12]

Enlightenment did not automatically translate into revolutionary action. On this point, see also Daniel Roche, *France in the Enlightenment,* trans. Arthur Goldhammer (Cambridge, 1998), 407–19; Henri Carré, *La noblesse de France et l'opinion publique au XVIIIe siècle* (Paris, 1920), 390–405; Guy Chaussinand-Nogaret, *The French Nobility in the Eighteenth Century,* trans. William Doyle (Cambridge, 1985), 23–38, 181–200, and Suzanne Fiette, *La noblesse française des lumières à la Belle Epoque* (Paris, 1997), 36–75.

10. The platform of the Society of Thirty has been examined in Daniel L. Wick, *A Conspiracy of Well-Intentioned Men: The Society of Thirty and the French Revolution.* (New York, 1987). See also Kenneth Margerison, *Pamphlets and Public Opinion: The Campaign for a Union of Orders in the Early French Revolution* (West Lafayette, Ind., 1997), 51–70.

11. On the concerted decision of the members of the Society of Thirty to stand for election for the nobility, see Georges Michon, "Essai sur l'histoire du parti feuillant: Adrien Duport" (Thèse pour le doctorat ès lettres, Université de Dijon [Paris, 1924]), 45–47.

12. *Archives parlementaires* (hereafter A.P.), 1st ser., V, 366. The entire of Péronne *cahier* 355–63.

Lameth was one of the forty-seven nobles who joined the Third Estate on 26 April and endorsed enthusiastically the suppression of noble privileges on the night of 4 August as well as the suppression of noble titles on 19 June 1790. He distinguished himself as a steadfast advocate of the preeminence of the legislative branch over the executive. This prompted him to vote always for measures meant to limit the power of the king, a stand that brought him frequently into conflict with Mirabeau.[13] He argued forcefully in favor of the suspensive veto and for the right of the Assembly to decide war by decree. Both were bound to weaken royal power and earned him the reputation of *enragé* and sworn enemy of the king. Even so, the progressive radicalization of the Revolution worried him and by early 1791 he was looking for ways to calm down the revolutionary fervor he had done so much to encourage two years before. Coming to fear, as Lord Acton put it, the king's weakness more than the king's power, he joined his closest friend Antoine Barnave in negotiations with Marie-Antoinette via secret letters. He hoped, along with Barnave, that a wise and conciliatory attitude on the part of the king and his court would appease the revolutionary firebrands, save the monarchy, and stop the radicalization of the Revolution. Such hopes remained unfulfilled.[14] Also unfulfilled were the hopes of the Feuillants, the club founded by the triumvirs shortly after the flight to Varennes as the party of order.[15]

After the disbanding of the Constituent Assembly in September 1791, Lameth became *maréchal de camp* in the Armée du nord, under the orders of General Luckner and of Lafayette. As an arrest mandate was issued against him after the republican revolution of 10 August 1792, Lameth surrendered to the Austrians together with Lafayette, Latour-Maubourg, and Bureau de Puzy. The captivity and a short exile in London, from which he was expelled as a potential troublemaker, led him to Hamburg, where he established a business with his brother Charles and the *ci-devant* duc d'Aiguillon. Back in France after 1800 Lameth became one of Napoleon's most trusted prefects and a baron of the empire. An active member of the liberal opposition

13. See Harriet B. Applewhite, *Political Alignment in the French Revolution* (Baton Rouge, 1993), 145–67; Kenneth Margerison, *Pamphlets and Public Opinion*, 149–82, and Allison Patrick, "The Second Estate in the Constituent Assembly, 1789–1791," *Journal of Modern History* 62 (June 1990): 223–52. See also Elizabeth Eisenstein "Who Intervened in 1788? A Commentary on the Coming of the French Revolution," *American Historical Review* 70 (October 1965): 77–103.

14. Antoine Barnave has been the subject of many studies. For the subject of his communication with the queen, see Pierre d'Amarzit, *Barnave, le conseiller secret de la reine* (Paris, 2000).

15. For an in-depth analysis of the activities of the Feuillants, see Michon, "Essai sur l'histoire du parti feuillant."

during the Restoration, he used the spare time parliamentary service afforded him during the unexciting government of Charles X to look back on his revolutionary days. The *Histoire de l'Assemblée Constituante* aims at presenting the first revolutionary assembly as a moderate, rational, and reasonable body, engaged in an orderly revolutionary process, which was to end in due time with the establishing of a constitutional monarchy. The Patriot nobles appear as key leaders in this endeavor, model citizens loyal to the end both to the king and to the principles of 1789.[16] That such exemplary patriotic actors in the main drama of the century ended up vilified by both sides struck Lameth as a terrible misunderstanding, a reasoning that connects his *Histoire* with the assumptions of unmerited punishment that lay at the foundation of all aristocratic memoirs of the time.

For Lameth, as for most like-minded deputies, there was little need to explain the philosophical basis on which Patriot politics were built. He took the content and worth of notions like freedom, equality, progress, or regeneration to be self-evident.[17] In numerous speeches he made clear that the legitimacy of the deputies, and through them that of the Assembly, came from their principles and from the correct understanding of the general will, which is why he believed that deputies should consult their conscience more often than their *cahiers*. After the king's flight to Varennes, however, Lameth was forced to confront the fragility of legitimacy based on supposedly self-evident principles rather than on clear mandates. He and his fellow triumvirs, frightened by the slide toward republicanism, proclaimed the *principes,* or principles, successfully integrated into the constitution and argued for an immediate end to the Revolution, for the sake of stability.[18] Robespierre, Pétion, and all the left of the Patriot party regarded this newly found moderation as a proof of corruption and a betrayal of the very principles that had validated revolutionary action up to that moment. In the case of Lameth,

16. Alexandre de Lameth, *Histoire de l'Assemblée Constituante* (Paris, 1828), 2 vols.

17. Mona Ozouf has analyzed the way regeneration was understood by most deputies as a spontaneous self-evident process: "The Revolution only needs to emerge and the Frenchmen only need to want it. Nothing here that resembles a task. It was a matter of grace: all it took was to look at old institutions with a new, free gaze and they would vanish under one's eyes." Mona Ozouf, "La formation de l'homme nouveau," in *L'homme régénéré* (Paris, 1989), 116–57.

18. For details, see Ran Halévi, "Feuillants," in *Dictionnaire critique de la Révolution française,* ed. François Furet and Mona Ozouf, vol. 2 (Paris, 1992), 341–53. The triumvirs defended so passionately the middle of the road that some historians believe that they had in fact become *monarchiens* in all but name. See Robert Griffith, *Le Centre Perdu: Malouet et les monarchiens dans la Révolution française* (Grenoble, 1988)102.

being a noble did not help, as Marat made clear with his customary brutality as he affirmed that the Lameths were "still courtesans."[19] Marat certainly did not err on the side of objectivity, but this time Madame de Staël, whose views otherwise were poles apart from his, corroborated his verdict: "These elegant leaders of the popular party . . . brought the peculiar mannerisms of the court to the democratic cause and many deputies of the Third Estate were simultaneously amazed by their decorum and captivated by their democratic doctrines."[20] But did Lameth himself come to perceive any incompatibility between his identity as a nobleman and his responsibilities as a revolutionary leader? With his revolutionary legitimacy called into question, did Lameth reconsider his political engagement?

The answers to these questions are scattered in the *Histoire de l'Assemblée Constituante*. Identity issues did preoccupy Lameth, but in his telling there was never a need to choose between noble heritage and revolutionary convictions. Nor did he find any inconsistency in claiming legitimacy on both accounts. In recounting the events in which he played so prominent a role he reaffirmed his unwavering loyalty to the notion of merit that prompted him to join the Revolution and to the principles that motivated all his subsequent actions. The mix of personal merit and dedication to the new ideas acted like an anti-aristocratic cleanser, a *savonette à aristocrate* of sorts, for it had the power, or so Lameth reasoned, to wash away the stigma of privileges, which in turn afforded the nobles the opportunity to demonstrate anew their utility to the nation.

In spite of repeated protestations of objectivity, Lameth writes not as a historian but as a witness of history.[21] Like all memoirs, his *Histoire* is the projection of a personal destiny onto the canvas of history.[22] The main interest of this text resides in the tension between the announced intention (writing an objective account of events) and the ever-present commentary illustrating the reasonableness of his positions at the Assembly, especially when it came to allegations of anti-noble behavior. Soon after a profession of impartiality comes a bitter denunciation of the aristocracy, setting the tone and the narrative frame for the entire work. From the very beginning Lameth tried to settle his accounts with the conservative wing of his order: "The aristocracy is like the armored chariots of the ancients, she cuts to

19. As quoted in Michon, *Essai sur l'histoire du parti feuillant*, 89.
20. Madame de Staël, *Considérations sur la Révolution française*, ed. Jacques Godechot (Paris, 1983), 195.
21. Gusdorf, *Les écritures du moi: Lignes de vie 1*, 250.
22. Jean Tulard, preface in Fierro, *Bibliographie critique des mémoires sur la Révolution*, 7.

pieces anybody who fails to follow her lead. In her eyes, the old duc de La Rochefoucauld is guiltier than Robespierre. Robespierre follows his interest, the aristocrats would say, while the duc de La Rochefoucauld betrays his order. The former succumbed to a natural impulse, the latter deserted our cause."[23] Lameth evoked the familiar reproach, best expressed by Joseph de Maistre, that prorevolutionary nobles betrayed their order not only by siding with the enemy but by renouncing the intrinsic qualities of honor, duty, and wise leadership that had justified their dominant position in society. It was in this sense that Patriot nobles were more to blame than revolutionary leaders from the lower classes. The nobles had obligations commoners did not have and thus were not allowed to indulge their fancies; put it simply, they should have known better, wrote de Maistre: "certain actions which were nothing but blunders or follies when coming from an obscure person suddenly showered with limitless power could be regarded as felonies when they came from a bishop or a duke and peer."[24]

Proving that nobles like himself and the "old" duc de La Rochefoucauld were guilty of neither frivolity nor treachery emerges as one of the main objectives of Lameth's narrative, which shows that he wrote in part for an audience of *ci-devant* nobles. But he also had in mind a prorevolutionary audience, who may or may not have harbored doubts on his ability to combine nobility and revolutionary allegiance. In reaffirming his bond with the estate he was born into Lameth also needed to prove that belonging to the nobility was not an inherent character flaw and surely did not inhibit one's aspirations for radical change. Lameth's views are in this way part of the large corpus of self-reflective aristocratic memoirs produced after the Revolution. Although Lameth wrote his *Histoire* primarily as a political memoir meant to settle political scores, he used the possibilities of the *écriture du moi* to also reflect on, redefine, and ultimately defend certain aspects of nobility. Along the way he also brought to light what he held as the positive attributes of his order and endeavored to show the social utility of such qualities.

Speaking for what he called his "party" Lameth agreed wholeheartedly with the general Jacobin indictment against irresponsible, frivolous, and

23. Lameth, *Histoire de l'Assemblée Constituante,* "Avertissement," IV. Further in the *Histoire* Lameth reiterated his contempt for what he viewed as shortsighted criticism: "He who opposes the abuses by defending good principles is a traitor, he abandoned his order. He is in their eyes more of a renegade than the Christian who converted to the Muslim faith." *Histoire de l'Assemblée Constituante,* 1:152.

24. Joseph de Maistre, *Considérations sur la France* (Geneva, 1900), 28. Lameth does not mention de Maistre, but he was certainly aware of his dark view of the Revolution as divine punishment for precisely the kind of behavior and beliefs displayed by Lameth.

backward-looking nobles, but not, of course, with the charges of rabble-
rousing directed against himself. He did, however, like most other nobles,
identify a crucial role for the nobility and did not hesitate to point fingers
in his turn. First, Lameth thought it important to clarify the terms of the
discussion and establish the difference between nobles and aristocrats. Lameth
made full use of the anti-aristocratic rhetoric of revolutionary writings, but
he insisted on limiting the reference of the term "aristocrat." He argued
that the label aristocrat belonged to all those, mostly nobles indeed, who
remained attached to the old order of things and thus came across as hostile to
the wishes of the nation. The nobles capable of understanding the magnitude
of the national movement, on the other hand, naturally placed themselves
on the side of the nation and took the lead.[25] Such nobles formed the avant-
garde of what Lameth called the Popular party and could not, without
abuse, be counted as aristocrats, in light of their resolute and consistent
stand for changes meant to benefit the nation, not themselves.[26]

Lameth developed his thoughts on the nobility in the introduction to the
Histoire by answering the accusatory writings of former members of the
Constituent Assembly who had opposed the Patriot party, such as the marquis
de Ferrières and the abbé Montgaillard. The denunciations of the marquis de
Ferrières distressed Lameth the most because Ferrières, although voting consistently on the right, seemed closer to the "new ideas" than many other
aristocrats and could claim some familiarity with the principles advanced by
the Patriot party.[27] That's why the response to this particular critic became a
veritable analysis of the state of the nobility before the Revolution.

Writing from the opposite political side, Ferrières also claimed impartiality
as the main virtue of his narrative and sharply criticized the aristocratic faction.
"The Grands used simple *gentilshommes* to reach their own goals," wrote
Ferrières, and he named Polignac as the chief villain among court nobles.

25. On the changing meaning of the term "aristocrat," see Patrice Higonnet, "'Aristocrate,'
'Aristocratie': Language and Politics in the French Revolution," in *The French Revolution,
1789–1989: Two Hundred Years of Rethinking*, ed. Sandy Petrey (Lubbock, Tex., 1989), 47–66.
26. In a short pamphlet published in 1790 Alexandre's brother Charles de Lameth has clearly
identified this political division, that cut across noble–non-nobles categories: "From the beginning
we saw two well-defined parties: one formed of open supporters of despotism, that we called
aristocrats, the other drawing together those who fought for liberty, that we called patriots."
Charles de Lameth, *Attention* (1790).
27. By 1789 Ferrières had published several works that criticized the clergy in Voltairian
fashion: *Le Théisme ou l'Introduction générale à l'étude de la religion* (1785) and *Les voeux* (1787). He
was also the author of a book about women titled *La Femme dans l'ordre social et dans l'ordre de la
nature*. His library numbered 3,000 volumes in 1800 when he put together a catalogue.

But, and this was less easy for Lameth to accept, Ferrières also accused Patriot nobles of manipulating fellow deputies of the Second Estate. The marquis revisited the atmosphere of generous sacrifice of 4 August, in which he seemed to participate quite willingly at the time, only to blame Patriot nobles of thoughtlessly conspiring with the radical elements of the Third Estate to force the hand of provincial nobles. With hindsight, Ferrières believed that 4 August, with its veneer of generosity and union of purpose was nothing but the bait for further despoliations, especially painful being the abolition of noble titles: "It was only the beginning of the sacrifices forced upon the nobles and the clergy. But, so that they won't be frightened from the start by demands that were too obviously unjust, it has been cleverly calculated how to extend indefinitely the dispossessions they initially consented to out of fear or out of generosity."[28]

In their eagerness to destroy the nobility, the deputies gave the unseemly spectacle of a bunch of drunkards ready to destroy everything they could get their hands on. As for the "union of orders," Ferrières rather believed that the deputies of the Third Estate were amusing themselves at the expense of the nobles and "with feigned enthusiasm, encouraged the delirium." Finally, the gravest error of judgment at the time belonged to the women of the nobility who, unlike their severe cousins from the provinces, indulged in inconsequential games and never measured the seriousness of revolutionary actions: "The women of the court, sitting in front of their dresser, lounging in their soft boudoirs were saying: a revolution is a charming thing, let's make a revolution. All the pretensions of sensitivity, of virtue, of charity, of religion faded before their real nature: the masks fell; the moral ugliness of some of them came to the surface and true monsters appeared in plain sight."[29] With this grotesque depiction of what he took to be the atmosphere of smart enlightened salons on the eve of the Revolution Ferrières executed the *coup de grâce*: Patriot nobles were not only irresponsible and frivolous, but also spineless enough to allow themselves to be governed by the whims of manipulative women, a rather commonplace anti-aristocratic cliché, employed here selectively against prorevolutionary

28. *Mémoires du Marquis de Ferrières. Avec une notice sur sa vie, des notes et des éclaircissements historiques par M. Berville et Barrère* (Paris, 1821), 1:185.

29. *Mémoires du Marquis de Ferrières*, 1:41 and 59–60. In the second volume of the *Histoire* Lameth treated at length the role women of the nobility played in revolutionary events and clarified that the ladies were moved by the prevalent spirit of self-sacrifice and enthusiasm for the general good: "Their actions, under the circumstances, were perfectly in accord with public opinion." *Histoire de l'Assemblée Constituante*, 2:8.

nobles only. The frivolity of Patriot nobles, however, did not make them less vicious at the Assembly. Far from engaging in the dignified process of making laws for a free nation, the various factions traded insults to the point that "the virtuous man" concluded Ferrières, "isolated in the midst of this multitude, dared not put his trust in any of those who surrounded him."[30]

These were the kind of accusations that made Lameth's blood boil. Ferrières lacked de Maistre's visionary breadth, but he echoed the familiar charge of frivolity and self-destructive irresponsibility. In so doing, he debased the Revolution by lowering it to the level of a trivial parlor game run amok. Such thinking, retorted Lameth, was nothing but the result of faulty understanding of the Revolution and of the nobility at the same time. The courtiers, "full of prejudices" and selfish, lacked any aptitude for measuring the true greatness of the Revolution as manifestation of the general will. Unfortunately, they still had the power of dragging vulnerable provincials down to their level.

By way of explanation Lameth emphasized the rivalries within the second order, which gave courtesans ample means for flattery and corruption with the sad result that many otherwise decent individuals remained deaf to the call to sacrifice for the nation. Thus it was true, Lameth wrote, that Ferrières, as an honest and educated person, had the foresight to condemn the abuses of *les* grands; it was equally true, however, that he could scarcely avoid being dazzled and manipulated by the *les grands* himself:

> He was seen accusing the errors and the injustices of the high aristocracy who, aided by the influence of the princes, resisted with great energy the establishment of a constitutional regime; Ferrières's frankness, therefore, passed for impartiality and was bound to inspire confidence. Unfortunately, those who reasoned in this way had no knowledge of the times that preceded the Revolution. . . . M. de Ferrières belonged to the provincial nobility. . . . His reproaches against the first ranks of the nobility are often justified, but since jealousy rather than candor prompted them, they cannot be accepted without further examination.[31]

Lameth traced the root of Ferrières's blindness to the thorny issue of privileges and, like Sieyès before the Revolution, he saw privilege as the

30. *Mémoires du Marquis de Ferrières*, 1:209–10.
31. Lameth, *Histoire*, "Avertissement," VI–VII.

central liability of the second order. Sieyès had argued forcefully and successfully that privileges defined the nobility as a separate entity and in the
end rendered the entire Second Estate foreign to the nation.[32] Lameth did
not disagree but saw a fundamental distinction between those nobles who
accepted to be defined in terms of privileges and those who did not, a
distinction that Sieyès preferred to bypass. On this note Lameth launched
a Tocquevillian argument *avant la lettre,* showing how the pressures of the
centralized state resulted in the perversion of noble values. Privileges, while
exposing all nobles to popular wrath, were byproducts of despotism and had
served no other purpose but to corrupt the nobility and, indeed, cut it off
from the nation. Hence, the problem with the nobility was that, through
privileges and royal favor, it tied itself closely to despotism. Lameth reminded
his readers that despotism has been established in France only since Richelieu,
and it was not, then, the work of the original nobility of the realm.

Lameth believed, with Sieyès again, that privileges molded the nobility
into a strange category at the same time dependent on, and hostile to, the
crown. This untenable situation ended up fostering a mix of rebellion and
selfishness: impatient with the despotic power of courts and ministers the
nobles defied both, an allusion to the concerted resistance of *parlements*
and the two assemblies of notables to royal domestic policies right before
the Revolution. The ensuing crisis of the executive power functioned, in
Lameth's view, as a litmus test that separated nobles concerned with the
public good from those uniquely interested in maintaining their privileged status: "At that moment the great division took place between the
men who only backed personal advantages and those who looked out for
the interests of the public. Among the latter there were several nobles,
especially from ancient families; several magistrates and rich capitalists,
some because of their opinions others because they bore with great impa-
tience the social superiority of the first orders; four or five members of the
clergy, and all the parish priests, as most of them had only to gain from
the coming changes."[33]

Lameth highlighted selflessness, absence of private ambitions, and devotion
to the public interest as his and his friends' unique motivation for engaging in
the Revolution. In doing so he splashed with a dash of contempt the "rich

---

32. Abbé Sieyès, *Qu'est-ce que le tiers-état?* was first published in 1788. Sieyès was one of the
only five non-noble members of the Society of Thirty. For a close analysis of this pamphlet, its
scope and influence on revolutionary discourse, see William H. Sewell Jr., *A Rhetoric of Burgeois
Revolution: The Abbé Sieyes and "What Is the Third Estate?"* (Durham, N.C. 1994).

33. Lameth, *Histoire,* "Avertissement," XVII.

capitalists" and others who had something to gain from the changes, while nobles gained nothing other than seeing their hopes for public good materialized. For nobles, then, the Revolution was an act of heroism, bound to impose respect and admiration, as much as it was a political engagement.

Indeed, what Lameth was most fond of, what he recalled with special relish and pride, was the spirit of unity and heroic disinterestedness of the first year of the Constituent Assembly. Such sentiments speak to his allegiance to the political culture of 1789, to the new idea of polity forged at the Constituent Assembly. There, politics was not supposed to be based on competition and compromise but on the consensus that came from instant recognition of the public good and reflexive abandonment of private interests. To paraphrase Keith Baker's succinct formulation, this amounted to doing politics without passions, without factions, without conflicts, without fear; in short, politics without politics. Even when individual members acquired a taste for politics and wished to pursue ambitious careers, they felt pressured to refrain from such aspirations, deemed unworthy by the ethos of disinterestedness.[34] In this atmosphere of selfless devotion to the public good, the nobles who sacrificed their private interests came across, in Lameth's narrative, as the most dedicated revolutionaries of all, the best members of a new political order articulated through altruistic dedication to principles. The reason was precisely that, belonging to the Second Estate, they had something to lose; their engagement was superior because altruistic, unlike that of various other categories who stood to profit from their political choices. Nobles earned their revolutionary legitimacy from the willing surrender of financial and social advantages granted them by the existing order. Moreover, Lameth firmly believed that Patriot nobles derived an unspoken, but palpable, moral leverage from such selflessness, easily translated into credible claims to leadership.[35]

---

34. Keith Michael Baker, *Inventing the French Revolution: Essays on French Political Culture in the Eighteenth Century* (Cambridge, 1990), 196. On the slow gestation of the spirit of altruism and generosity as guidelines for good political behavior, see Michael Fitzsimmons, *The Remaking of France: The National Assembly and the Constitution of 1791* (Cambridge, 1994), 47–67. See also Timothy Tackett, *Becoming a Revolutionary: The Deputies of the National Assembly and the Emergence of Revolutionary Culture* (Princeton, 1996). Barry Shapiro has argued that the ethos of abnegation and self-sacrifice compelled members of the Assembly to accept Robespierre's motion on the noneligibility of the deputies, although many did so with regret because they harbored political ambitions of their own. Barry M. Shapiro, "Self-Sacrifice, Self-Interest or Self-Defense? The Constitutional Assembly and the Self-Denying Ordinance of May 1791," *French Historical Studies* 25 (2002): 625–56.

35. The high opinion Patriot nobles like Lameth formed about their political activism was shared by Madame de Staël, who said out loud what Lameth only suggested, namely, that Patriot nobles were "vastly superior" to the deputies of the Third Estate: "These nobles held

Lameth did not forget to note that the most engaged nobles were those of great ancestry (*ceux qui l'étaient depuis longtemps*) who needed neither royal favors nor legal privileges to shine and rise above the multitude. There was a certain grandeur, a mark of superiority, in embracing high-minded principles that required sacrifices, which is why Lameth reserved the bulk of his contempt for the nobles who showed no eagerness for such concessions.[36] Lameth considered it petty and unprincipled to cling to privileges, but in his earnest attachment to the Patriot cause, he believed it was equally petty to try to profit from as great an event as the Revolution. Patriot nobles distinguished themselves by not doing either, and this was their greatest claim to the esteem of their fellow citizens. This did not mean, however, that they were prepared to melt into the indistinctive category of plain citizenry. On the contrary, there were plenty of identifiable opportunities for nobles to rise above and take the lead once they understood that what they were leading was a national movement, not an occasional rebellion: "Under the circumstances, all that the men supposedly better endowed with enlightened ideas, talent and character, could have done was to lead, up to a point, the course of this irruption, more or less successfully, in order to make it serve the public interest as they conceived it."[37]

With this short paragraph Lameth sketched out the concept of nobility as he understood it. Nobles stood above the multitude because of their superiority in "*lumières, talents et caractère*" (knowledge, talent, and character), qualities reinforced by a history of service to the nation that the Revolution reaffirmed. That's why true nobles did not allow themselves to be tied to despotism, did not separate themselves from the nation, and did not hesitate to make personal sacrifices for the sake of the general interest. Thus, for instance, Lameth's determination to dissolve the *parlements* did not mean that he scorned all Old Regime institutions and ignored their past merits. He acknowledged the *parlements* as "*des corps jadis utiles*" ("institutions useful

---

no private interest in the cause they supported and, even more honorably, they preferred the generous principles of liberty to the advantages they enjoyed personally . . . in spite of their virtues and of their talents, their small numbers rendered these nobles powerless. *Considérations sur la Révolution française*, 215. See also Patrice Higonnet and Antoin Murphy, "Les Députés de la noblesse aux Etats-Généraux," *Revue d'Histoire Moderne et Contemporaine* 20 (1973): 230–47.

36. Madame de Staël also made the observation that provincial and petty nobles were a lot more attached to their privileges than the great families of old nobility: "The latter were sure of their continuous existence, guaranteed by history, but all these gentilshommes with titles only they knew about saw themselves in danger of losing distinctions that did not command anybody's respect anymore." *Considérations sur la Révolution française*, 145.

37. Lameth, *Histoire*, "Avertissment," VII.

in the past") but obsolete because unable to keep up with the requirements of the new constitutional order.[38] In this and other similar circumstances Lameth was, in fact, teaching by example. In his view, members of the Second Estate were duty bound to make the effort of selecting those elements of their heritage that could be harmonized with the Revolution and nobly sacrifice those that could not. An admiring and grateful nation would then call on these truly noble nobles to put their qualities in its service, which opened new avenues for advancement that more than compensated for the abandonment of a few relics from the past.

The service that nobles traditionally provided was, of course, leadership; it was no opportunism, as Lameth saw it, to note that the Revolution also needed leaders. This was therefore a unique chance, not to be missed, for nobles to prove themselves as valuable assets to the national movement against despotism. All nobles had to do was exercise their traditional calling for leadership while putting into practice the principles so many of them claimed to hold in high esteem. In Lameth's telling, the aspiration toward merit, the ideas of the Enlightenment (his beloved *principes*), and the profound, though never directly expressed, belief in the natural superiority of the nobility came together to form a new representative type of elite. The Patriot noble portrayed in his narrative impresses as a natural leader dedicated solely to the public good, one who rises above inherited prejudices and self-interest, but also above the shapeless masses, to guide the nation toward an enlightened and well-ordered future. Such nobles expected that a nation of free citizens would freely put the reins of leadership in their hands, hence their profound disappointment and sense of injustice when this happy scenario did not materialize.[39] Furthermore, Lameth pointedly emphasized that patriotic nobles of the kind he described had nothing in common with the opportunistic rabble-rousers coming, incidentally, from the Third not the Second Estate. For this reason he dismissed Ferrières's suggestion of a certain similarity of positions between himself and Robespierre (who, unlike the triumvirs, deserved to be called a *révolutionnaire*). True, Robespierre was a member of the same deputation as Charles de Lameth,

---

38. A.P., IX, 664.

39. Lameth could find support for this line of thinking in the bluntest anti-aristocrat critic of all, since Sieyès himself predicted a brilliant future to well-intentioned nobles: "If the nation will achieve its freedom she will turn, I have no doubts about it, toward those patriotic authors of the two first orders who, as the first to abjure old errors, preferred the principles of universal justice to the murderous plots of corporate interests against the national interest." *Que'est-ce que le tiers-états?* (Paris, 1982), 54.

however: "all throughout the Assembly the most determined opposition existed and was daily manifested between that audacious leveler [Robespierre] and the Lameth brothers and Mirabeau, who constantly defended the constitutional monarchy."[40]

Reform, rather than Revolution, and constitutional monarchy, rather than a democratic republic, was the Patriot nobles' vision for the nation, Lameth maintained. It was to this ideal of public good that they, as dignified rulers, made exemplary personal sacrifices. The violent acts of the Revolution and the slip into republicanism and democracy violated both their ethics and their politics. But since Lameth was so keen on exculpating Patriot nobles while continuously lauding their prorevolutionary stand, he could not avoid the question of who was responsible for such colossal blunders if not the self-appointed leaders of the Popular party. Lameth's answer consisted in turning the tables, whereby he pointed the finger of blame against the very critics who showered him and his friends with opprobrium. The central message of his work is that the stubborn aristocratic opposition to the Revolution provoked the much-regretted excesses and led to the calamitous situation in which the entire nobility found itself.

The traitors were the real aristocrats who did not try to preserve the qualities that made a noble noble, but rather the privileges that made the nobility the object of popular hatred and scorn. Not engagement with the Revolution but, on the contrary, resistance to the Revolution provoked the exasperation of the masses and forced the radicalization of revolutionary leaders, which in time resulted in the catastrophic violence that destroyed the nobility and nearly destroyed the Revolution itself. In relating the events of the Constituent Assembly, Lameth answered his opponents' charges of conspiracy against the nobility by charging other nobles with conspiracy against the Revolution, the nobility, and the monarchy alike. The explanatory model of the conspiracy, so widely employed at the Constituent Assembly, extended to intra-noble disputes as well.[41]

The accusation of right-wing aristocratic conspiracy hardens throughout the narrative of the *Histoire,* which is mostly a verbatim reproduction of speeches by Lameth and other deputies in the Assembly, enriched with occasional annotations. All of Lameth's actions and positions are explained

40. Lameth, *Histoire,* 1:193. It is a telling sign of Lameth's eagerness to dissociate himself from Jacobins like Robespierre that he invoked Mirabeau to whose downfall he had greatly contributed.

41. Timothy Tackett, "Conspiracy Obsession in a Time of Revolution," *American Historical Review* 105:3 (June 2000): 691–713.

therein in terms of general interest, all his opponents' positions in terms of private interest, echoing his speeches during the sessions. Likewise, the comments on the nobility only reinforce the analysis of the introduction, namely, that unreformed aristocrats bore the responsibility for all that went wrong, but that the blame should not extend to the entire noble class: "All the historians, the poets, and the writers who discussed matters of morality directed their attacks against the very dangerous and pernicious class of courtesans. . . . No wonder then that reproaches against this class are frequent in the present work; but justice demands that these reproaches not be applied, not only to the entire nobility, but even not to the majority of those nobles who frequented the court."[42]

In keeping with the portrayal, drawn in the introduction, of a patriotic and engaged nobility, Lameth frequently draws attention to the good deeds performed by nobles in the early stages of the Revolution. Patriot nobles like the duc de La Rochefoucauld-Liancourt, for instance, averted the worst by convincing the king that the Revolution was indeed a national movement and not a plot, as his courtiers were telling him. It was Talleyrand, a member of the nobility and also of the high clergy, who called for the bold measure of confiscating the property of the clergy in the name of the general interest, a motion carried through by other nobles, such as the duc de La Rochefoucauld, who went one step further and called for the suppression of religious orders.[43] Similarly, well-intentioned nobles and clergy first gave the example of correct understanding of the general interest by renouncing their own privileges on the night of 4 August in a "cascade of sacrifices." Lameth only regretted that Noailles, a *cadet* with little fortune to give up, stole the thunder from the duc d'Aiguillon, for he thought that the disinterestedness of d'Aiguillon, the richest seigneur in France after the king, would have made a deeper impression on the people.[44]

In stark opposition to all these good deeds stood the activities of aristocrats on the right, a symmetry often called to mind to confirm Lameth's thesis of aristocratic opposition as the root cause of all that went wrong in the Revolution: "The nobility and the clergy, bold enough to believe they had the power to stop a movement whose entire force they failed to calculate,

---

42. Lameth, *Histoire*, 1:325.

43. "One recognizes in the work of M. de Talleyrand the progress of philosophical ideas. It is obvious that as a man and as a citizen he is profoundly convinced of the danger posed by privileges." *Histoire de l'Assemblée Constituante*, 1:151.

44. Ibid., 1:96–97.

put only obstacles against the torrent; they inflamed the situation and it [the torrent] broke all the dams vainly erected in its way. The deputies came to Versailles with the sole intent of reforming abuses; by calling the troops in to prop up the government and by *forcing the representatives of the nation to look out for their own security, France was precipitated into a revolution.*"[45]

The aristocrats, Lameth demonstrated again and again, not the engaged Patriot nobles, and even less the firebrands of the Third Estate, had to assume responsibility for the deplorable shift from reform to revolution, meaning from a rational and judicious movement to a violent and uncontrollable one. Take the disruptions of the *journées révolutionnaires,* for instance. After the night of 4 August, Lameth noted, many nobles lost heart (a point confirmed, coincidentally, by marquis de Ferrières's memoirs) and perhaps even regretted what they had done. In their distress, Lameth believed, such nobles thought nothing about inciting the masses to violence for the purpose of turning back the entire work of the Assembly: "A dizziness descended over the minds of the leaders of the aristocratic party and they flattered themselves with the thought that by means of a few manipulations, of the sort they had managed to do in the capital, and with the support of the personal guard and of the Flanders regiment, they would be able to provoke a *journée* and thus intimidate or maybe even dissolve the National Assembly."[46]

It all went downhill from there: the king lost prestige, the crowd escaped control by rational forces, mob instincts came to dominate politics, demagoguery replaced good thinking, and in the end the monarchy itself was overthrown. For Lameth, it was important to keep in mind that these disorders were unleashed by the aristocracy, who must accept all the blame for revolutionary violence and disruption: "We saw the sad results of these vain projects, which compromised the majesty and the security of the king and of the representatives of the nation at the same time. . . . It was from that time on that was put in motion the system of cunning and corruption that caused so many disorders and later brought about, in the midst of the storm, the overthrow of the throne."[47]

The vigorous scheming and plotting of the aristocracy created the conditions that allowed the Jacobins and their brand of revolutionary extremism to strive. Even after the abolition of feudalism and the promulgation of the

45. Ibid., 1:274 (emphasis added).

46. Ibid., 1:275.

47. Ibid., 1:276. Here Lameth condemns conservative nobles for the October Days; most aristocratic memoirs blame Patriot nobles like Lameth for the event.

Declaration of the Rights of Man and Citizen, the aristocracy was slow to disappear as a significant political force. On the contrary, aristocrats took it upon themselves to frustrate the work of the committees in the futile hope of turning back the wheels of history. When the aristocracy finally did disappear, it left the legacy of a strong and intransigent Jacobin faction which took the Revolution on the disastrous path of violence and republicanism. In the end the aristocracy did disappear, but not before grievously damaging the principles of 1789 and destroying the lives of those, mostly Patriot nobles, who promoted them.[48]

Lameth's work mirrors the narrative pattern of most other aristocratic memoirs in casting the nobility in the central role, positive or negative, depending on the author's point of view, in the unfolding of events. Lameth filled both the best and the worst roles with nobles. In his history of the Revolution the nobility determined the course of the events, either by leading the "torrent" in the right direction or, on the contrary, by steering it toward violence and destruction. The popular journalists and revolutionary leaders, the radical deputies, the Robespierres and the Marats, profited from circumstances created by irresponsible antirevolutionary nobles. Paradoxically, through the excessive blaming of the nobility, Lameth ended up agreeing with Joseph de Maistre who also considered the nobility the main guilty party, albeit for diametrically opposed reasons, that is, for flirting with the Revolution at all. The radical reformer Lameth and the arch-conservative de Maistre shared the same belief in the superior force of members of the nobility to initiate and direct major events.

Finally, there is in Lameth's *Histoire* a certain auctorial voice that echoes the tone of all memoirs written by nobles. The familiarity with which he recalls various meetings of like-minded nobles organized far away from the noise of the Assembly, the careful mentioning of titles, the fond description of intimate dinners with the duc de La Rochefoucauld, all give his narrative an unmistakably aristocratic *air de famille*. Writing in the 1820s, Lameth did not conceal his nostalgia for a bygone era of civilized debate inherited from

---

48. Lameth's views on the political muscle flexed by the aristocracy way beyond the night of 4 August confirm Timothy Tackett's conclusions that aristocrats on the right continued to undermine the work of the Assembly throughout 1790, which partly explains the radicalization of the left. Timothy Tackett, "Nobles and Third Estate in the Revolutionary Dynamic of the National Assembly, 1789–1790" in *The French Revolution: Recent Debates and New Controversies,* ed. Gary Kates (London, 1998), 192–236. On the political activities of the aristocratic faction during the National Assembly and beyond, see Jacques de Saint-Victor, *La Chute des Aristocrates, 1787–1792: La Naissance de la Droite* (Paris, 1992).

the republic of letters and which the Bourbon Chamber sorely lacked: "At the Constituent Assembly it seldom happened that a member launched an opinion from the podium without having it submitted to the judgment of some of the colleagues attached to the same principles as himself. During these useful conversations the proposal conceived by the author was discussed, considered on all its facets, its consequences were weighed with scrupulous attention. We sought to anticipate the objections of our adversaries and we distributed openly among ourselves the weapons which were to insure the happy resolution of the combat."[49]

The fondness with which Lameth invoked elements of the *douceur de vivre* is part of what Henri Rossi described as the "swan song" of a class in decline. The excitement of the Revolution did not make him forget that he had acquired his political education in salons, Masonic lodges, and such exclusive clubs as the Society of Thirty. So he praised the prerevolutionary "English" mores of the high society for teaching nobles and non-nobles to treat each other politely and according to merit: "one of the first articles of the regulations was to admit the elite of all classes of citizens."[50] As in all the aristocratic memoirs, the world evoked in Lameth's *Histoire* seems a very special place, a place where polite debate, generous sentiments, elegant manners, and daring new ideas combined to draw a luminous vision for the future, the vision that sent nobles like himself to the Constituent Assembly. From this point of view, there was something reassuringly familiar in the forms of sociability practiced at the Assembly. Deputies of the nobility and of the Third Estate treated each other with deference as members of the same "club" of leaders of the new nation, and behavior typical of the nobility, from polite forms of address to duels, quickly became the norm for all members of the Assembly. Nobles were only asked to share the burden of leadership with the cream of the Third Estate, which in 1789 seemed reasonable to all but the most conservative aristocrats on the right. For a short while it seemed entirely possible to be a gentleman and a revolutionary at the same time.[51]

Alexandre de Lameth had warned his readers from the very first page that his *Histoire de l'Assemblée Constituante* was part memoir and part history. The history examines the genesis, the initial success, and the ultimate defeat

---

49. Lameth, *Histoire*, 1:261.

50. Ibid., 2:6.

51. See the incisive remarks by Edna Hindie Lemay, *La vie quotidienne des députés aux Etats-Généraux 1789* (Paris, 1987), 94–105, and Patrice Gueniffey, *La Politique de la Terreur: essai sur la violence révolutionnaire, 1789–1794* (Paris, 2000), 109.

of constitutional principles championed by the triumvirs and their allies. The memoir buried within the historical narrative portrays the ambiguities and aspirations of those nobles who joined and sought to lead the Revolution. Against the Jacobins' accusations of *aristocracism* Lameth marshaled the triumvirs' many interventions at the Assembly, their voting record, activities, and sacrifices, and most of the time he let the facts speak for themselves. Against parallel insinuations of treason to the nobility Lameth tried to reformulate the notion of nobility in cultural rather than legal terms. His is a plea for living with, not against, the times. For this he found it desirable and necessary to abandon the legal notion of Second Estate, with its cohort of privileges and theories of difference. Once this outdated ballast was thrown overboard, the nobility could shine again and prove its suitability for leadership. Lameth wished to continue to belong to a regenerated nobility, cleansed of corporate privileges but proud of the ancient virtues of courage, sacrifice, patriotism, and service to the state.

More important, Lameth believed that these genuine qualities resonated with the new principles of equality, respect for property, and constitutional freedoms—so much so that nobles made ideal potential leaders in the new order of things. In other words, if nobles were astute enough to give up willingly and enthusiastically their privileges, they became free to compete as individuals in the race for leadership positions, as demanded by the revolutionary principle of open access to offices. The moral value most prized by the Revolution, selfless dedication to the cause, constituted an invaluable source of legitimacy on which nobles could draw in order to obtain leadership positions and generally maintain their preeminence in society. While Lameth believed that the nobility could not and should not form a corps apart, he had little doubt that nobles would eventually climb the ladder and form the upper crust of the new social order. Anchored by principles and merit, this was a legitimate move from the top of the Old Regime to the top of the new one. If the rich possibilities the Revolution kept in store for politically aware nobles never materialized, at fault was a foolish attachment to abhorrent privileges incompatible with the ethics of the Revolution, the intrigues of some and the arrogance of others, in short, the despicable process which turned the nobility into an aristocracy:

> It is undeniable that the generous and versatile resolution adopted then [on 4 August] by the nobles and the clergy earned them the public gratitude, as founders of a system that could well have passed

for freedom in comparison with the arbitrary regime that has oppressed us for so long. Thanks to important sacrifices, dictated by a wise political thinking, a great deal of consideration was given to a chamber of peers, composed of all the prominent personalities of France, of all backgrounds. In truth, the provincial nobility was entirely excluded from this first corps of the state; but the abandonment of its privileges and its siding with the new regime placed it at the head of the middle classes, always the most influential part of civilized nations, and opened to its members the door to the elective chamber, side by side with the notables of the Third Estate.[52]

There was no historical fatality or providential wrath: the Revolution had crushed the nobility not because the "torrent" could not be mastered but because too many nobles made too many bad choices: "it is to false ideas, to a misplaced stubbornness and to its reckless hostility that the nobility owes the loss of its influence, forever destroyed with help from the unfathomable error of the emigration."[53] The road not taken was the road of bold emancipation from the Old Regime toward a promising fresh start in the new one where nobles could have easily found their places at the top of the mixed elite forged by the Revolution. One can guess that the emigration had been so much more painful for Lameth and other like-minded nobles since they believed that their bright prospects for the future had been wrecked by their fellow nobles, their evil twins. This explains why the only truly irredeemable characters in this narrative are those backward-looking, devious, and obtuse members of the Second Estate, richly deserving of the moniker *aristocrate*, with all its negative connotations.

In conclusion, Lameth communicated to his readers his profound conviction that a regenerated nobility, proud of some of its ancestral attributes but unburdened by nostalgia, stood an excellent chance of being welcomed into the elite of the new social order. It was a straightforward enough process: ideas and principles had the power of making the nobles fit for the new era of civil equality, while targeted sacrifices earned them precious political legitimacy. To Lameth's chagrin, most of his fellow nobles failed to understand the difference between sacrifice and surrender, and simply refused to see the path toward their own salvation. To the end of his life Lameth

52. Lameth, *Histoire,* 2:2.
53. Ibid., 2:3.

remained persuaded that the nobility had squandered a unique historical opportunity. His remarks convey his vision of what the future might have been if, as he saw it, more nobles had resolved to act boldly and heroically, in other words, if they resolved to act more like nobles and less like aristocrats.

IV

NOBILITY AND MODERNITY

I I

FRENCH NOBLES AND THE HISTORIANS, 1820–1960

Jonathan Dewald

In this essay I will say little about real-life nobles or about the real functioning of Old Regime society. Instead, I will address a series of questions about how historians have approached the French nobility and about how these approaches have fitted into larger patterns in the historians' own culture. Such questions seem worth raising because novel ideas about the nobility have counted among the distinctive characteristics of historical writing since World War II. Whereas earlier scholarship stressed the group's failures to adapt to social change and its consequent decline, since 1960 historians have drawn increasing attention to nobles' successes and to the character-istics they shared with other groups. Nobles in Old Regime France, it is now generally agreed, were no less capitalistic than bourgeois, and they enjoyed only slightly more extensive privileges; they served the monarchical state willingly and participated fully in their society's intellectual life—and many of them welcomed the Revolution of 1789 as a chance to implement their liberal views of social improvement. Despite short-term ups and downs, during the century before 1789 they were in the main a rising social class rather than one in decline.

What has it meant for historians thus to relabel the Old Regime's ruling class a leading participant in processes of political and social modernization, rather than their principal victim? In exploring this question, I will leave aside the new facts and documents that have helped produce the revolution in nobiliar studies, not because they seem to me unimportant, but because of my adherence to the truism that historical facts acquire their significance only within larger systems of thinking. In the French case, I will argue here, before 1960 those larger systems rendered nobles at once central and invisible. On the one hand, nobles and the concepts surrounding nobility were deeply embedded in nineteenth- and early twentieth-century thought. To both professional historians and intellectuals writing after the Revolution, with fears of new revolutions much on their minds, the Old Regime nobility could not remain merely a topic for specialized historical investigation. In addition, many of the classics of French literary culture tended to depict aristocratic doings, so that the period's most important literary debates also raised issues about nobles and their place in French life. At the same time, however, the meanings that historians and other writers assigned the group were contradictory and shifting. Elsewhere in Europe, nobles might stand as symbols of conservative values and of national traditions. These ideas appealed to some French writers, but more typically they attached the traditions of national identity to the monarchy and presented its relation to the nobles as mainly hostile, dominated by a long struggle to eliminate the nobles' powers and lawless excesses. Celebrating the kings' role in French society necessarily raised questions about the nobility's opposition to the work of centralization, and nobles tended to become troubling symbols of a wider rebelliousness. They symbolized other failures to adapt to the conditions of modern life as well. For intellectuals seeking to understand the emergence of modern France, they ultimately had only negative meaning, as an embodiment of the social qualities that had to be overcome in the process of political and economic modernization.

The extent of the nobles' disappearance from modern French historical thought deserves emphasis: despite some exceptions, until the 1980s they played a strikingly small role in academic writing about the early modern period.[1] This fact is especially striking given the French historical profession's abundant research, conceptual daring, and wide influence from the 1920s onward. In this domain, intellectual influences tended to move eastward across the Atlantic, with French scholars eventually taking up themes first developed by American and British colleagues. Many of the elements that dominate contemporary visions of the nobility can be traced to the American Robert Forster's *Nobility of Toulouse in the Eighteenth Century,*

---

1. In this respect histories of the Old Regime contrast dramatically with those of the Middle Ages; French medievalists have given particular attention to the aristocracy.

which appeared in 1960.[2] Forster's book argued for the nobility's essential modernity. Feudalism (he found) meant little to most nobles. They had few seigneurial powers, and only about 8 percent of their income came from feudal rents; like contemporary English gentlemen, their money came from the grain and other products that their farms produced. They thought as capitalists, managing their farms for maximum profit and knowing that profit would come from the marketplace, not from the exercise of medieval powers. As such, over the eighteenth century they were a rising, not a falling class. They rose the more easily in that they enjoyed close relations with the royal administration, which assisted aristocratic families often and generously.

It is a suggestive footnote in publishing history that Forster's book appeared next to Robert Fogel's disruptive study of American railways, another Johns Hopkins dissertation, in the series "Johns Hopkins University Studies in Historical and Political Science."[3] Like Fogel's study, *Nobility of Toulouse* offered an early example of the quantitative approaches that would dominate American historical writing in the 1960s and 1970s. This new quantitative history, both works suggested, would have a skeptical, nominalist thrust, undermining certainties about how social categories corresponded to the realities they meant to describe and jumbling distinctions that had previously organized much historical writing—and pushing historical writing toward conclusions that had unsettling political overtones as well. Unlike Fogel's work, whose paradoxical arguments provoked immediate protests, Forster's book did not attract much notice on its appearance; there was no review, for instance, in the *Journal of Modern History,* and no debate in the middle-brow press, though there was a long and thoughtful review in the *Annales.* But Forster's book soon received attention from other historians, and in retrospect it can be seen to have inaugurated a rapid and surprisingly complete historiographical revolution. In 1964, Alfred Cobban referred warmly to it as one basis for his own revisionist views on the French

2. Forster, *The Nobility of Toulouse in the Eighteenth Century* (Baltimore, 1960). Other influences should also be noted: J. H. Hexter, whose collected essays appeared a year later and had less to say about the French case, argued forcefully for the continuing wealth, political influence, and sound educations of the nobility (Hexter, *Reappraisals in History* [Evanston, 1961]); R. R. Palmer also drew attention to the political and economic health of the eighteenth-century nobility and to similarities between French and British nobles, in contrast to a long historiographical tradition stressing their differences (Palmer, *The Age of the Democratic Revolution: A Political History of Europe and America, 1760–1800* [Princeton, 1959]).

3. Robert Fogel, *The Union Pacific Railroad: A Case Study in Premature Enterprise* (Baltimore, 1960).

Revolution. In the mid-1970s, François Furet and Guy Chaussinand-Nogaret presented similar ideas in France, and by the 1980s these views had become established orthodoxy. Other orthodoxies have clustered around them. In the 1980s, William Beik, James Collins, Roger Mettam, and others suggested that absolutist governments of the seventeenth century worked in close partnership with the nobility, rather than seeking to push it from power or domesticate it. Similarly, Norbert Elias's work on court society—written in the late 1930s but coming to historians' notice only after its republication in 1969—has drawn attention to the aristocracy's role in shaping modern values and modes of behavior.[4] Conversely, among the wave of great French regional studies from the 1960s, only Jean Meyer's addressed the nobility directly; it is scarcely visible in the great studies by Pierre Goubert, Emmanuel Le Roy Ladurie, Pierre Deyon, and others.[5]

To some extent, this neglect can be attributed to the political culture of French academia and notably to French academic Marxism during the post–World War II era. During these years French intellectuals were especially unsympathetic to the idea of a leisured and privileged class that believed itself entitled to rule. Jean-Paul Sartre, the iconic intellectual of the era, expressed this view with particular force in 1960: social differentiation "occurs in a society whose members produce always *a little less* than is necessary for the whole, so that the constitution of an unproductive group has for its condition the undernourishment of all, and that one of its functions is to select those who are to be eliminated. . . . The unproductive groups, always in danger of being liquidated because they are the absolutely Other . . . internalize this ambivalent otherness and comport themselves vis-à-vis the individuals either as though they were Other than man (but positively, like Gods), or as though they were the only men in the midst of another species."[6] Sartre's language echoes that of the abbé Sieyès, but it also parallels the neo-Malthusian interpretations that dominated postwar social history in France. Pierre Goubert, among others, sought to show that early modern France was indeed a society that produced less than it needed, and he sought to document the

4. A history discussed in Roger Chartier, *On the Edge of the Cliff: History, Language, and Practices* (Baltimore, 1997), 107–23.

5. Pierre Goubert, *Beauvais et le Beauvaisis de 1600 à 1730; contribution à l'histoire sociale de la France du XVIIe siècle* (Paris, 1960); Emmanuel Le Roy Ladurie, *Les paysans de Languedoc* (Paris, 1966); Pierre Deyon, *Amiens, capitale provinciale: étude sur la société urbaine au 17e siècle* (Paris-The Hague, 1967); Jean Meyer, *La noblesse de Bretagne au XVIIIe siècle*, 2 vols. (Paris, 1966).

6. From *Critique de la raison dialectique*, cited by G. Lichtheim, "Sartre, Marxism and History," *History and Theory* 3:2 (1963): 222–46, 235.

consequences: abundance for some meant starvation for others.[7] From such a perspective, it would seem, few historians could think seriously about nobles, and especially few could attempt a sympathetic reconstruction of their motives and potential contribution to society; Richard Cobb described Georges Lefebvre's "lack of understanding of the nobility" as bound up with a larger inability to understand the Old Regime's culture.[8] Conversely, the more sympathetic treatments of nobility that have come out since 1970 seem to show the influence of French historians' retreat from Marxism as a guide to either contemporary politics or historical research.[9]

But Marxism's declining intellectual appeal over the past generation does not fully suffice to explain the contemporaneous rise of nobiliar studies or the character that those studies have taken. For one thing, strong and explicit Marxist commitments have proven no barrier to studying the nobility and seem even to have encouraged some historians in sympathetic interest in the subject. Jean Nicolas's *La Savoie au dix-huitième siècle* was written from an explicitly Marxist perspective, and its author moved directly from that project to study working-class protest movements.[10] Lawrence Stone's *Crisis of the Aristocracy* likewise came out of the Marxist historical tradition, indeed, was undertaken in defense of that tradition.[11] Nor conversely were American historians of France especially hostile to Marxist analyses during the 1950s and 1960s. Postwar Anglo-American historians accorded immense respect to the work of Lefebvre, Albert Soboul, and other Marxist scholars. Lefebvre himself was invited to supply both an opening benediction to the newly founded *French Historical Studies,* in 1958, and the journal's first substantive article; in the same year, Richard Cobb (whose views were about to change dramatically) wrote in the *Journal of Modern History* that "any French specialist of the Revolution would accept the general premises laid down by MM. Lefebvre and Labrousse" about the nature of social structure.[12] Admiration of this sort ebbed after 1964, but interest in the alternative Marxism represented by E. P. Thompson rose to fill some of the gap thus created. Marxism's

7. See Goubert, *Beauvais et le Beauvaisis.*

8. Richard Cobb, *A Second Identity: Essays on France and French History* (London, 1969), 99.

9. For a compelling instance of this retreat, see Emmanuel Le Roy Ladurie, *Paris-Montpellier: P.C.-P.S.U., 1945–1963* (Paris, 1982).

10. Jean Nicolas, *La Savoie au 18e siècle: noblesse et bourgeoisie,* 2 vols. (Paris, 1978); Jean Nicolas, ed., *Mouvements populaires et conscience sociale, XVIe-XIXe siècles* (Paris, 1985). It is relevant to the argument that follows that eighteenth-century Savoy was not part of the French monarchy.

11. Lawrence Stone, *The Crisis of the Aristocracy, 1558–1641* (Oxford, 1965).

12. Richard Cobb, "The Era of the French Revolution: Some Comments on Opportunities for Research and Writing," *Journal of Modern History* 30:2 (June 1958): 118–30, 119.

changing fortunes, it appears, offer only a partial explanation for changing approaches to the nobility, either in France or in the United States.

Having pushed Marxism somewhat to the margins of this intellectual history, we might turn to a second line of explanation, resting on the nobility's real place in modern French society. Despite signs of the "persistence of the Old Regime,"[13] nobles held a weak position in nineteenth- and twentieth-century France in comparison with their prominence elsewhere in Europe. One element of weakness was the legal anarchy that surrounded their status. The Constituent Assembly abolished all titles in 1790, but after 1800 governmental policies oscillated. Napoleon reintroduced some of the terminology of nobility with his establishment of the Legion of Honor in 1802. There followed the creation of princes of the Empire in 1806, and finally, in 1808, the establishment of an imperial aristocracy—while at the same time all other claims to nobility, including the claim to have held noble status under the Old Regime, were declared illegal. The Bourbons' return in 1814 brought an ambiguous restoration of nobility: the Charter declared that "the former *noblesse* takes up again its titles; the new keeps its own." These privileges were also declared to confer no concrete advantages whatsoever, but the Restoration did establish a Chamber of Peers, numbering 184 nobles in 1814, expanding to 365 by the end of the regime, and it gave titled nobles real legislative power. The institution survived the Revolution of 1830, but its existence was debated from the outset: in 1831 the creation of hereditary peerages was abolished, and there was debate about the propriety of the government controlling false claims to nobility. Nobility itself was again outlawed in 1848, but Napoleon III restored it in 1852.

All of this legislation remained intact through the Third Republic—leaving in practice a confusion of usurped and authentic titles, uncontrolled by state authority and (with the disappearance of the Chamber of Peers in 1848) disconnected from any privileges or powers. Contemporaries believed that false claims to nobility were rising, particularly through the assumption of the *particule* "de" as part of a name, a practice that continued throughout the Third Republic. Napoleon III sought to control the process by fining unauthorized claims to nobility, but this had little effect, especially given the nineteenth century's profusion of periodical literature; "the great plague of the nineteenth century has been the proliferation of armorials," wrote an angry nobleman in 1939, adding that "this orgy of fantastical genealogies"

13. Arno J. Mayer, *The Persistence of the Old Regime: Europe to the Great War* (New York, 1981).

continued in his own time.[14] But such self-ennoblements apparently did not produce numerical growth in the order, partly because the nineteenth century's practices radically changed the nobility's structure. Formal titles became far more frequent during the nineteenth century than they had been during the Old Regime, aided by the altogether new practice of "decrescendo," by which the sons of a count, for instance, assumed the title viscount. Conversely, mere country gentlemen found themselves in a much more difficult situation, lacking clear claims to special status, and unable to claim higher rank without appearing ridiculous.

As the century progressed, then, nobility increasingly meant titled nobility, often with plutocratic connections; grandeur at the top of the order tended to go with decay at the bottom. In these circumstances, all numerical estimates were approximate, indeed acknowledged to be fictitious, but the numbers proposed were very low. On the eve of World War I, one authority claimed that there were only 5,000 noble families in France.[15] But in contrast to the Old Regime, when the vast majority of nobles had been undistinguished country gentlemen, these predominantly titled families were an ostentatious presence in French society, and new institutions added to their prominence: from 1815 through 1848, the Chamber of Peers, which gave them a political voice that they had not had during the Old Regime; the Jockey Club, founded in 1833, which explicitly sought nobles as members; even the Automobile Club, founded in 1895.[16] All of this might have very little meaning to outsiders. Proust's baron de Charlus uses his title to denote his family's very ancient origins; but at a luncheon party his wealthy bourgeois hosts understand nothing of this status and assume that a local marquis (his family ennobled only under Louis XIV) ranks more highly than a baron. The aristocratic world and its forms of distinction, so the novel suggests, were now little known to outsiders, indeed incomprehensible except to those directly concerned with living them out. Nobles themselves survived, but plenty of evidence suggests their loss of vitality as a group.

But—as both literary critics and historians have observed—the socially marginal may be symbolically central, and their small numbers did not prevent

---

14. Martial Pradal de Lamase, "L'idée de noblesse en France," *Mercure de France* 294:989 (1 September 1939): 322. My overview here of nineteenth-century practices regarding nobility is taken partly from this article; see also the excellent work of David Higgs, *Nobles in Nineteenth-Century France: The Practice of Inegalitarianism* (Baltimore, 1987).

15. Monique de Saint Martin, *L'espace de la noblesse* (Paris, 1993), 13.

16. Ibid., 147

the nobility from playing a large role in nineteenth-century imaginations.[17] As an illustration of both this centrality and the complexities that attended it, we may turn to one of the nineteenth century's best-known aristocrats, the count of Monte Cristo. Set in the France of 1838, Alexandre Dumas's novel abounds in aristocratic titles and doings. Alongside the count himself, its cast of principal characters consists of the count, countess, and viscount of Morcerf, the baron de Danglars, and monsieur de Villefort; many of the secondary figures carry titles as well. The characters refer often to military action: two have fought in Algeria, and the impact of the Napoleonic wars continues to resonate. Questions of honor arise often and often lead to dueling; the count himself proclaims that he will die if he fails to avenge a public insult, by killing the man who insulted him. Yet despite these surface trappings, the novel consistently undercuts the idea of aristocracy itself. "'He is undoubtedly some noble lord,'" a character says of the count, to the general agreement of others who have witnessed his manners and personal qualities. But of course the count is nothing of the kind. He is an altogether self-made man who happens to have a great deal of money, and he presents himself as such to his friends; "'I should never have passed myself off as a great nobleman,'" he tells one of them, "'were it not that I was repeatedly told this was absolutely necessary for anyone who travels a lot.'" The count de Morcerf, a successful military man, claims to be from "'one of the oldest families in the south of France'" and has the genealogies to prove it, but he is in fact another self-invented figure, a onetime fisherman who has made his way in the world through scheming and betrayal. Yet in a final twist, Morcerf's son—like Monte Cristo himself—displays a stereotypical aristocratic bravado and an intense commitment to maintaining his own honor; at the end of the novel he too embarks on a military career, to atone for his father's disgrace. Conversely, Maximilien Morel, the son of a Marseillais businessman who makes no claim to aristocratic title, embodies military valor and indifference to monetary gain.[18] *The Count of Monte Cristo* thus presents an aristocratic society from which authentic nobles are mostly absent. Aristocratic values and practices remain vigorous, but they have only weak connections to aristocratic persons—whose claims to ancient lineage in any case are usually fictional.

17. Judith Walkowitz, *City of Dreadful Delight: Narratives of Sexual Danger in Late-Victorian London* (Chicago, 1992); Peter Stallybrass and Allon White, *The Politics and Poetics of Transgression* (Ithaca, 1986).

18. Alexandre Dumas, *The Count of Monte Cristo,* trans. Robin Buss (London, 1996; first published 1844–45), quotations 393, 406.

The historian Ernest Renan supplies a comparable example of the nine-teenth century's fascination with the concept of aristocracy and its apparently paradoxical readiness to disconnect aristocratic values from persons of noble blood. Renan offers an especially compelling example because he was among the dominant figures in the historical culture of the later nineteenth century; in the next generation, Gabriel Monod (founder of the *Revue Historique* and Lucien Febvre's doctoral supervisor) would count him one of the nation's three "*maîtres de l'histoire*," the other two being Jules Michelet and Hippolyte Taine. Renan came from a modest social background; his father was a sea captain, born of peasant ancestors, and his mother kept a grocery store. He trained for the priesthood (first in Brittany, then at the Parisian seminary of Saint-Sulpice), lost his faith, and turned instead to a secular academic career, with dazzling success; in 1860 he was named a knight of the Legion of Honor, in 1861 professor at the Collège de France. The 1863 publication of his *Life of Jesus* made him one of the nineteenth century's best-selling authors, and its effort to historicize Jesus made him the particular target of conservatives. The government suspended his classes, and prominent clerics denounced him as an enemy of traditional values. For many of the same reasons, after 1871 he became a central figure in the culture of the newly founded Third Republic. He was gloriously restored to his position, and at his death in 1892 the government organized a state funeral. It also sought (unsuccessfully) to have his body buried in the Panthéon.[19]

Republican hero, provincial outsider made good, and the victim of both imperial and clerical power, Renan nonetheless turned to concepts of aris-tocracy to make sense of his own life in the modern world and for a political understanding of that world. This language could serve a variety of functions and moods, allowing him to express both embittered anxiety about where the world was heading and ironic detachment. "The idea that the nobleman is one who does not work for a living, and that all commercial or industrial enterprise, however respectable, diminishes the man who undertakes it and excludes him from the first circle of humanity—this idea is disappearing day by day. That's the difference that forty years can produce in human affairs. Everything that I once accomplished would today seem an act of lunacy; and sometimes, looking around me, I believe that I live in a world I no longer recognize."[20] The crisis that followed the Franco-Prussian War

19. For an overview of this career, Ernest Renan, *Souvenirs d'enfance et de jeunesse,* ed. Laudyce Rétat (Paris, 1973), 5–16; see also Gabriel Monod, *Les maîtres de l'histoire: Renan, Taine, Michelet,* 3rd. ed. (Paris, 1895), 1–49.

20. Renan, *Souvenirs,* 203.

brought more tragic and more practical expressions of these views. "The noble concerns of the old France—patriotism, enthusiasm for beauty, love of glory—have disappeared with the noble classes who represented the soul of France"; and his proposed remedies turned mainly on restoring aristocratic institutions. What he called "the basis of provincial life" in each corner of a restored France would be "an honest country gentleman"; in Paris, there would need to be "a permanent aristocratic center," combining functions of the House of Lords and the Académie Française, that would allow the survival of French superiority in the arts and sciences. The military would require even more direct infusions of aristocratic values, for "what is the nobility, in fact, if not the military function considered as hereditary and placed at the first rank of societal functions? When war disappears from the world, nobility will disappear as well, but not before." The restoration of France following its terrible defeats—"18 March 1871," he wrote, "is the day the French outlook [conscience] has been the lowest in the last thousand years"—could come only with the restoration of aristocratic values and institutions.[21] Comments like these defined the nobility as more than just a group of people or even a set of social roles; rather, nobles represented a full array of attitudes toward life, centering on neglect of economic calculation, refusal to subordinate honor to the market economy, commitment to family loyalty and to military pursuits. Yet in Renan's account (as in Dumas's) these attitudes and values had no necessary connection to any particular group of people; at no point did Renan suggest for himself any form of aristocratic lineage.

Renan stressed the incompatibility between aristocratic values and those needed for success in a modern commercial society, and this view was widely shared. Its prevalence had important implications for how the history of actual nobles was written in the nineteenth century. Defined as misfits within the market economy, they could scarcely be anything but a social class in decline, incapable of adaptation to a world that increasingly required individuals to evaluate their economic interests with care. As they looked at documents dating back to the Middle Ages, leading nineteenth-century historians claimed to discover that this in fact had been the case throughout French history. Tocqueville described the French nobility as visibly declining

21. Laudice Rétat, ed., *Renan: histoire et paroles, oeuvres diverses* (Paris, 1984), 601, 623, 624, 615. In his views of military valor, of course, Renan directly repeated eighteenth-century ideas to which David Bien and Rafe Blaufarb have drawn attention.

from the eleventh century to his own times.[22] François Guizot's lectures on the course of "French civilization" offered the same idea. For Guizot, "the most active and important [*décisif*] element" of that civilization, the one that determined its character, was the communes, bourgeoisie, Third Estate— terms that Guizot treated as synonymous. Thus for Guizot, in contrast to the tradition of Burkeian conservatism, the nation's essence lay not in its traditional great families, rising above and protecting the rest of the population, but rather in its active, changing, economically adventurous bourgeoisie. The development of this class constituted the central theme of French history, and that development was a story of ongoing struggle. "For more than six centuries, allied with the monarchy," it worked "without interruption to ruin the feudal aristocracy"—and once the aristocracy had been defeated, it moved on to attack its onetime ally, the monarchy. "It's the most powerful of the forces that have dominated our civilization," and its existence was a unique fact in world history. "Nowhere else will you encounter a social class that, starting from nothing, weak, despised, almost invisible at the start, rises by a continuous movement and unceasing labor; strengthening itself from one period to the next, to invade and absorb everything around it, power, riches, culture, influence; changing the nature of society and government; and finally becoming so dominant that one can say that it is now the country itself."[23]

Guizot's commitment to this view of his nation's history is especially striking in view of his contemporaries' keen awareness of French economic backwardness in comparison to England, with its cotton mill owners and iron masters. At a time when French landed wealth still mattered more than industrial or commercial, when even voting rights favored landowners, Guizot could nonetheless view the bourgeoisie as "the nation itself" (*le pays même*). As striking is his stress on the place of conflict in French social development. The Third Estate struggled "ceaselessly" (*sans relâche*) (a phrase he found apt enough to repeat), leaving no margin for even momentary alliances. This was a history in which real blood was shed, producing absolute gains and losses and ultimately "the ruin" of the aristocracy.

Guizot's vision thus detached the nobility from the nation's most important traditions, those that had come to fruition in his own times. Similar critiques emerged from nineteenth-century aristocrats themselves. The baron de

22. His views are discussed in Jonathan Dewald, *The European Nobility, 1400–1800* (Cambridge, 1996), 7–12.

23. François Guizot, *Histoire de la civilisation en France depuis la chute de l'Empire romain,* 3rd ed., 4 vols. (Paris, 1840), 4:211, 212.

Barante (a peer under the Restoration) argued in 1821 that aristocratic domination of society might have made sense in a purely rural society, "but commerce, industry, learning require another form of protection, and moreover have the force to insist on it."[24] For Barante as for Guizot, the story of the middle class was one of continuous advancement. "An intermediate class had been created, first weak and few, then endowed with power, wealth, and culture. It was thus necessary to give steadily more attention to its needs." As it rose, "the aristocratic edifice of feudalism, long besieged, weakened by so many attacks, everywhere undermined, collapsed completely beneath the blows of royal power."[25] For Barante, these processes had already begun during the seventeenth century, but the eighteenth century brought them to full flower. As "the nobility without any political function, without a real occupation, lost its energy from one generation to the next," "wealth, culture, and manners spread throughout the nation. Each day the inferior approached more closely the superior."[26] Tocqueville's best-selling *Democracy in America* would repeat these formulations a few years later.

Like Tocqueville, Barante assigned much of the blame for the nobility's loss of energy to the monarchy, which had limited its functions without restraining its privileges. But Barante was more impressed by the nobility's contemporary failings than by its sufferings under the Old Regime. The Restoration, he wrote, had converted honest landlords and small-town mayors, nobles who had adjusted in a constructive manner to the demands of the Napoleonic era, into pathetic office-seekers and connivers—in effect repeating the experience of the Old Regime itself, in which society's natural leaders had turned themselves into servile courtiers.[27] Barante's call for a liberal aristocratic regime, in which society's natural leaders would play preeminent roles, only highlighted the moral and economic failings of the actual French nobility.

Later in the nineteenth century, the duc d'Aumale's *Histoire des princes de Condé* used comparable language for somewhat different purposes. D'Aumale identified closely with the Condé family, and especially with Louis II de Bourbon, the Grand Condé. He owned Condé's estate at Chantilly, including the family archives on which his history was based; like several of the Condé princes he had been a successful general, and he peppered his text with

24. Amable-Guillaume-Prosper Brugière, baron de Barante, *Des communes et de l'aristocratie* (Paris, 1821), 26.
25. Ibid., 31.
26. Ibid., 43, 45.
27. Ibid., 77.

remarks about the enduring problems of generalship, suggesting that no absolute barrier separated the nineteenth century from the Old Regime; above all, he too was a Bourbon prince (a son of the deposed Louis-Philippe) who had been excluded by political circumstances from participating in the nation's public life.[28] D'Aumale was thus well situated to detect the continuities in aristocratic power that scholarship since 1960 has emphasized, but the brief and infrequent interpretive comments in his text stress instead decline. Of a moment in the Fronde, for instance, he wrote, "was this not a sign of the approaching [democratic] era? Do we not see here clearly the contrast between an impotent feudalism in decay and the imposing appearance of democracy in its cradle?"[29] But like many of his contemporaries, d'Aumale had little enthusiasm for the aristocratic politics of the Old Regime. Early in the reign of Louis XIII, he wrote, "the party of the *Grands*. . . , united only to destroy the remnant of authority that kept their petty ambitions in check, prepared itself for a new effort to reestablish in France a bastard form of feudalism."[30] Conversely, Richelieu's pacification of the aristocratic Huguenots ensured that "henceforth there were only Frenchmen in France," and that Protestants would contribute to "the great edifice of national unity."[31] Such comments show the extent to which d'Aumale too shared the nineteenth century's view of French state-building as a process that had continued through the early modern period, and which had set absolutist kings against aristocratic rebels. Whatever his admiration for the Grand Condé, his hero's turn to rebellion violated fundamental duties to the nation. "Shall we follow some," he asked, "in saying that the idea of the Fatherland [*Patrie*] . . . has only just now been revealed to modern societies? . . . No, whatever the claims, France was not born yesterday, and it's not just from yesterday that our ancestors began to love and serve her."[32] D'Aumale admired the Condés, but his historical perspective—like Guizot's—categorized their aristocratic politics as mere distractions in the history of French state-building.

These cases suggest how nobles might fade out of the nation's history, leaving them ghostly outsiders to the processes that mattered for French identity. A

---

28. M. le duc d'Aumale, *Histoire des princes de Condé pendant les XVIe et XVIIe siècles,* 2nd ed., 7 vols. (Paris, 1889–92), on contemporary generalship, 2:218; on similarities of seventeenth-century politics with those of the nineteenth century, 5:378.

29. Ibid., 6:16–17.

30. Ibid., 3:114.

31. Ibid., 3:224.

32. Ibid., 5:383, 384.

similar shifting can be detected in nineteenth-century discussions of race, a growing preoccupation among French intellectuals. The two topics inevitably intertwined, for "race" had been essential to the Old Regime's definition of nobility itself: although nobility could be acquired in other ways, its essence lay in purity of lineage, which allowed the development of such aristocratic qualities as courage and generosity.[33] These ideas survived among nineteenth-century writers: in Benjamin Disraeli's novel *Sybil,* the heroine is a descendant of medieval Saxon heroes, and she and her father display the characteristic bravery and honor of their lineage. But increasingly intellectuals attached such imagery to whole peoples, rather than just the stratum of the nobility, further reducing the nobility's importance as a repository of specific personal qualities. Comte Arthur de Gobineau's *Essai sur l'inégalité des races humaines,* whose first volumes appeared in 1853, represented the strongest expression of these views, in an emphatically emotional register, emphasizing pessimism about the future of France and of Europe more generally. Gobineau cared deeply about nobility, and some of his ideas indicated the survival into the nineteenth century of Old Regime ideas about its meaning. He had some claim to the status himself, since in the eighteenth century his family had held offices in the sovereign courts of Bordeaux, but his claim to a title was murkier; to support it, he spent several years assembling a half-fictional, half-historical version of his family's history, extending back to the Viking invasions of Normandy.[34] Ernest Renan's wife, possibly Gobineau's former mistress and in any case his passionate admirer, summarized the dynastic vision that dominated that work: "one sees a family developing, transforming itself, moving from place to place over the centuries, [yet] keeping its fundamental nature, remaining itself in all circumstances, reproducing long-dead ancestors, imprinted with pride and all the melancholy of ancient memories."[35] Here was the Old Regime's ideology of aristocratic lineage updated to new social circumstances: in his qualities and attitudes, the nobleman embodied historical survival, allowing medieval values to contribute to the modern world.

As with Alexandre Dumas and Ernest Renan, however, Gobineau's language of nobility concealed instabilities that ultimately left his readers uncertain both what nobility was and how it interacted with the surrounding society. Gobineau believed the races of humanity to be altogether dissimilar, so

33. Arlette Jouanna, *L'idée de race en France au XVIe siècle et au début du XVIIe,* rev. ed., 2 vols. (Montpellier, 1981).

34. Arthur comte de Gobineau, *Oeuvres,* ed. Jean Gaulmier, 3 vols. (Paris, 1983), introduction.

35. Roger Béziau, ed., *Les lettres de Cornélie Renan à Gobineau,* in *Archives des lettres modernes,* no. 75 (1967), 30.

much so as to raise the possibility of separate creations for each of them, but he also believed that they tended inevitably to intermarry. The result was a steady decline of human energy and achievement. When this process of racial mixing was completed (in the near future, he predicted), "men will all resemble each other," and this common humanity "will be of the most revolting baseness." Mankind would lose its capacity to dominate nature and instead would come to resemble the other animals. So reduced in energy and capacities, it would not last long, and indeed, signs of depopulation were already everywhere visible. China "has never had fewer inhabitants than today;" Germany, England, and France were no more populous now than during the late Roman Empire, while Italy and Spain had lost three-fourths of their populations.[36] Race dynamics thus explained "the fall of civilizations," which he described as "the most striking and at the same time the most obscure of all historical phenomena."[37]

Throughout Europe, this fatal tendency to racial mixture had begun early, as Germanic tribesmen intermarried with the conquered peoples of Roman Europe, and the tendency was especially marked in France, both because of its strong monarchy and because French territory grouped together a Germanic north and a Mediterranean south, giving special encouragement to racial mixing. "The ethnic decomposition of the French nobility began when Germanic tribes mingled their blood with that of the Gallo-Romans; but decline moved quickly, partly because the Germanic warriors died in great numbers in the incessant wars of the time, and partly because frequent revolutions replaced them with men risen from lower in society."[38] Thus Gobineau like Tocqueville and Guizot made decline the central narrative in the nobility's history, and like them he believed that the French monarchy contributed to the process. Already by the fourteenth century the monarchy had succeeded in coaxing the nobility "into habits akin to servility," which left the noble merely a "decoration" of the monarchy. "It hardly needs to be added that the nobles allowed themselves thus to be degraded because their blood was no longer sufficiently pure to allow them to feel the wrong, and to give them sufficient strength for resistance. Less romanized than the bourgeoisie, which in turn was less romanized than the common people, they were nonetheless very romanized."[39] Urbanization only completed this work of racial decline, for in the great cities the observer encountered "a

36. Ibid., 1:1164–65.
37. Ibid., 1:141; see also 1:170.
38. Ibid., 1:1091, note.
39. Ibid., 1:1091.

frightening spectacle of ethnic anarchy," with inhabitants showing traces of ancestry from throughout the world.[40] In the end, despite his aristocratic self-image, Gobineau's thinking led him to downplay aristocratic lineage and to stress instead the racial make-up of specific regions. Racial purity survived in the regions of the north (to which only France north of the Seine belonged), rather than among the nobilities. "Here subsist the last remnants of the Aryan element, disfigured, impoverished, but not altogether vanquished. Here too beats the heart of modern society, and consequently of modern culture [*civilisation*]."[41]

Gobineau wrote in a tense relationship with the intellectual establishment of his day. Unlike Renan's, his works enjoyed neither popular success nor the endorsement of established figures, and he suffered repeatedly for his readiness to make extravagant claims in fields that he did not know well.[42] Religious conservatives disliked the materialistic assumptions in his arguments, and Tocqueville considered their political implications pernicious.[43] French historians tended to view him as an overly enthusiastic autodidact, and in 1856 he continued to complain about the silence surrounding his book.[44] But if Gobineau was not entirely representative of his contemporaries' thinking, neither was he an outsider to Parisian cultural circles. Tocqueville noticed him early on, employed him as a secretary, secured him a place in the French diplomatic corps, and pushed him (unsuccessfully) for a place in the Academy of Moral and Political Sciences. They sustained a warm correspondence until Tocqueville's death, in 1859. Cornélie Renan likewise mobilized her husband on Gobineau's behalf, to secure reviews in prominent journals, and herself spoke warmly of his books in salon situations.[45] Years earlier, they had met at the salon of Cornélie's artist father, where he had also met the historian Augustin Thierry. To roughly the same degree, Gobineau's ideas also were in contact with those of his contemporaries. More respectable writers like Renan and Taine also made race central to their understanding

40. Ibid., 1:284.

41. Ibid., 1:1098, 1099.

42. Characteristically, in 1858, three years after the appearance of the *Essai,* he announced in a letter to Alexis de Tocqueville that he had discovered the proper reading of cuneiform texts, in the course of completing a six-volume history of Iran. "Jamais alchimiste n'a été plus heureux," he wrote to another friend, but the episode ended badly, with the Parisian specialist community rejecting his findings; *Correspondance d'Alexis de Tocqueville et d'Arthur Gobineau,* ed. M. Degros, in *Alexis de Tocqueville, Oeuvres complètes,* ed. J.-P. Mayer (Paris, 1959), 9:291.

43. Ibid., 9:199, 200, 203.

44. Ibid., 9:266.

45. Béziau, ed., *Les lettres,* 38–40.

of world history. Renan, whose good-humored self-identification with aristocratic values has already been noted, enthusiastically advocated French imperial adventures; France's working classes like its nobility (he wrote) descended from the warlike Franks, and the grand adventures of foreign conquest and rule alone could provide suitable outlets for these warrior instincts.[46] Elsewhere he spoke in comparable terms of the Celtic culture that survived in western Brittany. "If racial excellence were to be measured by purity of blood and inviolability of characer, no race . . . could compete in excellence with the surviving remnants of the Celtic race." The Celts' qualities paralleled those conventionally attributed to the nobility: a fierce opposition to modernity, a sense that the individual life constitutes "a link in a long tradition," a readiness to undertake arduous quests for idealistic purposes.[47] Despite his divergences from his contemporaries, Gobineau illustrates the variety of ideological schemes into which the vision of nobiliar decline might be fitted.

With varying emphases and assessments, the accounts traced here agreed in limiting the nobles' place in French national development, defining them as irrelevant to the emergence of both the state and the capitalist market. Other writers took these suggestions of nobles' inability to conform to modern life much further. For them, the noble was not merely unable to function successfully within bourgeois society, but was also unwilling to accept its constraints: the noble shaded into the bohemian rebel. The Goncourt brothers, whose family had been ennobled in the eighteenth century, spoke repeatedly of their inability to adapt to the nineteenth century's rules. "We feel ourselves . . . to be émigrés from the eighteenth century. We are déclassé contemporaries of that refined, exquisite, supremely delicate, rebellious [d'esprit enragé] society." On this view, nobles constituted a society of the disobedient, frondeurs unwilling to live by conventional rules. For the Goncourts, this view allied with an assertiveness about aristocracy as funda-mental to artistic excellence: "nothing beautiful in the arts has been achieved except by aristocracies. Works by the people and for the people . . . are only pyramids, roads, viaducts."[48]

46. Discussed in Jonathan Dewald, "'A la Table de Magny': Nineteenth-Century French Men of Letters and the Origins of Modern Historical Thought," *American Historical Review* 108:4 (October 2003): 1009–33.

47. Rétat, ed., *Renan: histoire et paroles*, 308–9, 311.

48. Edmond and Jules de Goncourt, *Journal: mémoires de la vie littéraire*, 3 vols. (Paris, 1989), 1:905, 1020.

Dumas's fictions suggested another form that aristocratic rebellion might take, a questioning of sexual and gender conventions. In his *La reine Margot* (first published 1844–45) the heroine's very aristocratic friend Henriette de Nevers proclaims herself "free, my queen, do you understand? Do you know how much happiness there is in this word free?" Henriette emphasizes that she is free from her husband's control, as well as from the rest of the world's, and that she is free in her sexual choices as in other matters. As a princess, Marguerite cannot enjoy the same degree of liberty, but she responds in similar terms: she and her friend, she acknowledges, are united in the untrammeled pursuit of pleasure.[49] During these years, the Old Regime's aristocratic women and their sexual outlawry fascinated professional historians as much as popular novelists. In the 1840s, both C.-A. Sainte-Beuve and Victor Cousin wrote significant studies of seventeenth- and eighteenth-century women; twenty years later the Goncourts themselves wrote a study of women in the eighteenth century.[50] All these authors portrayed women mixing illicit sexuality with politicking and learning. Sainte-Beuve showed Madame de Pompadour patiently tutoring an ignorant and boorish Louis XV in appreciation of the arts. "Arriving at that position, eminent but little honorable" of royal mistress, wrote Sainte-Beuve, she "considered herself as destined to aid, summon around her, and encourage, suffering merit and men of talent of all kinds. . . . It was not her fault that no one can speak of the 'age of Louis XV' as they do of that of Louis XIV."[51] Cousin came close to obsession with the beautiful, sexually adventurous *frondeuses* of the seventeenth-century, whom he found all the more attractive for their eventual middle-aged penitence. These themes continued into the twentieth century. In about 1902, the nationalist anti-Semite Charles Maurras reviewed the career of the aristocrat Mlle Coigny as an example of patriotic heroism: yet another in the series of atheistic libertines, entertaining multiple lovers, she nonetheless played an important role in bringing legitimate monarchy back to France in 1814. Maurras of course celebrated her political role, but also the absolute indifference she displayed to religious ideas. After death, she believed, there would be "nothing. No future. . . . This is what gives the brief elegy of her life and loves an intensity of interest and emotion."[52] Again, the

---

49. Alexandre Dumas, *La reine Margot* (Paris, 1994), 147.

50. Discussed in Dewald, "'A la Table de Magny.'"

51. C.-A. Sainte-Beuve, *Portraits of the Eighteenth Century, Historic and Literary,* trans. Katharine P. Wormeley (New York, 1905), 449.

52. Charles Maurras, "Mademoiselle Monk," repr. in Maurras, *Romantisme et révolution* (Paris, 1922), 206–26, quotation 216.

aristocratic woman embodied freedom from pious convention—and in this case personal nonconformity made possible political heroism.

These formulations came from intellectuals who exercised enormous influence on nineteenth- and early twentieth-century culture, and their vision of the noble as rebel was hugely popular. Dumas's books sold in legendary quantities, of course. Twenty years after *La reine Margot* appeared, the Goncourts overheard some men discussing the novel in a bar and concluded that Dumas "has truly been the history teacher of the masses."[53] A host of imitators produced other efforts drawn from the dramatic events and characters of the sixteenth and seventeenth centuries.[54] Even the sober duc d'Aumale drew attention to the overlap between his carefully documented exploration of the Gascon nobles who participated in the Fronde and that of Dumas: this "most seductive of narrators has engraved their image in everyone's memory."[55]

At loftier levels, Sainte-Beuve and Cousin exercised especially important influence on the institutional structure of nineteenth-century intellectual life; Cousin dominated philosophy teaching at the Sorbonne, served as minister of education, and had a say in most French academic careers through mid-century, while Sainte-Beuve's weekly newspaper columns helped determine literary careers. With this stimulus, their more scholarly contemporaries pursued and edited documents that displayed the early modern aristocracy's ungoverned lives. Marguerite de Valois's own memoirs were published, and from that publication there followed late in the nineteenth century a careful biography, by one of Ernest Lavisse's collaborators. Gédéon Tallemant des Réaux's immense collection of wild stories about seventeenth-century high society had remained almost unknown until the manuscript appeared on the market in 1803; a first edition (in six volumes) appeared in 1833–35, a second (ten volumes) in 1840, a third (nine volumes) in 1854–60—this last a complete edition, save for (a contemporary noted) "the suppression of some passages whose cynicism passes all bounds."[56] Tallemant's case typified how prurient fascination with aristocratic amorality intersected with intensive, careful scholarship, and with a nervous effort to contain the seditious effects of these examples. Reviewing in 1857 the third edition of Tallemant, Sainte-Beuve noted that "the seventeenth century is more in fashion than

---

53. Goncourts, *Journal*, 1:995.
54. Summary in Eliane Viennot, postface to *La reine Margot*.
55. D'Aumale, *Histoire des princes de Condé*, 6:13.
56. *Nouvelle biographie universelle*, s.v. Tallemant.

ever;" and that contemporary historians had absorbed Tallemant's Rabelaisian stories "without citing him . . . and pretending to despise him" for his vulgarity.[57] The sieur de Brantôme's works had been republished in the eighteenth century, but the nineteenth century saw two major new editions (the second in eleven volumes); an 1876 overview of "Brantôme the historian" praised the author's insights but added "we do not wish even to glance at" his *Dames galantes,* "the fruit of a perverted imagination, instruction in debauchery worth of Aretino."[58]

A more sober example of this interplay between literary imagery and historical documentation was the mid-nineteenth-century publication of a seventeenth-century account of the Grands Jours d'Auvergne by Esprit Fléchier. The events themselves took place in 1665 and represented an especially dramatic confrontation between the monarchical state and an unruly local aristocracy: in response to complaints about feudal lawlessness, Louis XIV sent a deputation of magistrates to the province (among the most backward in France) to execute summary justice on nobles who abused their local influence. The result was a wave of executions and lawsuits, and an affirmation of royal control over even remote regions. This was a confrontation very much in keeping with nineteenth-century ideas about the progress and achievements of absolutist monarchy. After a first edition in 1844, in 1856 the scholar Adolphe Chéruel (responsible for a number of other archival publications) superintended an annotated version of Fléchier's account of these events.[59]

The edition provoked widespread interest, hence the readiness of the already famous Sainte-Beuve to supply an introduction. Sainte-Beuve noted that the 1844 publication "obtained the greatest success in both the wide public and among cultivated readers [*esprits*]."[60] Taine also supplied a review in the middle-brow *Journal des Débats,* presenting the document as a narrative of cultural and social confrontation. Fléchier's "portrayal of provincial mores and Parisian elegance," he wrote, in its "authentic, instinctive contrasts indicates a revolution that is drawing to a conclusion: an aristocracy of petty

57. C.-A. Sainte-Beuve, *Causeries du lundi,* 3rd ed., 16 vols. (Paris, n.d.), "Tallemant et Bussy" (19 January 1857), 13:172, 188.

58. L. Pingard, "Brantôme historien," *Revue des questions historiques* 11 (1876): 218.

59. Adolphe Chéruel, ed., *Mémoires de Fléchier sur les Grands-Jours d'Auvergne en 1665* (Paris, 1862). The edition has served as a standard account; see, for instance, Arlette Le Bigre, *Les Grands Jours d'Auvergne: désordres et répression au XVIIe siècle* (Paris, 1976). I'm grateful to Albert Hamscher for suggesting that I investigate Fléchier and nineteenth-century responses to him.

60. Chéruel, ed., *Mémoires de Fléchier,* iii.

tyrants, men of action, is becoming a salon of cultivated, well-behaved courtiers." Taine's language suggested his dislike of the new dispensation, with its absolutist politics and neoclassical culture, but in keeping with the other historians considered here he mainly stressed the backwardness of the seventeenth-century aristocratic order, a world of "little private despotisms" and "little private wars" that preceded the monarchy's forcible entry onto the scene. "This robbery and killings of the weak, this regular exchange of ambushes and assassinations among the strong, this custom of affronting and murdering the forces of law and justice, constitute feudal mores through nearly the whole of the Middle Ages."[61] But both Sainte-Beuve and Taine expressed also an ambivalent view of the Parisian side of this encounter. A polished cleric and future bishop, a particpant in the salon culture of the hôtel de Rambouillet, tutor to an important family of magistrates, Fléchier himself perfectly embodied the new Parisian culture. But Sainte-Beuve's introduction draws attention to the complexities of this culture, noting the affinities between Fléchier's stories and the bawdy tales of another salon habitué, Tallemant himself. Sainte-Beuve found disconcerting the mix of gallantry and refinement with tales of wild behavior—and the visiting Parisians' ease in moving from festivities, dancing, and flirtation to torture and executions. In their discussions of libertine aristocratic women, historians and artists reflected a common mentality, and that mentality led directly to technical historical scholarship. The anarchic sides of the Old Regime nobility disturbed, but they were more fundamentally sources of fascination.

These examples help to explain the fact that conservative thinkers in France approached the nobility with considerable ambivalence. Of course French writers had available and intermittently used the social vision laid out by Edmund Burke, according to which nobles embodied important elements of the national character and served as living examples of the continuity between past and present. "By the sure operation of adequate causes," as Burke proclaimed, the British House of Commons was "filled with everything illustrious in rank, in descent, in hereditary and in acquired opulence, in cultivated talents, in military, civil, naval, and politic distinction that the country can afford"; no wonder that the country advanced so well toward political and social modernity.[62] In describing his hopes for French reconstruction after

61. Hippolyte Taine, *Essais de critique et d'histoire,* 14th ed. (Paris, 1923), 224, 232, 235.
62. Edmund Burke, *Reflections on the Revolution in France,* ed. Thomas H. D. Mahoney (Indianapolis, 1955), 50.

1871, Renan echoed some elements of this vision of the relation between aristocracy and nation: in both country and city, aristocracy was to be the foundation for a new, more solid national identity. But even he also noted examples of aristocratic disruptiveness, and others pushed these ideas much further. Nobles seemed fundamentally at odds with their society's most basic arrangements, and this from the early days of French history.

Hence conservatives proved surprisingly ready to speak critically of their nobles. Taine's famously critical history of the Revolution offered no defense of the French nobles, nor even of nobles elsewhere. To be sure, like Tocqueville he offered a positive view of their social role in the centuries before Richelieu, when they continued to reside in the countryside and their local influence remained strong. By the later seventeenth century, however, they had become pure influence-peddlers, concerned only to preserve the amenities that they and their relatives enjoyed. "If one looks at the castes and coteries, their isolation made their egoism," he wrote. "From bottom to top, the legal and moral powers that ought to have represented the nation represented only themselves, and everyone sought to advance himself at the expense of the nation." He viewed patriotism as another victim of this aristocratic self-interest; French nobles had never hesitated to betray the nation, and in defense of their interests they had regularly conspired with foreign powers, even helping them in their invasions. "The nature of an aristocracy that thinks only of itself is to become a mere coterie. Having forgotten the public, it comes as well to neglect its subordinates; having separated itself from the nation, it separates itself from its followers." Even nobles' much-praised indifference to monetary gain was not a sign of lofty ideals; it showed merely the debilitating influence of court life, in which "there was no time or taste for anything else, even for the things that touch a man most closely, public affairs, estate management, the family."[63]

Like Tocqueville, Taine blamed the monarchy for much of this disorder. In the seventeenth century it had destroyed the authority that nobles had exercised in the countryside, but for Taine the monarchy's culture impact was still more important. It had insisted on a rigid classical cultural, which disparaged discussion of the realities of life, requiring that all topics be reshaped so as to fit within the limits of polite, measured discourse. Because of this classicizing program, in the eighteenth century the French language "was unsuited to depict living things, the individual as he really exists in nature and history;" writers had simplified its subject matter until

---

63. Hippolyte Taine, *Les origines de la France contemporaine,* 2 vols. (Paris, 1986), 1:52, 58, 96.

there remained only "a residue, . . . an empty abstraction."[64] French classical culture had toxic effects on the aristocracy's outlook and behavior; still worse, it accounted for the dangerous abstractions of French enlightened philosophy—abstractions that the Revolution would eventually seek to implement. But unlike Tocqueville, Taine had doubts about the principle of aristocracy itself, which he viewed as a source of social dysfunction. "When the laws establish unequal social conditions," he wrote, "no one is exempt from insults; . . . human nature is humiliated at every level, and society is only an exchange of affronts."[65] The Goncourts disagreed with Taine about the value of the eighteenth-century nobility, whose amorality and indifference to convention they admired, but they shared some of his dislike of classicism: "Under every empire," they noted privately in 1863, "there is a move toward antiquity, toward classical sources. Tyrannies extend enslavement even to matters of taste."[66] They had in mind both Louis XIV and Napoleon III. Taine also contested the value of classicism for France, as impoverishing the nation's culture and emasculating its nobility.[67]

The conservatives who followed him tended to reverse these evaluations and to see the state as the maker of France—and the state-sponsored culture of French classicism as one of its principal tools. Men of letters and ideologues presented far-reaching versions of this idea. Thus Charles Maurras argued that France was not a natural entity, but the product of its kings' efforts, aided by the culture that the monarchy sponsored. When in 1898 Maurras listed the various qualities that marked "old France" before 1789, he left nobles off the list altogether, noting instead the old monarchy's sensible approach to religion, municipal government, and culture. He viewed the aristocratic Chateaubriand as precisely the figure in nineteenth-century culture who had most threatened this inheritance, another instance of the aristocrat as rebel. "From his ways of fearing demagogy, socialism, a Europe-wide republic, one comes to realize that he wanted them with all his heart. . . . This noble spirit . . . imagined the new regime with some horror. But he loved horror."[68] For Maurras, real conservatism lay not with these romantic "wreckers" (*naufrageurs*), but with the monarchy that had created the nation. "Our France is a work of art. It is a political work of art born of the collaboration of an obliging nature and the thought of our

---

64. Taine, *Les origines de la France contemporaine,* 1:149.
65. Hippolyte Taine, *Les philosophes classiques du XIXe siècle en France,* 4th ed. (Paris, 1876), 113.
66. Goncourts, *Journal,* 1:922; see also 1:821.
67. This is a principal theme of the first sections of *Les origines de la France contemporaine.*
68. Charles Maurras, *Trois idées politiques* (1898), repr. in *Romantisme et révolution,* 245–46, 248.

kings."[69] During the Occupation of the 1940s, the right-wing philosopher
Thierry Maulnier offered another version of this position: "Other nations
can have, as the principle of their unity, their territory, the form of their
work, and, at the very least, the relative homogeneity of their blood. Open
to numerous invasions, dedicated to very diverse activities, born of ethni-
cally disparate elements, France molded itself into a unique substance only
by the slow work of history. It is a nation forged by the hand of man. French
civilization has been one of the principal means by which the French nation
has been made."[70] To Maurras, as to his follower Maulnier, the essence of
French national identity lay not in the disruptive nobles, but in the dis-
ciplined forces of the French state and its culture.

I have argued that, despite the important differences among them, nineteenth-
century currents of thought rendered problematic many approaches to the
history of the nobility. The writers considered here detached nobles from
the main lines of French national development, whether political or social,
and they suggested that the nobles had no necessary relation to the positive
values commonly associated with them—valor, indifference to monetary
calculation, independence. Nobles seemed too rebellious to symbolize conservative values, yet they were clearly too privileged to stand for the political
left. If medieval nobles could be an important subject for investigation,
their counterparts during the early modern period, a period marked by the
development of state, capitalism, and a distinctive national culture, could
not. They could provide only victims of modernization, not participants.

These ideas remained a vigorous presence in French historical thought
into the 1960s. Here I can only briefly suggest this continuity—and the
accompanying discomfort with the topic of nobility itself—by considering
the work of three major historians. Lucien Febvre's 1912 dissertation offers
an especially significant example because Febvre played a leading role in
French academic life between the foundation of the *Annales d'histoire
économique et sociale* in 1929 and his death in 1956. Despite his advocacy of
historiographical innovation, in thinking about the nobility Febvre's views
fitted comfortably within the analytical framework sketched out in the
previous century by Guizot and Tocqueville. The work's real subject, he

69. Quoted David Carroll, *French Literary Fascism: Nationalism, Anti-Semitism, and the Ideology
of Culture* (Princeton, 1995), 71. Elements of this idea, with numerous anthropological and
scientific underpinnings, survive in Hervé LeBras and Emmanuel Todd, *L'invention de la France:
atlas anthropologique et politique* (Paris, 1981).
70. Quoted Carroll, *French Literary Fascism* 246.

explained, "is the struggle, the furious combat between two rival classes, nobility and bourgeoisie," a struggle that underlay the more superficial political conflicts of the period.[71] In the sixteenth century, "reduced to the revenues of his lands, the nobleman, amidst rising fortunes, remained stationary, and thus declined. He witnessed, powerlessly, the dislocation and destruction of the old system of estate management that once had made the grandeur and wealth of his ancestors."[72] The result was a tendency to violence and a hatred of the group's successful rivals, the bourgeois magistrates of the *parlement,* who enjoyed judicial powers over the nobles along with their economic successes. "The unruly nobility, . . . the daring esquires, the country gentlemen deep in debt . . . , satisfying on the highways their instincts for brutality and brigandage, found themselves face to face with the hated magistrates" of the cities.[73] Falling behind economically, unable to use violence as a means to economic recovery, wrote Febvre, "the whole nobility united against the common enemy, the magistrate [*parlementaire*]."[74]

After World War I, Marc Bloch (Febvre's colleague and cofounder of the *Annales*) presented a similar view of the nobility's evolution, though he expressed less interest than Febvre in the political ramifications of social changes. Bloch's *French Rural History,* first presented as a series of lectures in 1930, stressed the inappropriateness of feudal habits for the conditions of the late Middle Ages and the sixteenth century. Thus for Bloch as for Febvre, the essential social fact of this period was the nobility's decline, as the group's outmoded economic reasoning encountered new circumstances. Bloch stressed the importance of the correlative process, by which bourgeois landowners brought new values to the French countryside. Armed with the distinctive outlook required for success in the modern world, magistrates bought up properties from peasants and nobles alike, and in doing so they reconstituted the seigneurial system. "This advance by the bourgeoisie, followed by such rapid entrenchment," Bloch concluded, "was the most decisive event in French social history, especially in its rural aspect." Though ennobled, Bloch emphasized, these men and women "were accustomed to handling considerable liquid assets with caution, skill and even boldness. . . . In short, they had acquired the capitalist mentality. Such was the leaven which would transform seigneurial methods of

71. Lucien Febvre, *Philippe II et la Franche Comté: étude d'histoire politique, religieuse et sociale* (Paris, 1912; repr. Paris, 1970), 9.
72. Ibid., 145.
73. Ibid., 254.
74. Ibid., 431.

exploitation."[75] Bloch saw this renewed seigneurial system surviving to
1789, and a reinvigorated system of large properties surviving into his own
times. But these successes did not profit the French nobles. Rather, they
represented precisely the triumph of the French bourgeoisie, in much the
same terms that Guizot had used.

As a final example, we may turn to the historian Roland Mousnier, whose
dissertation on *La vénalité des offices* appeared in 1945, and who continued
to exercise an important influence on historical practice at the Sorbonne
into the mid-1970s.[76] In contrast to Bloch and Febvre, Mousnier held conservative political views, consonant with his early training at the French
military academy St-Cyr; and much of his work—in the tradition of French
conservatism—explored the process by which the French state brought its
civilizing influence to an unruly society. His differences of background and
orientation from Febvre and Bloch make all the more striking his essential
agreement with them on the history of the nobility. Indeed, Mousnier was
still more emphatic in presenting conflict between nobility and bourgeoisie
as central to French historical development; in his view, French modernization represented the bourgeoisie's triumph in this struggle. Mousnier explored
these questions with particular clarity in a 1958 article.[77] Against those who
might see convergence of interests between nobles and monarchy, he
argued that in the seventeenth century the high nobility wanted to "ruin
the entire work of the monarchy [*l'oeuvre monarchique*], and truly return
to the feudal order which, in fact, no longer existed."[78] The fact that many
of the crown's own servants held aristocratic titles did not change the character of this struggle, he argued, because their formal status fell well short
of real nobility; the administrator was "a noble, but not a gentleman or a

75. Marc Bloch, *French Rural History: An Essay on Its Basic Characteristics,* trans. Janet Sond-
heimer (Berkeley and Los Angeles, 1966), 125–26.

76. Roland Mousnier, *La vénalité des offices sous Henry IV et Louis XIII,* 2nd ed. (Paris, 1971).
In some ways Mousnier's influence on the French historical profession probably equalled that of
Lucien Febvre himself, for he directed a wide array of dissertations during the 1960s and 1970s.

77. The article was his entry into a prolonged debate with the Russian historian Boris
Porshnev, a debate whose implications dominated the last two decades of Mousnier's academic
career. Porshnev had argued that early modern France was dominated by an aristocratic state,
which channeled tax revenues to an alliance of nobles and magistrates, in effect replacing the
revenues that nobles lost as the seigneurial system fell apart. In important respects, this idea is
basic to contemporary understanding of absolutism.

78. Roland Mousnier, "Recherches sur les soulèvements populaires en France avant la
Fronde," first published in *Revue d'Histoire Moderne et Contemporaine* 5 (1958); repr. in Mousnier,
La plume, la faucille et le marteau: institutions et société en France du Moyen Age à la Révolution (Paris,
1970), 335–68, 364.

member of the feudal hierarchy. . . . An official, ennobled by his position, was
a bourgeois. . . . In fact the officials of the seventeenth century had habits and
customs that sharply distinguished them from the gentlemen, even when they
acted as seigneurs."[79] Real assimilation of bourgeois into nobility thus
remained an illusion, whatever the new nobleman's properties or even his
behavior. In Mousnier's view (as in Guizot's) the French state relied on this
group in its work of constructing the French nation: "I see nothing to
change," he wrote, "in the theory according to which the progress of the
absolute monarchy was advanced by the possibility of opposing bourgeois
against nobles [gentilshommes] . . . in reconstructing the state, the monarchy
relied on the bourgeoisie, and I maintain that it left to the bourgeoisie a
signficant share in political and administrative power."[80] For Mousnier as for
other French conservatives, thus, the genuine nobility remained essentially
irrelevant to understanding the real nature of French society. He too saw
France as the creation of its kings, and the nobility mattered in this story
mainly for its efforts to block the monarchy's work. To be sure, the French
bourgeoisie also required disciplining by the monarchy, but for Mousnier its
place in the nation's history was altogether different from that of the old
nobility. For if bourgeois had to submit to the state's disciplining, they also
participated in its powers; they were the king's agents, and this position
made them in the end the real makers of the nation.

That historians of such varied professional and ideological commitments as
Febvre, Bloch, and Mousnier shared essentially the same view of the French
nobility suggests the importance and durability of the literary traditions
that this essay has examined. These traditions influenced popular novelists,
professional historians, and public intellectuals alike. Though these writers
disagreed on specific points, they shared a coherent view of what nobility
meant within French history. At its core was the idea that, by the seventeenth century at the latest, nobles had essentially been removed from the
important stories of French national development.

  Given the strength of this consensus, it is not surprising that alternatives
to it arose first among American historians. Only outsiders to French culture,
it seems, could set aside ideas that (I have argued here) had been part of
French historical culture over the 150 years between Guizot and Mousnier.
More speculatively, one may suggest that the American context itself made

79. Ibid., 365.
80. Ibid.

American historians especially receptive to thinking about social roles as easily put on and taken off, sites for reinvention and adaptation, rather than rigid identities; and of course it is noteworthy that French scholars have themselves taken up some of these views during a time of increasingly close contacts with American life. Whatever its sources in historians' lived experiences, though, rethinking the French nobles has required a significant revision in ideas about social identity itself. Despite their differences, nineteenth-century writers shared the belief that there might exist a collection of people somehow resistant to the influences of modernity itself. Nobles served nineteenth-century writers as an example of natural anticapitalists and natural opponents of the conventional and utilitarian ethics that seemed to dominate the modern world. Since the 1960s, both radical and conservative social theorists—both those who celebrate market economics and those who hold Foucauldian beliefs in the pervasive influence of modern power—have looked critically at this idea that one might stand outside the social order. Our changing ideas about the nobility can be thus seen as an element in a broader shift in our understanding of how societies function.

FOR FURTHER READING

References to archival collections and to many specialized studies relevant to each of the book's themes can be found in the footnotes to the individual essays. The book's common historiographical frame of reference was established by a relative handful of canonical works reflecting the approaches and priorities of Marxist, revisionist, and what can now be called postrevisionist historians. Fine, and still valuable, examples of the old Marxist "orthodoxy" are Albert Soboul, *La Révolution Française* (Paris, 1962), and Georges Lefebvre, *Quatre-vingt-neuf* (Paris, 1939; translated by R. R. Palmer as *The Coming of the French Revolution*).

Three highly influential books written from the revisionist perspective, by François Furet, Guy Chaussinand-Nogaret, and Robert Forster, are discussed in the introduction and throughout the book. But most of the important findings of the Marxists' revisionist critics were actually conveyed in article form, including the following: C. B. A. Behrens, "Nobles, Privileges, and Taxes in France at the End of the Ancien Régime," *Economic History Review* 15 (1963): 451–75; Elizabeth Eisenstein, "Who Intervened in 1788? A Commentary on the Coming of the French Revolution," *American Historical Review* 70 (1965): 77–103; Colin Lucas, "Nobles, Bourgeois, and the Origins of the French Revolution," *Past and Present* 60 (1973): 84–126; David D. Bien, "La réaction aristocratique avant 1789: l'exemple de l'armée," *Annales: Economies, Sociétés, Civilisations* 29 (1974): 23–48, 505–34; and George V. Taylor, "Non-Capitalist Wealth and the Origins of the French Revolution," *American Hisorical Review* 72 (1967): 469–96.

Among the important postrevisionist works that have begun to turn the lens of American historical analysis back toward the nobility, social class, and the fraught relations between "nobility" and "bourgeoisie" (or various constructions of the same), readers may especially wish to consult Colin Jones, "Bourgeois Revolution Revivified: 1789 and Social Change," in *Rewriting the French Revolution*, ed. Colin Lucas (Oxford, 1991), 69–118; David Garrioch, *The Formation of the Parisian Bourgeoisie, 1690–1830* (Cambridge, Mass., 1996); Mathieu Marraud, *La Noblesse de Paris au XVIIIe siècle* (Paris, 2000); Michael Kwass, *Privilege and the Politics of Taxation in Eighteenth-Century France: Liberté, Egalité, Fiscalité* (Cambridge, 2000); Christine Adams, *A Taste for Comfort and Status: A Bourgeois Family in Eighteenth-Century France* (University Park, Penn., 2000); and Sarah Maza, *The Myth of the French Bourgeoisie: An Essay on the Social Imaginary, 1750–1850* (Cambridge, Mass., 2003).

RAFE BLAUFARB is associate professor of history at Auburn University. The author of articles and essays on nobility, the military, and absolutism, he has also written two books: *The French Army, 1750–1820: Careers, Talent, Merit* (2002) and *Bonapartists in the Borderlands: French Exiles and Refugees on the Gulf Coast, 1815–1835* (2006). His current research is on the history of noble tax exemption in early modern France.

GAIL BOSSENGA is associate professor of history at the College of William and Mary. A specialist of finance, institutional history, and eighteenth-century political culture, she is the author of *The Politics of Privilege: Old Regime and Revolution in Lille* (1991) and has written articles on taxes, guilds, citizenship, and the origins of the French Revolution.

MITA CHOUDHURY is associate professor of history at Vassar College. She is the author of *Convents and Nuns in Eighteenth-Century French Politics and Culture* (2004). She is also coediting the Prentice Hall series *Microhistory Series in Western Civilization* with Steven Ozment. Her current project is on the 1731 trial of Catherine Cadière and Jean-Baptiste Girard, which will be published in that series.

JONATHAN DEWALD is UB Distinguished Professor of History at the University at Buffalo. His books include *Aristocratic Experience and the Origins of Modern Culture: France 1570–1715* (1993), *The European Nobility, 1400–1800* (1996), and *Lost Worlds: The Emergence of French Social History, 1815–1970* (forthcoming, 2006). He is also editor-in-chief of *Europe 1450 to 1789: Encyclopedia of the Early Modern World,* 6 vols., (2004).

DOINA PASCA HARSANYI is assistant professor of history at Central Michigan University. Her main interests are the history of the French nobility and the evolution of French-American relations during the revolutionary era. On the latter subject, she has edited a volume titled *Lettres de la duchesse de La Rochefoucauld à William Short* (2001); she is also preparing a book manuscript about French noble exiles who traveled to America in the 1790s.

THOMAS E. KAISER is professor of history at the University of Arkansas at Little Rock. He has published on many aspects of eighteenth-century French political culture, including the refashioning of the royal image, finance and public opinion, and royal mistresses in the court of Louis XV. He is currently coediting a book on conspiracy in the French Revolution and writing another book provisionally entitled *Devious Ally: Marie-Antoinette and the Austrian Plot.*

MICHAEL KWASS is an associate professor of history at the University of Georgia. He specializes in the broad social and cultural history of economics and finance in the eighteenth century. Recipient of the David H. Pinkney Prize for *Privilege and the Politics of Taxation in Eighteenth-Century France* (2000), he is currently working on the politics of consumption in the Enlightenment.

ROBERT SCHWARTZ, E. Nevius Rodman Professor of History at Mount Holyoke College, has written *Policing the Poor in Eighteenth Century France* (1988), which was awarded the David H. Pinkney Prize from the Society for French Historical Studies; *History and Statistics: The Case of Witchcraft* (1992); and articles on rural history, one of which appeared in a recent collection of essays he coedited with Robert A. Schneider, *Tocqueville and Beyond: Essays on the Old Regime in Honor of David D. Bien* (2003). He is currently incorporating his research on rural communities in Burgundy in a comparative study of railways, uneven geographic development, and a crisis of globalization in France and Great Britain, 1830 to 1914.

JOHN SHOVLIN is an assistant professor of history at New York University. He is the author of several recent articles on luxury and social thought in prerevolutionary France and has a book forthcoming from Cornell University Press that explores French political economy and its articulation with politics in the latter half of the eighteenth century: *The Political Economy of Virtue: Luxury, Patriotism, and the Origins of the French Revolution.*

JAY M. SMITH is professor of history at the University of North Carolina at Chapel Hill. A specialist of early modern French political culture, aristocratic self-perception, and the methodologies of cultural history, he is the author of *The Culture of Merit: Nobility, Royal Service, and the Making of Absolute Monarchy in France, 1600–1789* (1996) and *Nobility Reimagined: The Patriotic Nation in Eighteenth-Century France* (2005).

JOHNSON KENT WRIGHT is associate professor of history at Arizona State University. An intellectual historian who specializes in the period of the Enlightenment, he is the author of *A Classical Republican in Eighteenth-Century France: The Political Thought of Mably* (1997) and many essays on eighteenth-century political thought and twentieth-century historiography.

INDEX